The Tragic Abyss

Studies in Genre

Louise Cowan, *General Editor*

The Terrain of Comedy
The Epic Cosmos
The Tragic Abyss

The Tragic Abyss

edited by

GLENN ARBERY

with an introduction by

LOUISE COWAN

The Dallas Institute Publications
The Dallas Institute of Humanities and Culture
Dallas

Cover: Mark Rothko, *No. 14, 1960.*   1960; oil on canvas; 114 1/2 in. by 105 5/8 in. (290.83 cm x 268.29 cm).   Reproduced with permission from the San Francisco Museum of Modern Art.   Helen Crocker Russell Fund purchase.   © Kate Rothko Prizel & Christopher Rothko / ARS, New York.

Cover design: Patricia Mora

Library of Congress Cataloging-in-Publication Data

The tragic abyss / edited by Glenn Arbery ; with an introduction by Louise Cowan.
     p. cm. ~ (Studies in genre)
Includes bibliographical references and index.
  ISBN 0-911005-41-2 (alk. paper)
  1. Tragedy~History and criticism.   I. Arbery, Glenn C. (Glenn Cannon), 1951- II. Series.
  PN1892.T68 2003
  809.2'512~dc22

                        2003016171

The Dallas Institute of Humanities and Culture
2719 Routh Street   Dallas, Texas   75201

To the memory of Donald A. Cowan

'A was a man, take him for all in all,
I shall not look upon his like again.
Hamlet

Contents

Contents (cont.)

Editor's Preface

Most of the essays in this volume, The Dallas Institute's third on genre, are the work of the students of Louise Cowan, who is both the general editor of the series and the principal theorist of the four "kinds" (tragedy, comedy, epic, and lyric) that form the *mundus imaginalis*. The others are by Dr. Cowan herself. Her theories of genre have shaped curricula at the University of Dallas, Thomas More College in New Hampshire, The Thomas More College in Fort Worth, Mobile University, the Honors Programs at Southeastern Louisiana University and Louisiana State University, and the Dallas Institute's Teachers Academy. Directly or indirectly, her ideas have influenced thousands of undergraduates, graduate students, and secondary school teachers, as well as tens of thousands of their students. This is theory that does not feel theoretical in the current sense. It does not distribute sprigs of pungent jargon: it lets in the native air of the great homelands of the poetic imagination.

The first two volumes in this series—*The Terrain of Comedy* (1984) and *The Epic Cosmos* (1992)—dealt with the genres most in need of exploration at the time. Now, in this third decade of the project, with many fashions in criticism having come and gone in the meantime, we turn to tragedy, the most theorized of all, in the hope of seeing tragedy afresh. One of the truths about tragedy always sounds unfeeling. Whenever a newspaper or television account of some disaster describes it as "tragic," the response out of Aristotelian theory, delivered with a certain rue, is that this incident must be distinguished from a tragedy, whatever the anguish involved. Strictly speaking, the word "tragedy" should not be applied to every terrible thing that happens, but only to "an action that is serious, complete, and of a certain magnitude ... with incidents arousing pity and fear, wherewith to accomplish its catharsis of such emotions." The word describes a particular kind of action, and, more to the point, a poetic distillation of that action. Yet

this insistence on accuracy might also carry a faint air of deroga-
tion, as though these lives were darkened by misfortunes that did
not quite manage, after all, to be *tragedy*. The undeserving dead
and the bereft survivors might take on an air of aesthetic failure,
unoriginal and déclassé, as if they had claimed to rival Sophocles
but had relied, in the end, on mere accident to produce the effect
of pathos—and as if the event were being judged on its capacity
to arouse and purge the emotions of an audience.

When terrible events are daily news, the real urgency is to
find the language adequate to reality, because repetition and cliché
obscure the very truth of these events. The word "tragedy" itself
has become a cliché, but it helps to ask what is meant by it in
common usage. In his new book on tragedy—too recent to impact
this volume—Terry Eagleton points out that the question is "why
we use the same term of *Medea* and *Macbeth*, the murder of a
teenager and a mining disaster" (3). Although Eagleton argues
that "no definition of tragedy more elaborate than 'very sad' has
ever worked" (3), the word seems most common in circumstances
when the emotions engaged by some terrible occurrence seem
emblematic of larger forces and therefore likely to continue to
deepen and grow more complex. Part of the complexity lies in
the recognition that what happened was not accidental, but deliberate. Moreover, it was enacted for an implied audience, and
some mystery of its local, private harm centrally grips public
awareness after the fact as part of the intention in the act itself.

The terrorist attacks of September 11, 2001, were described as
a "national tragedy," and no one wanted to quibble over the
term. In the context of high grief, only such a term could
approximate the conjunction of perpetrators and victims: that cal-
culus of destruction in which a terrible shadow of Allah found
its intelligent agents, and the thousands of lives brought into a
single, encompassing symbolic form in the twin towers. Even so,
upon reflection, tragedy does not seem to be quite the appropriate word. The image of a huge airliner penetrating the World
Trade Center high above New York City and a globe of jet fuel
exploding through the other side exceeds the human scale of
tragedy. Louise Cowan rightly described it as a "theomachy," a
war of the gods, such as occurs in the epics—the *Ramayana* or
the latter books of the *Iliad*. It has a mythological look; it was
planned in such a way that its very spectacle would summon the

Western technology of vicarious simultaneity to frame and endlessly reproduce this densely symbolic image for a world audience.
The unfolding destruction as an image is not tragedy but reli-
giously charged mythopoesis.

More appropriately, incidents of terrible domestic violence
(especially murders of children) are called tragedies—that term
from literature—but they take place in a context of such dark passion that, in the immediate wake, "literature," like Cordelia, can
say nothing. It would be sentimental, on the other hand, to think
that miseries in the news do, in fact, trump the meaning of
tragedy in its high and ancient, entirely unsentimental sense. In
its serene refusal to yield its place to the agonies of the age, an
Oedipus or *King Lear* checks the emotional appetites that real
events often arouse—primarily, appetites to pity (with perhaps
unrecognized *Schadenfreude*) and to fear (if one is not in actual
danger). When something truly wounds the communal imagination, however, only tragedy can distance it sufficiently to make it
recognizable. Medea kills the children she loves because Jason will
understand her only if she does so; their dead bodies become
writings, as it were, of savage power. Greek tragedy asks us to
imagine still more terrible intimacies of anguish. Atreus not only
kills his own brother's children, but also prepares them as his
brother's meal, erasing the central distinctions between animal
and human life in a premeditated sacrament of hatred. Were it
not for the actuality of the horrors from contemporary experience—and each year provides its own—such vengeance might seem
an absurdly conceived worst case. Actually to imagine it, however,
is to enter a zone of emotional symbolism that tragedy has made
its own and elevated into form, not so much as an imitated
deed, but as an action of consciousness brings into the open the
possibilities that people ordinarily will not let themselves admit.
In the *Republic*, Socrates claims that it actually awakens the
tyrannical part of the soul, what Freud called the *It* (more
uncanny in ordinary English than the distanced Latin *Id*), best
left to Itself in its own dark places. If the tyrant performs in
waking life what others only do in their worst dreams, then
tragedy risks too much, Socrates suggests, by bringing tyrannical
deeds before the waking imagination. A mother's murder of her
children onstage, for example, might provoke similar things, either
in real life or in the soul—what we now call "copy-cat" reactions.

Aristotle, of course, argued that tragedy does not lead to similar acts; his theory of catharsis answers Socrates by showing that the imagination is purged of pity and terror—the sources of identification with such deeds—rather than aroused to action. Plato's Socrates worries that the medicine and the disease are the same thing. This similarity is surely the point also of the confusion between terrible events and the term tragedy. Strictly understood, tragedy acts almost medically upon the psyche, but more like a modern vaccine, I suggest, than the purge of superfluities that Aristotle found the best analogy from ancient medicine. If every vaccination unforgettably intensified and condensed the essential experience of the disease, then people would gradually begin to use it to describe the real thing. To call an outbreak of ebola a "vaccine" would be immediately comprehensible, like calling a terrible event a "tragedy."

Great tragedy does not awaken the dark passions indiscriminately. Rather, it speaks in the unmediated language of deepest emotional symbols—children, mothers, fathers, kinsmen, lovers—in ways that bring the most terrible actions enacted in that language into a removed, symbolic form and let them come before the mind to be contemplated otherwise than in actual blood, even to be understood with pleasure. Socrates knew very well what tragedy did, I think. His great concern was whether the tragedian himself was deep enough, wise enough, central enough, to expose other people to the most virulent strains of human nature in the context of poetic pleasure. Tragedy as *pharmakon* invokes every kind of ambivalence, from Plato to Freud to Derrida. With Euripides, one often senses real danger, as though a live psychic virus were somehow left uncontained by the play; but those suspicions never occur in the same way with Aeschylus, Sophocles, or Shakespeare.

One accounts for the difference, not medically, however, but in terms of literary criticism, that maligned and misunderstood discipline on which good judgment nevertheless depends. Even if literary criticism were only the technical assessment of literary texts or the application of sophisticated analysis to cultural constructs in language, it would have great value. Obviously, though, it would not have enough. With the most potent texts, criticism needs every available avenue of insight, every kind of knowledge; it has to be capable of judging the adequacy of particular achieved forms to the permanent human truths. The orthodoxy of current criticism hotly denies that any human truth is permanent, given "the social construction of reality" and the always-shifting forces of cultural power. Nevertheless, the constructions always work from the same prior realities in our nature—male and female, parent and child, individual and community. There are relational truths that require "constructions," particular social interpretations—for instance, what it means to be "a man" in Periclean Athens as opposed to Renaissance Venice, or what it means to be Priam's god-haunted Cassandra or to be the daughter of a Yoruba chieftain in contemporary Nigeria. These particulars of social reality are certainly constructed socially. Indeed, tragedy assumes that there is a profound constructedness to lived reality: what else is the Oedipus story about?

But the generative relational realities hold fairly steady. Otherwise, we could not even ask what it is that makes Sophocles' *Antigone*, for example, seem more centrally true than Strindberg's *Miss Julie*, even though burial rituals are far more remote from early twenty-first century concerns than questions of sexuality or class. Why does *Miss Julie* seem dated? Is it the disappearance, since the 19th century, of a large servant class, with all the tensions, sexual and otherwise, that informed the relations between masters and servants? Is it the relative freedom of our own age in addressing sexual matters? Surely those cultural changes are less profound than the disappearance of kings and blood sacrifice. Yet *Antigone* remains fresher, in her more essential defiance, than Strindberg's rebellious heroine, who lacks a similar metaphysical urgency.

The distinction seems to require unfashionable considerations. In this volume, the contributors frequently return to the "abyss" of this volume's title in probing for clues about what constitutes tragedy as a commentary on existence. There would be something unapologetically "essentialist" about the endeavor if one could take abysmal absence as an essence. In general, the abyss can be understood as the sudden emptying of all expected meaning from everything taken for granted, everything familial, marital, communal, political, or religious that has become so customary that it has never been recognized as constructed. "Such is the influence of custom, that, where it is strongest," writes Hume, "it not only covers our natural ignorance, but even conceals itself, and seems

not to take place, merely because it is found in the highest
degree." In tragedy, the supposedly solid footing gives way. Everything one took for the truth was a lie. One feels a rending of
the fabricated order—fabricated not only *out there*, but most intimately *as oneself* and therefore most deeply interior.

But the abyss has to be distinguished from its simulacra. Perhaps when the customary world gives way, one merely finds oneself on the ground for the first time, as in a comedy. Tragedy,
on the contrary, does not simply expose the difference between
the constructed floor and the naturally prior ground, or between
the cultural "world" and the "earth" in Heidegger's terms; it rends
the ground itself and exposes one to groundlessness simply—the
abyss. Yet the abyss is not simply negation, as some moderns
believe, but a yawning into the indeterminate out of which ground
itself stabilizes, an exposure of depths mysteriously astir with terror and healing, a revelation of the blackness-to-us of the divine.
It does not nullify reason so much as it crucifies it, to use one
of Louise Cowan's figures. Tragedy involves a felt metaphysics in
which primal significance obliterates constructed meaning, as Job
discovered. In tragedy, the poet resorts to speech in very natures,
to terrible symbolic action, to means of expression that in life constitute horror and in religion the most profound ritual.

❧ ❧ ❧

We hope, then, to see tragedy afresh, but freshness does not
mean novelty for its own sake. These essays approach what is
most salient about tragedy in terms of its theories, its periods,
and its texts. Louise Cowan scans the whole field of study in her
introduction, and the volume itself is organized into four sections.
In the first, the primary philosophic thinkers about tragedy—Aristotle, Hegel, and Nietzsche—come up for stimulating reappraisal.
Robert S. Dupree lucidly recasts the standard understandings of
such Aristotelian terms as *hedone*, *mimesis*, *praxis*, and *catharsis* in
ranging over art and music, ancient and modern, in exploring the
"tragic bias." Bainard Cowan, assessing the place of Hegel and
tracing the understanding of *Antigone* through philosophers after
him, concludes that what Hegel intuited about the darkest, most
resistant dimensions of spirit in tragedy was finally what he was
least able to put in the language of dialectical synthesis. My own

essay on Nietzsche concentrates on Nietzsche's Dionysian understanding of "primal unity," not as ground but as abyss, tolerable only in the sublimity of art.

The second section concentrates on tragedy in the ancient world. Daniel Russ argues persuasively that the Book of Job, often interpreted in terms of justice, should instead be understood as a tragedy of divine love in the sense that the love of God does not preclude "untold suffering." In her essay on the *Oresteia*, Louise Cowan speaks of the primordial horror in Aeschylus as "a poetic calling up of ancient wrongs" and "an aesthetic recurrence of their atrocities." Two essays on Sophocles deal with different dimensions of his final healing vision—Dennis Slattery with the theme of the wound in *Philoctetes*, and Bainard Cowan with the grove of the Furies in *Oedipus at Colonus*. Slattery focuses on Philoctetes' wound as emblematic of the reconciliations of tragedy—the capacity of the victim to praise the origin of pain and receive the blessing of its pollution. Cowan shows that Oedipus' action at Colonus creates a space of revelation that is the gift of tragedy, but that remains outside any application to a progressive dialectic, "even in the name of greater freedom." Virginia Arbery, in her essay on *Medea* and *The Bacchae*, argues that Euripides bracingly counters in advance those moderns who believe that bad fortune can be avoided by the clever exercise of freedom.

Shakespeare occupies the third section, and for the purposes of this study of genre, we have returned to the four tragedies that A. C. Bradley singled out in *Shakespearean Tragedy* a century ago: *Hamlet*, *Othello*, *King Lear*, and *Macbeth*. Judith Stewart Shank, reading *Hamlet* in its densely Christian context, finds in the title character a figure who has plumbed the depths of the tragic abyss to find a restoration of identity through "the divinity that shapes our ends." Mary Mumbach's notes on *Othello* find that the influence of epic on tragedy in the ancient world is repeated in the relation between the epic world of Dante and the tragedy of Othello's loss of faith in Desdemona. My work on *King Lear* is an attempt to read this play, which Bradley found, as drama, "decidedly inferior as a whole to *Hamlet*, *Othello* and *Macbeth*," in terms of depths that become comprehensible only as ritual rather than representation. James Walter concentrates on what he calls the "intervals of risk" in *Macbeth* that decide the nature of "human finitude measured against the dark of metaphysical mystery."

The final section of this volume takes up the vexed question of what has happened to tragedy in modernity, and in particular, its destiny with respect to the emergence of other popular forms, such as opera and the novel. Robert S. Dupree explores a divergence that begins in about 1600, resulting in the rise of popular opera, which engages the crowd at the expense of the theater's real communal power, and the northern turn (ultimately issuing in the works of Ibsen and Strindberg) toward dark, personal drama without a collective emphasis. Paul Connell accounts for the "strange upward draft" of affirmation and re-sacralization of the world that keeps novels with apparently tragic actions, such as *Madame Bovary* and *The Possessed*, from being ultimately tragic in effect. Gregory Marks examines Lorca's successful appeal to Andalusian folk traditions that sustain the tragic view in *Blood Wedding* but that evaporate in *Yerma* and *The House of Bernarda Alba*. In his essay on Faulkner, Larry Allums recovers Faulkner's tragic vision from those who decry the offensive aspects of Southern culture that become most visible precisely in his tragic actions. Kathleen Kelly Marks concludes the section and the volume by meditating on the apotropaic dimensions of Toni Morrison's *Beloved* in their fertile tension with tragedy—a tension that goes back to the earliest origins of the genre itself.

This book, long in gestation, would not have come about at all without the play of ideas that those of us in the Teachers Academy of the Dallas Institute have shared over the years with the teachers in our Summer Institutes. We thank them, as always, for their great spirit of generosity and their dedication to a noble calling. Joanne Stroud, the founder and director of Dallas Institute Publications, has given us the timely encouragement and support necessary to complete the book. Patricia Mora's professional expertise took us past many rough spots in the production of the volume, and the skill of Kathryn Smith brought this endeavor in tragedy to a comic conclusion at last.

Introduction
The Tragic Abyss

LOUISE COWAN

So blind, in so severe a place
(All life before in the black grave)
The last alternatives they face
Of life, without the life to save.
Allen Tate, *"The Cross"*

Despite its sinister revelations, tragedy stands virtually unchallenged in the Western world for moral and artistic supremacy. And though its pure lineaments surface only rarely, it remains in the poetic canon a privileged model, if only as an unattainable ideal. Aristotle lists it in the Poetics as one of the four "kinds" and assumes its superiority over the other three in artistic economy and power (Butcher 116-117). But his authoritative analysis of its formal elements, almost slavishly adopted in every epoch since the fifteenth-century rediscovery of his treatise, left the meaning of tragedy essentially undefined. What are its dark secrets that even the rumor of them so fascinates and enthralls? For, despite its few appearances, this most absolute of genres seems always hovering in the background in Western society. It manifests its presence as a potentiality of the psyche, and though seldom embodied—and then, apparently, only in drama—appears like a kind of fractal design in the margins of our music, our films, our news media. It punctuates our conversations; it governs our relationships and exhales in our dreams what Max Scheler calls tragedy's "heavy breath" (249). It is one of the supreme human icons, borne with us on the shared journey of civilization, much as Aeneas carried his household gods—or, it might be more appropriate to say, as Perseus carried his shield. Despite the critical disagreements it spurs, its infrequent manifestations are universally recognized. Only by some sort of theoretical timidity do we stop short of acknowledging behind them the presence of a tragic essence, an archetypal idea that takes on form at intervals throughout history.

Unlike the other modes of which Aristotle speaks, tragedy cannot really be said to be a *mimesis* of a *praxis*, an imitation of an action. Certainly it has a plot, characters, and the other elements he names as imitating an action "serious, complete, and of a certain magnitude" (Butcher 63). In both epic and comedy, however, that action, the underlying "movement of spirit," as Francis Fergusson expresses it (Introduction 4), is an image of some such movement in life. It is in this large analogy that those genres are mimetic, not simply in their characters and plots. But tragedy, rather than being a model of life experience, seems absolute—like a diagram or a recipe. It evokes something rather than reminds us of something. As raindancers strive in their ritual not so much to imitate human action as to make gestures that, reaching beyond the human, cause rain to fall, so tragedy bends all its efforts toward producing a result. And in this purpose it stands in contrast with comedy, whose long-drawn-out episodic turns mimic in distorted guise the trials and narrow escapes of daily living. Viewed in this light, tragedy is less a simulacrum of human action than a liturgical confrontation of a deep-seated dread which, when brought to light, can be borne only through the medium of poetic language. Its plots, then, should be recognized for what they are: not really, as Aristotle would have it, structures with a complication and resolution—with a beginning, middle, and end—but dramatizations of single moments of unmasking, accompanied by whatever is necessary to reach that chilling and epiphanic event. For a moment in the tragic vision one looks beyond the boundaries of ordinary awareness and glimpses the caverns of a lightless abyss. The tragic protagonists who find themselves in this severe place—Job, Prometheus, Oedipus, Hamlet, Macbeth, Ahab, Joe Christmas, among others—discover that they are transfixed, as though caught in a trap. They face the immediacy of an ultimate choice. For, in the dead air of this unmoving time, they are unable to go forward or backward. They have reached a point of no return. These chosen protagonists *qua* victims confront the final alternatives. This is the tragic moment.

But it seems less an analogy of anything that happens in life than an unconcealing of the substratum of human existence. Thus in the tragic world, for all its otherness, one is somehow in familiar territory—the setting of dreams and nightmares. But tragedy presents a nightmare from which the dreamer cannot awake. Its vision has a finality that leaves not only the protagonist but the audience changed. It rends the curtain of intelligibility to reveal another kind of reality, so deep that it seems to the viewer an abyss. For the spectator, what remains is not the specific action represented onstage so much as the drama aroused in the underworld of the spirit, that deep well of darkness in the human psyche in which joy and pain are mingled. Many twentieth-century thinkers have been concerned with this hidden aspect of the person. Freud has directed his attention to the "dark, inaccessible part of our personality" (19:36); and Jacques Maritain has spoken of "the nocturnal kingdom of the mind" (94). But tragedy goes even deeper than these statements would indicate: it dredges up something from the bottomless pit. Like the gorgon's gaze, what it brings up ought not be faced directly, as one knows instinctively, but is better viewed at a slant, through a mask or an image. To see the thing itself could mark the fulfillment of the *dies irae*, the day of wrath, the whisper "Thou art the man." And because this final accusation is never quite realized in actual life, no matter how dire one's circumstances, it is likely to be kept in abeyance as an undischarged fear in the back of consciousness, its terror and pity doled out in small doses.

An impressive number of twentieth-century thinkers have attempted to isolate tragedy in one of its elements, such as suffering,[1] paradox,[2] the destruction of a value,[3] or the confrontation with the irremediable.[4] Others consider it to issue from the ritual of sacrifice,[5] the boundary situation,[6] or the incarnation of political order.[7] These theories—and there are hundreds more—advance single elements as keys to the tragic. Yet no one of them completely captures its forbidding though oddly exhilarating power. In seeking the sources of this power, however, one must first acknowledge that tragedy seems not to have a definable content or a specifiable structure. As we have been suggesting, it presents itself almost as a kind of mechanism—or a sacrament—something that *does* something, that has an effect *ex opere operato*. And though what it does may be fearfully important for the *polis*, as Aristotle made clear twenty-five hundred years ago, it channels its power through the medium of one protagonist—the scapegoat, victim, tyrant, or hero—who must go alone to face the abyss. It is as though tragedy opens the door to Tartarus, activating the pattern of the soul's possibility and exposing the threat buried at the bottom of consciousness. But it is a threat from another realm and hence represents something beyond the human, something essentially metaphysical, rather than the distillation of actual experience.

But without its art form, the tragic is likely to be kept in abeyance, an undischarged terror in the psyche. And the creation of tragedy is not simply subject to the author's will: modern tragedy, for instance, has been infrequent and, when it occurs, incomplete. It is hardly evocable in the novel. As readers of novels, we lack the viscera for tragedy; we are all minds and sensibilities. However terrible, Kurtz's famous cry, "The horror! The horror!" stops short of the genuinely tragic, even though it is the dying voice of a tormented soul that has exceeded human bounds in "stepping over the edge." But, as readers, we do not see with him what he sees but are told about the experience retrospectively. "Heart of Darkness" is a superb novella about the abyss, but it is not tragedy. It wisely makes no attempt to trace the grammar of Kurtz's vision. We are not present at the moment that the trap springs.

Such a sight as Kurtz saw, unless it is to overwhelm entirely, would have to be brought into consciousness as communal experience in full view of an audience. There, secure within the tragic form, and not as solitary reader, one might look directly upon the face of the gorgon and live to tell the tale. Otherwise a Marlow must interpret for us—or, in *Absalom, Absalom!* a Quentin Compson, who goes with Miss Rosa Coldfield into the deserted Sutpen mansion, the house of death, to find Henry Sutpen, his brother's murderer, locked away in darkness. Horrifying as this moment is, however, it is still questionable as tragedy. Quentin *reports* the experience to us, and our minds and sympathies give assent to it. We recognize it and thrill in vicarious horror. But what we experience is removed from the fullblown tragic experience. For in the confines of the novel, we are shielded by mediation from the unfathomable contradictions of the act. It happened somewhere else, to someone whose interiority we do not know. We know *of* it intellectually and can contemplate it in complete safety. Another person is telling us about it, which is another kind of experience entirely—possessing its own *frisson*, no doubt, but not the full-bodied pity and terror that come of being there, or even when we read the Greeks or Shakespeare, of *feeling* that we're there. Unalleviated tragedy provides no protection for us, no way out by means of psychological detachment. In its authentic appearances, the tragic experience is irreducible, inexplicable, offered directly to the audience.

During the two epochs of its generally agreed-upon appearance in Western history, it was within the safety of cities that the tragic epiphany occurred. The tragic pattern was harrowed up into the light of recognition, with all levels of the populace looking on in the same fascinated horror and *jouissance*. And the dramas produced during those two epochs are still capable, centuries later, among strangers, of generating the tragic event. Like the Bible, these Greek and Shakespearean texts remain potential sources of unmediated catharsis in ages and climes far removed from their origin, belonging to succeeding eras as much as to their own. Even solitary readers can experience the shared pity and terror arising from their pages. For in their essence, these works were conceived communally and expressed in language that carries with it primordial implications, recognizable—even longed for—in whatever medium. But the Greek and Shakespearean dramas do not exhaust the tragic; they *educate* us about it. They have shown us that it is a pattern in reality, not of our own making; hence we can recognize in works of art its partial appearance as well as oblique patterns signifying its presence, hieroglyphics that we would otherwise miss. For, though not every age can or even should try to produce full-blown tragedy, a *sense* of the tragic seems a necessary ingredient of the Western mind.

Tragic Theory

Tragedy in itself is unarguably communal, but its relation to the *polis* has frequently been considered problematic. Plato saw it as the poetic kind most dangerous to the city, a condemnation Aristotle attempted to offset in his *Poetics*, with his emphasis on the ethical and the ameliorative. In the Aristotelian view, the tragic action results from a castigable blindness—*hamartia*, the same word Christians were later to use for *sin*—a myopia affecting the judgment and will of an otherwise predominantly virtuous leader. Further, a reversal of fortune and its consequent recognition brings about a counterpoint of pity and terror leading to insight and effecting a catharsis, with a subsequent restoration of order. This conception of tragedy dominated the poetics of the Middle Ages, even though, steeped in Horace and Cicero, medieval writers were familiar with Aristotle only through a Latin translation by the Arabic philosopher Averroes.

After the late fifteenth-century rediscovery of the *Poetics* in a Greek manuscript, it became almost the sole arbiter of tragic drama, though it was blended with an already established Roman didacticism.[8] For a couple of centuries afterward, neoclassical theorists tended to view tragedy in the light of poetic justice, conceiving of tragic conflict as the dramatization of a threat against not only morality but decorum, ending, however, with the ultimate vindication of right order. Not until the nineteenth century, when Hegel advanced his philosophy of the conflict of good with good, or *kollision*—his term for the painful attempt of Spirit to embody itself in space and time—was there a theory to rival Aristotle's, though, unlike the Greek philosopher, Hegel was chiefly concerned with the significance of tragedy rather than its art form.[9] Hegel considered certain human powers as making up an ethical substance binding a person to various "goods." The most poignant situation in which one can find oneself, according to Hegel, is to encounter these goods in conflict with each other in one's own life.

Nietzsche continued this view of tragedy as representing forces in conflict with each other—as he expressed it, between the Apollonian and the Dionysian poles in human culture and in individual persons (Birth 143). As Gerald Else comments, Nietzsche saw the rise of tragedy "out of the dark womb of the 'Dionysian,' that indispensable, all confounding Primal Unity of joy and pain which lies at the heart of life itself" (9). And in the twentieth century, Max Scheler, building on Hegel and Nietzsche, reiterates the idea of tragedy as representing a conflict between two values in which, though such a clash generates new meaning, it nonetheless destroys something keenly valuable. Scheler is adamant about the necessity of acknowledging a potential tragic presence in the depths of existence. As he comments, "it is impossible to arrive at the phenomenon of the tragic through the art product alone... The tragic is rather an essential element of the universe itself. The material made use of by the art product and the tragedian must contain beforehand the dark strain of this element" (249).

The tragic, then, according to Scheler, "is not the result of an interpretation of the world and the important events of the world" but inheres in events, in people, in fortunes. It is given off by them "like a heavy breath, or seems like an obscure glimmering that surrounds them." Scheler continues, "In it a specific feature of the world's makeup appears before us, and not a condition of our own ego, nor its emotions, nor its experience of compassion and fear." What he calls the "tragic knot" occurs in the "inner entanglement between the creation of a value and the destruction of a value as they take place in the unity of the tragic action and the tragic event. When we can see the catastrophe as a "species of transcendent necessity," for which no blame can be attached, then and only then do we have tragedy (262).

Lionel Abel in America and Roman Ingarden in Poland proceed in this vein, viewing tragedy with an ontological rather than an ethical, psychological, or aesthetic concern. For Abel, tragedy provides a vision of the irremediable. The tragic vision, he maintains, results from a direct act of seeing rather than from holding any particular view. The tragic writer provides the noblest view of human adversity, portraying a world wherein supreme values collide, "one in which we know we could not live" (187). Ingarden is openly metaphysical in his conception of the literary work of art in general. The tragic, in his view, is among those essences which "are not properties in the usual sense of the term, nor are they in general 'features' of some psychic state but instead they are usually revealed... as an atmosphere which... penetrates and illumines everything with its light" (291). In realizing them, Ingarden maintains, "we enter into primal existence..." (292). We have a secret longing "for their realization and contemplation—even if they are to be frightful" (293). Tragedy, both of these writers would say, is primarily concerned not so much with examining philosophical ideas or ethical standards as with discerning a tension at the heart of being, to which mortals resonate in their depths.

The Tragic Art Form

If the tragic vision has given rise to great diversity of interpretation, the tragic structure, in contrast, has been regarded
throughout history with a surprising rigidity. Of course the Aristotelian "rules" dominated the theory and practice of tragic
artistry for several centuries. But even after the nineteenth-century
break with the unities, critics (and dramatists themselves) have
constantly felt the need to demand certain specifics of the tragic
art, giving rise to basic imperatives concerning the proper form
for tragedy. Many have thought there is a prescribed shape to its
plot—that it should be condensed, limited in time and space, with
a *peripeteia*, a reversal, and an *anagnorisis*, a recognition, ending
in the death of the protagonist. But then questions have arisen:
Is the protagonist necessarily male? Must he commit a "terrible
deed," make an egregious mistake? Should he always be guilty of
hubris? Is he a scapegoat—Isaiah's "rejected, despised of men"? Or
should he be a public leader, a magnanimous soul, our highest
representative, our bravest contender? Are divine presences essential to tragedy? Does it need a chorus?

These questions are, of course, unanswerable if not perhaps
irrelevant. All one can say is that if the tragic action means ending in a certain place—a black hole—then any way one gets there
seems sufficient. We have been suggesting that the tragic, rather
than being a primarily aesthetic phenomenon, is a metaphysical
occurrence given form, to be judged by its ability to call down
upon its viewers a certain response. Admittedly, in its infrequent
appearances throughout the centuries, one can observe certain
strategies it has employed to secure its effect, certain themes and
situations, images and symbols. Whatever constants we find, however, are neither necessary nor sufficient, even though many of
them have recurred with notable regularity in the tragic canon.
Largely Greek in their origins, they are absent from the Book of
Job, for instance, as from *The Iliad*, Lorca's *Blood Wedding*,
Faulkner's *Light in August*, Allen Tate's lyric poem "The Cross,"
Robert Penn Warren's *Brother to Dragons*, and Toni Morrison's
Beloved, all of which are in some measure versions of tragedy.
Hence, one must infer, the traditional themes and conventions of
tragedy are not its absolute essentials. However we may analyze
the parts of a tragic drama, the conviction persists that something

beyond its separable elements is responsible for its tragic nature. It takes place in a tragic world, for one thing; and in that world no action, even if comic in itself, can dispel the ominous shadow. For all his quips, Hamlet must die the death.

Some of the observables one can note from examples of the tragic tradition could be regarded as purely dramatic conventions; yet they are perhaps clues to the essence we seek. In all the paradigmatic models, for instance, tragedy takes place in a disturbed realm that has only recently begun to question its established *doxa*. It makes use of few characters and even fewer incidents in the unfolding of the plot; it tends to observe an inexorable cause and effect, single out a lone—and in most instances, male—protagonist and move toward a shattering conclusion, usually concluding with his death and the deconstruction of the established regime that has revolved around him. It moves with extraordinary rapidity: tragic time is brief, swiftpaced, demanding immediate action, leaving little room for alternatives for those moving to destruction. Yet somewhere in it there is leisure for lamentation: the chorus or one of the victimized characters manages to stop time and utter cries and protests that in rising from the depths demand a lyric, primordial language. Its wailing has something always to do with lost unity, with the earth, with the gods. Further, tragedy tends to portray the victimization of the feminine; to concern the relation of fathers and children, down-playing or ignoring the maternal. Its total effect is usually to portray the collapse of the myth of order; and, though it may offer some sort of reconciliation, it leaves its audience with the vision of a denuded world and only a faint hope for any possible far-off restoration of civil harmony.

As the tragic action has been conceived in Greek and Shakespearean drama (its two high points), it describes an arc divided into three parts. Francis Fergusson, basing his analysis on Sophocles' *Oedipus the King*, has designated these three portions of the action as purpose, passion, and perception (Fergusson, Introduction 10-13). The Greek trilogies themselves testify to this tripartite structure, though we have to extrapolate somewhat from the *Oresteia*, the only complete surviving trilogy, in order to discern the underlying action of the triple structure in other Greek cycles. In the first stage of tragedy, as we can see in the *Agamemnon*, the first drama of the *Oresteia*, the catastrophe occurs at the end,

producing a violent reversal, a fall from happiness to misery. This
is the portion of tragedy described in the *Poetics*, with the more
than ordinarily good man coming to misery; his *hamartia* causing
the tragic misstep that leads to *atē* (madness) and finally, to a
peripeteia and *anagnorisis* (reversal and recognition), with pity and
fear producing a *catharsis* (purgation). Aristotle analyzes Sophocles'
Oedipus the King as the paradigmatic example of tragic art, but, in
fact, rather than encompassing the entire range of tragedy (as we
can see from an encounter with *Oedipus at Colonus*), this play represents only the first "moment" of the tragic movement, the stage
in which the "terrible deed" is done. In Aeschylus's *Oresteia*, the
opening drama, *Agamemnon*, traces out this movement; and one
might be justified in speculating that the lost play of Prometheus
(*The Firebringer*) takes place in this stage, like *Oedipus the King*,
The Bacchae, and *Othello*.

In the second stage, the catastrophe occurs at the beginning
or has just occurred: this is a time of stasis, marked by tension,
conflict, suffering, paradox, indecision. Tragedies that fit this category are *The Libation Bearers* (the second drama of the *Oresteia*),
Job, *Prometheus Bound*, *Electra*, *Hamlet*, *Macbeth*, and the Oedipus
play that Sophocles did not write, which would have had to
depict the time between Thebes and Colonus, his hero's period
of helpless wandering after blinding himself. In the third stage,
the catastrophe has occurred long before; the movement of the
plot is upward, *de profundis*, toward redemption and reconciliation.
One finds this pattern in the third part of the *Oresteia*, the
Eumenides, as well as in the lost *Prometheus Unbound*, *Oedipus at
Colonus*, and *King Lear*.[10]

Looking back over the tradition, one can see that, in contrast
with comedy, tragedy has an immediate and powerful impact on
the reader or viewer. The effect of comedy is developmental, lifting spirits and enlightening intellects, so that the audience can
see better how to compromise and endure in a damaged world.
Tragedy in contrast is cataclysmic, granting its recipients a terrible and exalted kind of wisdom then and there, at that very
moment. And in any profound questioning of tragedy, it is the
character of this revelation that one seeks to know. What is it,
one wonders, that the viewers of—or, perhaps more accurately,
participants in—this most mysterious of genres see and understand?
Is it at base what Wole Soyinka claims for Yoruban tragic ritual,

a taming of the abyss? (Myth 2). Or is it a surrender to it? Are participants in tragedy being swallowed up for a moment in "outer darkness"? a glimpse of uncreation?—of *nihil*? a *Blick ins chaos*? Is it that their being is contingent, that they did not create themselves; that they stand convicted before a primal power unimaginable in its grandeur? Is Kafka's *Trial* a proper delineation of the tragic fear?—that one is accused of a nameless crime by a faceless judge, to be tried at a time and place, with evidence of which one is kept ignorant?

We should have to say, rather, that Job's, Oedipus', or Lear's situation is much worse. What each confronts is something that elicits his *self*-condemnation—something that makes him "repent in dust and ashes," or dash out his eyes, or take leave of his reason. "I am bound / Upon a wheel of fire," the old king declares to his daughter Cordelia, "that mine own tears / Do scald like molten lead" (4.7.45-47). He is carried, in Yeats's words about tragedy in general, "beyond time and persons, to where passion living through its thousand purgatorial years, as in the wink of an eye, becomes wisdom" (239). But to attain this wisdom the hero must go down into the abyss, and the audience is brought as near as possible to its brink.

The Borderland of Tragedy

What is first discernible in the no-man's-land that surrounds the abyss is its menacing and horrid aspect. When one comes finally to the dark tower (as Browning would have it in "Childe Roland to the Dark Tower Came"), it has been by enduring "ugly little rivers," containing possible corpses of infants. Ancient memories of human sacrifice, long hidden out of sight, remind the audience of a shared communal guilt. Cassandra in the *Oresteia* acknowledges this liminal region and intuits the abyss beyond it, when—caught like an animal and prodded to go in to her own slaughter—she looks up at the rooftop and makes out the apparitions of horror: the mutilated children, their bodies half-eaten, their blood staining the palace roof. She cries out against "the house that hates god, / an echoing womb of guilt, kinsmen / torturing kinsmen, severed heads, slaughterhouse of heroes, soil streaming blood" and calls upon the murdered children:

See, my witnesses—I trust to them, to the babies
wailing, skewered on the sword,
  their flesh charred, the father gorging on their parts.

(Aeschylus, *Agam.* 1095-97)

Human sacrifice and torture are border images implied in all
the tragedies, sometimes made overt, as in the *Oresteia*, sometimes
hidden, as in the *Oedipus*. Robert Miola, speaking particularly of
Renaissance revenge tragedy and "the *disiecta membra* of hands,
tongues, and other bodily parts," makes clear that "the expression
of such *thymos* in action rends the human body and the human
soul" (12). But even further, in this shadowy no-man's-land verging
on the abyss lie not only human sacrifice and torture, but that
most unspeakable *sanctum sanctorum*, cannibalism—the ritual eating
of human flesh—at once the most sacred of practices and the most
heinous of crimes. This is a portion of the tragic knowledge shared
by the human race in its Great Memory. But even the horror of
torture, child murder, and cannibalism—only a few of the unspeakable things mortals have done to each other—cannot entirely
account for the tragic response. Cassandra not only apprehends this
fearful past but at the same moment recognizes the power of the
gods: she herself is inexorably to be slain, along with the man who
has captured and violated her. In *King Lear* we witness onstage an
atrocity beyond language in the blinding of Gloucester and then
later, a mute acceptance in the calm eloquence of Cordelia's dead
body. Yet an abiding presence hovers over these unspeakable acts
and modifies their horror. An open-eyed view of necessity characterizes the tragic vision and gives it a willing acquiescence to what
has been and what must be. Standing on the brink of the abyss,
Oedipus commands the herdsman to relinquish the final bit of
information that will send his king hurling into the darkness. "Oh
God, I am on the verge of frightful speech," the hapless shepherd
protests. "And I of hearing," Oedipus replies. Then later, emerging
after he has put out his own eyes, "Darkness! / Horror of darkness, enfolding, resistless, unspeakable," he exclaims, to our pity and
our mesmerized joy. "Look there!" are the dying words of the old
and maddened Lear.

Peering over from the edge, the chorus and the audience watch
the inescapable, transported to the realm of the unsayable. Authentic experience of the tragic threshold, in its enactment before us,

is so stark and so demanding as not to be governed by the imagination, that ingenious mediator between spirit and flesh. The devastating effect of tragedy, in fact, may be related to the utter separateness in it of the mind and the senses. Tragedy, as it is experienced, is of the innards, as Ruth Padel translates the Greek word *splanchna* (the brain, the liver, the heart, the bowels). "Tragedy's language," she writes, "stresses that whatever is within us is obscure, many-faceted, impossible to see" (77). And it is this impossibility that tragedy takes as its challenge. Its task is to transport us to this inside-outside and to strip away the veil concealing the dread secret. Greek tragedy in particular, according to Padel, "with its dialectics of seen and unseen, inside and outside, exit and entrance was a simultaneously internal and external, intellectual and somatic expression of contemporary questions about the inward sources of harm, knowledge, power, and darkness" (77).

But its damage is perceived not only by the body; the spirit, too, is deeply implicated in tragic knowledge. When the hidden is brought back from the abyss, revealed in the art form of tragedy, the mind recoils in pity at the body's suffering; and the body is wracked by fear at the mind's recognition. The imagination, which is essentially a comic alleviator, has no part in unifying the experience and hence is paralyzed by what seems inevitable. In the tragic realm, the protagonist cannot triumph, can only submit. The trap is sprung, the jig is up. The audience stands on the rim, so to say, and participates in the peculiar doubleness of the moment of discovery, wherein the realization remains unassimilated and unresolved, retaining the full force of its painful contradiction.

The Tragic Abyss

But if the chorus and the audience remain on the rim, the tragic protagonist has to descend into the deepest crevices of the universe—into Tartarus itself. Caught in its depths, he can go neither forward or backward. He finds himself in a pit at the bottom of an underworld where gravity is so heavy that nothing can escape. In this no place—this stony cliff, this bloody ground, this blasted heath, this dungheap, this pit for beasts (poets have exhaustively explored the variety of metaphors that can express the absoluteness of the tragic *khora*, this place that is the final end of all things), the laws of the land dictate that one is in an ultimate situation, that everything hangs on the next few seconds. Time has run out, in direct contrast to comedic time, which is elastic enough to allow sufficient leisure for working things out or slipping by and evading the consequences. But in tragedy, suddenly *no time at all* exists and hence no escape is possible. When Birnam Wood can be seen coming to Dunsinane, nothing can be done but to arm oneself for a battle one is fated to lose. Comedy, in contrast, has recourse to an alternative world, so that, instead of heading straight for disaster, one can avoid it long enough to dream up narrow escapes—to don a disguise, or leave a misleading note, or hide behind a bush.

The prospects of tragedy are so thoroughly unsettling that—yet again—one must wonder at our fascination with it. What does the tragic protagonist accomplish in the abyss that is worth our attention? Why do we long so for tragedy; why do we watch it at all? Is it that we are fulfilled in this glimpse of the irremediable? Is it that matter itself is a triumph? That we cry out for the reality of blood? That darkness affirms life in ways that light and harmony cannot do? Whatever the answers to these questions, the one thing agreed upon in discussions of tragedy is that its effect is strangely therapeutic. As art form tragedy helps its viewers (not its protagonists!) look upon violence and turn away from it freed and content. It enables them to rise from the devastating experience with a sense of having been fulfilled and liberates them to shape their lives into the wisdom of comedy. But tragedy supplies the knowledge with which they shape that wisdom. Without the tragic there could be no comic resolution. Further, it is important to note that tragedy itself never simply turns into comedy. If it effects a reconciliation—as in the *Oresteia*—its harmony comes about still within a tragic terrain. And that terrain is elsewhere. For the situations and characters of the tragic world make us see not our own lives but rather something in the universe that, though it affects our world, has no counterpart in the daily lives we lead.

Is tragedy, then, simply a vision of human destiny and the dramatization of our dread at confronting it? Certainly there is a dread that lies dormant at the bottom-most portion of our psyches, suppressed throughout life, since life could not be lived if it were confronted directly. It has to do with our being caught in the flesh, of daring to exist as a spirit incorporated in matter, of believing in the "blind hopes" Prometheus planted in the human race. Uncovered, it reveals itself as a dread of seeing in one fearful instant of *Aufklärung* the vast distance between temporal consciousness and the realm of essences. Yet something in the iconic gaze of tragedy evokes a corresponding image in our depths: for a moment we glimpse ourselves as full participants within the accused and splendid human race. And for a moment we see that the gods look on, with bright interest and admiration, watching the suffering of mortals that elevates them to an almost godlike standing.

To adopt so apocalyptic a vision of tragedy is of course to abjure the employment of the word in its ordinary usage as catastrophe, or disaster, or personal loss. For if the tragic consists, as I have been arguing, of the experience of the abyss, as if one had fallen into a black hole in inner or outer space, then it would seem unsuitable to speak of even the most severe actual suffering as tragic. If we adopt this distinction, it is with some wonder at how a form so remote and forbidding has assumed its supreme power over the art of poetry and the lives of mortals. The answer has to lie, of course, in the experience of the tragic art itself, which in some mysterious manner is *not* forbidding, not removed from daily life but rather lights it up from within.

A clue to the solution of this enigma is offered in Aristotle's doctrine of *catharsis*, which seems nearer the mark than his frequently cited *mimesis*. To emphasize the cathartic nature of tragedy implies that the tragic art accomplishes its task apart from any resemblance to life. That is, if its essence is to be located in what it *does* rather than what it *emulates*, then it is a kind of *leitourgeia*, a liturgy, a public ceremony; and its elements have to be assembled in such a manner as in the end to achieve the right effect, or, to change metaphors, to make the right kind of compound—a purgative remedy that discharges the poisons afflicting the psyche. Tragedy, then, as we have been saying, would have to be judged by neither its plot nor its characters but, like a cathartic, by its results, which, we are hazarding, effect a cleansing of the soul and a regeneration of the *polis*. The tragic effect is absolute and final. As Job laments, "What I feared has come upon me." And Oedipus can only stand in stunned silence as the last piece of the puzzle fits into its inevitable place.

Perhaps one might further hazard that the tragic work of art, as a ritual conveying the sudden intuition of outer darkness, surprisingly reveals that shadowy realm to be, not chaos as uncreation, as one might think, but a *ruin*—creation after the fall. In it order is confounded, goodness marred. Putting it simply, then, we could say that tragedy results from a final *anagnorisis*—a recognition of the harm done by some primordial event. But this vision is dependent upon an instantaneous revelation in which the tragic protagonist—and the viewers of tragedy—see what creation was like before its ruin and at the same moment recognize that they themselves have been responsible for the loss. Confronted with their imperfection, which they discern as an external depth into which they have fallen, and finding themselves to blame for everything, they are stunned into immobility as from a sudden blow.

But it is only from within the deep chiaroscuro of the divine, in the perspective of eternity, that this culpability can be apprehended. In ordinary life, human beings have a secret but unexamined awareness of an imperfection in the frame of things and of their own implication in it—along with the intuition that they will ultimately be held accountable for it. Tragedy dramatizes this potential judgment—a dreaded experience that in actual life can only be intuited. The reference point of tragedy is from the deeps. Humanity is viewed from the outer darkness, as in his *Comedy* Dante portrayed his characters from the outer light. But his view of them, being comic, was external, through observation and conversation. The view of tragedy is internal; through its agency one is made to see from within the soul a potential experience as though it were taking place.

Perhaps we can begin to delineate what that potential experience consists of, that experience that lies behind and beyond tragedy: can we not say that it is the dread of eternal loss, along with a simultaneous recognition of one's full value? Lucien Goldmann quotes an anonymous seventeenth-century Jansenist text:

> There is in our heart so deep an abyss that we cannot sound its depths; we can scarcely make out light from dark or good from evil.... But the affliction that God, in his infinite mercy, sends down upon us is like a two-edged sword that enters into the very depths of our hearts and minds. There, it cleaves our human thoughts from those

which God causes to rise up in our souls, and the spirit of God can then no longer hide itself. We begin to have so clear a knowledge of this spirit that we can no longer be deceived. (66)

Is it not this sudden switch from one universe to another that causes the vertigo in tragedy that we call catharsis? And is not the center of that alternate universe that we have suddenly glimpsed, the center from which all radiates, the "deep but dazzling darkness" of the divine, as in the *Commedia* it is its dazzling light? Tragedy might thus be seen as the *aporia* that allows a momentary glimpse of the ruined cosmos, whereas comedy provides, in contrast, a glimpse of its redemption. At the center of the tragic abyss, at the opposing pole from Dante's sun in comedy, is the event that staggers the imagination: the agony of a god, an event sensed preveniently from *illo tempore*. Thus the terror of tragedy stems from the sudden vision of our implication in this sacrifice, with its resultant imperative to choose for or against the bottomless abyss of love—which has to be witnessed as though it is from beyond this life.

Hence the tragic vision seems to have to do with facing both the origin and the end of things: the veiled Chaos and Old Night that surround the divine author of the cosmos. "I seed the beginnin and now I sees the endin," as Dilsey professes in *The Sound and the Fury*. The endeavor is something like the way in which Einstein conceived of modern physics, as bringing one "closer to the secret of the Old One." To become aware of a vast all-fathering darkness and a suffering god is to see something that reminds the audience, uncomfortably, of the act of creation—its own rootedness in matter and its gravity and guilt in the downward pull toward the ancient mother. Jahweh's answer to Job is to remind him of the secret ways of the earth; Oedipus's murky path leads him to the grove of the Furies, "ladies whose eyes are terrible"; Lear's wanderings in the storm teach him something repugnant but humbling about the reproductive fertility of nature.

Wole Soyinka laments the gradual loss in Western drama of the earth and cosmic consciousness, attributing its absence to Platonic and Christian thought (Myth 10), though such a radical shift seems more probably related to the dominant modern view of the universe as mechanism. In discovering the existence of a "dark energy" in the universe that devours whole galaxies, postmodern cosmologists are coming to view our little planet as insignificant indeed, a small point in the blankness of infinite space. If a requirement for tragedy is guilt toward a precious earth and humility toward a vast outer darkness which, though we cannot comprehend it, beckons to us with love—along with a sharp awareness of the ruin we have made of the human enterprise—then twenty-first century writers may once again be able to evoke the necessary shared pity and terror that tragedy demands.

But not without the one secret ingredient. Without Job's lamentations, Oedipus' grave and noble protests, Lear's howls of remorse, Hamlet's anguished, theatrical meditations, there could be no tragedy. The tragic hero suffers not in silence but in the most opulent and expressive language the world has known. From these cries arising in the center of the soul, the secret dwelling-place of language—in a darkness corresponding to the abyss—bursts the poetry that raises human suffering to the level of contemplation and, to a stunned and gratified audience, conveys the liberation of tragic joy.

NOTES

[1] "Tragedy's one essential is a soul that can feel greatly. Given such a one and any catastrophe may be tragic. But the earth may be removed and the mountains carried into the midst of the sea, and if only the small and shallow are involved, tragedy is absent" (Hamilton 142); "The suffering of a soul that can suffer greatly—that and only that, is tragedy" (143).

[2] D. D. Raphael, passim.

[3] See Scheler 255.

[4] See Lionel Abel, "Is There a Tragic Sense of Life?" (Abel 177).

[5] See Fergusson, Harrison (Themis), and Muller.

[6] Originally Karl Jaspers' phrase, it was adopted by Tillich: "The human boundary situation is encountered when human possibility reaches its limit, when human existence is confronted by an ultimate threat" (197).

[7] See Voegelin (Order 143-147).

[8] For a thorough treatment of tragic theory after the Greek and Roman epochs, see Henry Ansgar Kelly.

[9] See Gellrich 23-93.

[10] Shakespeare combines all three stages in the single arena of each

of his tragic dramas, though he may emphasize one stage and merely imply the others.

Part One

TRAGEDY

AND

THEORY

Happiness extends, then, just so far as contemplation
(theoria) does, and those to whom contemplation more
fully belongs are more truly happy, not as a mere con-
comitant but in virtue of the contemplation; for this
is in itself precious. Happiness, therefore, must be
some form of contemplation.

ARISTOTLE, *ETHICS*

1

Aristotle and the Tragic Bias

ROBERT S. DUPREE

Though Aristotle doubtless had more information about Greek tragedy than we now possess, his *Poetics* is far from representing an eyewitness account of its subject. To be sure, fourth-century Greeks continued to attend theatrical performances and new plays continued to be staged. However, the great era of tragic art was long over; the need to revive the plays of Aeschylus, Sophocles, and Euripides had long reflected a decline in the quality of their successors' efforts. While Aristotle's analysis remains firmly in touch with the performing traditions of the plays, it is distinctly retrospective. The focus of his treatment is the tragic effect, the emotional impact of tragedy on its audience. He takes full account of the extraliterary aspects of tragic art—of spectacle, music, and dance—but treats them as auxiliaries that assist the tragic effect without themselves producing it. What he provides is not, as has sometimes been asserted, a manual for the writing of tragedy but an inquiry into why it has such an impact on participants in the theatre or even on readers at home. He shows no inclination to recognize what modern scholars have called "the vision of tragedy," that perspective on man's place in the cosmos that genuine tragedy seems to present wherever and whenever it emerges. Yet such a vision is implied throughout the *Poetics*, even though it is never explicitly evoked. That is likely because, for Aristotle, the tragic perspective was not one of many possible ways of seeing reality; it was the only way of seeing it.

Aristotle assesses various genres against the background of an implied hierarchy of values. He speaks first of the varieties of imitation produced by the means of voice—that is, speech, harmony, and rhythm rather than colors and shapes—and include epic, tragedy, comedy, dithyrambic poetry and lyre or aulos music. Though not all of these have the same elements in common, he seems to suggest that they all point to the same reality; otherwise, they would not be comparable and capable of ranking according to their degrees of success in producing a certain impact on the audience. Ultimately, Aristotle wishes to demonstrate that tragedy is superior to all other genres in producing the effect proper to it. This preferential ranking, which I am calling "the tragic bias," has loomed large in the way literature has been understood subsequently in the Western world, especially beginning with the Renaissance.

The end of art, according to Aristotle, is pleasure, *hedone*, not intellectual understanding. It is, however, a peculiar kind of pleasure, and each art has its own particular variety that is best suited to it by nature. The word *hedone* is more concrete in Greek than our word "pleasure" in English. Our word is derived, through French, from Latin *placeo*, which is based on the notion of agreement, acceptability. Something pleases me because I find it to my liking. It is associated with appeasement, reconciliation, or satisfaction. But the Greek word is more like Latin *voluptas*, which implies an appeal to the senses, even though etymologically it also refers to fulfillment of desire (Latin *volo*). The family of words to which *hedone* belongs, however, is anchored in the sense of taste; it includes the adjective *hedus*, "sweet" and the verb *heduno*, "to sweeten or season." The Latin and English words are focused on the subject, the Greek on the thing experienced. *Hedone* is a property of the thing that gives pleasure, not an agreement between it and the enjoyer. Thus our Latinate minds, at least as reflected in the word origins of our mongrelized English vocabulary, tend to think of pleasure in terms of an accommodation between subject and object—a problem related to that of knowledge—rather than in terms of something naturally and inherently good within a thing. While knowledge is not opposed to pleasure in Aristotle—indeed, it gives its own particular kind of pleasure—his purpose in the *Poetics* is to determine not what kind of wisdom tragedy provides (its "vision" or "insight") but what kind of pleasure (its "effect"). That pleasure seems to be closely tied to a phenomenon he calls "*catharsis*."

The concept of *catharsis*, central to the main argument of the treatise and to the tragic effect, has elicited numerous interpretations of its exact meaning among commentators from Scaliger to Else, Lucas, Harbison, and Golden. It has been interpreted as a medical or quasi-medical phenomenon (purgation), a term from the harvesting of grain (winnowing), or on a more abstract level as insight (clarification). All these meanings can be supported by examples of usage from Greek writers other than Aristotle; what remains controversial is the meaning Aristotle himself intended.

Scholars have long had recourse to a passage in the *Politics* that appears to be directly linked to the section on *catharsis* in the *Poetics*. However, even that does not offer the clarity of intention which certainty of interpretation demands. In their presentation of the passage, Russell and Winterbottom warn: "Some caution is... necessary in applying the notion of musical *catharsis* to tragedy" (133). However, Aristotle offers a succinct and clear definition of what he means by *catharsis* in general; he speaks of "a sort of *catharsis*, a relief accompanied by pleasure." Music and tragedy alike seem to be capable of producing this relief; likewise, if epic, comedy, and dithyrambic poetry are also comparable in effect, they must be capable of producing it as well. They are all cathartic to some extent; all produce both relief and pleasure. Perhaps the problem with our understanding of *catharsis* is that we try to make more of it than Aristotle intended. It seems clear enough that he means something rather straightforward that applies to all the arts mentioned in the *Poetics*: a structure that consists of a building of tension followed by a pleasurable release from it.

The ancient Greeks reflected extensively upon music; they recognized in it a social and cultural role far greater than we would expect, though music plays just as important a role in our own society. Nietzsche was not mistaken in titling his treatise *The Birth of Tragedy from the Spirit of Music*. Each of the ancient modes (or scales) that the Greeks recognized as the building blocks for their music was associated with a different effect, much as we associated the major mode with joy and the minor mode with sadness. In Greek music, as in Chinese or Indian music, however, the range of emotions associated with the modes was far greater and

far more subtle. In the 1950s parents worried about the delete-
rious effects on their children of rock and roll music, as their
parents, in turn, had worried about jazz. The twentieth century
was mostly characterized by dissonance in its music, by a steady
onslaught of unrelieved musical tension. We currently pay little
heed, for the most part, to the effects of music on the young
(apart from sometimes worrying over the shocking lyrics that
accompany it); perhaps we should. In any event the ancient
Greeks were convinced that one should.

Any treatise on music, whether Western or not, makes the
same fundamental points about its nature. Music works by inducing and then releasing tension. The Greek word *tonos* (the source
of our word "tone") does in fact mean "tension." It is defined
in the dictionaries as a stretching or tightening. In musical terminology, it also refers to the modes, the *tonoi*. In versification
it refers to "stress." To us, a tone is a thing. To the Greeks it
was a straining between two things. All music, whatever its origin, works in the same way. A mode or scale establishes a sense
of pattern and order. The musician creates sequences of tension
and relaxation by moving away from and back to the home base
established by the mode. One can accomplish this effect through
unaccompanied melody alone, and the Greeks did so exclusively.
We do so through more elaborate means involving simultaneously
sounded notes. The effect, however, is the same, even though
from era to era the implications of degrees of tension may be
different. Yesterday's dissonance may become today's consonant; in
music, all is truly relative. In the *Politics* Aristotle himself notes
that there are different kinds of music for different classes of people. The vulgar, artisans, laborers, and so on ought to have their
own music, since "just as their souls are warped from the natural state, so there are deviations from the modes and high-strung
melodies with smaller intervals than normal, and what produces
pleasure in any set of people is what they find naturally akin to
them; so we should allow the contestants to use such music to
such an audience" (133). But somehow it is possible to represent,
indeed to provoke, emotions through the creation of sound-ten-
sions, even when different classes of people are involved. The
release from those tensions promotes a peculiar pleasure that is a
universal aspect of human nature, whatever the means employed
to obtain it.

Nevertheless, the means to that peculiar pleasure are not without importance. We tend to extract from the *Poetics* those aspects that interest us and ignore those that don't. Why does Aristotle find it necessary to go into detail concerning elementary linguistic and rhetorical properties in a work that is so overtly centered on tragedy? There are stretches of the treatise that seem unnecessary, if not exactly out of place. Yet the analysis of tragedy does not take place in a literary or social vacuum. If Aristotle sometimes seems to say too much, at other times he doesn't say enough to satisfy our fascination with the tragic. In many ways it is fortunate that he doesn't; otherwise, Hegel, Nietzsche, Scheler, Jaspers, and other modern philosophers would not have had much to say. At the same time, we must acknowledge that what Aristotle states only obliquely or not at all (because presupposed) may be even more important than what he makes explicit. These presuppositions point to his and the ancient Greek's vision of tragedy, which is the culmination, rather than simply a component, of a whole philosophy of existence.

Throughout the document one is aware that the author has in mind certain hierarchies of excellence. He is not only interested in analyzing the elements that make up each kind but in showing which are essential and which non-essential, which tend to contribute to or intensify the tragic effect and which are merely further enhancements of its peculiar excellence. That excellence is of a purely aesthetic nature, and the point of the aesthetic experience is to give pleasure. *Mimesis* or imitation (I do not intend to engage the interpretive tangles to which this concept leads) gives pleasure, even when the thing imitated would be fearful, disagreeable, or disgusting if experienced in itself. The example he gives is a painting of a dead body. The spatial arts provide a pleasure that is directly mimetic. Aristotle thinks that we learn through recognition: this is that. The pleasure that is the product of the verbal and musical arts, which are time-based in nature, is tied to release from the very tensions generated by the work of art itself, quite differently from the pleasure that arises out of a "this is that" kind of recognition.

The direct form of *mimesis* practiced in the visual arts operates not through a process of building and relaxing tension in the sequential and temporal order (though, of course, all painting and sculpture use balance, contrast, and tension in a simultaneous order) but through a process of allowing viewers to connect a representing "this" with a represented "that." The pleasure associated with this recognition issues from the knowledge that the viewer gains, according to Aristotle. One could also see it as the resolution of a different kind of tension, an epistemological tension that is eliminated when one sees how two things relate to one another or fit together. To bring them together in the mind is to see a pattern; though not, strictly speaking, a *catharsis*, the result is a near cousin to it: clarification. While the emotions and the intellect are both engaged to some degree in all the arts, Aristotle suggests that the pleasure proper to narrative, drama, and music is connected with their emotional impact. The pleasure proper to non-representational arts and to direct *mimesis* alike is connected with our perceptions of similarity and difference.

Tragedy is, however, unique in the way it represents. Aristotle says that it is the imitation of an action, by which he means not a representation of a physical object, such as a painter might depict, nor the physical actors on a stage nor sets and costumes, nor even the qualities or character of a person such as a prose writer might describe, but of something not immediately perceptible. This particular object of imitation he calls *praxis*, which, though usually translated as "action," implies a great deal more. As in English, the Greek word is contrasted with "passion" or "suffering" in the manner that active is opposed to passive. To act is to make things happen, not to allow them to happen *to* one. The Greek verb corresponding to *praxis* is *prasso*, "to pass through" or "to finish." In common usage this verb meant something like "to achieve" or "bring about," "effect," "accomplish." In the epic world, *prassein kleos* means "to achieve or win glory" or "to take charge of a thing," according to Liddell and Scott. In this latter sense it leads to the notion of practicing a trade or business, managing affairs, or behaving well or ill towards someone.

This choice of vocabulary has certain ramifications. *Praxis*, a doing or acting well or ill, can also refer to the progress or result of something done. It points towards accomplishment, results. It is engaged in by movers and shakers, by responsible people who have an impact on the course of things. Little wonder, then, that Aristotle insists that the tragic protagonist be a person of consequence, of high status and moral stature, not simply one of us but a man in charge. *Praxis* is not just any occurrence, any common act. It indicates purposiveness, direction, consequence. In short, the imitation of a *praxis* must point to a teleology, a goal-oriented action that is characterized by a beginning, middle, and end because it commences, passes through, and concludes in some significant achievement. As M.E. Hubbard glosses Aristotle's word *prattonton*, things people do, it "means, for him, 'people performing responsible and morally characterizable actions'" (Russell and Winterbottom 92).

Contrast this term with another Greek word, *drama*, which means "a deed" or "act." All drama is about action in this broader sense, as both the English and Greek words make clear. But tragedy, in its imitation of a purposeful action, has something to do with human participation in the direction of the cosmos. Further, the word *praxis* seems to suggest more of what we mean in English when we speak of something as "dramatic," meaning full of anticipation and tension or startling surprise. A dramatic turn of events is one that creates new tensions and problems as a result of sudden change. All narratives function through the building of tensions, followed by release from them, whether they be epic, tragic, or comic in character. Comedy works the same way as tragedy. It too has a *catharsis*, or moment of consonance and relaxation of tension, though not of the same order as in tragedy. How it truly differs I wish to defer until the end of this essay, but I would note that no time-based art, not even lyric poetry and twelve-tone music, can really escape this rhythm without seeming pointless and aimless.

Obviously, it is not enough to move from tension to release over and over again without engaging this movement in a more comprehensive pattern. It is in considering how this basic rhythm is used to build a larger structure that Aristotle differentiates the kinds of *praxis* imitated in epic, comedy, and tragedy. His famous definition of tragedy includes the following aspects: *praxis* (a responsible action of some magnitude that causes something to happen, brought to its fulfillment with moral consequences); *logos* (speech) enhanced with elements pleasurable in themselves (such as rhythm and music) that appear in different sections of the play (some recited in verse, others, such as the choral odes, sung); *dramatic* rather than narrative *form*; pleasurable *catharsis* effected through pity and fear by way of imitation. Of these the first and the last are central to an understanding of Aristotle's notion of a tragic vision and his contribution to the tragic bias.

A *praxis* implies agents, Aristotle goes on to explain, and they must have moral qualities and reasoning minds if they are to attempt their goals, whether attaining them successfully or not. It is presented as a *muthos* (plot or story), a selection of key incidents presented in a suitable order and chosen from all that may have occurred during a particular period of time so that we may discern the causal connection between them without being distracted by unimportant or irrelevant details and events. Furthermore, the poet must include some representation of the way his characters think, argue, speak, and exhibit moral qualities by justifying their choices. Consequently, tragedy, as distinguished from other literary kinds, has a total of six elements: plot (the ordering and selecting principle); depiction of moral character (good or evil); verbal expression (high or low style of speech); quality of mind (intelligent, ignorant, etc.); scenery, costumes, masks, and other stage equipment; and musical composition (for the choral odes).

Of these, the *muthos* is the most important, since without it the tragedy falls apart, whereas one could dispense with the last two altogether (e.g., in reading) and the other three could be flawed to some extent or even absent in some cases without necessarily ruining the whole. Tragedy is not primarily about what kind of person a character is but what happens when he or she does something. The *muthos* is the most difficult element to get right, and the two most attractive aspects of it are *peripeteia* and *anagnorisis*. It is the *muthos* that gives life to a tragedy because it is the central structural principle.

The order of the events is crucial to an effective *muthos*. Moreover, it must take place in a sufficient period of time to give ample exposure to all its elements without being so long that we lose track of their relationships. The way individual events contribute to the cumulative effect of the *muthos* must never be lost sight of, otherwise the tragic effect will be weakened or non-existent. In addition, the fact that a *praxis* is performed by one person is no guarantee of that unity of *muthos* and its contribution to the total effect. Rather, it is necessary to construct a tragedy so that no episodes can be added to or taken from or transposed within the *muthos* without affecting the whole. Finally, it is important that there be a plausible connection between them as we experience event after event. This last requirement, as I shall argue later, is both intellectually and formally indispensable to both tragic effect and tragic vision. It comes into play especially as Aristotle examines the role of the unexpected in tragedy. There even chance events must look as though they were meant to happen. This last point is crucially related to the role of destiny in tragedy, a feature of the tragic vision that Aristotle never evokes.

There are two sorts of *muthoi*; Aristotle calls them "simple" and "complex." Both are characterized by a clear beginning, middle, and end and consist of causally-linked episodes. The simple is best described in the words of Lewis Carroll's King of Hearts: "Begin at the beginning, and go on till you come to the end: then stop." Its main defining aspect is its linearity. The principal defining aspect of the complex *muthos* is surprise. With a simple linear presentation we watch the inevitable march of events as they lead to their terrible climax without interruption. Aristotle considers the incorporation of surprise to result in a superior structure. It consists, first of all, of a *peripeteia*, a sudden change (literally a turnaround). What gives this device suggestive power is the way it combines a reversal of direction (things seem to be getting better and suddenly take a turn for the worse) with the probability that such a shift was inevitable. This element of surprise (which, to judge by Aristotle's examples, could be either pleasant or unpleasant for the protagonist) can make the causal links between the episodes all the more terrifying by suggesting an underlying ignorance on the part of both protagonist and audience of what is really going on. This *muthos* is rightly called "complex" because its structure suggests two orders of events: the one that we think is occurring and the one that is really occurring. As an analogue to our knowledge of our own destiny, it can contribute mightily to the tragic effect.

The other element of surprise in a complex *muthos* Aristotle calls *anagnorisis* or "recognition." The word means literally "to know again" or even "to own up" to something. Curiously, it also has the meaning of "reading." If we combine all these senses, what emerges is a coming to knowledge about events or about oneself where there had been ignorance. Clearly, *anagnorisis* is an effective companion of *peripeteia*. Once you truly know where you are going, you recognize yourself and your destiny for the first time. You have known yourself twice: first erroneously and

now correctly. You must now confess—as Oedipus does—to all the
terrible things you have done. You are reading or interpreting
what has been written down for you from the beginning and has
only now come to light. Though *anagnorisis* does not necessarily
presuppose *peripeteia*, and the latter does not necessarily demand
being followed by it, their tandem operation seems almost
inevitable. Nevertheless, Aristotle speaks of both as though they
may occur in less portentous contexts.

Aristotle adds a third element, *pathos*, which is "an act involving destruction or pain." The word was understood in opposition
to *prasso* and *praxis*; it referred to anything that befalls one, especially suffering, misfortune, or unavoidable calamity. It could
include passions or feelings, again especially those beyond one's
control. It might also mean simply "an incident." Unlike a *praxis*,
which is willed and managed by its agent, *pathos* is an involuntary passive condition that often accompanies the *peripeteia*.
Indeed, it is a component of the reversal of fortune: he who
seemed to be in control is now suffering under the control of
another, superior force. The helpful one with a plan of action
(one thinks immediately of Oedipus) is now the helpless one with
nowhere to turn. Again, as in the case of the other two parts,
pathos need not be directly linked in a major way with other
elements of the *muthos*, but Aristotle sees it as one that ought
to be used in connection with them for full effectiveness. Thus
he finds the complex arrangement to be the best and the more
elements brought into play within it the better. At the same time,
he finds a *praxis* with a double conflict—that is, one with different outcomes for the evil and the virtuous—to be unsatisfactory
for tragedy, though quite proper for comedy. The only *pathos* that
evokes pity and terror is one unjustly imposed, though not totally
undeserved. There must be a disproportion between the suffering
and its cause; were tragic protagonists to be utterly guilty of acts
that precipitated a well-deserved fate, they would still seem in control of a personal destiny. The *pathos* must be tied to the *praxis*
but must not be determined by it.

In comedy, by implication, one gets what deserves or better
than one deserves. In tragedy, there is a conspicuous disproportion, a tension between the *pathos* imposed and the *praxis* leading to it. The resultant pity and fear that emerge must be a
consequence of the way the *muthos* is structured, not from some

direct *mimesis* arising out of theatrical spectacle. Thus the often-told story of the terrifying stage appearance of the Furies in Aeschylus' *Choephoroe* and *Eumenides* that caused women to give birth prematurely is not an example of the kind of terror Aristotle means; but their pursuit of Orestes, which is the consequence of his *praxis*, the killing of his mother, is.

Unfortunately, at several points Aristotle seems to contradict himself. He calls Euripides "the most tragic" of the dramatists, though elsewhere he implies that Sophocles' *Oedipus Rex* is a better tragedy than those of the younger playwright. In his analysis of recognition, knowledge, intention, and the tragic effect (1454a), he calls the best combination the one involving a character who ignorantly intends to kill someone related to himself and recognizes the victim in time to avoid doing so, a situation that leads to a happy ending. The examples he gives are all from Euripides. Some scholars have suggested that this inconsistency is the result of a later change of heart, a shift in preference towards tragicomedy on the part of an aging Aristotle and therefore a later addition (e.g., Bywater, Hubbard). In their edition and French translation of the *Poetics*, Dupont-Roc and Lallot propose a distinction between "tragedy" as an ideal model of the perfect play and that kind of dramatic situation which promotes the "tragic," of which this example would be a specimen. Neither explanation seems convincing, simply because no evidence exists for the first and the second introduces yet another inconsistency: Aristotle insists clearly on the indissoluble relation of part to whole that such a distinction denies. Perhaps the answer lies in the context of the statement. He is speaking of traditional stories that cannot be changed but must be used unaltered as effectively as possible. The ending of *Iphigenia in Tauris* does, in fact, include an evocation of pity and terror followed by a resolution and, in that way, illustrates the main lines of the tragic effect. It also illustrates the element of surprise. As Hubbard remarks (109, n.5), there is little else to do with this odd inconsistency in the *Poetics* but to accept it. Perhaps it simply demonstrates that Aristotle is more interested in analyzing the tragic effect than the tragic vision.

It is true, however, that a tragic vision and a view of destiny are implied throughout the treatise. They emerge as a result of Aristotle's final ranking of the literary genres according to excellence. Early in his analyses, the author makes clear the

inferiority of comedy to tragedy. He notes that the kind of character imitated in tragedy is superior to that appropriate to comedy; the comic hero is one like us or lower in status, while the
tragic hero is something of an ideal type, flawed though he may
be in some respect. Comedy tends to make use of an episodic
structure or of one with double issue, both of which lack the
concentrated linear unity of the tragic *muthos*. Though the comic
muthos consists of tension and release, just like its tragic counterpart, it does so in a looser, less rigorous fashion. It does not
lead to the profound terror and pity that tragedy is capable of
inducing, even when these qualities are succeeded by a happy
ending. Comedy is broad and dilated where tragedy is narrow and
concentrated. Though they share common elements, including
spectacle and music, they are unlike in intensity of grandeur.

The comparison with epic is less schematic but no less favor-
able to tragedy. The two kinds have many aspects in common,
of course: both should have *muthoi* that structure one whole or
complete action. Both present protagonists of high status and
noble character. Taking Homer as exemplary, the author notes
that epic can be just as linear in design and unified in form as
tragedy. Both can be simple or complex; they can focus on character or on *pathos*. Both are most effective when they make use
of *peripeteia*, *anagnorisis*, and *pathé*. Both are capable of excellence
in verbal expression and psychological penetration. They are also
different in several ways. Their modes of presentation are distinct.
The epic poet can narrate or he can speak, dramatically, by
impersonating the voice of one of his characters. The narrative
mode offers certain benefits: it allows considerable extension in
length, and as Aristotle puts it,

> one can tell of many things as at the moment of their accomplishment,
> and these if they are relevant make the poem more impressive. So it
> has this advantage in the direction of grandeur and variety for the
> hearer and in being constructed with dissimilar episodes. For it is sim-
> ilarity and the satiety it soon produces that make tragedies fail... for
> the narrative mimesis has itself a sort of abundance in comparison with
> the others. (Russell and Winterbottom 125).

In tragedy, "it is impossible to represent many parts as at the
moment of their occurrence, since one can only represent the

part on the stage and involving the actors" (125). Yet tragedy, in avoiding narration and presenting action directly, gains in vividness what it loses in flexibility. Both epic and tragedy use meters appropriate for their purposes, the steady, weighty, and more inclusive heroic hexameter for the epic, the iambic trimeter and trochaic tetrameter for drama, both meters "of movement, one of the dance, the other of action" (125). In an earlier passage, Aristotle points out that in "plays episodes are brief, but epic uses them to increase its length" (114). He adds later that one ought "not make an epic body of material into a tragedy" (115) because of the disproportion in length between them. He points out, in a passage praising Homer's practice, that "epic is more tolerant of the prime source of surprise, the irrational, because one is not looking at the person doing the action" (125); yet later he suggests that one should "not compose one's argument of irrational parts" and that preferably "there should be no irrationality at all" (126). Though the comments are not meant to suggest a qualitative difference, they do point towards later conclusions about the respective merits of the two genres.

It is in the last section, finally, that Aristotle reveals his hand. He asks which is superior, the epic or the tragic genre. He begins by paraphrasing those who oppose tragedy (i.e. among others, Plato): "Epic, they say, is directed to a cultivated audience which does not need gesture, tragedy to a low-class one; so if it is vulgar, it must obviously be worse" (131). His answer is that the charge is directed against the art of the performer rather than that of the poet. Tragedy can produce its effect even without movement, just as can epic, since both can be satisfactorily experienced through reading. In fact, tragedy is superior to epic for a number of reasons. First,

> tragedy has everything that epic has (it can even use its meter), and moreover has a considerable addition in the music and the spectacle, which produce pleasure in a most vividly perceptible way.
>
> Moreover, it has vividness when read as well as when performed.
>
> Again, it takes less space to attain the end of its *mimesis*; this is an advantage because what comes thick and fast gives more pleasure than something diluted by a large admixture of time—think, for instance, of the effect if someone put Sophocles' *Oedipus* into as many lines as the *Iliad*.

Again, the *mimesis* of the epic poets is less unified, as we can see from the fact that any epic *mimesis* provides matter for several tragedies. The result of this is that if they do make a single plot, it either appears curtailed, when it is only briefly indicated, or follows the lead of its lengthy meter and becomes dilute; I mean here the poem made up of several actions, in the way in which the *Iliad* has many such parts and also the *Odyssey*, and these parts have extension in themselves (and yet these two poems are as admirably composed as can be and are, so far as possible, the *mimesis* of a single action).

If tragedy is superior in all these respects and also in artistic effectiveness (for these arts should produce not just any pleasure, but the one we have discussed), it would obviously be superior to epic as it is more successful in attaining what it aims at. (132)

In claiming that tragedy has everything epic has, Aristotle forgets about the narrative mode, which is not very effective on stage. For all that, his point is obvious: tragedy can do everything epic can and does it better.

In praising Homer, Aristotle singles out those qualities that make his epics like tragedies: "he did not undertake to make a whole poem of the war..., even though it had a beginning and an end. For the plot would have been too large and not easy to see as a whole, or if it had been kept to a moderate length it would have been tangled because of the variety of events" (123). It is this ability to grasp the whole that identifies the great advantage of tragedy. It is a more concentrated and intense form that leads more efficiently to the complex pleasure produced by the *catharsis* of pity and terror. In spite of its compactness, it is rich in elements. Moreover, the very structure of tragedy is an exact mirror of the insight it embodies. It is here that Aristotle's tragic vision becomes apparent. The most profound imaginative experience—an emotional rather than an intellectual one—is for him one that leads down a narrowing corridor that promises certainty but turns into an unpleasant surprise, a revelation of the dark horrors we have tried and failed to hide from ourselves. The causally linked episodes of the complex tragic *muthos* set up a rhythm that makes us feel this tightening noose which awaits us at the end of the journey without our knowledge or power to escape it. Pity and terror are the products not of an idea but of a movement, the outcome of a *praxis* that we feel bound to perform but helpless to implement. And yet, because this terrifying experience is not randomly thrown in our path but calculatedly structured to fit our very human contours, it is passed through (*prasso*) and looked back on with relief. For ultimately knowledge of the most terrible things that can happen to us brings with it a kind of relief and even a release from uncertainty. That is what *catharsis* is about—the knowledge that comes not from a knowledge of history—what actually happened—but from imitation—that which could happen and that we have already experienced emotionally. We enter the theatre at one end of the narrow tunnel that leads to terror and we leave it at the other, having learned not the meaning of suffering but what it means to experience it truly and unexpectedly for the first, though not the last, time.

The tragic vision is only one of the several that readers of literature, in the relativity of imaginative experience, can explore in their quest for a full view of human nature. I suspect, without being able precisely to prove it, that Aristotle saw tragedy as offering a more truthful view of reality than its competitors. But even if we post-moderns see tragedy as only one of a choice of pleasures with equal claims on our leisure time, the eminence of tragedy still remains, to some extent. The formal ideal Aristotle presents in his description of tragedy gave it a prestige that was to last for centuries. If the great ambition of the poet from the sixteenth through the eighteenth centuries was to compose a great national epic, the gauge of the moral stature of a society in those following was its ability to revive the tragic theatre. While that ambition has been disappointed in playwright after playwright, it has continued to shape our aesthetics and our literary ideals. The modern novel, from Flaubert and Henry James to their successors in the last years of the twentieth century, has been shaped, indeed dominated, by the tragic ideal of compactness, variety of elements, and unity of vision. The tragic bias has infiltrated philosophy, theology, and philosophy. It has made us value organic form over the "loose, baggy monsters" of popular fiction, as Henry James put it, and consistency of structure and point of view over playful literary acrobatics. Beyond the realm of the merely literary and theoretical, it has given the idea of tragedy a life with far greater longevity than the theatre itself was able to sustain. Profundity, intensity, realism, discipline, craftsmanship, all are measured by the degree to which they conform to the tragic bias of our criteria. If tragedy still matters to us, it is less because we are inclined to attend performances of Aeschylus, Sophocles, or Euripides than because we have been taught to care by Aristotle.

2

Tarrying With the Tragic:
Hegel and His Critics

Hegel's thought on tragedy is central to his entire system of the self-development of spirit in the world. For this reason it has been the subject of a great deal of scrutiny since Western philosophy has undertaken to cross-examine, not to say prosecute, its own tradition. It is perhaps fitting that the reassessment of tragedy (and of one particular tragedy especially, Sophocles' *Antigone*) lies at the heart of the transition from the Eurocentric, secularized Christian world—whose vision Hegel so consummately expounded—to the world in which we now live, whose "paths to thinking" contemporary philosophy is struggling to articulate. Croce's title, *What Is Living and What Is Dead in Hegel's Philosophy*, still poses the apposite question, for Hegel's analysis of tragedy constitutes an enormous advance over earlier critical models that must be fully comprehended before one can go on to address his failures. The way to any synthesizing of a new understanding of tragedy for our brave new world—no doubt a way of pain—still runs through Hegel; and consequently I propose here to review his thought historically and sympathetically before sketching some prominent recent critiques.

Hegel's generation was the first to overthrow the "prejudice of Enlightenment" against the past. Fed by the first stirrings of a poetic revolution and by a historical movement in scholarship that was bent on retrieving ancient mythology, art, and culture, Hegel (along with his fellow philosopher F.W.J. Schelling and the poet Friedrich Hölderlin) sought in the great works of the past a wisdom profounder than the recent products of European culture. They laid the foundations for the twentieth-century view of the literary work of art as meaningful in itself, as incorporating a cognitive act, and as conferring on the reader a kind of knowledge with its own integrity, distinct from philosophical or religious knowledge and, if less explicit, more authoritative in that it has not had to desert its solidarity with human experience in order to know that experience. This was the generation that had to rescue art from the manacles of classicist theory, which had located the chief worth of aesthetics in its study of nature. In its place Schelling, Hölderlin, and Hegel conferred on art the same distinction given to philosophy (and, in their estimation, to religion): all, they maintained, are adventures in thinking. They thereby reinstated, at a level that converted them into aspects of thought, the old Aristotelian modes of life: art (*poiesis*); religion (*praxis*); philosophy (*sophia*). Each was to yield its truth about the revelation of spirit in its gradual incarnation in the world.

For this the dimension of history was crucial. Hegel and his coevals collectively came to see history as the path that spirit traces in its journey through the world. They found that the study of history allows one to see the unity of culture. And not only unity but its ruptures as well: seen in its proper light, a past work of art, religion, or mythology has already confronted aspects of human existence that the modern reader may have been unable or unwilling to face. Encountering these moments and returning to them will make one deeper: this idea, familiar in Matthew Arnold, is distinctively Hegelian, following from the way Hegel sees the works of art he discusses. The historical study of culture thus reveals both positive and negative dimensions, and the two together point to that "higher unity" so often identified with German thought. In the approach of these German Idealists the humanities curriculum obtains its modern rationale; and if Kant, that giant of two generations prior, has been credited with the basis for the New Critics, one can see that Hegel's approach leads no less strongly to their affirmation of poetry as knowledge. As Hegel puts it in his *Lectures on Aesthetics*, man "must know what the powers are which drive and direct him, and it is such a knowledge that poetry provides in its original and substantive

form.... Poetry... is the original presentation of the truth, a knowing which does not yet separate the universal from its living existence in the individual... but which grasps the one only in and
through the other."[1]

Hegel's introduction of the historical dialectic into art is
accompanied by a new attitude toward art, one of "seriousness"
(*Aesth.* 204) where before—in Kant and Schiller, notably—the
keynote was "play," a suitable note for the eighteenth-century
world of Pope, Mozart, and Fragonard. This new seriousness—
whether one welcomes it or bemoans the loss of a freer, more
Olympian attitude and possibly of enjoyment itself—is owed to art
because art can yield meaning and insight into history and into
one's own historical moment. For Hegel the signature of this historical content is *"Kollision"*: "the seriousness and importance of
the situation in its special character can only begin when its def-
initeness comes into prominence as an essential difference and,
by being in opposition to something else, is the basis of a collision" (*Aesth.* 204). The violence implied in this moment calls for
an attitude of seriousness in response and makes tragedy the central model of art as historical significance. Furthermore, the concept of collision is especially suited for drama. The most
architecturally complete Greek tragedy, Aeschylus' *Oresteia* trilogy,
presents a threefold scheme of assertion, collision, and resolution
that Hegel found most congenial to his general theory of the
working of the world.

Hegel writes allusively—not to mention elusively—with very few
direct references in his text. The index of names to the
Suhrkamp edition of his central work, the *Phenomenologie des
Geistes*, lists only thirty-seven, and thirteen of those are names
found in Greek or Shakespearean tragedy. More indicative is the
shaping of his thought by tragedy in transparent though not
explicitly acknowledged ways—specifically, by the *Oresteia* and the
Theban cycle of Sophocles. In this latter, episodes that deliberately are not portrayed by Sophocles also play important roles: the
mutual fratricide of Eteocles and Polyneices, and Oedipus' vanquishing of the Sphinx, which becomes the key schematic image
later in the *Aesthetics*.

Perhaps the greatest indication of the congeniality of Hegel's
thought with tragedy is the program he announces in the Preface to his *Phenomenology of Spirit*. Building on the great focus of

attention of the Romantic idealists—the Absolute in which all things are one—and intent above all on healing the fundamental split between knowledge and truth effected by Kant, Hegel announces that "The True is the whole" (*Das Wahre ist das Ganze*).[2] He then adds his essential contribution, the single great idea expounded by his *Phenomenology*: the necessary dynamism of truth. "But the whole is nothing other than the essence consummating itself through its development." The whole, the truth, does not exist ultimately apart from its understanding, and understanding is a labor of the negative, encountering its opposite, everything in the world resistant to understanding. Hegel was equally eager to refute the romantic irrationalist belief that the truth is best intuited rather than reasoned, for again that would presuppose that the whole exists apart from the understanding and the labor required to achieve it. So he declares that our thinking of the whole, "the life of God and divine cognition," sinks into "mere edification, and even insipidity, if it lacks the seriousness, the suffering, the patience, and the labor of the negative" (*Phen.* 19). Mere intuition must pass on to its "becoming-other" (*Phen.* 20; *Anderswerden* 3.25) in rationality.

To this thought must be added a further essential advance: Hegel conceives of thought as carried out not simply by the head-work of philosophers but by the human race, and even by nature, in the serious choices all beings make. Thought is lived commitment, not empty analysis. For Hegel "analysis" as Kant conceived of it is trivial, simply procedural; what is of far more importance is the kind of analysis that the world performs in the sphere of real interaction among its denizens.[3]   For by making choices and acting on them, intelligent beings thereby manifest the essence of spirit, which is "active movement and development" (*Aesth.* 178). "But," he hastens to add, "development is nothing without onesidedness and separation.... Spirit, complete and whole, abandons its repose *vis à vis* itself and enters the opposition of this chaotic universe, where in this rift it can now no longer escape the misfortune and calamity of the finite realm." Charles Taylor comments that Hegel's "negativity is opposition, and since opposition is essential to everything, everything is in contradiction, contains negativity, and thus is in movement" (Taylor 110). The awareness of what a particular manifest form in history *is not* is bought only through suffering, for we, limited beings that we are, must and gladly do every day place our trust in limited things, in manifest forms, about any of which one might well say as Faust says, "*Verweile doch, du bist so schön*" (translated by Philip Wayne as "Remain, so fair thou art, remain!" *Faust* 87)—or, more ruefully, "It seemed like a good idea at the time."

Yet tragedy arises from a commitment so deep to a partial good that one who holds on to it through all opposition undergoes a kind of crucifixion. As ultimate example of this "misfortune and calamity" Hegel quotes the abandoned cry of Christ on the cross, "the grief of soul in which he had to cry: 'My God, my God, why hast thou forsaken me?'" Clearly, tragic experience is the nuclear core of Hegel's dynamical system. For the reconciliation of the individual person with God does not enter as a harmony directly, but as a harmony proceeding only from the infinite grief, from surrender, sacrifice, and the death of what is finite, sensuous, and subjective (*Aesth.* 1.537; see Knox's note on 1.522 that the phrase "infinite grief" in Hegel refers to the Crucifixion).

In the Introduction to the *Phenomenology*, Hegel describes his project as tracing "the way of the Soul which journeys through the series of its own configurations as though they were the stations appointed for it by its own nature, so that it may purify itself for the life of the Spirit, and achieve finally, through a completed experience of itself, the awareness of what it really is in itself" (77). These "stations" invoke the Stations of the Cross, as Hegel's English translator A.V. Miller notes here, giving further indication that Hegel's ultimate model for the journey of mind and spirit he portrays is the incarnation, crucifixion, and resurrection of Christ. The stage to which he most frequently alludes is the passion: Gethsemane, the *via crucis*, Golgotha, the seven last words—what one is tempted to say constitutes the kernel of tragedy as understood in a Christian culture. It is, in short, the wisdom and suffering of Greek tragedy, stretched across the open sky of the Christ story, that forms the model for the journey of spirit that Hegel outlines.

Tragedy is also the ultimate test of Hegel's dynamical system, however, for the going out from self that spirit must endure in order to progress is nothing if it remains safe and self-contained; it must be a true abandonment of self; it must include the profound experience of loss to its absolute dimension. If this occurs, however, can spirit then return to itself, reflect on itself as changed, and progress? Just after quoting the cry of Christ in the *Aesthetics*, by a series of gradations Hegel modulates unfathomable loss into what almost seems a kind of cosmic game: "[Christ's] mother suffers a similar agonizing pain, and [*und* 13.234] human life as such is a life of strife, struggles, and sorrows. For greatness and force are truly measured only by the greatness and force of the opposition out of which the spirit brings itself back to unity again." This "and" is surely a hastily constructed bridge over the abyss of infinite pain to get to the more conventional vale of tears.[4] An essential of tragic suffering is the loss of the possibility of return or restoration, and Hegel has staked his entire system of the self-development of spirit on this return. The difficulty Hegel manages to face with only middling success is articulating a world system that is not closed but pre-supposes on the one hand self-loss, the precondition for unknowing development and genuine discovery, and, on the other, the knowing predestination by absolute spirit of all discoveries.

This is a crucial problem because Hegel's breakthrough in realizing the thought value of human action leads inexorably to his insistence that thinking is carried out through suffering: "the life of spirit is not the life that shrinks from death and keeps itself untouched by devastation (*Verwüstung* 3.36), but rather the life that endures it and maintains itself in it. It wins its truth only when, in utter dismemberment (*Zerrissenheit*), it finds itself" (32). The unstated model for this endurance in devastation is the Greek tragic hero: Orestes' steadfastness and the Aeschylean watchword, *pathei mathos*—through suffering comes learning; Antigone's embrace of death to be true to her brother and the chthonic gods; but preeminently Oedipus, who, more than any other figure on the Greek stage, claims the true life of spirit as his own in the blindness and exile that issue from his action. Hegel goes on to say that spirit is the power of enduring "only by looking the negative in the face, and tarrying with it. This tarrying (*Verweilen*) with the negative is the magical power that converts it into being. This power is identical with what we earlier called the Subject." Tragic experience is thus the crucial element in realizing the human spirit; for the negative must be met not simply by "disselecting" it but by a metamorphic change bringing the negative into the heart of spirit.

The word *Verweilen*—tarrying, enduring, dwelling—contains

much of what in Hegel's philosophy is congenial to art and the tragic. *Verweilen* is his word of choice for denoting process and experience as ineluctable dimensions of the truth. It hence implies, as he says above, the dynamization of the essential, a process identical with the making of the thinking subject as an active, even heroic, principle. *Verweilen* is also important for its connotations, its overtones of intentional choice, implying whim, contingency, leisure—"tarry a while yet"—and hence the freedom of reflection, possibly enjoyment and delight, as in the famous wager of Faust that if ever he says to the fleeting moment, "*Verweile doch! Du bist so schön,*" the devil may take his soul. As Goethe's apostrophic form demonstrates, *Verweilen* also implies a certain dialogical relation that is rich in implication for tragic suffering as not simply a solitary and mute gauntlet but a working out of crucial matters in an exclusive conversation with the abyss, a colloquy with the power that has brought one's destruction. The model for such a dialogue, of course, is not Greek at all but rather the Job of the Bible and the Christ of Gethsemane.

Alongside this profound implication, however, remains a persistent connotation of *Verweilen* as more suitably describing the "seasoning" of a crown prince among the commoners and their everyday woes, like Shakespeare's Prince Hal, a model for Goethe's Wilhelm Meister. If so, Hegel's drama of spirit might at worst seem only to mime tragedy and to fit much more aptly the form of a *bildungsroman,* as many commentators have called *The Phenomenology of Spirit.* The aspect of voluntariness is not just a fortuitous association of *Verweilen;* it bespeaks well the character of its agent Spirit, in its journey toward self-realization, a journey undertaken freely. Hegel's overall interpretation thus often seems to be split between the tragic form and tone of the contest, wherein faithful and suffering individuals destroy each other, and the bildungsroman overtone of the larger picture, whose more unscathed journey no one individual, only Spirit, experiences. The question then becomes what Hegel's understanding of the retention or erasure of the tragic remainder is. One may well point out that for any reader of Hegel the encounter with tragedy is most likely to be exactly the way Hegel has described it—a framed witnessing of the tragic spectacle by one whose journey of education is underway. So perhaps Hegel is simply being more honest, seeing the big picture better than bourgeois readers who are quick to accuse him of bourgeois inauthenticity. Yet his theory is not supposed to be a theory of reading but of how tragedy exposes the way the world works.

Does he foreclose on the abyss-opening power of tragedy? Comparing the *Aesthetics*, put together from students' notes at the end of Hegel's career, to a work Hegel wrote in his youth, Peter Szondi finds that in the later work he has changed so that "the Tragic is no longer an essential part of the idea of the divine, since in the religious consciousness the divine lies beyond the Tragic" (Szondi 53). Even by the time of the *Phenomenology*, Szondi argues, "the dialectic [is] at the same time the Tragic and the means of transcending the Tragic" (Szondi 54-55). Yet to an attentive reader the question is far from settled by a biographical evolutionary narrative, as important as such perspectives may be. In fact, one finds it inescapable to conceive of Hegel as caught in a dualism reflecting a larger reality than he could account for, a pull between two forces, or scales, or world views, that he could not resolve in synthesis.

Hegel remains a stimulating commentator on literary works, however. In the *Aesthetics* he goes on to present "Romantic" (meaning belonging to Christian civilization) tragedies—i.e., Shakespeare's—as crowning the expression of suffering in an exploration of the interior life.[5] Most cross-disciplinary commentators, however, have considered Hegel's most far-reaching analysis to be his treatment of ethical conflict in the *Phenomenology*, in which he maps the forces impinging on human life by uncovering them in the fully externalized conflicts between Greek tragic characters wholly devoted to a single side of spirit.

Before considering tragedy as a specialized art form, Hegel first employs its data as an aid to understanding human relations: in his schema, a crucial stage of the development of the spirit is through its recognition of the ethical order. He quotes Antigone's line in Sophocles' drama as a signal of this validation: "For these have life, not simply today and yesterday, but for ever, and no one knows how long ago they were revealed" (*Antigone* 456-57). The conflict of the *Antigone*, in fact, becomes the template for his discussion of the development of this consciousness, for here spirit becomes conscious of the ethical on two levels at once. In the Thebes of Eteocles' and Polyneices' fatal conflict, the community is the field of "ethical substance conscious of what it actually does"—what one might call the public sphere; and it stands over against a realm less aware of widespread consequences but more intimately conscious of immediate demands, namely the family, "an *immediate* consciousness of itself... in an 'other'" (450). The ethical life of the family is "immediate, elemental, and there-fore, strictly speaking, negative" (458), expressing itself most mean-ingfully in honoring its dead.

This intimate and negative awareness is found "in its unmixed form... linked to the equilibrium of the blood and... devoid of desire" in the relation of brother and sister (457). Furthermore, this equilibrium finds itself split dialectically into an unconscious feminine awareness—"the highest *intuitive* awareness of what is eth-ical"—and a conscious masculine awareness. "The loss of the brother is therefore irreparable to the sister and her duty to him is the highest." Here he cites *Antigone*:

> In virtue of what law do I say this? If my husband had died, I could have had another, and a child by another man, if I had lost the first, but with my mother and my father in Hades below, I could never have another brother. Such was the law for whose sake I did you special honor, but to Creon I seemed to do wrong and to show shocking reck-lessness, O my own brother. (908-915)

Creon's understanding of this opposition is carried out to its complete fulfillment. But here Hegel brings into focus the law of fate, the mysterious cosmic law of balance and retribution that stands behind the action of Greek tragedy and is expressed in what Heidegger called the earliest saying in Greek philosophy, Anaximander's fragment, which regards the becoming and passing away of existing things "according to necessity; for they pay penalty and retribution to each other for their injustice according to the assessment of Time" (Kirk/Raven/Schofield 118).[6] Hegel's method of reasoning from the Absolute—"The True is the whole"—allows him to transform this dark inhuman truth into a crystal-clear law of spirit: since "the two laws [are] linked in the essence, the fulfillment of the one evokes the other and—the deed having made it so—calls it forth as a violated and now hostile entity demanding revenge" (469).

One can see how the nineteenth century is bracketed by Hegel at the beginning and Freud at the end. For Hegel, as for no one before him (although it does evoke Newton's third law of motion by analogy), action always contains a contrary unconscious dimension. Alluding to Oedipus he remarks that "actuality... does not reveal the whole truth about itself to consciousness; the son does not recognize his father in the man who has wronged him and whom he slays, nor his mother in the queen whom he makes his wife. In this way, a power which shuns the light of day ensnares the ethical self-consciousness, a power which breaks forth only after the deed is done, and seizes the doer in the act." The tragic action is thus resolved to a pattern as absolutely rational as Newtonian vector analysis: both sides cancel each other out. "The victory of one power and its character" is only an "incomplete work which irresistibly advances to the equilibrium of the two. Only in the downfall of both sides alike is absolute right accomplished" (472).[7]

Together taking the part of the family over against the community, the duality of brother and sister presents part of a larger set of oppositions that Hegel explores here and later in the *Phenomenology*: the claims of man *versus* the claims of woman, in which are contained levels of opposition in human experience: respectively, the universal against the individual, the self-conscious against the unconscious, the human against the divine (463). Moving beyond *Antigone* to consider Greek tragedy in general—surely Hegel is thinking primarily of Agamemnon facing the fleet of the Argive alliance on one side and Clytemnestra with her daughter Iphigenia on the other—he expands these levels. One side contains the human law, the law of the upper world, the state power, and the masculine character; opposing it, the divine law, which is the law of the nether world (the old gods who hold a law that is "for ever"), the power of the family, and the feminine character (736). At this level the protagonist of ancient history, the male lawgiver, meets his tragic opposition in the alliance of woman with the gods, especially the chthonic deities whose power is devoted much more to the element of necessity than to freedom. Necessity entails acknowledging everyone with either the honor or the punishment due them, leaving no one out for the sake of some supposedly larger cause.

Thus a striking new component in the understanding of truth emerges, which can no longer be completely understandable rationally. *Das Wahre ist das Ganze*, and fully half of the whole is the resistance that spirit incorporates in matter, the earth, the spirits of the dead, and woman. Such a view is hardly idiosyncratic or original to the romantics; besides constituting the wisdom of Chinese culture for millennia in *yin* and *yang*, it expresses well the cosmos of the Hellenic Greeks as expressed in tragedy.[8] It is conspicuously foreign to the Western philosophical and the Christian traditions, however; and so its return in philosophy is particularly notable; and when it does return it takes the form of the unconscious.

The alliance of women with the gods appears most explicitly in the *Oresteia*, where the Furies arise in defense of the destroyed and disgraced Clytemnestra. The fierce tenacity of the chthonic gods alters the outcome of everything and, in Aeschylus' presentation, gives rise ultimately through their dogged persistence to the civic order of Athens as the sole response that can placate them. It is in the *Oresteia* that one can see his dialectic of history being born in his mind. "the tragic poet whose world view most closely resembled Hegel's was Aeschylus" (Kaufmann 203), as one finds the conflict of right with right in the *Oresteia*, the *Prometheus*, and even his less often discussed works. That conflict rather than a character's suffering is the central subject of Aeschylus' plays.

Hegel construes the "religion of the underworld" as the belief in two things: "the terrible, unknown night of Fate," which is "pure negativity in the form of universality," and "the Eumenides of the *departed spirit*," which is "the same negativity in the form of individuality" (*Phen.* 674). These older gods of the dead are not superseded by the higher order of the Olympic gods, any more than woman is superseded by man. Womankind is to Hegel "the everlasting irony in the life of the community" (475) and changes everything. Hegel's strong androcentric bias makes her secondary but ineluctable; his insight accords her the role of ironist without specifying where that power stops.

Only by concentrating on Sophocles' plays, however, can one come to a more personalist conception of tragedy and allow the inner dimension of the transformative power of suffering to emerge. Aesthetically the plays of Sophocles were Hegel's favorites, and among them as well he clearly had a preference. Hegel calls *Antigone* "one of the most sublime and in every respect most excellent works of all time" (*Aesth.* 471), "the absolute triumph of tragedy" (*Lectures on the Philosophy of Religion*, quoted in Kaufmann

195); he once termed its protagonist "the heavenly Antigone, the most glorious figure ever to have appeared on earth" (Kaufmann 201).[9] So tragedy may be set up to put on display the kind of knowledge that one's imagination (in this case Hegel's) cannot grasp, though reason leads one ineluctably to conclude it must be true. Interestingly, this is how Kant defines the sublime. In general Hegel insists that "the chief thing in drama is not the objective action, but the exposition of the inner spirit of the action in... the dramatis personae and their passion" (*Aesth.* 2.1170). Where Aeschylus delineates a cosmos of balanced forces, Sophocles shows Spirit in action in the figure of heroic suffering who must stand forth while those forces destroy her.

In the *Aesthetics* the balance of the forces is "logical": two instances of personal "pathos," or dedication to an essential truth: and the absolute collision of those two truths. Hegel does not dwell on microscopic analyses of Creon but rather, asserting that both he and Antigone represent absolute right, clearly avows that what makes the play great is Antigone's revelation of that essence which the state in its daydream of order has left out. Creon's command "concerned only the public weal" and it is then left to Antigone to "fulfill the holy duty of burial." Pointing to Antigone's defense of her transgression—"Yes, for it was not Zeus who made [Creon's] proclamation, nor was it Justice who lives with the gods below" (*Antigone* 451-52)—he denotes the gods she worships as "the inner gods of feeling, love, and kinship, not the daylight gods of free self-conscious national and political life."

Hegel has examined these two favorite examples in discussing the conflict of "old" and "new" gods in ancient Greek religion. For Spirit to develop in history the new gods must take the stage with justice. But of all Greek tragedies what the *Oresteia* and the *Antigone* are best conceived to show is that the new gods are no less one-sided than the old. "The old gods are assigned the right of family situations in so far as these rest on nature and therefore are opposed to the public law and right of the community." Athene explicitly resolves this impassable conflict in the *Oresteia*. If one looks for a resolution in the *Antigone*, however, it is that Creon's wife and son "perish owing to the death of Antigone" (*Aesth.* 471). Yet this revenge is hardly a resolution. Not even "sustainable damage"—the bruised heel endured in order to administer the crushing of the head of the retrogressive principle—these deaths leap up like judgments on Creon's character and path of action. Here again the *Oresteia* is the perfect map of the Hegelian triad of thesis, antithesis, synthesis, with an *Aufhebung* that both preserves and cancels, constituting the final leap into that synthesis. It is the *Antigone*, Hegel's favorite, that presents the greatest challenge to his master system, not because it is so unlike his terms of analysis but because it fits them perfectly but refuses to lead to an affirmative outcome.

It is for this reason that Hegel's treatment of *Antigone* has been a focal point of French deconstructive and feminist thought, because it finds Hegel at a most intensely assertive and least textually attentive moment and thus seems a strategic place to attack his project of envisioning the ultimate rationality of the world. Here that kind of thinking that places the sexes in series of polar oppositions (Cixous/Clément 63-64) is well in evidence, and Hegel moreover tends to resolve them in favor of the male (Chanter 94). He insists on the mediating role of woman, who becomes the mere means whereby the man achieves self-consciousness (Irigaray *This Sex* 167-68, Benhabib 41), and who in *Antigone* "reconciles the dead man with himself *by taking upon herself the operation of destruction*" (Irigaray *Speculum* 214-15).

A closer look at Sophocles' Antigone, argues Victoria Burke, reveals a figure unique in Greek tragedy in being "the only virgin who takes her death into her own hands" (Burke 538), a pure death that can be taken as evidence of Antigone's victory over Creon (Loraux 31). This of course makes her something other than a mediator who enables self-consciousness' attainment of itself. Burke observes that Sophocles' Antigone "is acting out of a deliberate allegiance to something which she takes to be higher than the law of the land, higher than rationality" (Burke 539).

Hegel's perceived failure to give Antigone and hence woman her due may be part of a more general intolerance of disorder that has been remarked about him for some time. Walter Kaufmann, for instance, finds in Hegel "a singularly restless and at bottom quite unsystematic spirit that is scared of its own pluralistic bent and tries, never twice in the same way, to organize the chaos of its observations, insights, and ideas" (206). Michelle Gellrich argues that Hegel construes tragedy in a way that will affirm his notion of the historical process as set forth in his *Phenomenology of Spirit* and especially in his *Philosophy of History*. As he observes in that latter work, "But even regarding History as the slaughter-bench at which the happiness of peoples, the wisdom of States, and the virtue of individuals have been victimized—the question involuntarily arises—to what principle, to what final aim these enormous sacrifices have been offered" (21). His project of a "philosophical history" answers the "need of the beholder to eliminate contingency, to find rational meaning in the apparent aimlessness, conflict, and destruction of the past" (Gellrich 38). The dramatist resembles the philosopher of history in that where "for ordinary sight only obscurity, accident, and confusion seem to have control, for him is revealed the real self-fulfillment of that which is in and for itself rational and true" (*Aesthetics* late). The reality, Gellrich argues, is quite the opposite: tragedy puts literary theory in question because tragic conflict undermines the stable categories on which critical thought would base itself (Gellrich 10). For her the conflict in tragedy better fits Foucault's model of an "insurrection of subjugated knowledges" (*Power/Knowledge* 78-92).

This direction of antisystematic critique finds its ne plus ultra in Jacques Derrida and Georges Bataille. To Derrida Antigone represents "pure singularity: neither the empiric individual that death destroys, decomposes, analyzes, nor the rational universality of the citizen, of the living subject" (*Glas* 143). This singularity links Antigone to the abyss: "What if the inassimilable, the absolutely indigestible, played a fundamental role within the system, abyssal, rather, the abyss playing... a quasi transcendental role and letting be formed above it, like a sort of effluvium, a dream of appeasement? Is there not always an element excluded from the system which assures the space of the system's possibility?" (*Glas* 151a). Unlike Hegel's Spirit, which in Derrida's view takes on a calculating character in the *Bildungsroman*-like plot of the *Phenomenology*, Sophocles' Antigone presents an absolute model of the ethical, acting in disregard for the consequences of her action "in much the same way that Abraham does in Kierkegaard's reading of the Abraham and Isaac story" (Burke 540). As Simon Critchley explains, "by exemplifying the essence of ethical life, of *Sittlichkeit*, Antigone marks a place ('an impossible place') within the Hegelian system where an ethical moment irreducible to dialectics is glimpsed. Such an ethics would not be based upon the recognition of the other, which is always self-recognition, but would rather begin with the expropriation of the self in the face of the other's approach" (Critchley 14).

Derrida places Bataille's radical irrationalism favorably over against Hegel's rationalism. To Bataille Antigone's action concerns "the moment in which the sacred enters into a relation of identity and difference with the profane" (Burke 541). Such a moment "proclaims legitimacy for the sacred within the realm of the human," and the only conclusion can be that "reconciliation of these two domains is both impossible and, according to Hegel, necessary."[10] Bataille calls the act of bringing the divine into contact with the human "transgression" (Burke 541, Bataille *Eroticism*). Antigone's burial of her brother is "an essentially transgressive action; it opens the political sphere to the divine" (Burke 542). Michel Foucault writes of Bataille's concept of transgression:

> Perhaps it is like a flash of lightning in the night which, from the beginning of time, gives a dense and black intensity to the night it denies, which lights up the night from the inside, from top to bottom, and yet owes to the dark the stark clarity of its manifestation, its harrowing and poised singularity; the flash loses itself in this space it marks with its sovereignty and becomes silent now that it has given a name to obscurity. (Foucault "Preface" 35)

Transgression "opens the individual to an alterity so profound that it cannot be comprehended, yet so absolute that it knows no compromise with the world of the profane" (Burke 542). Antigone's action "brought the unregulated force of death and the sacred into a sphere which cannot function unless that force is contained. Uncontained, it results in the destruction of the world of immediate Spirit. This force, absolute negativity, is beyond sublation and exceeds any effort to circumscribe it by enfolding it into a higher stage of Spirit" (Burke 542). Transgression, in Bataille's thought, opens up a "continuum" that, Derrida says, "push[es] itself toward the nonbasis of negativity and of expenditure":

> the experience of the *continuum* is also the experience of absolute difference, of a difference which would no longer be the one that Hegel had conceived more profoundly than anyone else: the difference in the service of presence, at work for [the] history [of meaning]. The difference between Hegel and Bataille is the difference between these two differences. (Derrida "From Restricted" 263)

This continuum occupies the place of but is radically different from Hegel's bridge over the abyss. Thus, Julia Kristeva observes, Antigone's action shows the movement of consciousness not to be Hegelian, "on the path leading to the constitution of unity," but on a path leading to "its consummation, its annihilation" (Kristeva 243)—in the Bataillean continuum.

In another vein, Mitchell Breitwieser notes that Hegel sees the conflict in the *Antigone* "as a struggle over representation, specifically over the power to control the proper manner of remembering the dead"; Creon wants to "promote a socially accepted genealogy of virtue to which he is the remaining heir" (Breitwieser 127). In denouncing Polyneices Creon thus relies on what Derrida has identified as a Hegelian habit of choosing concept over being, mind over reality, the project over existential authenticity—a reliance on the "power of exemplification" (*Glas* 29-30) in which Creon creates a simulacrum of Polyneices as negative example of social virtue. Antigone opposes Creon's politically motivated exemplification with an organic process of representation, namely mourning.

Drawing on Freud's "Mourning and Melancholia" and Lacan's discussion of Antigone in *The Ethics of Psychoanalysis*, Breitwieser points out that mourning is "abject and gradual... like the labor of the slave [discussed] earlier in the *Phenomenology*" (Breitwieser 130) and that it "works on an inscrutable schedule"; in mourning "desire and love are operating under a stern injunction that Hegel calls divine and Lacan calls the law of the unconscious, an injunction to take account of what was rather than of what the mourner might otherwise want to have been the case" (Breitwieser 131). By contrast, exemplification "*mimics or simulates* mourning instead of advancing it" (Breitwieser 134); it does not oppose or seek to eliminate mourning but "is hostile only to certain contrary directions in which the energy [of mourning] might flow" (Breitwieser 135). The suppression of this free flow of mourning that it authorizes leads to melancholia, as Freud's analysis would dictate—to Hamlet's experience of the world as either an "unweeded garden" or a "sterile promontory."

This Freudian-Lacanian reading of Hegel is of enormous help in thinking about the action of tragedy. From Clytemnestra's response of rage at Iphigenia's sacrifice to Hamlet's emotionally accented confusion at his father's demise, tragedy seems to emerge not from mourning but from its refusal or blockage. Frustrated from their proper occurrence, the interior "second deaths" that Lacan locates in the mourning process become externalized, "demonized," in the tragic situation—the unappeased ghost, the inexplicable decision.

Where Hegel is most flawed is not in failing to intuit the unqualified existential nature of tragic suffering but in failing to find a way to express it, because of his need to preserve his treasured notions of conflict and resolution in a dialectical synthesis. It is his own work that gives rise to his most perceptive critiques, for Hegel is ineluctably drawn to those realms in which spirit manifests itself in darker, more resistant ways. No other philosopher has so consistently emphasized the rational and spiritual consequences that are enacted by an unthinking instinctual or passionate choice. So it is ironic that criticism may have to part company with his judgments because of his not seeing beyond philosophy. More than a century ago Dostoevsky sounded the key note in this resistance movement, as the hero of his "Dream of a Ridiculous Man" concludes, "'The consciousness of life is higher than life, the knowledge of happiness is higher than happiness'— that is what we have to fight against!" (Dostoevsky 322). The battle between tragedy and philosophy is thus resolved by shattering the modern dream of a programmatic philosophy for the completion of spirit and returning to the tragic "impossible place" of existence that Hegel first enabled readers to see.

NOTES

¹ G.W.F. Hegel, *Aesthetics* 2.973, cited parenthetically in the text as *Aesth.* in further references. (German wording cited is taken from the *Theorie-Werkausgabe*, vols. 13-15.) In this section of the *Aesthetics* Hegel is concerned with distinguishing the nature of poetry over against prose in the arts of language. Sir T.M. Knox, the translator of Hegel's *Aesthetics*, writes: "For Hegel, art has a vocation of its own ... It shares with religion and philosophy the vocation of revealing the truth" ("The Puzzle of Hegel's Aesthetics" 2).

² Hegel, *Phenomenology of Spirit*, paragraph 20; *Die Phänomenologie des Geistes, Theorie-Werkausgabe*, 3.24. Further references to the Miller translation, cited parenthetically in the text as *Phen.*, also cite paragraph instead of page number.

³ Compare the views of contemporary scientists integrating the three

great natural sciences through information theory. According to this perspective, the molecular form in which atoms organize themselves constitutes a choice over other possible forms, and this choice constitutes information that is then communicable throughout the system in which it is embedded. See Werner Loewenstein, *Touchstone of Life*.

4 On the figure of the bridge over the abyss in Hegel see Chiurazzi, "Il 'ponte sull'abisso' come metafora dell'essere artificiale."

5 Perceptive commentators on Hegel's treatment of "Romantic" tragedy include Anne and Henry Paolucci, Introduction, *Hegel on Tragedy*; and Leonard Moss, *The Excess of Heroism in Tragic Drama, passim*.

6 Michelle Gellrich sees Hegel as drawing on Anaximander and Heraclitus for his notion of tragic *Kollision* (*Tragedy and Theory* 13).

7 Inevitably something is gained and something lost in Hegel's reading of the darkest corners of human existence as obeying the laws of spirit. At the same time that one becomes able to think about and relate to these incomprehensible irrational realms, the general picture of the world tends to become less mysterious, to never stop making sense, and to be increasingly tellable from the single point of view of Spirit. This gain/loss is itself a dialectical equilibrium, of course, but it places a great burden on the ability of writing to represent with poetic sensitivity and negative capability the realms explored. To the extent, again inevitable, that one does not do so one is drawn into a kind of false shadow that is thrown by Hegel's philosophy but is no less a part of his effect: this is the claim, whether espoused consciously or not, that one is speaking for Spirit and knows in advance what it is finding in its journey outward toward its other—a claim that runs so counter to twentieth-century historical experience that Hegel has drawn fire from all sides: the conservative tradition of commentary has stigmatized his stance as secular humanism, while the left has branded it as imperialism. At bottom the issue is whether the whole, "Absolute Spirit," contains the abyss still potentiated, not annulled through dialectical cancellation but an ever potential, and potentially endless, moment.

A case in point is his misreading of a line in *Antigone*. Antigone too acts in response to Creon's legislation, and the main event of the play is her confession of responsibility for her deed. Ascending to the level of the ethical consciousness in general, Hegel asserts that it "must, on account of this actuality and on account of its deed, acknowledge its opposite as its own actuality, must acknowledge its guilt" (470), and in support he quotes *Antigone* 926: "Because we suffer we acknowledge we have erred" (Miller's translation of Hegel's citation)—a line that fits Hegel's point very well but seems strange coming from Antigone. *"Weil wir leiden, anerkennen wir, daß wir gefehlt"* (3.348). The original passage reads rather:

What justice of the gods have I transgressed?... Whom can I call on to protect me? For by acting piously I have been convicted of impiety. Well, *if* this is approved among the gods, *I should forgive them* [= Creon and his officers] *for what I have suffered, since I have done wrong; but if they are the wrongdoers,* may they not suffer worse evils than those they are unjustly inflicting upon me! (921-28, emphasis added)

Antigone would never unconditionally acknowledge any wrongdoing on her own part. Hegel's misrepresentation, reversing the cause-effect relation of wrongdoing and suffering, points to his tendency to seek a unitary consciousness, which amounts to trying to convert Antigone into a philosopher who can "see the larger picture." This despite his explicit declaration of women as the unconscious intuitive spokespersons of the ethical and the divine.

[8] Kurt Leidecker judges that Hegel's dialectic "was the trailblazer for the synthesis between Orient and Occident" (Henry Paolucci, Introduction, *Hegel: On the Arts* xvi).

[9] See Steiner on the era 1790-1905 as the ascendancy of the *Antigone* in European thought. Hegel's recent critics have returned to his analysis of *Antigone* to find both his profundity and the kind of double bind that leads him to expose, without letting him affirm, the otherness of the other to any incorporative schemes and the grounding of tragic knowledge in the abyss (*Abgrund* or no-ground).

[10] In a similar spirit Heidegger calls Antigone "the supreme uncanny [*unheimlich*]" (Heidegger 102).

3

The Mystery Doctrine of Tragedy:
Nietzsche's Sublime

GLENN ARBERY

With the exception of such terms as *catharsis* and *hamartia* from Aristotle's *Poetics*, the governing ideas of Nietzsche's first book, *The Birth of Tragedy from the Spirit of Music*, are in all likelihood more familiar than those from any other theory of tragedy. The Dionysian and the Apollinian (to accept Walter Kaufmann's spelling) "appear coupled with each other," writes Nietzsche, "and through this coupling ultimately generate an equally Dionysian and Apollinian form of art—Attic tragedy" (BT 33).[1] Once articulated, the pairing seems intuitively obvious, perhaps because analogous oppositions or contraries—feeling and rationality, in all their permutations—so often occur. The ideas of earlier philosophers in Germany also seem transparently similar, if one considers the finished tragedy as the successful synthesis of contraries. Schiller's sensuous drive and formal drive converge in the play drive; Schopenhauer's will and idea join in the universal particular of the work of art—and it is hardly difficult to understand why Nietzsche would say, in a late comment on the book, that *The Birth of Tragedy* "smells offensively Hegelian" (EH 726).

Familiar as its ideas are, the book itself is irreducibly strange. If one comes to it from the Greeks, whose deepest truths it claims to reveal, one might very well ask what this book has to do with Aeschylus or Sophocles, much less with Homer. In the Greek poets, Apollo is associated with dream interpretation and prophecy (Chryses, Calchas, Cassandra, Tiresias), but in *The Birth of Tragedy* he represents "dream" per se and the entire visual understanding of art, especially the idealized images of the gods. M. S. Silk and J. P. Stern accuse Nietzsche of inventing the dream-functions of Apollo in order to sharpen the contrast with Dionysus, who more plausibly stands for "intoxication" and music (Silk and Stern 170-71). But John Sallis argues that the objections of Silk and Stern stem from

> [a] reduction of the structure of Nietzsche's discourse, as though it were simply a matter of establishing a philologically complete inventory of the god's features and then determining the Apollinian on the basis of such an inventory; as though it were not a matter of recovering through the figure of the god a certain understanding of art that is made perceptible in that figure. (Sallis 23, n.9)

If it is true that the Greeks themselves conceive of Apollo as the embodiment of "a certain understanding of art," then Sallis' correction is sufficient. But in that case, "Apollo" would merely be the name of an idea or the personification of an "understanding," and this is perhaps too large a concession, perhaps even an instance of what Nietzsche himself calls "Socratism." Imagining the gods differs from either making understandings perceptible or from making perceptions understandable, though it does both of these things. Poetic experience of the gods bristles with privilege and terror and exaltation, an openness to the onset of immortal beauty, yet one of the first moves of Greek philosophy is to neutralize this experience of the imagination. Sallis considers it legitimate philosophically, as it were, for Nietzsche to erase the figure of the god and treat "Apollo" as an understanding of art; he suggests that Nietzsche moves "through the image of the god to an impulse that it mirrors."[2]

But this justification of Nietzsche's practice does not account for the genuine strangeness of his tone and posture in *The Birth of Tragedy*. Nietzsche enacts a ritual of display; his assertions scorn protocols of scholarly proof and restraint, because he means for the book to be potent rather than correct. In effect, he *reinvents* Apollo and Dionysus out of his own experience. He is not approaching these gods as products of Greek culture to be recovered by careful scholarship: Sallis is certainly right about that.

Rather, when he speaks of the Apollinian and the Dionysian as "nature's art impulses" that have no dependence on "the mediation of the human artist" (Birth 38), he is reflecting upon the way that nature itself produces *in him* the "image world of dreams" (with its corollary sense that appearances might be illusion) and, on other occasions, the quite distinct "intoxicated reality... [that] seeks to destroy the individual and redeem him by a mystic feeling of oneness" (38). The Greeks, experiencing these same *natural* art impulses, disclosed them "not, to be sure, in concepts, but in the intensely clear figures of their gods" (33).

❖ ❖ ❖

Nietzsche's way in *The Birth of Tragedy* is to speak with hubris, and not as one of the scholars. Because he knows the creative matrix out of which the gods themselves took their first form, he can speak confidently of the origins of all the Olympian gods in "the same impulse that embodied itself in Apollo." The way to understand such gods is to recover the "terrific need" that produced them.

> Whoever approaches these Olympians with another religion in his heart, searching among them for moral elevation, even for sanctity, for disincarnate spirituality, for charity and benevolence, will soon be forced to turn his back on them, discouraged and disappointed. For there is nothing here that suggests asceticism, spirituality, or duty. We hear nothing but the accents of an exuberant, triumphant life in which all things, whether good or evil, are deified. And so the spectator may stand quite bewildered before this fantastic excess of life, asking himself by virtue of what magic potion these high-spirited men would have found life so enjoyable.... (41)

What makes the book so disconcerting, in other words, is that Nietzsche himself wants to break through the constraints of merely talking about the "exuberant, triumphant" act of deifying all things and to make the book itself into a summoning of gods. What would it serve merely to recognize the origin of Greek tragedy in a certain historical fusion of the visual imagination with musical depth? Only *a re-deification of what would otherwise be merely conceptual* can begin to reach into the origins of the tragic art—only a new creation of tragedy. The last sentence of *The Birth of Tragedy* imagines an old Athenian with the eyes of Aeschylus saying, "But now follow me to witness a tragedy, and sacrifice with me in the temple of both deities!" (144)

Nietzsche invents the Apollo he needs, because for "a genuine poet," as he puts it, "metaphor is not a rhetorical figure but a vicarious image that he actually beholds in place of a concept. A character for him is not a whole he has composed out of particular traits, picked up here and there, but an obtrusively alive person before his very eyes" (Birth 63). In this book, as in many of his later ones, Nietzsche writes as something at least *approaching* a poet. In the 1886 "Attempt at a Self-Criticism" appended to a new edition of the work as a preface, he writes that what spoke in this work "was something like a mystical, almost maenadic soul that stammered with difficulty," and he adds that "It should have *sung*, this 'new soul'—and not spoken! What I had to say then—too bad that I did not dare say it as a poet: perhaps I had the ability" (20). His descriptions of Apollo and Dionysus do not follow from his interpretation of Greek texts but from his beholding the "obtrusively alive" gods and setting about to explain his revelation. Through this very act of invention Nietzsche becomes most Greek, certainly more than those (beginning with Wilamowitz-Mollendorff) who condemn him for his philological deviations—and most Romantic as well as most Greek.[3] If Nietzsche can write, in the same year that he published *The Birth of Tragedy*, that "The Greek is envious, and he does not consider this quality a blemish but the gift of a beneficent godhead," if he can argue that Xenophanes (and later, Plato) attacked Homer out of "an overwhelming craving to assume the place of the overthrown poet and to inherit his fame," his own recognition of Apollo through his experience of "nature's art impulses" would move him to rival the Greeks—not simply to understand *their* Apollo and Dionysus, but to create the gods anew, with attributes now recognizable in the originals who share the names. What he later does in re-creating Zarathustra is already anticipated in his first work.

In *The Birth of Tragedy*, the Apollinian emerges as visual image, as dream, as healing illusion—the idealization and divinization of appearance or "shining." Nietzsche associates it with statues of the gods, with painting, with any visualization, such as the images one inhabits "inside" a poem. When Keats writes in "To Autumn" of a reaper and imagines her "drows'd with the fume of poppies, while [her] hook / Spares the next swath and all its twined flowers," the theme might be intoxication, but the visual experience is Apollinian. As art, the Apollinian consoles through the beautiful image; Sallis argues that such an image "is a perfection, a truth, whose shining provides a certain release from the negativity of the everyday, a certain relief from that fragmentariness, a healing" (29). Through this capacity associated with Apollo, art brings phenomena into more perfect shining, but not simply by imitating appearance. If one imagines, for example, an athlete photographed in some gesture that beautifully combines power and repose, the image might still remain too literal; it might retain too much of that athlete's particular identity or foster too personal a speculation. Simply by being tied to historical reality, it could not approach the shining that "bursts like a star" from Rilke's "Archaic Torso of Apollo."

Originally, according to Nietzsche, the Apollinian arises in response to terror, and some of its power must derive from what it holds at bay. Never "naive" in Schiller's sense, it is rather the result of a culture which "always must first overthrow an empire of Titans and slay monsters" (43). If this terror of primal existence gives rise to the Apollinian, and if Apollo is father, in a sense, of the whole Olympian order, as Nietzsche argues (41), then the overthrow of the Titans by the Olympians must be understood as an "Apollinian" achievement. The original terror of the Titanic was overcome, in effect, by beauty, understood as this shining that characterizes the images of the Olympian gods, even the remnant torso "still suffused with brilliance from inside," as Rilke puts it. This restraining beauty is evidence that "the body of the gods shines with such an intense brilliance that no human eye can bear it. Its splendor is blinding," writes Jean-Pierre Vernant (Vernant 44). Although the Apollinian impulse seeks definite, limited forms and protects the *principium individuationis* (a term that Nietzsche takes from Schopenhauer), it also fosters the necessary illusion that the phenomenal world (essentially subject to change) can be made eternal. If the mortal body grows old and dies, there is nevertheless an immortal body—the body of the god—that exists in unoccluded shining. Apollinian art brings the things of nature that emerge from nothing and exist for a day into a greater truth that is, at the same time, a kind of healing illusion. Lord of the radiance of the image, Apollo prevents the beholder from being consumed by a recognition of the monstrous impersonal forces that underlie the phenomenal world.

*   *   *

Yet these forces make their inevitable return in the Dionysian. Unlike Apollo, Dionysus can hardly be grasped at all in a figure. One cannot gaze at an "archaic torso of Dionysus" in anything like the same sense as one gazes at Apollo: he exceeds and defies representation in any image. As the other natural art-impulse, this one associated with intoxication rather than dream, the Dionysian medium is music, "the emotional power of the tone, the uniform flow of the melody, and the utterly incomparable world of harmony" (40). This hardly sounds monstrous or Titanic, and to understand why its effect is so catastrophic, one needs to imagine what it means that Dionysian music resounds the "primal unity" beneath all appearances. "In the Dionysian dithyramb man is incited to the greatest exaltation of all his symbolic faculties; something never before experienced struggles for utterance—the annihilation of the veil of maya, oneness as the soul of the race and of nature itself" (40). Even in writing about it, Nietzsche struggles against the fact of his own text:

> Language can never adequately render the cosmic symbolism of music, because music stands in symbolic relation to the primordial contradiction and primordial pain in the heart of the primal unity, and therefore symbolizes a sphere which is beyond and prior to all phenomena. Rather, all phenomena, compared with it, are merely symbols: hence language, as the organ and symbol of phenomena, can never by any means disclose the innermost heart of music.... (55-56)

Reading *The Birth of Tragedy*, then, means always being summoned toward an experience that no text can ever disclose. The Dionysian cannot be made into language, and what we ordinarily take as tragedies—the texts of the Greek plays, or even these plays performed without music—are to the actual experience of tragedy what librettos are to operas in full performance. Without the music, one understands little of what actually underlies the genius of tragedy or the real terrors and pleasures that it aroused in the Greeks. "It is through music," Nietzsche says, "that the tragic spectator is overcome by an assured premonition of a highest pleasure attained through destruction and negation, so he feels as if the innermost abyss of things spoke to him perceptibly" (126). This "innermost abyss" contains "a hidden substratum of suffering and of knowledge, revealed to [the Apollinian Greek] by the Dionysian." Since it threatens the beauty and moderation of the Apollinian world, the Dionysian is "titanic" and "barbaric" to the Greek, but it is also "in the last analysis as necessary as the Apollinian" (46).

By means of its uncanny innerness, music can mirror the undifferentiated unity of being before the emergence of phenomena. In tragedy—and in tragedy alone—this pre-imagistic depth emerges *as* the Apollinian image in the spectacle of the play, the actors, the poetic language, the plot as the imitation of an action. The Apollinian makes visible and brings into a kind of shining the primal energies of Dionysian reality in tragedy, which weds or couples these contraries.[4] From the first sentence of the book—in fact, from the title itself—Nietzsche understands the development of art as dependent on this duality, "just as procreation depends on the duality of the sexes" (33). The relation between Apollinian and Dionysian, dream and music, is best understood through a sexual analogy. Nietzsche summarizes the history of the "Hellenic genius" as a series of "new births ever following and mutually augmenting one another" until they reach a consummation in tragedy:

> out of the age of "bronze," with its wars of the Titans and its rigorous folk philosophy, the Homeric world developed under the sway of the Apollinian impulse to beauty;... this "naive" splendor was again overwhelmed by the influx of the Dionysian; and... against this new power the Apollinian rose to the austere majesty of Doric art and the Doric view of the world.... And here the sublime and celebrated art of *Attic tragedy* and the dramatic dithyramb presents itself as the common goal of both these tendencies whose mysterious union, after many and long precursory struggles, found glorious consummation in this child— at once Antigone and Cassandra.[5] (47)

A word such as "consummation" should not be taken as mildly

metaphorical. Nietzsche emphasizes in *Twilight of the Idols*, published sixteen years after *The Birth of Tragedy*, that the Greeks believed in "true life as the overall continuation of life though procreation, through the mysteries of sexuality. For the Greeks the sexual symbol was therefore the venerable symbol par excellence, the real profundity in the whole of ancient piety. Every single element in the act of procreation, of pregnancy, and of birth aroused the highest and most solemn feelings" (TI 561). Even more to the point for tragedy,

> *pain* is pronounced holy: the pangs of the woman giving birth hallow all pain; all becoming and growing—all that guarantees a future—involves pain. That there may be the eternal joy of creating, that the will to life may eternally affirm itself, the agony of the woman giving birth must also be there eternally. All this is meant by the word Dionysus: I know no higher symbolism than this *Greek* symbolism of the Dionysian festivals. (TI 562).

This passage illuminates much of what is implicit in Nietzsche's imagery in the earlier book. Tragedy itself should be understood through this *higher* (not lower) sexual symbolism of a pleasure and pain that hallow life.

What is the great pain of tragedy? The annihilation of the individual, the terrible destruction—in a day, an hour—of the whole construct of meanings and relations and beliefs. And what is tragedy's great pleasure? This same annihilation of the individual. Re-creating the way that one comes to understand the joy in *making nil* the individual through the spirit of music, Nietzsche seems at first more Schopenhauerian than Greek: "The metaphysical joy in the tragic is a translation of the instinctive unconscious Dionysian wisdom into the language of images: the hero, the highest manifestation of the will, is negated for our pleasure, because he is only phenomenon, and because the eternal life of the will is not affected by his annihilation" (104). But as Nietzsche goes on to distinguish the "lies" implicit in any Apollinian glorification of the *"eternity of the phenomenon"* (his emphasis) from the Dionysian truth, the language rises once again toward the sexual symbolism he finds everywhere among the Greeks. In Dionysian art, nature cries "with its true, undissembled voice" that she is "the *eternally creative primordial mother*, eternally impelling to existence" (104, my emphasis).

Those who enter the Dionysian experience become "for a brief moment primordial being itself, feeling its raging desire for existence and joy in existence" (104). "Primordial being" should be read in terms of the whole range of sexual elements—attractions, rivalries, couplings, ecstasies, painful births. When one *is* primordial being, one participates in this range as though simultaneously: "the struggle, the pain, the destruction of phenomena, now appear necessary to us, in view of the excess of countless forms of existence which force and push one another into life, in view of the exuberant fertility of the universal will." The tragic agonies of conflict become comprehensible when one ecstatically embodies—that is, embodies while *beside oneself*—the "raging desire for existence." What already exists as completed form, including oneself as a distinct, important individual, is subject to destruction in the primordial being's eternal pregnancy and birthing and clearing away.

Yet the annihilation of any individual narrative, any meaning to a particular life, is unbearable: "We are pierced by the maddening sting of these pains just when we have become, as it were, one with the infinite primordial joy in existence, and when we anticipate, in Dionysian ecstasy, the indestructibility and eternity of this joy" (104). This crossing of biographical pain with natural rapture gives the distinctive tragic pleasure, and *not* because it is cathartic: "In spite of fear and pity, we are the happy living beings, not as individuals, but as the one living being, with whose creative joy we are united" (105).

※ ※ ※

"Primal unity" or "primal being" in Nietzsche is experienced, then, as ecstatic. It is a self-exceeding and self-forgetting whose metaphors can only be sexual, because the "primal being"—far from being the stillness or rest of the unmoved mover—is in fact a ceaseless "impelling to existence," sheer becoming, an exceeding of boundaries (like childbirth) that painfully rends individual forms in bringing forth new ones. Nietzsche speaks of this "primal being" not as God or substance or ground, but as *Abgrund*, abyss. With respect to the individual or the *principium individuationis*, Dionysus is the abyss. Inside the experience, one feels that "the innermost abyss of things" is speaking, but the aftermath reveals a different kind of abysmal character. "For the rapture of the Dionysian state with its annihilation of the ordinary bounds and limits of existence contains, while it lasts, a *lethargic* element in which all personal experiences of the past become immersed" (59). "Lethargic": its roots besotted in Lethe. Rapture, in other words, induces self-forgetting: "This chasm of oblivion separates the world of everyday reality and of Dionysian reality." But its effects are temporary. "And as soon as this everyday reality re-enters consciousness, it is experienced as such, with nausea: an ascetic, will-negating mood is the fruit of these states" (59-60). From the perspective of everyday consciousness, Dionysian reality is the abyss, because it exposes the emptiness of the everyday, the meaninglessness of one's *particularity*.

For this reason, Nietzsche finds a surprising analogy between Dionysian man and Hamlet, surprising because what resembles the effect of Dionysian rapture must be Hamlet's unsettling—ungrounding—recognition that his brilliant personal particularity became irrelevant as soon as he was cast into the stock role of the avenger by his mother's remarriage and the fearful revelations of his father's ghost. Nietzsche's Hamlet is inhibited by nausea. Like the Dionysian man after the experience of the primal unity, he knows that "action could not change anything in the eternal nature of things." Because the self is already trapped in the "nature of things" (cultural and otherwise) that governs all phenomena, it is already a repetition-in-advance, always a stock role and never a genuinely original part. In this sense, Hamlet begins at the point with which Stephen Greenblatt ends *Renaissance Self-Fashioning*: "to let go of one's stubborn hold on selfhood, even selfhood conceived as a fiction, is to die. As for myself,... I want to bear witness at the close to my overwhelming need to sustain the illusion that I am the principal maker of my own identity" (Greenblatt 257).[6] For Nietzsche, such an "overwhelming need" is Apollinian, but tragedy begins with the Dionysian destruction of this illusion, in the ecstatic moment when it becomes unsustainable. How, for example, can the Dionysian reveler (like Hamlet) not regard his own mother as the local evidence, so to speak, of his own origin in a ceaseless "impelling to existence"? In this sense, the dismemberment of Pentheus by his own mother has an archetypal inevitability. The very fact of one's mother's participation *in* and *as* the "primordial being" already renders personal identity in a sequence of generations meaningless: as womb, she was already the abyss. "True knowledge, an insight into the horrible truth, outweighs any motive for action, both in Hamlet and in the Dionysian man" (60). The disparity between oneself as shining form, on the one hand, and the raging desire and pain of the primordial mother from whom one came, on the other, discloses nature itself as both source and abyss.

Or perhaps it is a mistake to identify "nature" with "primordial being." Nature might be described as the visible order of phenomena, whereas the "primal unity" does not appear as an order and cannot be classified. Strangely, the abyss revealed in nature is not itself nature. It is no wonder that Nietzsche begins to speak explicitly of the abyss in his discussion of the Oedipus story. Its movement from patricide and incest toward a "supraterrestrial cheerfulness" in *Oedipus at Colonus* is "nothing but that bright image which healing nature projects before us after a glance into the abyss" (68). Nature, in fact, seems more Apollinian in its preference for the healing image; the Dionysian abyss threatens in such a way that nature must heal its effects. A violation of nature nevertheless somehow in nature—Nietzsche finds in the Oedipus story a very ancient popular belief

> that where prophetic and magical powers have broken the spell of present and future, the rigid law of individuation, and the real magic of nature, some enormously unnatural event—such as incest—must have occurred earlier, as a cause. How else could one compel nature to surrender her secrets if not by triumphantly resisting her, by means of something unnatural? (68)

One should notice, however, that the "unnatural" is *Dionysian* and that it is also spoken of a few pages later as "the philosophy of wild and naked nature" (74); the Dionysian resembles the Promethean for Nietzsche in that it posits "the necessity of sacrilege imposed upon the titanically striving individual" who reveals the truth:

> It is this insight that I find expressed in that horrible triad of Oedipus' destinies: the same man who solves the riddle of nature—that Sphinx of two natures—also must break the most sacred natural orders

by murdering his father and marrying his mother. Indeed, the myth seems to wish to whisper to us that wisdom, and particularly Dionysian wisdom, is an unnatural abomination; that he who by means of his knowledge plunges nature into the abyss of destruction must also suffer the dissolution of nature in his own person. (BT 68-69)

Such an individual becomes the hero of tragedy, but only because "all the celebrated figures of the Greek stage—Prometheus, Oedipus, etc.—are mere masks of this original hero, Dionysus" (73). The sacrilege of the hero echoes that of Dionysus himself, "the god experiencing in himself the agonies of individuation," and the annihilation of the hero repeats in a ritual way the dismemberment that befalls the god when the Titans tear him to pieces. Nietzsche writes that in this state of dismemberment Dionysus was worshiped as Zagreus—an intimation that "this dismemberment, the properly Dionysian suffering, is like a transformation into air, water, earth, and fire, that we are therefore to regard the state of individuation as the origin and primal cause of all suffering, as something objectionable in itself" (73).[7] For Nietzsche, the hope of Dionysian religion lies in a third birth of the twice-born god that will reunite "a world torn asunder and shattered into individuals" (74). That hope underlies what Nietzsche calls "*the mystery doctrine of tragedy*: the fundamental knowledge of the oneness of everything existent, the conception of individuation as the primal cause of evil, and of art as the joyous hope that the spell of individuation may be broken in augury of a restored oneness" (74).

The central paradoxes of tragedy are these: that only the individual par excellence who strives sacrilegiously against nature can break the spell of individuation, and that nature, which generates the lie of the individual, also tells the truth of primal unity and heals the devastation of that truth with the healing image that is the aftermath of looking into the abyss. Individuation and appearing are Apollinian, but the tragic hero, far from being Apollinian, is actually Dionysus himself undergoing in this disguise *the agony of appearing at all*, having to be and act in this circumscribed and limited mode of being. Appearing in this sense does not mean simply appearing to others in a body, but above all *appearing to oneself*. The deeper problem lies in the consciousness of consciousness, a doubleness that paradoxically constitutes the singular. Dionysian truth overcomes this inner doubleness.

How? By plunging consciousness into the abyss with its "lethargic element" where one forgets oneself and ceases to appear before one's own consciousness. In tragedy, too, one forgets oneself. So engaging is the terrible action on the stage that it momentarily displaces self-consciousness. The destruction of the tragic hero reenacts and focuses the near-annihilation of individual selves that constitutes an audience as a single being in the Dionysian reality. But the return from this experience means a re-dispersal back into individuals, whose painful self-consciousness necessarily returns with the return to everyday life. Each one experiences the everyday as a sudden emptying out and loss, an agony of individuation—but also as a relief, since one has not been destroyed.

John Sallis summarizes Nietzsche's understanding of the effect of tragedy by arguing not only that "the danger is pessimism, the onset of the wisdom of Silenus,"[8] but also that "tragedy alone knows how to turn these disgusting thoughts about the horror of existence into representations with which one can live: the *sublime* as the artistic taming of the horrible" (Sallis 92, 93).[9] The experience of art transfigures meaninglessness into sublimity. Sallis' discussion of what "the sublime" means for Nietzsche (see 94-95) needs no supplementing here, but one should perhaps underscore his remarks about the nature of the abyss or *Abgrund* in Nietzsche's text. The sublime interpretation of Dionysus is crucial for an understanding of Nietzsche's rejection of Socratic philosophy and his preference for art. According to Sallis, Dionysus is the god of excess, the god of difference. He ruptures the limit: "The Dionysian state is one of being impelled beyond the limit, driven on beyond the very limit that would delimit every state of the individual. Such transgression cannot but disrupt the limit and the delimitation that it effects" (Sallis 54).

If one imagines the self as a kind of enclosure, then the Dionysian takes the individual outside it—except that the self was only "an individual" inside it. To transgress the limit is to go outside, to cross the boundary, but the idea of transgression requires that there still be the limit of the enclosure. Going "outside" disrupts the enclosure itself, because it is not just any enclosure; one has been "outside *oneself*." If nothing else, "the self" to which one returns is now less than what has been experienced; it is now felt as "an enclosure." But its very nature has already been called into question and made to seem arbitrary by being

exceeded. What is the reality, then? The excess in which one is—
what? Not *oneself*. The reason that Dionysian excess "resist[s] sta-
bilization along the metaphysical axis" (Sallis 54) is that it cannot
be the truth by which all others would be grounded. One could
take Dionysian excess to underlie all truths or things as the origin from which they arise in their individual determination only
by ignoring the way in which the would-be ground disrupts the
very ordering that belongs to the concept of ground. It dissolves
the very determinateness that ground would produce.

What Dionysus reveals is not ground but abyss.[10] (Sallis 58)
"Primal unity" or "primordial being" in Nietzsche's text is an
abyss for reason. Yet it was not this recognition that moved
Socrates, at least in Nietzsche's depiction of him, to reject tragedy:
it was that Socrates never experienced the Dionysian intoxication
(witness his sobriety in the *Symposium*) and therefore had no
experience of the Dionysian truth. Nietzsche imagines Socrates as
deprived of the doubleness of vision that makes a tragic hero like
Oedipus capable of understanding the "Sphinx of two natures,"
the union of Apollinian dream and Dionysian frenzy. Socrates
has, as it were, a single nature, a single intellectual eye: "Let us
now imagine the one great Cyclops eye of Socrates fixed on
tragedy, an eye in which the fair frenzy of artistic enthusiasm had
never glowed. To this eye was denied the pleasure of gazing into
the Dionysian abysses" (BT 89). Denied—because one eye cannot
perceive depth. In Nietzsche's early interpretation of Socrates,
then, the philosopher builds everything upon a "profound *illusion*... that thought, using the thread of causality, can penetrate
the deepest abysses of being, and that thought is capable not only
of knowing being but even of correcting it" (95). This illusion,
so profoundly different from the Apollinian one that it displaces,
shapes the history of the West, according to Nietzsche. And it
becomes possible to understand tragedy again only when science,
the child of Socratism, finally comes upon the Dionysian abyss
and once more "needs art as a protection and a remedy" (98).

Nietzsche always insisted that the genius of *The Birth of Tragedy*
was its disclosure of the Dionysian. Although he later criticizes the
book as "badly written, ponderous, embarrassing, image-mad and
image-confused, sentimental, in some places saccharine to the point
of effeminacy, uneven in tempo, without the will to logical cleanliness, very convinced and therefore disdainful of proof" (BT 19),

he also recognizes in it two "decisive innovations." He claims in *Ecce Homo* that these are "its understanding of the Dionysian phenomenon among the Greeks... as one root of the whole of Greek art" and "the understanding of Socratism... as an instrument of Greek disintegration" (EH 727). At the heart of the Dionysian was tragic affirmation:

> Saying Yes to life even in its strangest and hardest problems, the will to life rejoicing over its own inexhaustibility even in the very sacrifice of its highest types—*that* is what I called Dionysian, *that* is what I guessed to be the bridge to the psychology of the *tragic* poet. *Not* in order to be liberated from terror and pity, not in order to purge oneself of a dangerous affect by its vehement discharge—Aristotle understood it in that way—but in order to be *oneself* the eternal joy of becoming, beyond all terror and pity—that joy which included even joy in destroying. (TI 562)

In his other writings, Nietzsche would be far less convinced that *life* was an adequate guide to nature. He would see the universe as essentially dead, and life itself as a peculiarly rare type of its deadness.[11] No longer would he speak of a "primal one," yet he would understand the will—the "impelling to existence" that can be characterized as "the will to power"—as the fundamental nature of all beings. There is a continuity between his early work and his later thought in this respect: he always rejects any notion of a rationally knowable ground to existence, anything in which the mind could come to rest, any more than it could rest in orgasm or childbirth. One does not come upon *logos*, in other words, but upon a will that has no *telos* but its own protean becoming. If knowledge is a form of mastery, then the search for meaning is evidence of the will to power, instead of evidence that the universe is rationally knowable; rather than philosophical truths, in other words, there are constructs—interpretations—that can be analyzed as symptoms of the quality of will at work in them.

In *The Birth of Tragedy*, there is a truth that one can know, but not with the distancing intellect; it is irrational, a truth of passion, artistically accessible through music. It can only be encountered outside rational self-awareness—that is, not encountered *as what it is* by reason, a fact that makes it impossible to ground one's thought upon it. The "primal one" is not a meaning, though it is possible through Dionysian art to penetrate (unnaturally, by sacrilege) to the truth of this innermost abyss. In order to do so, one must abandon the self–the contained individual mind–because it is impossible to hold Dionysian truth "within oneself" except as the remnant of an experience that calls individuation profoundly and permanently into question. Still, unlike Schopenhauer, Nietzsche *affirms* existence, because he understands art, in its double sense as image and music, to be the natural mode of accommodation to the irrational truth of things. In tragedy, Apollinian art makes possible a survival of this innermost abyss that leaves the individual deepened by Dionysian truth but fundamentally intact, because healed by the formal image. Only tragedy, in which healing images arise from the penetrations of music, and dream succeeds intoxication, truly addresses the world as it is, through this highest union of artistic instincts.

❊   ❊   ❊

> Whoever fights monsters should see to it that in the process he does not become a monster. And when you look long into an abyss, the abyss also looks into you.
>
> *Beyond Good and Evil*

Without the tragic abyss, then, there is only illusion. Terrible as it is, it is also the source of all fertility, all power. Nietzsche's insistence on this kind of passionate intuition, not to mention his obliteration of the boundary between philosophic and mythical thinking, made tragedy the choicest mode of post-Enlightenment, post-Romantic, post-Hegelian, post-Darwinist, post-positivist knowledge. It both precedes the "Socratism" of the West and follows it as the postmodern artistic solution for those who loathe modern democracy's small-souled fascination with the security and comfort of the many.[12] In a letter to Benjamin Bailey, Keats wrote, "The imagination may be compared to Adam's dream,–he awoke and found it truth. I am more zealous in this affair because I have never yet been able to perceive how anything can be known for truth by consecutive reasoning" (365). Nietzsche's understanding runs in the same vein: he awakes from annihilation to find the truth of the image.

What is difficult to understand from *The Birth of Tragedy*, how-ever, is *why* it is so devastating to be plunged into self-forgetful jouissance. Perhaps when Thomas Mann's Aschenbach in *Death in Venice*, smitten by the beauty of a young Polish boy, dreams about the onset of Dionysus, he is close to the truth of what Nietzsche might mean. Smitten in waking life by the beauty of this boy whose face is "reminiscent of Greek statues from the noblest period of antiquity" (Mann 21), the dreaming Aschenbach is caught up among the Dionysian revelers by the drum beats and the primal smells of bodies and blood; he finds himself in this scene, as the great phallic image of the god's worship appears before the maddened throng:

> Their obscene symbol, gigantic, wooden, was uncovered and raised on high, and they howled out their watchword all the more licentiously. With foam on their lips they raved; they stimulated each other with lewd gestures and fondling hands; laughing and wheezing, they pierced each other's flesh with their pointed staves and then licked the bleed-ing limbs. Now among them, now a part of them, the dreamer belonged to the stranger god. Yes, they were he, and he was they, when they threw themselves on the animals, tearing and killing, devouring steaming gobbets of flesh, when on the trampled moss-covered ground there began an unfettered rite of copulation in sacrifice to the god. His soul tasted the lewdness and frenzy of surrender. (Mann 57).

If this description glosses what Nietzsche means by "Dionysian abysses," then it is easy to see why it would overwhelm the self-contained man—the Apollinian man (or his successor, the Socratic man)—and send him back to the everyday with a sense of nau-sea. The body as a boundary gives way entirely; "the lewdness and frenzy of surrender" approximate, perhaps, the "primal unity." The soul of Socrates, of course, would never taste this frenzy, as the *Symposium* reveals. But for Aschenbach in Mann's novella, this Dionysian vision obliterates his integrity and plunges him into a headlong erotic pursuit. As Mann puts it, it leaves "his whole being, the culmination of a lifetime of effort, ravaged and annihilated" (56).

Mann clearly means this passage as an exact reversal of the divine dynamics at work in Nietzsche's *The Birth of Tragedy*—and also as a critique of Nietzsche. In Aschenbach's case, the Dionysian annihilation of the individual comes through the dream, not through music; in fact, it comes into the dream through the god-like, Apollinian perfection of the image of young Tadzio. The very beauty of the godlike boy—the perfection of the Apollinian—leads Aschenbach to his destruction. As a kind of Socrates musing on the relation between form and desire, he imagines a dialogue in which he addresses Phaedrus: "But form and ingenuousness, Phaedrus, lead to intoxication and to desire, might lead the noble soul to horrible emotional outrages that his own lovely discipline would reject as infamous, lead him to the abyss. Yes, they too lead to the abyss" (Mann 61). The experience of the abyss, in other words, is not only musical and therefore not limited to Dionysus in that sense.

Neither is it only sexual. Jonathan Shay's book *Achilles in Vietnam* recovers for our times the recognition of what battle—particularly an overwhelming, devastating rage in battle—does to the hero who undergoes it. The Norse term "berserk" has clear parallels in Homeric Greek (for example, the kind of rage called *lussa*), and, as Shay shows, men who have experienced this berserk state in battle use the similes of beasts and gods, as Homer does. Why the comparison to beasts? Because these warriors lose all human restraint, mental, ethical, and social, and they do things that—outside the berserk state—they remember, if at all, with horror. But they are also like gods: they exceed all human limits, all vulnerability, and it is difficult afterward not to consider that experience of excess superb.[13] Great deeds in battle are done in such a state, and warriors—Achilles most of all—have always been honored for their almost superhuman accomplishments against the enemy. The great difficulty, as with the experience of the Dionysian abyss, lies in going home. Those who have gone berserk have had the framework of character "ravaged and annihilated," to use Mann's terms, and they can never go back (even physiologically, Shay argues) to what they were before. The war hero might fit the description that Aristotle gives in the *Politics* of the man "who is unable to live in society" and who must therefore "be either a beast or a god" (*Politics*). Perhaps, having been both, he finds it difficult to live in the everyday according the limited human measure.

As a philologist, Nietzsche appeared to his contemporaries—and perhaps he appears to us—as something of a berserker. Not only was he reinventing tragedy, but also putting philosophy itself into a position that separated it much more profoundly from its own surrounding society: "To live alone one must be a beast or a god, says Aristotle. Leaving out the third case: one must be both—a philosopher" (TI 467). Everything about his argument assumes not only a "twisting free from Platonism," as Sallis, translating Heidegger, puts it (Sallis 2 and passim), but at the same time, an attempt to get out from under the shadows of the death of God[14] "that must soon envelop Europe" (GS 279) and find the means of affirmation. "And herewith I again touch that point from which I once went forth: *The Birth of Tragedy* was my first revaluation of all values" (TI 562). In his later writings, Nietzsche forthrightly undertakes the task of making mere Enlightenment unbelief into tragic annihilation by proclaiming the "death of God." He does so by finding in tragedy a new form that is also the recovery of the old; he conceives of tragedy as both pre-Socratic and postmodern, a return and a new horizon.

The question is whether, in his encounter with the abyss, he has not experienced a shattering of his own boundaries that makes thinking itself into an ecstasy and frenzy such that it ultimately eludes his artistic control and becomes a kind of *sparagmos*. Where, one might ask, is this jouissance of the abyss resolved, for Nietzsche's own work, in the Apollinian image?[15] For all its energy, Nietzsche's theological re-invention of tragedy might be faulted for eroticizing the tragic abyss and giving it a particular philosophic appeal, a glamour of sublimity. Against such an appeal, Dante looms large in the aftermath of the ancients, since even damnation is part of the whole Christian design of the *Commedia*—the dark glamour of earthly tragedy recontextualized and re-imaged: no longer Ugolino starving in the sublime cannibalistic gloom of the tower, but Ugolino embedded in ice, gnawing his archbishop's neck like a dog with a bone. In the greater vision, sardonic ironies of rejected good emerge from the very graciousness of offered love, and needlessly chosen miseries of the self-justifying stud the abyss in its orderly declensions. Faith regrounds any conceivable tragedy, and any bottomless darkness appears as an illusory fissure in the greater Mercy. To be real, however, the tragic abyss cannot be regrounded; it must *be* the abyss, an absence of ground that absorbs the whole capacity of faith. But if the mode of its reality is a poetic one, as Louise

Cowan argues in the Introduction to this volume, when she writes that tragedy "evokes something rather than reminds us of something" (Cowan 2), then the greatest danger will lie in making tragedy the measure of human life. If tragedy after the Greeks requires the profound unsettling and ungrounding that only the annihilation of God as the individual of individuals could effect, then, as what Cowan calls "a diagram or ritual," this drama might be imagined and taken in, but it should not in the end be taken as more than a nightmare. Otherwise, one might stare too long into the abyss one reifies by one's own glamorous posture at its brink—and so become monstrous oneself. The Greeks themselves—"profoundly superficial," Nietzsche called them—opened the depths to listen, like Oedipus at his death, for a calling beyond the abyss.

NOTES

[1] Nietzsche's individual texts will be cited as follows: *The Birth of Tragedy* (BT); *Ecce Homo* (EH); *The Gay Science* (GS); and *Twilight of the Idols* (TI). Page numbers for TI refer to *The Portable Nietzsche* and those for EH to *Basic Writings of Nietzsche*.

[2] Sallis goes on to defend Nietzsche's scholarship by demonstrating the implicit interpretation of the Apollo of the *Iliad* that underlies the exposition in *The Birth of Tragedy*. Sallis' emphasis on "shine" or "shining" as the translation of Schein, instead of "appearance," gives what seems to me a Heideggerian cast to Nietzsche's interpretation of Homer, but it is one that accords with Nietzsche's praise of the Greeks for loving surfaces: "Oh, those Greeks! They knew how to live. What is required for that is to stop courageously at the surface, the fold, the skin, to adore appearance, to believe in forms, tones, words, in the whole Olympus of appearance. Those Greeks were superficial—out of profundity" (GS 38).

[3] In the "Preface" to *Prometheus Unbound*, Shelley asserts that the Greek tragic writers employed "a certain arbitrary discretion" in their treatment of traditional stories: "They by no means conceived themselves bound to adhere to the common interpretation or to imitate in story as in title their rivals and predecessors. Such a system would have amounted to a resignation of those claims to preference over their competitors which incited the composition."

[4] Nietzsche might be thinking of the way that the essentially image-

less powers of retribution, the Furies, emerge as images in the presence of Apollo in the *Eumenides*. Not so much what they look like, but the fact of their being made visible at all is the crucial point.

5 One could pause over this pairing: Antigone so singular in her stance, so high, yet so primitive in her insistence on law, so absolute in blood (but Apollinian in this respect, or Dionysian?); and Cassandra so personally obliterated—helpless, unbelieved, unresisting—and at the same time so illuminated by Apollo's vision, possessed entirely by Apollo's images.

6 Greenblatt's statement follows upon his earlier declaration that he had begun his work because he thought he saw a high degree of autonomy in the "shaping power" that Renaissance men had over their own lives: "But as my work progressed... the human subject itself began to seem remarkably unfree, the ideological product of the relations of power in a particular society" (256). Nietzsche sees in Hamlet something more: a lack of freedom that stems from the nature of becoming that underlies and necessitates the structure of power relations as such.

7 In this dismembered state, Dionysus is also (like Apollo) the origin of the gods: "From the smile of Dionysus sprang the Olympian gods, from his tears sprang man" (BT 73). The gods thus come both from shining appearance and from the joy of *sparagmos*.

8 Nietzsche recounts the fable of Silenus in Section 3, where the satyr-demigod and companion of Dionysus tells King Midas, who captured him, what is best and most desirable for man: "What is best of all is utterly beyond your reach: not to be born, not to be, to be nothing. But the second best for you is—to die soon" (BT 42).

9 This sentence sums up what might be taken as the movement of Melville's *Moby-Dick*, from Ishmael's abysmal meditations ("faith like a jackal feeds among the tombs") through a displacement of his self-consciousness by Ahab's, to the sublime battle with the White Whale.

10 Compare Martin Heidegger's comment on the abyss in "What Are Poets For?" Heidegger appears to reject Nietzsche's mythological thinking and to focus instead on recovering language etymologically to find a different kind of pre-conceptual thinking:

> The word for abyss–*Abgrund*–originally means the soil and ground toward which, because it is undermost, a thing tends downward. But in what follows we shall think of the Ab- as the complete absence of the ground. The ground is the soil in which to strike

root and to stand. The age for which the ground fails to come, hangs in the abyss.... In the age of the world's night, the abyss must be experienced and endured. But for this it is necessary that there be those who reach into the abyss (Heidegger 92).

[11] In Section 109 of *The Gay Science*, he writes that we should beware of thinking of the world as a living being, because "we should not reinterpret the exceedingly derivative, late, rare, accidental, that we perceive only on the crust of the earth and make of it something essential, universal, and eternal, which is what those people do who call the universe an organism" (GS 167). Neither, he adds, should we call it a machine, since it was not constructed for any purpose. This meditation, of course, follows from his first pronouncement in the previous section that "God is dead." If this thinking remains an exploration of the Dionysian, then a passage later in the same section becomes particularly important: "Once you know there are no purposes, you also know that there is no accident; for it is only beside a world of purposes that the word 'accident' has meaning. Let us beware of saying that death is opposed to life. The living is merely a type of what is dead, and a very rare type." To say that God is dead—not only that belief is no longer possible, but that the fundamental characteristic of "being" is death—theologizes "what-is-dead." The Dionysian, so much associated with the endless becoming of life in *The Birth of Tragedy*, becomes in this later vision an access to the primal, original "unity" of what is dead. In experiencing this unity one has touched, not the deadness that waits for all life, but the very origin of life. The word "dead" must now describe the source of all that happens to live, neither on purpose or by accident.

[12] "A people," he writes in *Beyond Good and Evil*, "is a detour of nature to get to six or seven great men.—Yes, and then to get around them."

[13] One Vietnam veteran describes going berserk and firing madly at the North Vietnamese from an exposed position: "I felt like a god, this power flowing through me. Anybody could have picked me off there—but I was untouchable" (Shay 84).

[14] He glosses this statement with the appositive clause, "that the belief in the Christian god has become unbelievable" (*Gay Science* 279). But see also note 10 above.

[15] Arguably, he means for the circle, the ring of eternal recurrence,

to be such an image: meaninglessness redeemed by the affirmation of endless repetition.

Part Two

SUFFERING

AND WISDOM

...In the day when the keepers of the house shall tremble, and the strong men shall bow themselves, and the grinders cease because they are few, and those that look out of the windows be darkened,

And the doors shall be shut in the streets, when the sound of the grinding is low, and he shall rise up at the voice of the bird, and all the daughters of musick shall be brought low...

Ecclesiastes 12:3-4

4

Job and the Tragedy of Divine Love

Job was a man beloved by all the people of the land of Uz. He loved his children, for whom he offered sacrifices after all of their feasts, fearing that they might sin and curse God in their hearts. According to his testimony in his final speech, he loved his people and served them, including the slaves, the poor, and the orphans. Most of all he loved God and was God's beloved. In fact, when the prologue renders a rare glimpse of God's activity in the heavenly place, we are told that God boasted of his servant Job to the accusing angel, Satan. Job not only did nothing wrong to deserve his unbearable suffering, but as the story indicates, his very goodness made him the object of God's admiring gaze and, therefore, the target of the Accuser. The opening description implies that if God had not boasted to Satan about Job, "a blameless and upright man, who fears God and turns away from evil" (Job 1:8),[1] the Accuser would not have challenged God to let him take away all that Job had. Can it be that the heart of this tragedy is the love of God for Job? Job suffers, not because God holds him in contempt, like the "creatures of a day" in *Prometheus Bound*, whom the King of the gods disdains; Job is afflicted because the Almighty God's love of him and belief in him arouse the envy and attention of Satan.

Job loses everything but his soul and integrity. His wife advises him to curse God and die. His friends accuse him of bringing the losses on himself by some sin, which they have not witnessed, but which their theology tells them must have been committed. The story advances largely through a cycle of accusations by these friends against Job; they take turns trying to wear a confession out of him. Again and again Job denies wrongdoing and demands to plead his case before God. When the three "wise men" finally bring Job to the brink of despair and blasphemy, young Elihu comes to Job's defense while cautioning Job to be careful in what he says about God. At this point, when Job almost loses hope of ever being vindicated, the Creator speaks out of a storm: "Who is this that darkens my counsel with words without knowledge?" He then asks Job where he was when God created the heavens and the earth, graphically describing aspects of the created order from the macrocosm to the birth of mountain goats. God then concludes his song of creation with this question to Job: "Will the one who contends with the Almighty correct Him? Let him who accuses God answer him!" Job answers that "I am unworthy—how can I reply to you? I put my hand over my mouth. I spoke once, but I have no answer—twice, but I will say no more." The story ends with God accusing Job's accusers, vindicating Job's good name, and restoring to him double everything he once had, except, of course, children.

Many readers have difficulty understanding Job as truly tragic, because of the folktale-like envelope that surrounds the drama. They know the hidden truth of what went on at the throne of God and they know the ending. Thinking of the work a tragedy of divine love calls into question the way many interpreters of it have understood tragedy and the way they have conceived of the relationship of the human to the divine. But to understand the Book of Job fully and to probe its most profound tragic meaning, one must read it as it has been received in the synagogue, in the church, and in Western culture. The faith and imagination of peoples and persons have been formed and transformed for over two millennia by this sacred and poetic text. Many contemporary biblical and literary scholars advocate dropping the prose narrative that frames the speech cycles written in dramatic verse. They justify these exclusions not only because the larger core of the book is lyric and dramatic, but also because they believe that the prologue and epilogue depict a much older legend and turns an otherwise existential depiction of suffering into a pious tract.

Many of the same scholars would also drop the final speeches of God, and some would drop Elihu's speech and rearrange some of the final cycles of speeches so that Zophar could have a third speech and so that Job would not appear to speak the praise of wisdom in Chapter 28. Of course, among the scholars who would rewrite and rearrange the received text, there is little agreement about what belongs where. What they do agree upon is that the framing narratives mitigate the suffering, legitimize the theology, and extend the primitive text beyond its earliest form.

In the meantime, generations of astute scholars and careful readers have read and made sense of the traditional book of Job rejected by these post-enlightenment scholars. For the characters and themes of the epilogue and prologue resonate throughout the central speeches, with the speakers taking up each other's very wording, often sarcastically. As Moshe Greenberg has observed, "We must gain an awareness of the complexities and interplay among the elements of the book...and [see] that the literary complexity of the book is consistent with and appropriate to the nature of the issues with which it deals" (Alter and Kermode, 283-84). This view does not preclude the possibility that the Job poet may have taken up an ancient story and given it poetic form centuries after a historical and now legendary Job lived. But the greatness of Job's tragic persona and the ambiguities about God's mysterious character make less sense without this framing narrative. Indeed, as I will explain later, these narratives make Job more fully tragic than would the central speeches alone.

※　※　※

First, however, I must also answer those who would deny that the Book of Job is tragedy, indeed that any religious work can be tragic in that religion presents the hope for a solution to the problem of evil. Such critics concur with I. A. Richard's famous assertion that "Tragedy is only possible to a mind which is for the moment agnostic or Manichean," because "The least touch of any theology which has a compensating heaven to offer the tragic hero is fatal" (Sanders 46). Their logic is that the hope of a beneficent deity "working all things together for good" or of a Nirvana where good and evil are as one makes impossible tragedy which, in the words of D.D. Raphael, "treats evil as unalloyed evil...and does not think that innocent suffering can be justified" (Sanders 55). This peculiarly modern view of tragedy as utter despair not only declares that "Tragedy is hardly possible against a background of Biblical religion" (55) but calls into question some of the greatest tragedies of the Greeks such as the *Oresteia*, *Prometheus Bound*, and *Oedipus at Colonus* as well as Marlowe's *Dr. Faustus* and Shakespeare's *Hamlet*. This categorical exclusion of religious tragedy in general and of Biblical tragedy in particular is not only made questionable by the existence of the tragedies I have listed above, but it also reveals more about the existential and secular perspectives of the critics of the last century than about the meaning of tragedy.[2]

Another group of critics, among them Jewish and Christian scholars, deny for formal reasons that the Book of Job is tragedy. Some, such as Leland Ryken, point out the fact that Job has a happy ending, which characterizes comedy with its "U-shaped plot in which events begin in prosperity, descend into tragedy, and rise suddenly to a happy conclusion" (Ryken 109). Some would argue that tragedies must always be written for a dramatic performance, and that since Job is a dramatic narrative, not a play, it is therefore not a tragedy. While it is true that tragedy as we have come to know it was born in the Greek theater and that most of the greatest and purest tragedies are dramas, it is still possible to render in narrative form all the elements of tragedy described by Aristotle and expanded by later critics. Nor can we forget that Aeschylus, the father of Greek tragedy, began writing for a theater that was still religious liturgy and only later became secularized, partly because the Greeks were calling into question their deities and sacred beliefs. Perhaps the Hebrews never conceived of a secular theater, because they never fully lost a sense of their temple, synagogue, and Seder liturgy as sacred drama. As to the argument that Job follows more the pattern of comedy than of tragedy, let me suggest that the brief ending in which Job's reputation and fortunes are restored hardly constitutes a "happy ending." Perhaps this strange ending only deepens the mystery of the affliction of Job. Moreover, to suggest that any drama with such a U-shaped plot is *ipso facto* a comedy implies that *The Eumenides* and *Oedipus at Colonus* are comedies. While comedies usually contain certain conventions and tragedies are characterized as well by particular elements, these characteristics and conventions are not the essence of either genre. Often, in fact, some of the greatest works of literature test the limits of a genre while remaining some of its highest expressions. Job expands the horizon of pure tragedy, and understanding it as such deepens our understanding of this marvelous and terrible story.

❖ ❖ ❖

William Lynch has said that tragedy explores "the most finite moments of the finite; it discovers its most limited points. These are final moments and points of weakness, collapses of energy, failures of the human will to raise itself, of itself...." (65). Lynch concludes that the most beautiful images of human beings in literature are tragic ones, revealing the glory of the human person at the point in life where he is most helpless.

But Job's tragic beauty lies not in his being a docile victim but in his daring to contend with God. Like his counselors, he started out with a neat and tidy theology, but between their rather formulaic use of theology against Job and Job's unspeakable suffering, his theology fails to sustain him. What does sustain Job in this time of suffering is that he believes, somehow, that a mere mortal in all his finite weakness can plead with, cry out to, and demand the help of the very God who has afflicted him. He has the audacity to believe that the Creator of the universe will hear him and become his defender. He even believes that God watches over his petty life and cares about his affliction. He contends to the point of presuming to correct and accuse God, which is apparently why God intervenes in the life of this man on whom the divine honor depends. Moreover, while Job protests and rails against the injustices which he must suffer, his speeches actually move from cursing the day he was born to pleading with God not only for himself but for all those who suffer through no fault of their own.

Job, his family, and friends do not know of God's great pride in Job (though they may have speculated) nor of the Accuser and his malevolence. This privileged knowledge of how things turn out can cause readers to want to jump ahead, not dwelling with Job and his accusers in their incessant dialogues and diatribes. The idea that tragedy must end in unmitigated suffering and disaster not only overlooks such tragic heroes as the Oedipus of

Oedipus at Colonus or the Orestes of the *Eumenides,* but more importantly fails to take into account that, in the meantime, the unbearable loss, humiliation, suffering, and abandonment of Oedipus, Orestes, and Job are no less tragic because they obtain redemption in the end.

Job faces the abyss as much as and perhaps more than any tragic hero did. Indeed, he fits the description that the Prophet Isaiah gives of the Messiah as suffering servant:

> He was despised and rejected by men,
> A man of sorrows, and familiar with suffering.
> Like one from whom men hide their faces,
> He was despised, and we esteemed him not.
> Surely he took up our infirmities and carried our sorrows,
> Yet we considered him stricken by God,
> Smitten by him, and afflicted. (53:3-4 KJV)

While Job is no doubt not perfect, he is righteous before God, looked up to as patriarchal priest by his family, and the wisest among the wise of the elders of his world. In his world, a mere man can be no higher; he is not in this elevated position, like Oedipus or Orestes, because of murder or bloodline. He is exalted among men by his uprightness, as one exalted by God. He is blessed with wife and children, property and friends, wealth and power. He takes none of these blessings for granted. Then, for no reason, all he possesses is ripped away from him. He is not merely suffering pain; he is *afflicted.*

Simone Weil aptly describes Job's condition when she writes that "Affliction is an uprooting of life, a more or less attenuated equivalent of death, made irresistibly present to the soul by the attack or immediate apprehension of physical pain" (118). Job, upon hearing of the loss of his property and children, tears his robe to symbolize his "torn heart" and shaves his head to express "the conscious loss of his dearest ones" (Keil and Delitzsch 64). He then falls down to the earth as both an act of worship to the God who gives and who takes away, and an act of falling back into the dust from which he came. Job's life has been torn away; everything he loved and lived for on this earth is dead. He embodies Weil's assertion that "There is no real affliction unless the event that has seized and uprooted a life attacks it, directly

or indirectly, in all its parts, social, psychological, and physical"
(Weil 119). What Job cannot know, numbed as he is by unbearable grief, is that there is a second round of affliction being prepared for him by the Accuser. He will not only feel the pain of
the loss of children, servants, herds, and property, but lose the
comfort of dwelling in his own body, being at home in his own
skin. Left devastated and abhorrent to others, he takes refuge in
the ash heap, becoming part of the refuse of life and burying
himself in the dust of the earth. He has lost everything, including the support of his wife, who instructs him to renounce his
integrity, "to curse God and die" (2:9). Spared by the Accuser,
she has taken the Accuser's role. Job is left with no person or
thing, not even his own healthy body, to reflect back to him his
intimate identity as a person of worth in the world. He is left
with only the integrity of his will and his ultimate trust in God.
Job surely must think that this suffering cannot be made worse.

Enter Job's friends—those comrades who share his pious faith
in God and his love of wisdom. They will at least be able to
affirm to him the spiritual and psychological truth of his faithfulness to God and God's ultimate faithfulness to him. Of the
latter they are certain and can speak endlessly. But they cannot
affirm Job's faithfulness, since they cannot reconcile Job's affliction with their theology. At the point that they follow Job's lead
by beginning to speak after a week of silence, they join Job's wife
as the prosecuting team representing the Accuser.

From the depths, Job breaks the silence by lamenting the day
of his birth and the existence of everything associated with it:

> Let the stars of its dawn be dark;
> let it hope for light, but have none,
> nor see the eyelids of the morning,
> because it did not shut the doors of my mother's womb,
> nor hide trouble from my eyes. (3:9-10)

In one sense, he simply wants to join his children and servants
by being annihilated. They are gone; he longs to be gone. Better
yet, if he never existed then they would not exist and none of
them would have suffered. His longing resonates with that of
many tragic heroes at the first moment of agony, like Oedipus in
the passion of blinding himself. But Job's affliction has only

begun, as his friends begin to accuse him of some secret sin that
would explain why God has rightly punished him. Like waves battering a drowning man, their words move from patronizing sagac-
ity to scathing accusation to contemptuous condemnation. At first,
Eliphaz simply suggests that if God reproaches his angels, why
should Job be surprised that he is being punished for some sin:
"But now it has come to you, and you are impatient; / it touches
you, and you are dismayed" (4:5). Then Bildad tells him that perhaps his sons also sinned, but things will probably be better in
the end after he receives his due punishment. When Job forthrightly denies that he has done anything to justify such punishment from God, Zophar gives him a lecture on the vastness of
the wisdom of God and the puniness of Job's understanding. Not
only must Job listen to his friends accuse him of sin he knows
he has not committed, but also he must hear them do so in a
theology that up to now he has shared and probably taught them.

Job has suffered the death of his family and the death of his
dignity. As his accusers become more vitriolic, Job becomes more
desperate to present his case to the only one who knows his
heart and who can answer his cries. He increasingly responds to
his accusers by appealing to or railing against God. They are actually instruments of the Accuser, whom Job believes to be God.
Job begins to speak of God no longer as only his advocate but
also as his adversary. Weil rightly asserts that "If Job cries out
that he is innocent in such despairing accents, it is because he
himself is beginning not to believe in it; it is because his soul
within him is taking the side of his friends" (121). There is no
doubt that Job is becoming more desperate, for his integrity is
inseparably bound to his faith in God. If Elohim, the Creator,
and Yahweh, the Covenant maker, is not who he is, then Job is
nothing—neither beloved creature nor redeemed man. Perhaps one
of the reasons that the third cycle of his accusers' speeches is
never complete is that they no longer matter. The contest is
between Job and God.

Thus far, God has been silent. "Affliction," writes Weil,
"makes God appear to be absent for a time, more absent than
a dead man, more absent than light in the utter darkness of a
cell." If we are to believe God's words of boasting of his servant
Job, this man has communed with the Creator in ways unfathomable to Oedipus, who fled the gods and would earn their

approval only at the end of his penance. Some have suggested that Job presumed in his religious piety and worldly success that God favored him; but God affirms in the end that Job has indeed been righteous, presuming nothing. And yet during these days or weeks of affliction, God chooses not to speak. In such circumstances, maintains Weil, "The soul has to go on loving in the emptiness, or at least to go on wanting to love, though it may only be with an infinitesimal part of itself." God does finally show himself to Job "to reveal the beauty of the world," but, Weil argues, there was yet the possibility for Job to stop loving, and "if the soul stops loving it falls, even in this life, into something almost equivalent to hell" (121-22). Job's words to God and about God in response to his accusers reveal a man who has fallen from the object of God's delight to one who fears he is about to be sucked into some spiritual and moral maelstrom: "the terrors of God are arrayed against me" (6:4).

Then a silent young observer intervenes as the interlocutor for God and the prelude to the words which Job has all but despaired of ever hearing. In what could be the oldest book of the Bible, Job begins the great tradition by which Jacob will be transformed and for which God's people will be named: "Is-ra-el: he wrestles with God." For at the point of life when time stands still because human grief has become unbearable, the only hope is that human beings can contend with a loving and good God who loves to contend with them. The poet of Job, like most biblical writers, offers no easy answer to the question of why the innocent suffer. But if we live in a fallen world that seems to parcel out its pain and suffering indiscriminately, the response of Yahweh is to enter into the suffering of his creation.

This contentious God with whom Job contends is, unlike Zeus, both Creator and Lover of humankind. While the opening scene in which God permits Satan to take away everything but Job's life may infuriate a reader like Carl Jung (see Jung's *Answer to Job*), all the characters in the world of Job believe that the Almighty can do as he pleases with his creation. What gives him pleasure is his servant Job. Indeed, one of the many ways which Eliphaz and his cohorts speak falsely of God is when they say:

'Can mortal man be in the right before God?
Can a man be pure before his Maker.

> Even in his servants he puts no trust,
>> and his angels he charges with error;
> how much more those who dwell in houses of clay,
>> whose foundation is in the dust,
>> who are crushed like the moth. (4:17-19)
>
> [or]
>
> Behold, even the moon is not bright,
>> and the stars are not pure in his sight,
> How much less man, who is a maggot,
>> And the son of man, who is a worm? (25:5-6)

These pious platitudes and obsequious admonitions sound humble, but we know from the beginning that Job pleases God. We know that God even trusts the accusing angel, Satan, with real but limited power. And we learn from the theophany when Yahweh describes creation from the macrocosm to the microcosm that he takes pleasure in everything He has created. This God who delights in his creation and who boasts from his throne about his servant Job, this Almighty Creator whose absolute power no one calls into question, pervades this tragic story. He is inseparably involved in Job's suffering—and in suffering with Job.

The name used for God in the dramatic speeches is some variation of *Elohim*, the Creator God. While Israel understands their God as the only true God and the one who created the entire universe, this word for the divine was common among Semitic peoples. Many of Israel's neighbors worshiped El or Elohim. In this sense, the God of these central chapters is the God of all and the God above all. However, in the prose prologue and epilogue, as well as when God speaks to Job in 38:1 and 40:1, he is called *Yahweh*, the covenant name by which he revealed himself to Israel alone. As Yahweh he is the one who is with and for his people. He is free to be who he will be. He is not to be defined by the priests and cults and icons of either the gentiles or of Israel. He will love Israel and through them the nations at his pleasure and in his way.[3] At first, in the prologue, Yahweh is *for* Job but *above* him, present only through sacrifices and worship. Then God chooses, like Job's friends in their first week on the ash heap, to remain silent. But if one accepts and hears the story as it is written, God is present for those days and weeks where he is the subject of conversation, the object of Job's rage, and the victim of Job's friends and their "prosperity gospel." God listens patiently while Job denounces his own life and God's goodness and justice. God listens patiently when Job's wife tells him to curse God and commit suicide. God listens patiently while Job's friends falsely accuse his beloved servant, denigrate his angels and his creation, and defend his infallible holiness with half-truths and outright lies. And God listens patiently, waiting his turn, when Elihu defends Job's integrity against his friends' accusations and warns Job not to blaspheme God.[4] God, in short, is present throughout the speeches by his silence, not his absence. He does not speak until everyone has exhausted the silence, the outrage of grief, and the platitudes of comfort, prepared to hear God's word.

The proverbial wisdom of Job and his friends had reduced God to abstractions about "God." But they did not know about the accusing angel, about God's sheer delight in his servant Job, or about God's granting Satan the freedom to strip Job of the fruits of his righteousness, which Satan believed to be the reason Job was a good man. It is intriguing that when this patient God finally answers Job out of a whirlwind remembering his creation, he is called Yahweh, not Elohim. It is as if two aspects of God's character and of his relationship to man, to Job, are reconciled in this loving litany of his creatures. Jung, in his profound though total misreading of Job, sees God here as merely a bully. According to Jung, God is perhaps trying to assert his omnipotence to Satan, his "double." Jung protests, "What has all that to do with Job?" (544). While he answers his own question through a Jungian analysis of a God who lacks reflection and individuation, the text and the reality it represents to us answer very differently. The obvious problem that many readers have with God's "answer" is that it does not address why Job has suffered unjustly and why God permitted it. Job is satisfied with the answer, and it is Job who has suffered the indignity and humiliation of loss, rejection, and condemnation. Why is Job satisfied?

Some would say Job is simply overpowered by the Almighty. But Yahweh's description of his creation overpowers Job not only with God's omnipotence but also with God's love for his creation. Just as God bragged about his servant Job, here he is to be found boasting about intricate details of the world he has wrought. We should recall that Job answers Zophar's early accusations by invoking God's creation as a witness for Job and against God:

> The tents of robbers are at peace,
>> And those who provoke God are secure,
>> Who bring their god in their hands.
> But ask the animals, and they will teach you;
>> The birds of the air, and they will tell you;
> Ask the plants of the earth, and they will teach you,
>> And the fish of the sea will declare to you.
> Who among these does not know
>> That the hand of the Lord has done this? (12:6-9)

Job, like his accusers, attempts to save the appearances as he "darkens counsel by words without knowledge" (38:2). God begins his interrogation of Job, as we might expect, asking this mortal where he was when the Creator laid the foundations of the earth, when the morning stars sang together, when the angels shouted for joy, when he shut in the sea with doors and clothed it with clouds, when he commanded the sun to rise, the rains to fall, the lightning and thunder to go forth, the stars to move through the heavens, and the cycles of weather to continue.

These cosmic images of creation and Creator are awesome, but then God's description takes a strange and tender turn. He begins to ask Job what he knows about satisfying the appetites of young lions and ravens, about how and when the mountain goat gives birth, about the beauty of the wild ass running free, about his relationship with the wild ox, the ostrich, the hawk, the eagle and their young. These are not the words of a divine bully or of a dispassionate and distant deity, but of a loving Creator who is invested in his creation. And Job knows, for good and evil, that he and his fellow humans are the crown of that creation. Job gets it, whether or not the reader does. To be the beloved of such a Creator is even more humbling than merely to be his servant. If God can speak with such passion and specificity about the details of the cosmos, can Job not trust that God will speak with passion and specificity on behalf of Job? On the other hand, if God is the force that created every detail of the macrocosm and the microcosm, why does he not use such unfathomable power to prevent a righteous man from unspeakable affliction?

Jung is deeply disturbed, as are so many readers, because Job suffers unjustly and is reduced to an ash heap, metaphorically returned to the earth from which he came. Job is as good as dead. But when the covenant-making and almighty-creating God finally speaks forth from the storm, Job is created anew. Job's response to God infuriates the modern ear: "My ears had heard of you, but now my eyes have seen you. / Therefore I despise myself and repent in dust and ashes" (42:5-6). God recreates Job from the ashes in which he repents. After all, this deity is not Job's shadow, his alter ego, his double, or his household idol. This is the Creator God speaking out of a storm about the vastness of his creation of which Job is one speck. People in our time are awed by a glance or a touch of mere mortal celebrities. Is it so hard to understand why a man who has personally encountered the Creator of all things, against whom he has been railing for days or weeks, should "repent in dust and ashes"? Is it surprising to those who know the biblical God, that when Job, like Isaiah, feels overwhelmed by the presence of the Almighty, God should then speak on his behalf, not "remembering his sins against him"?

While God never explains to Job or his friends why Job was permitted to suffer, he does say that Job spoke of him "what is right" and his three friends did not. What does God mean? He cannot mean that everything Job said of him was right, because Job made accusations against God that were by measure of his own theology bordering on blasphemy. He calls God unjust, a friend of thieves and the unrighteous, an oppressor of the righteous, one who contradicts his own word. While Job avows that he will not give up his integrity, he accuses God himself of lacking this quality. But just as God never answers the question of why Job suffers, likewise he never mentions Job's accusations.

In what sense, then, does Job say what is right about God? First, Job believes that God does know and hear him, even when he almost despairs of God's justice and love. While Job and his friends believed much the same *quid pro quo* theology that characterizes most of the wisdom tradition, Job never demeans man, the angels, or the rest of creation as do his friends. Their god takes no pleasure in his creation, does not trust his angels, and takes no pride or joy in the righteousness of man. Their god derives his transcendent majesty by virtue of how diminished and meaningless is his creation on earth and in heaven. But this is not the God to whom Job cried out and against whom Job declared his own integrity and innocence. Walter Brueggemann describes this diminished theology as the "royal consciousness," created by the domestication of God in the static religion of the Solomonic tradition. It sought to make God the accessible deity of priests and kings who would sanction the illusion that the kings and their kingdoms are eternal and deny the sufferings of their subjects.

God responds to these illusions of power and oppression through the prophets, who call the people back to the God who is free from their definitions and controls and free to be for them. Brueggemann asserts that this "the task of this prophetic ministry is to nurture, nourish, and evoke a consciousness and perception alternative to the consciousness and perception of the dominant culture" (13). Job might be the prototypical prophet, whose story precedes the Mosaic tradition but whose experience and theology liberate his people, the people of "the east," from a God imprisoned in their theology, declaring a God who is free to "be who he will be," who is for his creation, and who wants to wrestle with man. This intimate grappling between creature and Creator does not preclude human suffering. Indeed, it is merely another revelation of the mystery that God's "solution" to human misery is to enter into it.

Brueggemann explains that "energy comes from the embrace of the inscrutable darkness." He goes on to say, in discussing a situation analogous to Job's, that "something is 'on the move' in the darkness that even the lord of the darkness does not discern" (23). Job's friends would explain away the suffering, the evil, and the darkness and thereby miss the opportunity to wrestle with God. Job refused to relinquish his integrity, which now must include the suffering and death that have afflicted him, and he refuses to lose hope in the God whom he believes to be both Elohim, his creator, and Yahweh, his redeemer.

※ ※ ※

The gentile Job, who knows the true God and anticipates the God of Moses, also fits Aristotle's ideal of the tragic hero, as Richard B. Sewall proposes:

> He was "unaccommodated man," moved in his first moment of bit-
> terness to give up the struggle, but for some reason making a "ges-
> ture" first. It is this action, and the action, which follows from it,
> which establishes Job as hero. It had what Aristotle called "magnitude":
> it involved Job totally, and he was a man of high estate on whom
> many people depended; it involved Job's world totally, since it ques-
> tions its beliefs and modes of life; it transcended Job's world, hori-
> zontally as well as vertically, as the perennial relevance of Job's
> problem, from his time to ours, shows (Sanders 27).

Sewall rightly argues that Job's life fits the tragic ideal that Aristotle saw in Oedipus, only Job is not finally guilty of sins against
man and the gods, as was Oedipus. The tragic irony of Job's life
is not that the gods cursed him before his birth, but that God
blessed him for his righteousness before the angels—and that the
blessing became his curse. Moreover, while we never are told that
Oedipus could have been free from the fate which was given him,
Job is cursed by the God who is perfectly free to prevent the
Accuser's afflictions, which God chooses not to prevent for reasons of his own. That the curse is transformed by God back into
a blessing deepens the mystery of the abyss of divine love.

What are we to make of this God who loves and vindicates
his servant Job but allows such violence to be done against him?
René Girard probes this question in his essay "Violence in Biblical Narrative." He begins by saying that we cannot deny that the
violence described in the historical narratives, the imprecatory
psalms, and sections of the prophets surpass most of what we find
in classical literature. It would be foolish to deny that the violence exists; rather, we should ask what it means. In Girard's
view, "the persecutors are in charge" in pagan cultures and "we
never hear the victims." Those who suffer in such stories, even
Prometheus, being guilty, suffer justly, even if there is more to the
story than their guilt. It is the Biblical witness to violence and
injustice that is almost always an outcry of the victim. "Whereas
in myth," says Girard, "we learn about lynching from the persecutors who maintain that they did the right thing in lynching
their victims, in the Bible we hear from the victims themselves."
He adds, "These victims feel exactly the way Job does." Girard
then explains that "The Book of Job must be defined... as an
enormously enlarged psalm of malediction" (391-92). Although the

Book of Job should properly be considered a tragedy and not a "psalm of malediction," nevertheless Girard's insight—that the Biblical tradition gives voice to the victim as no other tradition does—helps us understand one of the distinctives of Biblical tragedy and, perhaps by extension, Christian tragedy. Whatever else can be said about the God of the Bible or, if you please, the religion of the Bible, it depicts a vision of the human that is not afraid to cry out and complain to God, and it reveals a God who does not crush those who complain, a God who, indeed, argues with them, changes his mind, and takes pleasure in every detail of his creation—not least in his servant Job.

If Girard adds the dignity of victimhood to our perspective on Job, Soren Kierkegaard's *Works of Love* can shed some light on the dynamics of a Biblical tragedy of love. Kierkegaard's understanding of love, derived from reflections on the Bible in general and the New Testament in particular, resonates with the way tragedy enables human beings to apprehend the mystery of life: "The hidden life of love is in the most inward depths, unfathomable, and still has an unfathomable relationship with the whole of existence" (27). He goes on to explain that the deep source of human love is God's love, but that "love's mysterious grounding in God's love prevents you from seeing its source," since "it is a reflection which deceives you, as if it were the bottom, this which only conceals the deeper bottom" (27).

Kierkegaard shows that love covers sin in three ways. First, love is silent in the face of sin. It refuses to accuse the sinner, even when it seems absolutely clear that the beloved has sinned. Job's friends begin lovingly in this way, in silence, covering their suspicions about Job's sin by grieving with him. But when Job breaks the silence and curses the day he was born, his words unleash the piety in his friends, making them his accusers, along with Satan and Job's wife. Even here they sound at first as though they may be moving to what Kierkegaard regards as the next phase of love's covering sin: the mitigating explanations of lovers who try to understand their beloved's sin in the best possible light, attempting to understand what drove them to such sins. In reality, Job's friends are actually presenting mitigating explanations that would save the theologies and the successful lives that they love more than they love Job. It is God alone who comes up with the truly mitigating explanation: I am the creator and you are not, and I love my creation, including you, Job, and even your proud accusers, if you will pray for them. God breaks his silence to explain not Job's suffering but his place in God's creation. This is enough for Job. But this is not enough for God, who goes on to the third and highest way, according to Kierkegaard, to cover a multiplicity of sins: forgiveness. Whatever Job has said while wrestling with God in his suffering, God has forgotten. And whatever injustice Job's friends have inflicted on Job, God forgives as Job forgives. It is an amazing moment that the writer does not explain, because it is an unfathomable mystery.

Kierkegaard writes that "When God forgets sin, forgetting is the opposite of creating, for to create means to bring forth out of nothing and to forget is to return it into nothing" (275). In light of these insights, the beauty of the Book of Job is that the Creator God permits, for reasons we are not told, to allow the Accuser to de-create Job's life, that with which God has blessed him. The end of Job is the ultimate covering of sins and, thereby, a reversal of the de-creating acts of the Accuser. God does not accuse Job. Job does not accuse his accusers, and so God forgets their sins against Job and himself.

✿   ✿   ✿

Sewall rightly considers Aeschylus and the poet of the Book of Job to be the seminal tragedians:

> Suffering itself, as the Poet of Job defines it, has been made to yield knowledge, and the way has been plotted out. After this achievement by the Poet of Job and after the similar achievement by Aeschylus in what may have been in the same era (the fifth century), the tragic form was permanently available. No subsequent artist whose imagination was attracted to this mode of writing could ignore it. (32)

Sewall's insight is akin to Louise Cowan's recognition that tragedy is not merely about catastrophic suffering in the life of noble persons, but it is about such suffering being given a permanent form so that human beings can face the unfathomable depths of suffering, darkness, and the abyss, which they represent in the lives of tragic heroes. Job is such a hero, and perhaps more so than any other. For Job truly contends with the Almighty, the loving and forgiving creator of all things.

The Book of Job renders a vision of God who is the Alpha and the Omega of history. But the tragedy of Job also tells us that the suffering and affliction even of an innocent man who serves an omnipotent and loving God does not do away with the indignities of life in the meantime. This is why the epilogue is not a happy ending; it is a just ending that reflects God's love of Job. God is the creator of this world, he created it as a good world, and he promises good things to good men in this life. There are hints of immortality, or more accurately of resurrection, in Job's assertion that "though the maggots eat me, in my flesh I shall behold God." But salvation is for and through and in this world, where the tragic hero has suffered. As Sewall points out, Job is tragedy even with the epilogue: "But the universe seems only secure to those who do not question too far" (34). For Job has lost all of that property and all of those beasts and all of those servants, even though he now is blessed with replacements. Job lost seven sons and three daughters, and this God who created man in his image does not presume to double their number, as if twice as many children would replace those lost. They are lost to Job and his wife forever in this world, and this world is all they know for now.

Like Lazarus being raised from the dead, Job's restoration is a mixed blessing, for he cannot know that he will not lose everything again. He must live the rest of his life, one hundred and forty years, knowing what it is to lose everything. Yes, he knows as never before that he can trust God, even if God kills him. But he also knows that the love of God does not preclude untold suffering. Perhaps the final mystery is that the love of God is both the source and the abyss into which Job fell in his affliction.

NOTES

[1] Unless otherwise indicated, Scripture quotations are from *The Holy Bible*, English Standard Version, copyright © 2001 by Crossway Bibles, a division of Good News Publishers. Used by permission. All rights reserved.

[2] To the contrary, Joseph Wood Krutch contends that tragedy can only be written when a religious sense "that something outside his own being, some 'spirit not himself'—be it God, Nature, or that

still vague thing called a Moral Order—joins him in the emphasis that... his passions and his opinions are important" (24). Without some sacred and moral sense of life, whether Biblical or otherwise, there can be no tragedy written and there can be no poetic catharsis for that deep dread of the abyss and that deep longing for vindication. Job is tragic because of, not despite its depiction that human beings can cry out to and against a God who is there.

[3] As Walter Brueggemann has reminded us, "the freedom of God is always in considerable tension with the accessibility of God" (35).

[4] Elihu's speech is perfectly placed. It not only sums up the best of what has been said by all four men, but it allows someone to represent us, the listening audience, who have wanted to jump in and assert our convictions and opinions. Elihu is the antistrophe to Job's counselors.

5

Tragedy's Bloody Borders:
The Oresteia

LOUISE COWAN

> *"Who can redeem the blood that wets the soil?"*
> Choephoroe, ll. 66-67

According to Robert Fagles, the classical scholar who has rendered what many consider the finest translation of Aeschylus, the Parthenon and the Orestes trilogy are the two noblest achievements of the Greeks' high period, following upon their triumph over the Persians at Salamis and Plataea.[1] Both of these masterworks were created in honor of the gray-eyed goddess Athena, patron of Athens and sponsor of wisdom and excellence. Both bring about a union of the terrestrial and the heavenly in an order of *sophrosyne*, a harmony encompassing an entire cosmos. Further, the crumbling marble edifice and the still intact dramatic trilogy include in this cosmos not only earth and sky, but the chthonic realm under the earth, so that Hades' region of fertility and death is part of the transfigured order. But here the resemblance ends: language can evoke what sculpture cannot even suggest, something that must remain essentially imageless. Aeschylus' drama intuits a place more deeply hidden than the Underworld, a negative region where, as the Furies say, "the terrible is good." Aeschylus is able to make his audience envision a realm of recrimination and chagrin, a black hole in the universe, more deeply hidden even than Chaos and Old Night. Out of this pit, into the murky ground surrounding it, erupt things ordinarily regarded as obscene, as not to be viewed onstage. During the first performance of the *Oresteia*, we are told, the audience fled the theater in horror at the onslaught of these female figures in black with snakes for hair, blood dripping from their eyes. And their visceral impact has little diminished over the centuries. For through these obscenities the creator of Greek tragedy introduced into drama a gargoylian asymmetry that, far from marring the classical balance so marked in the Parthenon and in most of Aeschylus' own lines, enlarged the sphere of imagined space and enhanced its clarity with the deep gloom of the abyss.

The Erinyes, the grim and avenging Furies whom Aeschylus first brought onstage in 458 B. C. and who thereafter form the ground of Greek tragedy, have permanently affected the Western poetic mind. Their origin is obscure. Andre Lardinois informs us that they are mentioned on three Linear B tablets from Cnossos and suggests the possibility in Mycenean times of "a real cult of demons who bore the name of Erinyes" (330-31). According to R. P. Winnington-Ingram, they were once thought of as the "vengeful dead themselves, intent on retaliation" (156). Homer mentions the Furies several times, referring to them as upholders of divine justice. Hesiod declares that they were originally ancient earth goddesses, born from the blood of the castrated Uranus and appointed the task of guarding reproduction and family bonds. By the time Aeschylus encountered them in the arena of his mythopoeic imagination, however, they had long forsaken the positive duties of their role. As he saw them, they inhabited the dark regions of outrage, emerging only from time to time in the bloody territory surrounding the abyss to track down and torment those guilty of crimes against blood kin. In the *Eumenides*, the last play of the Oresteian trilogy, they speak of themselves as the "great fulfillers," who, working with "memories of grief," drive men who have been "banished far from god to a sunless, torch-lit dusk" (392-95). Apollo characterizes them in the same drama as cosmic outcasts. "Born for destruction only, the dark pit," he says scornfully, "they range the bowels of Earth, the world of death, / loathed by men and the gods who hold Olympus" (74-76). And in driving them away from his shrine, he exhorts them:

Go where heads are severed, eyes gouged out,
where justice and bloody slaughter are the same,
castrations, wasted seed, young men's glories butchered
extremities maimed, and huge stones at the chest.... (183-86)

As Winnington-Ingram writes, "An audience which made its first acquaintance with these infernal powers in the opening scenes of Eumenides—hideous in aspect, cruel in method, truculent in speech, narrowly intent upon avenging a wicked woman, might incline to share the simple detestation of a civilized Apollo for these barbarous creatures and, later, might wonder by what sleight of hand the dramatist transforms them into worshipful and benev- olent divinities" (Winnington-Ingram 154). The ambiguity of the Furies thus is central to Aeschylus' vision of tragedy; in them he confronts the chief tragic enigma: the transformation of the painful individual parts into what Gerald Else has called the "redemption-centered whole" (100).

Behind the terrifying eruption onstage of these "gorgons shrouded in black, their heads wreathed, swarming serpents" (*Eum* 1948-50) are implied the depths from which they emerge. They come from "the dark pit," an abyss that indicates a rift in being, a void in the ordered universe, and, if we are to trust Apollo's aversion, a place not of origins but of cast-offs. This repellent region hardly seems the same as Homer's or Virgil's underworlds of shades; rather, as Apollo testifies, it is a realm of mutilation, of mixed parts, of bitter pain and unappeased *ressentiment*. It was during a time of high aspiration and prosperity, the Greek golden age, that Aeschylus discovered its ominous presence. In a kind of ironic recompense, as it seems, tragedy makes atonement for suc- cess by opening up a terrifying gulf until then hidden from con- sciousness. In both periods of its greatest flowering (fifth-century Athens and sixteenth-century England), the societies out of which it arose were in a heady state of success. We might speculate that the cost of amassing such power and the threat of its misuse prey on the poetic imagination, giving rise to a probing examination of human greatness. According to C. J. Herington, author of the Aeschylus volume in the Yale Hermes series, Aeschylean drama could have come only out of a mind that "at some point had looked on chaos—chaos intellectual, political, and religious" (19). Fifth-century Athens provided such a perspective. But whatever the connection between poet and culture, we have to agree with Gilbert Murray, Gerald Else, and other authorities that Aeschylus "invented" tragedy[2] and that this soldier-hero-poet discovered in the human psyche a region that no inhabitant of the West has been able to forget. Several authorities, however, among them

Robert Corrigan, maintain with some persuasiveness that Aeschylus' plays are something other than tragedies—actually, that they are dramas about the gods, divine dramaturgies depicting something more like theomachies than tragic struggles. Aeschylean drama does indeed take place in a different territory from the profoundly human world of Sophocles and Shakespeare. Even so, it seems hardly just to speak of it as pre-tragic, for that label would reduce Aeschylus' grand conceptions to a mere phase in a developmental process. It may be more accurate to think of his dramas spatially, in terms of their location in tragic territory, rather than to view them as part of a temporal sequence, incipient forms of something later to come.

The seven surviving Aeschylean dramas are lyric pageants, apparently all of them parts of trilogies consisting of three related tragic dramas followed by a satyr play. Aeschylus's earliest—*Persians* (472), *Seven against Thebes* (467) and *The Suppliants* (463?)—are quite different in style and focus from the later four, the undated *Prometheus Bound*[3] and the *Oresteia* (458), this latter a trilogy: the *Agamemnon*, the *Choephoroe* (*The Libation Bearers* in Fagles), and the *Eumenides*, or "kindly ones." All Aeschylus's plays, except the *Prometheus*, are about the conflicting drives within the human psyche that trouble both the family and the city. It is not simply that particular families have hidden crimes that, disgracefully, will out. Rather, it is that the mortal condition in itself entails persistent violence. Humanity is made up of borderline creatures, subject to two warring forces and doomed to destroy themselves unless a reconciliation can be effected between such oppositions as male and female, reason and blood loyalty, *polis* and *oikos*. The record of that struggle toward harmony is overtly recorded in two of Aeschylus' trilogies—one, the *Oresteia*, which survives intact; the other, the *Prometheia*, of which only one play remains. In both, Aeschylus uses his powerful lyric sense as a means of exploring the communal source of pain and dread. In probing the roots of myth, he discovers the unlighted caverns of the tragic abyss. Since his time, if tragedy is to be authentic, it must make its way, by whatever means, to this region that he first realized. Some four hundred years earlier Homer had implied Achilles' confrontation with it, and a Homeric hymn had recounted Hera's wrathful flight to this cavernous and forsaken region, but Aeschylus—who wrote some ninety tragedies, introducing a second actor and, in the *Oresteia*, a third—probes the intrusion of this realm into the civic order. His works establish the metaphysical bounds of the tragic in works of art that reveal a fundamental conflict in the nature of being. Some things are so because they cannot be otherwise. And it is by uncovering the hidden horror of the tragic necessity that humanity suffers into wisdom: *pathei mathos*—the terrible insight of the Aeschylean vision.

Once Aeschylus had uncovered the existence of the tragic region, Sophocles and Euripides were not long in looking into its depths. And, two thousand years later, Shakespeare, though he focused more than Aeschylus on the intricacies of character, still based his tragedies not so much on his heroes' individual traits as on their entry into an experience of impenetrable darkness. For tragedy, as Aeschylus first reveals it, is about the invitation of a chosen person into the dimension of the gods, though the way into that dazzling ambience is through the blindness of tragic insight. Those who are marked for such immolation but who refuse the call spend their time, generation by generation, in the bloody ground surrounding the abyss, where they maul and tear each other in acts of retribution. At the heart of the tragic, then, we could say, is the summons to divine inclusion, though it is hardly recognized as such by the victim. The site of entry is made ready by the suffering of a god. There could be no tragedy without the firebringer Prometheus, who crossed over immortal boundaries to bring mortals the gift of comprehension.

Aeschylus thus prepares the tragic ground, and two of his trilogies lay out its parameters. The *Oresteia* describes the horizontal extension of tragedy and the *Prometheia* its vertical heights and depths, though only one part of this latter group of dramas, *Prometheus Bound*, has been preserved. Fragments of a second play, *Prometheus Unbound*, and mention of a third, *Prometheus the Firebringer*, remain to tantalize the scholar. Though most authorities think otherwise, the play that survives seems logically to be the middle play of the trilogy, the one in which the theft of divine fire has already been accomplished, so that the action of the drama consists in the suffering that leads to the final plunge into Tartarus. The setting of the drama is at the world's end, the "jumping off place" in farthest Scythia, where the Titan's servants and fellow gods, at the command of Zeus, nail Prometheus to a rocky cliff. This is the edge of the earth, the cragged region bordering the gulf into which at the end of the drama this heroic, foreknowing Titan will be hurled. Nailed to the ledge, Prometheus thus is the iconic figure of tragedy, becoming the visible sign of a suffering that heretofore unknown to the gods can no longer be viewed as the exclusive and ignominious burden of mortals. It is as though he prepares the way for tragic human suffering, leads the way, so to speak, for mortal being to enter into an immortal ground. Until the final age, the drama makes clear, when a reconciliation will occur, a god is undergoing agony for the human race.

The Prometheus drama seems the absolute paradigm of both the tragic *mythos* and the tragic *ethos*. The protagonist has crossed the line between the human and the divine, has attempted to remake the human project and redefine the ideal concept of justice, and for his hubris is now isolated on a rocky cliff. This "stony place of justice," of which the chorus in *Antigone* later speaks, is, in mythic time, first brought onstage in *Prometheus*; but it recurs perennially in the tragic region of the psyche and in tragic drama as liminal space: the crossroads, the heath, the brazen doorsill, the woods at Dunsinane, the dark halls of the castle at Elsinore. It is the region where the ultimate opposing powers are probed and the necessity of the descent into darkness discovered. The elements of tragic illumination come together in *Prometheus Bound*, not as conscious knowledge but as an icon—an image of suffering divinity that has haunted the Western mind since the play was first performed. *Prometheus Bound*, then, is about the splitting open of the abyss, this rift in being, where those specially called may be brought for their suffering. In it we apprehend the vertical axis of the cosmos, with the protagonist touching (so to say) both the deepest regions of Tartarus and the highest regions of Olympus. The *agon* takes place within this cosmos: Zeus, the principle of intellect and order, struggles with Prometheus, principle of freedom and compassion. As viewers, the audience actually sees neither Tartarus nor Olympus but experiences their location as transcendent psychic terrain.

In contrast, the *Oresteia* takes place in the flatlands surrounding the dread chasm, in a murky territory where mortals make their futile attempts to attain justice by evening the score. The chief concern of this sole existent Greek trilogy is the work of art that we call civilization. Depicting the exchange of wrongs in which mortals engage, it goes on to show the possibility of redemption and the way back from the void. It presents the ultimate human dilemma; mortals contend with two laws in their members, two different inheritances: the necessity of living up to the father's code, an urgency primarily of the mind, of ideals, of *nomos*; and the necessity of honoring the mother's heart, a burden primarily of the body, of the vitals, of *physis*. Clytemnestra's baring of her breast to her son is not simply a melodramatic reproach but a reminder of his obligation to the maternal body—all that Apollo disdains. Aeschylus is the first to discern what seems the impossibility of resolution. Mortals being what they are, the gods themselves cannot agree on their proper role. Only stopping and starting over in a renunciation of rights can ensure the continuance of the race.

Steeped in Homer (who preceded him by nearly four hundred years), Aeschylus took the plot of the Orestes trilogy and its main characters from the *Iliad* and the *Odyssey*. But, as Fagles tells us in "The Serpent and the Eagle," the introduction to his translation, Aeschylus "deepened Homer with even older, darker legends and lifted him to a more enlightened stage of culture" (14). Perhaps this is a key to the tragic: the poetic calling up of ancient wrongs and, in a ritualized art piece, spreading their contagion so that they infect the ground around them, bringing about an aesthetic recurrence of their conflicts—which can then, in the simulacrum of an art piece, be resolved. Ultimately, from a new protagonist's making his way through the tragic territory and daring an encounter with the void (in which he either calls upon the gods for help or allows himself to be engulfed by the darkness) emerge the beginnings of a new order.

In the grim story of the House of Atreus, the turbulence of the present actions stems from a "spirit" (*daimon*), a curse, that has fallen on the entire family line. It apparently can have no ending, since it is passed on from person to person, generation by generation, giving birth to fresh abhorrences and the renewed necessity of retaliation. The Chorus of old women declares at the beginning of *The Libation Bearers*, the second play of the trilogy: "the blood that Mother Earth consumes / clots hard; it won't seep through / it breeds revenge; and frenzy goes through the guilty / seething like infection, swarming through the brain" (LB 66-69). They are describing the dark and bloody foreground of

the abyss, those borders in which people must continue to live
until the curse is lifted. In the driving force of this seminal
drama, we witness the ongoing of the curse until it turns against
itself and is finally exorcised by the practical wisdom, the courtesy, and the persuasion of the goddess Athena.

Herington has written of Aeschylus' plays that they "invoke the
entire environment—human, divine, and... inanimate." He sees
"ranked side by side, with impartial reverence" the different elements of the playwright's cosmos: "the political community, the
natural elements, the powers of the bright sky, the powers of the
dark earth who hold the dead in their keeping, and finally the
god whom Aeschylus most often names, Zeus" (1). For, though it
is Athena who accomplishes the specific action of the trilogy, yet
it is the mysterious and powerful Zeus who is over all in Aeschylus' drama, governing the world, both in its inner and outer
aspects, and drawing all to unity. The chorus chants:

> Zeus, great nameless all in all
> if that name will gain his favor
>   I will call him Zeus.   (Agam 161-63)
> . . . .
> Zeus has led us on to know
> that we must suffer, suffer into truth.
> ...drop by drop at the heart
> the pain of pain remembered comes again,
> From the gods enthroned on the awesome rowing bench
> there comes a violent love.   (Agam 177-84)

The "violent love" of the gods is what impels mortals forward,
though the buffeting is recognized as love only after suffering has
stripped away any purely human aims. For Aeschylus, Zeus is the
author of this healing suffering, the enveloping cloud of divinity
that gives life value. From human imperfections, from unspeakable
deeds, from suffering into truth, even from an encounter with
nothingness comes the turbulent divine love intuited by this Greek
poet who in his old age, after having fought at Marathon and
Salamis, turned to the writing of tragic dramas to be performed
before the altar of Dionysus, the god of destruction and renewal.

The trilogy, divided into its three separate plays, enacts the
completed drama of the curse on the house of Atreus. The

perpetuation of that curse is portrayed in the first play of the trilogy, which depicts the ironically triumphant return of a hero, King Agamemnon, expecting the welcome due a victorious warrior. He is greeted instead by an adulterous wife who has planned her vengeance against him during his ten-year absence. Her chief grievance is the sacrificial death of their daughter Iphigenia, whom Agamemnon slew on the altar at Aulis so that the winds might blow to carry the Achaean ships to the Trojan battlefields. Clytemnestra and her lover Aegisthus—Agamemnon's cousin and bitter enemy—have been living together in the royal palace and contriving the death of King Agamemnon. For it is not only Clytemnestra who holds a grudge against Agamemnon. Aegisthus too has the obligation of revenge, according to the old laws. Atreus—Agamemnon's father—perpetuated the family curse in a feud with his brother Thyestes. The son of Thyestes, Aegisthus, nurses a murderous hatred of Agamemnon and—whether out of natural lust or unnatural desire for vengeance—has become Clytemnestra's lover during the long years of Agamemnon's absence. An evil spirit of revenge indeed lies on the House of Atreus; but Aeschylus is at pains to show that not only this inherited curse but Agamemnon's own actions bring him down. He has heartlessly sacrificed his daughter, has, according to some accounts, slain his wife's first husband and married her by force; stayed away on the battlefields for ten long years; spoiled the altars of the gods at Troy; taken maidens as "meeds of war"; and brought home a royal captive, daughter of King Priam and favorite of Apollo. As the final stroke, in the immediate action onstage, he commits the confirming sin of hubris by stepping on the crimson carpet unfurled before him by his treacherous wife.

In Aeschylean tragedies, the chorus represents the unease of the communal mind, veering alternately from practical, almost platitudinous, advice to haunted conscience, the long-remaining memory of guilt and remorse. In particular, the *Agamemnon* hints of this double mind, this knowing and not knowing, beginning with the watchman's lament about "the hard times come to this house" as he waits for the signal of fire that will announce the fall of Troy and the return of Agamemnon. And the chorus of old men, going through its litany of grief and horror, recalls the death of Iphigenia, sacrificed to propitiate the goddess Artemis that the winds might blow to carry the warships to Troy. Agamemnon had

agonized at the thought of staining his hands with his child's
blood, but he conceded to it, as the chorus recalls:

> And once he slipped his neck in the strap of Fate,
>   his spirit veering black, impure, unholy
>   once he turned he stopped at nothing,
>   seized with the frenzy
>   blinding driving to outrage (Agam 217-221)

But Iphigenia is not the only child victim by parental murder
in this family. A long sequence of atrocities against its members
taints the history of the House of Atreus. Savage retaliation has
accompanied savage deeds, all the way back to the earliest ances-
tor Tantalus, who slew his own children to serve to the bright
and appalled Olympian gods. This monstrous crime is repeated in
a later generation, when Atreus butchers Thyestes' children as
food for their unsuspecting father. Aegisthus fulminates against
the atrocity, revealing an imagination sickened by horror:

> He cuts
> The extremities, feet and delicate hands
>   Into small pieces, scatters them over the dish (Agam 1624-26)

These lines indicate the savagery that haunts the terrain surrounding the dread abyss, its ominous and horrid foreground,
soaked with blood. Within this no-man's-land lies a hint of an
even darker curse than murder, one that descends from generation to generation, involving an unthinkable evil—a secret that
only tragedy dares recall. Lurking in the shadows at the boundaries of this landscape are ancient memories of familial violations
so intimate and dark that cannibalism becomes their symbol.
Nothing else could induce the primordial dread that tragedy
arouses and then exorcises. Nothing else could so account for the
appalled recoil it awakens within us.

This is the terrible root of tragic knowledge that the human
race shares in its Great Memory—that we ourselves, not only the
gods, are implicated in the horrors that befall the human race.
We have it in us to devour each other, but, as Aeschylus knew
long before Dante, the human mind immeasurably deepens the
abyss, because it can plot a greater horror even than eating

another's flesh: not only can intelligence calculate the effect of
an unsuspecting kinsmen discovering that he has eaten his own
children, but it can also anticipate the satisfaction of revealing
through these means a bottomless malice that is absolute and
essentially unanswerable.

Some hint of the inevitability of long-hidden things emerging
out of that abysmal darkness into light is revealed not only in
overt recollections but in the choral chanting of ancient and
indefinite wrongs. It is with the ghastliness of this hidden realm
that Cassandra is struck as she stands outside the palace, silent
and unmoving. Her prophetic insight (a gift of Apollo) enables
her to see into the shadows of the invisible. Confronting what
she knows will be her own death, penetrating the veil of the
underworld with her second sight, she sees the slain children on
the housetops, polluting the air with their unavenged injuries:

> ... the babies
> wailing, skewered on the sword,
> their flesh charred, the father gorging on their parts (Agam 1095-97)

Recognizing the pattern of the old wrongs, Cassandra knows them
to be perpetuated in the present. She utters a bone-chilling cry.
On the housetop are the loathsome Furies, who have crept out
of the pit, "a dancing troupe / that never leaves":

> flushed on the blood of men
> their spirit grows and none can turn away
> their revel breeding in the veins—the Furies!
> they cling to the house for life... (Agam 1192-95)

But if these repellent hags are shocking, they have come, as Cassandra knows, on official duty. More familial blood is to be shed.
Later, when the dreadful vengeance has been accomplished and
Agamemnon lies dead in his bloody robes—Cassandra with him—
Clytemnestra speaks of her "masterpiece of justice" and attributes
it to a fulfillment of the law: "By the child's Rights I brought
to birth / by Ruin, by Fury—the three gods to whom / I sacrificed this man" (Agam 1459-61). She is speaking of Themis, Ate,
and the Erinyes, all principles of retributive justice. A few lines
later she boasts that "fleshed in the wife of this dead man" lives

the "savage ancient spirit of revenge" (Agam 1528-30). But, as the chorus predicts, a further avenger will come—her own son. What Clytemnestra fails to see in this complicated tapestry of justice is that death cannot wipe out death. From the old law of revenge will spring her own death and that of her lover—and the city will be torn with strife until the long chain of repaying wrong with wrong is broken.

If Clytemnestra is deluded about the effects of her own actions, even more deluded is the man she kills. The herald announcing Agamemnon's arrival speaks with an unconscious irony when he recounts Agamemnon's accomplishments:

> He hoisted the pickaxe of Zeus who brings revenge,
> he dug Troy down, he worked her soil down,
> the shrines of her gods, and the high altars, gone!
> and the seed of her wide earth he ground to bits. (Agam 516-19)

In his view, "the man is blest" (521). When Agamemnon comes onstage, he is thus praised as conqueror, as sacker of a city. One recalls that the chorus had earlier proclaimed, out of its prophetic double-edged wisdom, "God takes aim / at the ones who murder many" (Agam 455-56). And now, as though to confirm his hubris, this mighty king treads the crimson carpet Clytemnestra cunningly spreads before him. Yet Agamemnon is neither fool nor villain; he is a man of some nobility who essentially intends the good but who, like most mortals, has inherited ugly secrets, faced ugly choices, and, lacking the courage and discernment to go against the current, has participated in ugly deeds.

The great theme of the trilogy is justice (*dike*), shown to be crowned not in retaliation but in its embrace of all aspects of life in their right order, requiring the help of the gods. The complete tragic cycle, as Aeschylus discovers and as Shakespeare later incorporates into single dramas, moves from destruction to cleansing to building anew. Most tragedies depict only one stage of the completed arc, so that tragic drama seldom enables its viewers to reach the third stage of rehabilitation. But the *Oresteia* devotes its entire last play, the *Eumenides*, to that reconciliation. In it the gods make actual physical appearances and state their arguments, pro and con. This reintegration is the highest reach of the play, the theomachy, the battle of the gods, rendering the trilogy a metaphysical drama—a ritual in which the regal presences of Apollo and Athena themselves are depicted onstage, along with those of the frenzied and cacophonic Furies.

At the center of the *Oresteia*, near the middle of *The Libation Bearers*, Aeschylus has his chorus pause from the action and reflect:

> Marvels, the Earth breeds many marvels,
> terrible marvels overwhelm us. (LB 572-73)
> . . . .
>> Oh but a man's high daring spirit,
>> who can account for that? Or woman's
>> desperate passion daring past all bounds?
> She couples with every form of ruin known to mortals.
> Woman, frenzied, driven wild with lust,
>> twists the soft, warm harness
>> of wedded love—tortures man and beast! (LB 579-585)

Here then is indicated, among many in the trilogy, a crucial conflict: the battle between the masculine and feminine elements in the cosmos, the city, and the soul. Briffault and other anthropologists have maintained that the societies formed when agriculture was first learned were matriarchal, overthrown by the warlord culture that swept down from the north and settled in the Aegean basin. Agamemnon's sacrifice of Iphigenia and his apparently unloving marriage to Clytemnestra (whom he abducted after slaying her husband, Tantalus, the King of Pisa) could be viewed, as some critics point out, as a condensation of that historical memory. Froma I. Zeitlin turns to an interpretation that seems more likely: "Far more compelling," she writes, "is Joan Bamberger's theory of the myth of matriarchy as myth, not 'a memory of history but a social charter'" authenticating the oppression of women (90). Thus Zeitlin would read the mythical awareness at the back of consciousness, the seeming "memory" of a time when women ruled, as a collective collusion in deception. The memory serves, she feels, to authenticate the patriarchal conception that women are unfit to rule. But the moral tilt of the trilogy seems to favor women rather than discourage them. And one of its remarkable features is the extraordinary power it gives to the *kore*, the feminine virginal figure.

The chief *kore* in the *Oresteia* is, of course, the goddess Athena, who at the end of the trilogy exhibits both power and forbearance in the building of her city. But there are also the Furies, ancient goddesses of the family, who, like ill-humored maiden aunts, can rage if neglected and dishonored, but turn arch and benevolent when flattered. Another powerful virginal figure dominates a good portion of the Agamemnon, the first part of the trilogy—the seeress Cassandra, forced to give her life for a city and a man alien to her, for both of which she feels only distaste. Still further, the presence of a paradigmatic virgin, though dead, haunts the city and the family—Iphigenia, the innocent sacrificial victim of her father's masculine pride. In contrast to these strong *kore* types are two married women. One is not present but frequently invoked: Helen of Troy, the unfaithful wife, the epitome in both Trojan and Greek minds of lawlessness and disorder. The other is her sister, Agamemnon's powerful queen Clytemnestra, whom the chorus many times refers to as "manlike." She seeks her own justice, she uses one man to kill another, and she murders another person's daughter to avenge her own. In this dramatic trilogy, it is married women who cause the trouble.

For the Homeric and Athenian Greek, the great metaphor of harmony has been the wedding of earth and sky, the fertilization of the earth by the rain, the planting of the semen in the womb— the *hieros gamos*. But what we have in a dynastic city in its final stages such as Argos is rather a battle in all its institutions between the masculine and feminine elements. Near the end of the first play of the trilogy, as she stabs her husband in his bath, Clytemnestra expresses both her skewed courage and her hubris:

> So he goes down, and the life is bursting out of him,
> great sprays of blood and the murderous shower
> dyes me black, and I, I revel
> like the earth when the spring rains come down,
> the blessed gifts of god, and the new green spear
> splits the sheath and rips to birth in glory. (Agam 1410-15)

At the moment of slaying her enemy-husband, her exultation reaches a terrifying height. She envisions something even more destructive than murder: the splitting apart of this union that holds the cosmos together, the "soft warm harness of wedded love / that strengthens man and beast." She would divide the world into open warfare between male and female, between *oikos* and *polis*, between custom and law (*themis* and *dike*), between culture and civilization. Clytemnestra here reverses the metaphor of fertility: it is the husband's deathblood that fertilizes; and in her destructive capacity (rather than in the creative receptivity of the female earth) she revels at the act that will bring to birth "the new green spear," failing to foresee that what splits the sheath and rips to birth in her seminal action is rather a new shoot of the same plant—the bloody vengeance that will destroy the destroyer.

But the drama is named after Orestes. It is, after all, his task, as it later is Hamlet's, to come to terms with an erring mother and a murdered father. Thus the central issue of the *Oresteia*, despite the focus on Agamemnon's downfall, despite the very real theme of the battle between the sexes, concerns the contest over the fugitive from justice, Orestes. And we need to remind ourselves that he is a specially chosen one of Apollo, so that, like Cassandra, he is called to a special suffering, though the audience was not allowed to view it. He exhibits the human paradox, the piety toward both mother and father, and, further, he has the courage to go against his own blood and follow the god's command in being, as Hamlet would say two thousand years later, "scourge and minister." After he has slain his mother, the chorus cries out,

> Death calls and she is gone.
>   But oh, for you the survivor,
> suffering is just about to bloom. (LB 2002-4)

Apparently the Chorus cannot see the Furies; Orestes must enter his torments alone. Aeschylus does not attempt to portray this portion of the tragic arc; we are allowed to see only Orestes' stunned gaze when he first views the dark ladies, the hounds, as he says, of his mother's hate: "Women—look—like Gorgons, / shrouded in black, their heads wreathed, / swarming serpents!" (LB 1048-50). The chorus falls back appalled, seeing now the whole pattern of the curse:

> Here once more for the third time

the tempest in the race has struck
the house of kings and run its course.
    First the children eaten,
the cause of all our pain, the curse.
And next the kingly man's ordeal,
the bath where the proud commander,
lord of Achaea's armies lost his life.
And now a third has come, but who?
    A third like saving Zeus?
Or should we call him death?
Where will it end?—
where will it sink to sleep and rest,
    this murderous hate, this Fury? (LB 1064-1077)

When we next see Orestes, it is through the eyes of the priest-
ess of Apollo at Delphi. She sees, she says, a man, "an abomination to God / he holds the seat where suppliants sit for
purging; / his hands dripping blood, and his sword just drawn"
(Eum 42-44). He holds an olive branch, as she sees; but he is
surrounded by a ring of women—gorgons, she would call them—
black, repulsive, with "heavy, rasping breathing" (Eum 56). We
must assume, then, that Orestes, having survived the torments of
the abyss, makes his way to Apollo's shrine at Delphi, is cleansed,
and from there, still pursued by the Furies, hastens to Athens,
where he prays to Athena for help, declaring that he has "suffered into truth" (Eum 274). Though she is on Scamander's
banks, claiming the fallen Troy, the goddess hears his prayer and
comes to his aid.

    There in Athens not only Orestes but Athena as well and the
fate of her entire city are caught between two extremes: bright
Apollo and the dark Erinyes. These are irreconcilable poles of
existence, sky and earth, masculine and feminine; but more
broadly they represent the contest between reason and passion,
the conscious and unconscious mind, the Apollonian and the
Dionysian. Apollo demonstrates an abstract and uncluttered vision
of principle at the expense of life itself. In stark contrast, the
Erinyes are drinkers of blood, "children of the night." Yet both
the contending powers engender violence. Neither can be taken
as the sole guide to action. In the very blood humankind inherits lies a curse, *atē*, a furious spirit of rebellion. And yet, at the

same time, abstract principles of the mind, blindingly pure and simple, goad people into unspeakable deeds. Ruth Padel uses the phrase "blood in the mind" to describe the obstacle against which the spirit of reconciliation must battle in the *Oresteia*. For the actual life of the soul (as well as the city), Apollo must be replaced by the wise and practical Athena. [The Furies must be persuaded by courtesy and concern to seek out the real reason for their frenzy—not vengefulness and resentment, but pious outrage at the damage men do to the living stuff of life and at their forgetfulness of earth's claim to human piety.] Thus the conflict between man's "high daring spirit" and woman's "desperate passion" is only one aspect of the discord that produces the bloody foreground of tragedy.

The single remedy for this ruinous battle would be the "soft warm harness of wedded love that strengthens man and beast"— if it could be achieved. But for the actual life of the damaged and failing community, wedded love and loyalty to the family must be replaced by the clear-eyed, practical wisdom of the virgin Athena. The Furies must be persuaded by courtesy and concern to seek out the real reason for their frenzy—not vengefulness and resentment, but pious outrage at the violence done to the living stuff of life and at mortal forgetfulness of earth's claim to human piety. And if the *hieros gamos* has been set against itself, then a new construction, a *polis* that aims at deliberative justice must attempt the balance—and a virgin must lead the way. The path out of this abhorrent terrain for Orestes (and for the new city Athena is forging) does not have to be bloodshed, but courtesy and cool rationality, the way of harmony and wholeness, wherein each of the powers is given its due. The new order of the city "straight and just" (Eum 1003), however, is no longer familial; the pristine virginal element has triumphed. Thus a defense of civic justice rests on a defense of justice for the person. But the things of the *oikos* will have their place in the *polis*; and after Athena's cajoling, the Furies are persuaded to be part of the general harmony. "No home can thrive without you," Athena tells them (Eum 903). "Make the seed of men live on," she exhorts. "The more they worship you the more they thrive." (Eum 919-29).

Thus, in the last third of the last play, the ugly Furies are transformed into the Eumenides, the Kindly Ones; and some hope begins to dawn that humankind, "loved by the loving vir-

gin girl" (Eum 1008), can transform the bloody ground of the
tribal city into a city of justice and peace. The ingredients for
such a metamorphosis have been set before us: a chastened hero-
victim, who, in daring to confront the abyss, has acted out the
violence within the familial order and in effect destroyed its dominance; abstract Apollonian principles modified into practical wisdom; dark drives of the blood changed into blessings of the
hearth; the lex talionis replaced by the jury system; a tribal city
transformed into the work of art that is a *polis*, despair relieved
by hope for the human race. It is a farewell and a prophecy. It
points the way from the bloody borders surrounding the abyss to
the cool, clear air of the *polis*.

NOTES

¹ All citations of *The Oresteia* refer to the Fagles translation.
² Most authorities agree on this point. Else and Murray have been
  particularly definite in their statements concerning it.
³ There is no general agreement concerning the dating of the extant
  Prometheus drama. Some scholars place it at the beginning of
  Aeschylus's career, some at the end. A few are unwilling to concede that it was written by Aeschylus. For an analysis of current
  critical opinion on this embattled play, see Herington (*Prometheus
  Bound*) and Griffith. It seems plausible to follow scholarly tradition and consider the play Aeschylus', written at the end of his
  career, though it is about beginnings.

    Whatever the date of this play's composition, its mythic time is
  far prior to Aeschylus' other tragedies, since it traces the opening
  up of the abyss. Bernard Knox argues for Sophocles' influence on
  Aeschylus in the portrayal of the Titan's interiority (see his discussion in *Oedipus at Thebes*). His argument is plausible, since
  Sophocles had probably produced many of his tragedies before
  Aeschylus wrote his Promethean trilogy and well could have influenced the older dramatist in his portrayal of the suffering Titan.
  But before Sophocles Aeschylus had divined the presence of the
  ominous region of the abyss. Writing a bit later, Euripides, with
  little inkling of the nobility to which characters must aspire if
  they are to enter into immolation, either destroys his ill-fated protagonists outright or carries them away by means of a *deus ex
  machina*. Nietzsche may have been right in his dissatisfaction with

Euripides, seeing in him the decline of the Greek moment of tragic vision, though the great philosopher may not have entirely understood the reasons for his discomfort.

6

Bowing to the Wound:
Philoctetes as a Tragedy of Compassion

DENNIS SLATTERY

More than Aeschylus or Euripides, Sophocles seems interested in the body's tendency to be marked by the world. Being wounded is a paradoxical action in Sophoclean tragedy, for it bears witness to our vulnerable and easily extinguished nature while it allows powerful forces to surface that might not otherwise appear. Through being wounded, we cross a threshold and gain a strange metaphysical strength. As the genre of afflictions *par excellence*, tragedy is also the most immediate and intimate of all the genres, perhaps because of what its mythopoetic figures call up. Borrowing from Jung's insights on mythic realities, James Hillman suggests that "these mythical figures, like my afflictions, are 'tragical, monstrous and unnatural,' and their effects upon the soul, like my afflictions, 'perturb to excess'" (*Revisioning Psychology* 99). This sense of a shared affliction binds audience to action, certainly in Sophocles generally, but most poignantly in this play in which a wound is as much a character in the action as it is a characteristic of the protagonist.

In *Philoctetes* Sophocles teases our imaginations by having Philoctetes brood and remember his injury on the island of Lemnos. He suffers there for nine years with two opposing gifts: a bow bequeathed to him by Heracles on his funeral pyre, and a suppurating wound from a snake bite inflicted on him by a water snake at the temple of the nymph Chryse. Sophocles asks us to imagine these two images—one a wound that never ceases its painful assault on Philoctetes' foot, relentlessly oozing pus and gore from the injected poison and emanating an insufferable odor; the other an object used to inflict wounds, Heracles' bow. The bow and the wound are two of the most compelling images of tragedy itself: armed with the bow, especially that of a divinity, one gains power and deadly accuracy, yet the wound disarms and makes one almost helpless. It also links Philoctetes forcefully with the animal world; in the years spent alone, he has become, like an animal, intimate and conversant with earthly objects—rocks, caves, trees, birds, precipices. These objects in nature have taken on their own lives as companions; they have cared for him. The bow, on the other hand, connects him with a cultural world and thus intensifies a dramatic tension close to the heart of what tragedy is.

Charles Segal perceptively observes that in his plays Sophocles often finds a visual image "which expresses in the condensed, evocative way of symbols, the major concern of the work" (114). Symbols, in other words, are efficient and economical ways to transmit a quality, character, or condition from one realm to another. Hillman writes that for the Greeks all things "had a second sense" and moreover that "Each problem contains a secret, is the emblem of a secret or, better said, is a secret emblem, secretly an emblem" ("Culture and the Animal Soul" 13). The wound and the bow are the residua of "the female spirits of nature" who "were often the nurses of the gods" ("Nymphs" 1) and of the immortal, Heracles himself. This demigod will appear at the end of the play to guide Philoctetes through forceful and persuasive speech. Through Heracles' words, the wounded warrior will heal into glory when he arrives at Troy. Divinities, spirits, and the natural order all participate in the pain and suffering of Philoctetes as he inhabits the wilderness of Lemnos.

Suffering through tedium and pain to a transformed relation to the world—one resting in compassion—is a large part of the dramatic move through which Sophocles understands the value of human misery. His exploration of suffering never allows us to forget that we are embodied; through our flesh, we feel pain and confront anguish. How characters are wounded offers one way of tracking their destiny. This somatic reality, what Morris Berman rightly calls "body literacy," is ignored in most disciplines' explorations, even while the body's presence can inform us of what he terms the "somatic" or "visceral history" of a people (110) or an individual. On the island of Lemnos, where Philoctetes subsists alone for almost a decade, he shoots birds with his bow in order to maintain the barest existence, as he cleans and dries the rags that cover his oozing wound. It is as if the body in its battle to cleanse itself from the poisons of the snake's venom wishes to drain from itself more than physical toxins. The wound of Philoctetes has shaped and transformed him into a figure of suffering who at the same time has gained solace from the wild austerity of his surroundings. Carl Jung believed that the gods have gone indoors and become diseases, in which case we are asked to think of the wound as an aperture into another realm of being. And as Sophocles' play unfolds, the wound of Philoctetes reveals in Odysseus and Neoptolemos, the ambassadors from Troy, their own forms of woundedness.

Tragedy's deepest metaphysics resides in wounding; it establishes an ineradicable link between physicality and destiny. This tragic terrain is the most afflicted of geographies, which slowly eventuates into a resolved healing. Where there is a wound, there is also a promise of cleansing, a *catharsis*—a word which means both a clarifying and a cleansing of the wound in healing. The wound assumes its own voice and becomes an accomplice to the act of healing on several levels. In a condition like that of Philoctetes, we *see through* the instinctive body response of the wounded warrior; he responds to an archetypal condition that serves in its own right as an aperture to some deeper recognition. According to Jung, the instincts "are not vague and indefinite by nature, but are specifically formed motive forces which... pursue their inherent goals. Consequently they form very close analogies to the archetypes, so close, in fact, that there is good reason for supposing that the archetypes are the unconscious images of the instincts themselves,... They are *patterns of instinctual behavior*" (*Archetypes* 43-44, my emphasis). Divinely wounded, Philoctetes inhabits a place deserted but not desolate. In the center of nature's spirits, he is comforted by the wilderness that isolates and encloses him.

✣ ✣ ✣

As Sophocles' drama opens, Neoptolemus and Odysseus have just arrived on the island—in this play, deserted, untamed, isolated, harsh, and marginal to all human traffic. They plan to recover the bow and sail immediately back to Troy so they can be victorious over the city. Philoctetes himself concerns them only as an impediment to the possession of the bow, since it never misses when he wields it. But both the island and Philoctetes in his own person, as the abandoned sufferer, take on a major importance, as the play reveals.

It was on the island of Lemnos that Hephaestus fell when Zeus cast him out of Olympus for his deformity; here the Sintians nursed him. Since then this uninhabited region has been sacred to Hephaestus, who divinely foreshadows Philoctetes' grotesque malady. Lemnos is where both divinities and mortals land because of their wounds. As a wilderness it offers sparse comfort to Philoctetes who suffers here, nursing himself and remembering his abandonment at the hands of those with whom he was prepared to fight. It is the terrain of tragedy, like his wounded painful body. The harsh landscape and the wounded body are both dramatic ways in which Philoctetes remembers his treatment by the Achaeans. The island is also a place of incubation, of meditation, and of transformation, an alchemical container out of which bubbles up a fuller creative potential of the individual, for it is linked to a more intimate relation with the elements, both divine and natural. It becomes is the site of changed imaginations, a place where a creative shift occurs in these figures of Hephaestus and Philoctetes, the womb out of which emerges a creative energy or development in both. This setting of tragedy in the terrain of suffering Jake Berry calls "a mythopoeic site origin," which he defines "as the location of the mythic impulse prior to its establishment in a finite structure" ("Mythopoeic Site Origin" 417).

The body itself, I would add, is the other geography of mythic origination. Peter Hays observes that in ritual societies pain was "the price that many individuals paid for initiation into secret mysteries· of nature" (126). To be marked bodily in tragedy, as Philoctetes strongly is, carries the paradoxical condition of being blessed and cursed simultaneously, feeling the limitations of nature and the boundlessness of divinity through the same wound. This marking is the genesis of a way of seeing and knowing that pains one as it cures. The grand paradox of his nine solitary and painful years of suffering on Lemnos is that Philoctetes is, according to a prophecy, an essential source of victory over Troy that the gods have chosen. Like Oedipus, wounded in the feet at birth and moving toward a transcendent destiny at the end of *Oedipus at Colonus*, Philoctetes, wounded in the foot, gradually discovers his mysterious divine chosenness.

❊   ❊   ❊

In one of the most imaginative essays on this play, Edmund Wilson suggests that Philoctetes "is a man obsessed by a grievance; he is to be kept from forgetting it by an agonizing physical ailment" (427) that in another place he calls a "mystery" (421). Philoctetes' ulcerated foot corresponds to his unyielding, unbending nature. Through the deceit, then the guidance, of Neoptolemos, and finally the intercession of the god Heracles himself, he surrenders to a higher purpose and destiny. In the wounding itself is some mystery of divine election, as well as the memory of transgression and abandonment. When Philoctetes violates sacred ground, when he steps into divine territory, he is made to suffer the pain of that transgression and simultaneously to draw that divine nature into himself through the wound's opening. The source of the wound, Chryse's guardian snake, connects the poisonous bite at once to the most intimate relation to the earth, to the natural order, and to divinity.

Outraged at being left behind by the Achaeans with only the most basic sustenance, Philoctetes suppurates venom as he obsesses over being abandoned. This rage at his treatment is also part of his destiny; his is a sacred outrage. Something sacred in the natural order is in the bite of the snake that both wounds and initiates Philoctetes, as the tusk of the boar both wounds and initiates the young Odysseus on his inaugural hunting expedition, or the white whale wounds and initiates Ahab into both a rage and a vengeance that cannot be quelled without destroying almost all the inhabitants aboard the Pequod. The natural order engulfs, comforts, and embraces Philoctetes.

The action of the tragedy will develop the wound as a

metaphor for a deeper affliction felt profoundly by the young Neoptolemus, as he suffers a metaphysical injury to his own heroic nature. In Sophocles' play, the wound in its decaying stench includes the pollution of deceit and the shame of the loss of honor that comes from violating one's essential nature—what is natural to one's being, most conducive not just to winning glory but to becoming part of a larger heroic tradition. More than the fields of Troy, Lemnos is Neoptolemus' tragic place, where the deepest truth of his own heroic nature will be tested. Odysseus tells Neoptolemus as they begin the search for Philoctetes: "This is where I marooned him long ago, /...his foot diseased and eaten away with running ulcers" (ll. 4-6). They find his cave and outside it Neoptolemus locates the remnants of clothing the injured warrior uses to bandage his wound: "And look some rags are drying in the sun / full of the oozing matter from a sore" (38-39). Here at the site of these rags the other wounding appropriately begins; Neoptolemus' honor has found its sore spot, where the offensive odor of self-betrayal, even self-mutilation, begins.

Duplicitously, Odysseus tells the young son of Achilles: "Ensnare / the soul of Philoctetes with your words" (56-57). The word "ensnare" suggests an animal that needs trapping. It conveys Odysseus' disdain for Philoctetes and makes it easier for Neoptolemus to steal the bow by deceit. Odysseus recognizes that, as he tells the younger man, such duplicitous behavior "is not your natural bent" (78). But he nonetheless persuades Achilles' son to trick the bow of Heracles from Philoctetes by directing his attention to glory and victory:

> But the prize of victory is pleasant to win.
> Bear up: another time we shall prove honest.
> For one brief shameless portion of a day
> give me yourself, and then for all the rest
> you may be called most scrupulous of men. (80-85)

What Odysseus is calling for is *a contained pollution*, but the nature of pollution is to move from the source of the affliction to infect first the entire body, and then an entire world. He assumes, perhaps, that its long-lasting effects will be minimal or non-existent. But Neoptolemus already smells a certain corruption in Odysseus' method:

> I have a natural antipathy
> To get my ends by tricks and strategems. (88-89)
> ...I would prefer even to fail with honor
> than win by cheating. (94-95)

Odysseus' tongue moves more quickly and deceitfully to convince him:

> You are a good man's son.
> I was young, too, once, and then I had a tongue
> very inactive and a doing hand. (96-97)

But Odysseus has learned that "everywhere among the race of men / it is the tongue that wins and not the deed" (98-99). But shame keeps Neoptolemus from acquiescing. He questions Odysseus:

> Neoptolemus: Do you not find it vile yourself, this lying?
> Odysseus: Not if the lying brings our rescue with it.
> Neoptolemus: How can a man not blush to say such things? (107-09)

At this point, as the son of Achilles begins to move more deeply into the island, he also moves towards suffering a wound potentially as lethal as Philoctetes' affliction. When he violates Philoctetes' cave, he repeats the boundary violation that brought the guardian of Chryse to attack Philoctetes in the first place; in doing so, he suffers the sting of Odysseus' deceitful and deeply wounding speech. Odysseus persuades Neoptolemus to suspend his shame, to help him win the bow, and then to return to virtue as if nothing had happened. Odysseus tells him, "You shall be called a wise man and good" (119), and Neoptolemus replies, "Well, then, I will do it, casting aside all shame" (120). But shame can no more be cast off than the poison clothing worn by Heracles or the wound suffered for so long by Philoctetes.

✳ ✳ ✳

As Neoptolemus yields to temptation, Philoctetes enters the action directly, dragging his infected foot, and illustrates by contrast his unyielding nature, an antidote to the surrender of honor that Neoptolemus has just suffered. The chorus of Greek sailors wonders how he has existed for so long with so little, there on "his crag at the edge" (147). Pitying him his suffering, they muse on his isolation without human community, with spotted shaggy beasts for neighbors.

> His thoughts are set continually on pain and hunger.
> He cries out in his wretchedness;
> there is only a blabbering echo,.... (187-89)

Mythically, his neighbor is Job, or perhaps Adam. According to Northrop Frye, "the tragic hero is typically... half-way between human society on the ground and something greater in the sky.... The tragic hero hangs between heaven and earth, between a world of paradisal freedom and a world of bondage" (*Anatomy* 207). As the relation between the wounded Greek and the son of Achilles deepens, their roles will reverse. Neoptolemus, newly-shamed but determined nonetheless to win back his sense of honor and heal his own self-wounding, becomes most fervid in his relations with Philoctetes. The wound of Philoctetes mutates into the wound of shame. The link between Neoptolemus' shame and Philoctetes' outrage binds the two of them in the tension of tragic awareness. One might say that the pain of Philoctetes' wound is transformed into the suffering in Neoptolemus' soul. Newly slain in Troy by Paris' arrow in his foot, Achilles apotheosizes unyielding virtue and heroic conduct, but shame is now the festering wound carried directly to the heart of his son.

It is natural as well as rhetorically appropriate that Philoctetes is wounded by the mouth of the snake and Neoptolemus by the mouth of Odysseus. The respective mouths of the animal nature and the human order may be Sophocles' way of playing with the origin of these two characters' respective myths, for one is wounded with poison and the other with the toxicity of words. Hank Lazer asks, "if we take 'myth' to its root word, *muthos*, mouthing, won't all modes of mouthing have something of the mythic to them?" ("Poetry and Myth" 403). The suffering one undergoes in tragedy often begins in the mouthing of a knowledge that afflicts one ontologically. The scar from such a wound gathers around words heard or overheard.

When Philoctetes first appears, he seeks out a human community both to hear and to be heard by. One of the first of his

utterances is "Friendliest of tongues! / That I should hear it spoken once again" (234-35). He relates his outrage and his unbending nature as he recounts the shame of those who put him
ashore, including Odysseus. His wound, he admits, has its own
appetite, its own needs. His story spills out of him to the young
Neoptolemus: "I must drag my foot, / my cursed foot, to where
the bolt / sped by the bow's thong had struck down a bird"
(287-89). Some deep connection to Being is reached at this
moment in Philoctetes' telling. He is an emblem of those who
have "plumbed the depths of their own misery, of their own
apparential insubstantiality, their own nothingness," as Miguel de
Unamuno puts it, and who, "having turned their newly opened
eyes to their fellows" (150), have related their woes to "whoever
is moved by the narrative" (151).

Hearing this story, Neoptolemus' own wound begins to fester
in him. The play maintains a constant tension from this point
onward, with Achilles' son negotiating between the words of guile
uttered by Odysseus and the bilious language of Philoctetes,
whom Neoptolemus will soon promise to take home. For Neoptolemus, Philoctetes' self-revelation acts like an antibody to the
poisonous persuasion of Odysseus' words. Meeting the wounded
warrior gives him a chance to tell his own story to Philoctetes:
how he was cheated out of his father's weapons at Troy after
Achilles was slain, and how they were given to Odysseus, who
promised never to part with them. In a sense, the stories of each
are expressions of their deepest wounds, and purging them
through narrative is the first stage, if healing is to occur. The
wound, as a presence, seems to fold back on itself in self-narra-
tives as Neoptolemus begins to realize what I would term a
mimetic intimacy between his story and Philoctetes' that centers
on the wound and the bow. As the bow gains tension when its
two ends bend towards one another by means of the string's
strength, so the play's tension increases as these two stories bend
towards one another. Philoctetes pleads, with the same intensity
of passion shown by Odysseus earlier, for Neoptolemus to take
him home, even if it means putting him deep in the hold of
the ship. He calls to Neoptolemus for pity: "meanness is shameful, decency honorable. / If you leave me it is an ugly story"
(474-75). Growing within Neoptolemus as he listens is a deepening sense of his own shame that, like Philoctetes' own wound,

begins to suppurate: "I should be ashamed / to be less ready than you to render a stranger service" (524-25).

Philoctetes, elated, turns then, not to escape, but to pay homage to the earth, to his natural dwelling that has sustained him throughout a decade of suffering: "Let us go, boy. But let us first kiss the earth, / Reverently, in my homeless home of a cave" (531-32). Although their desire is to sail immediately from Lemnos, the tide is out, and as Philoctetes has done for almost a decade, they must yield to the natural order's rhythm of ebb and flow. This waiting and yielding to nature is an action evident throughout the drama. The orders of nature and divinity situate the human existence between them, and this human order must be willing to yield to the larger forces of the natural and divine orders. There is an herb, Philoctetes tells Neoptolemus, that he wants to fetch from his cave before they leave, for it gives relief from his ebbing and flowing pain. This first mention of some natural tonic that can appease his affliction appears directly after a sailor, disguised as a trader, informs Philoctetes of the prophecy that Troy cannot be conquered until he is persuaded to accompany Odysseus and his men in order to assure victory for the Achaeans. But just at this juncture, when his future begins to take shape, the pain in his wound attacks Philoctetes. Neoptolemus asks him: "What is this thing that comes upon you suddenly, / that makes you cry and moan so?" (752-53) to which Philoctetes, afraid of being abandoned because of his increasing agony, responds: "Do not be afraid and leave me. / She comes from time to time, perhaps when she has had her fill of wandering in other places" (756-59).

He downplays the pain, for he wishes to sail from the island, but at this moment the pain becomes too intense: "the blood is trickling, dripping murderously / from its deep spring. I look for something new, / It is coming now, coming. Ah!" (782-86). Threatened with unconsciousness, Philoctetes turns the bow over to Neoptolemus for protection. Sophocles' artistic genius in many of his plays is to describe that point, often through the relation between body and language, in which a bursting of some boundary, including both knowledge and the flesh together, is necessary. What has been hidden just below the surface of the skin and below the level of full conscious awareness erupts and scatters, releasing tremendous tension in the dramatic action. Such is the case here with the wound. Philoctetes' wound howls to break its boundaries further. The body as container is incapable of holding back the spirit of the wound. Chryse's semi-divine presence intensifies the pain in the wounded nature of Philoctetes and demonstrates what Bernard Knox believes is a poetic element included most frequently in Sophoclean tragedy: "The gods are presences felt at every turn of the action... and by some mysterious poetic alchemy we are made to feel... that the gods have more concern and respect for the hero, even when... he seems to fight against them, than for the common run of human beings who observe the mean" (6-7).

Here the boundaries are burst as a parallel in the body to Philoctetes' wish to leave the island and return home. The skin breaks open; the festering wound pushes farther into the world as its stench carries its presence well beyond eyesight. Like any crucial violation of divinity or humanity, it cannot be contained to that one incident, as Odysseus tried to convince Neoptolemus earlier could be done. No, it spills into the collective myth and alters it, as Oedipus' afflicted origins and polluted life spill across the land at the beginning of *Oedipus the King* to inhibit the natural order from all attempts at regeneration.

Crippled by the pain's intensity, Philoctetes pleads with Neoptolemus to place him on a funeral pyre in a gesture of pity, as Philoctetes himself did for Heracles before, and then to become the keeper of the bow, which will be handed down in another act of compassion for the suffering of another. Neoptolemus' change of heart is evident in his response to the suffering man: "I have been in pain for you; I have been / in sorrow for your pain" (805-06). His compassion acts as a salve to the suffering Philoctetes. The wound's discharge prompts Neoptolemus to offer a healing in words, a response almost medicinal in nature; he begins to become Philoctetes to the latter's Heracles. Charles Segal writes that in this moment "a spirit of heroic generosity still radiates from the bow" (122) and is passed down, like a scepter from king to prince. The bow is metonymic of the entire code of heroic largesse. The younger man's compassionate presence is transforming him into a heroic figure, first through the deep wound of his shame, and now through witnessing the honor and heroism implicit in the suffering man's ability to suffer and still pay homage to the gods. He becomes much more deliberate and unyielding in his ability to honor himself by honoring another's suffering. Called forth at this instant is the heroic ideal of compassion, perhaps given only to those characters in tragedy who have "plumbed the depths of their own misery" (151), in Unamuno's sense.

❧ ❧ ❧

As Philoctetes calls on the Earth to take him and so allow his suffering to end, Neoptolemus, sounding in his words more mature and resolute, more akin to a physician than one who promised to take Philoctetes from the island, speaks of the wound's condition:

> The sweat is soaking all his body over,
> and a black flux of blood and matter has broken
> out of his foot. Let us leave him quiet, friends,
> until he falls asleep. (822-25)

The sweating suggests a fever trying to break, an infection coming to its limits before healing, but not before bursting forth. Perhaps the chorus gives us the best word to apply here—"*Ripeness that holds decision over all things* / wins many a victory suddenly" (836-37, my emphasis). The wound has ripened into a form of knowing expressed most cogently by Neoptolemus as his focus shifts from the bow, the object of Odysseus' obsession, to the man Philoctetes himself: "His is the crown of victory, him the God said we must bring. / *Shame shall be ours* if we boast and our lies still leave victory unwon" (841-42, my emphasis). As in the Oedipus tragedy, the focus narrows from the "many" to the "one," in this case from the broad and mythic tradition of the heroic to the enfleshed, historical suffering of one person.

When Philoctetes awakens from his sleep, a sense of blessedness surrounds his words. He has for the moment been purged of his anguish:

> Blessed the light that comes after my sleep,
> blessed the watching of friends.
> I never would have hoped this,
> that you would have the pity of heart to support
> my afflictions. (867-71)

His vocabulary is crucial at this stage of his turn to a more healing presence: the words "blessed," "pity," and "hope" characterized
his speaking. These are words of renewal rather than continued
toxicity. Nonetheless, Neoptolemus remains in his original shame,
for he carries with him the earlier oath sworn to Odysseus to
help steal the bow from Philoctetes. But he now regrets having
compromised his own nature, and he sees himself more clearly
in the mirror of Philoctetes' heroic suffering. Neoptolemus' words
pollute his will, and he finds himself in that tragic state of need-
ing to choose between violating his words either to Odysseus or
to Philoctetes. He has promised the latter, again deceitfully, to
take him straight home from Lemnos rather than to Troy, where
the destiny of being whole and victorious awaits him.

Philoctetes senses the wandering words of Neoptolemus and
assumes they are because of his own foul-smelling wound. But
Neoptolemus has already taken that disgust into himself, and he
recognizes the odor of his own polluted nature:

> Philoctetes: Is it disgust at my sickness? Is it this
> That makes you shrink from taking me?
> Neoptolemus: All is disgust when one leaves his own nature
> And does things that misfit it. (899-902)

When Philoctetes calls on the honorable nature of the young
man's father, Achilles, and through that name, to the tradition
of the heroic ideals embodied in his figure, Neoptolemus immediately feels the sharp point of the wound of self-betrayal: "I shall
be shown to be dishonorable: / I am afraid of that" (904-05).
Caught between two allegiances, one of which carries the stench
of dishonor, Neoptolemus feels the increasing pain of his condition and asks that most tragic of questions which often arises out
of a moral checkmate: "Zeus, what must I do? Twice be proved
base, / hiding what I should not, saying what is most foul?" (907-
08). Recognizing this condition, Neoptolemus begins to suffer on
a level he could not have imagined. He suffers both for himself
in his vulnerability and for Philoctetes in his helplessness;
tragedy's taut bow bends. The foul wound and fouler words now
engulf both heroes in pollution.

But this pollution is necessary for there to be even a possibility of some break into a new order. The word "pollution,"

Dudley Young explains, has its own paradoxical nature. It "points to something essentially bad, even horrible; and yet, because its root meaning is 'a coming into presence of the usually absent divinity,' it also carries an ambiguous shadow." Pollution may include and embody "an injection of strength which disorders" (232). In another section, Young adds to our understanding of the action of Philoctetes by exploring, the Greek word for scape-goat, *pharmakos*, which "like the dirtying *katharma* that also prom-ises cleansing, *katharsis* is essentially ambiguous, akin to *pharmakon*, a poison that may be a cure" (302). One could per-haps not find a more inclusive image for tragedy itself.

※　※　※

The suffering of Philoctetes is not yet completed when his agony passes, for he has given the bow to Neoptolemus out of good faith to honor him for agreeing to take him home. But he senses that Neoptolemus is split in his own mind and not to be trusted, so he pleads for the bow to be returned. With no response from Achilles' son, Philoctetes turns again to that harsh terrain which has been both austerely present and strangely com-forting to him. The earth's fierce geography offers him a basic solace:

> Caverns and headlands, dens of wild creatures,
> You jutting broken crags, to you I raise my cry—
> There is no one else that I can speak to—
> 　　And you have always been there, have always heard me,
> Let me tell you what he has done to me. (934-38)

Having incorporated the nature nymph into himself through the wound, Philoctetes has grown intimate with the landscape, and it has returned his affections by offering him clarity of vision—a see-ing through the wound—that he never before possessed. Now, instead of violating the spirit of nature, which brought forth the wound, he is in harmony with it. He is, in a sense, *in* his own nature, which is why he is so wounded by Neoptolemus, whom he knows to be outside *his*. So not only is the earlier event—Her-acles bequeathing the bow to Philoctetes for lighting the funeral pyre—repeated here, but the earlier violation is as well, and

Philoctetes, having suffered into this way of knowing, can witness it and be stung once again.

Further, he knows that the bow does not suffer *hamartia* or "missing the mark," but rather with deadly accuracy, divinely inspired, hits its mark every time; without it, he will die of starvation. He is put into the same position as Neoptolemus was earlier: "I have been deceived and am lost. What can I do?" (948-49). Instead of addressing Zeus for guidance, as did Neoptolemus, Philoctetes once again turns for solace to the one character he feels has never and would not ever deceive him, the places of the natural order herself.

> Two doors cut in the rock, to you again,
> again I come, enter again, unarmed.
> Here in this passage
> I shall shrivel to death alone. (952-55)

He utters the cry of desolation and hopelessness that echoes across time to King Lear's naked woeful cries of nothingness on the heath: "Then I am nothing" (951) and "I am nothing now" (1030). At the same time, Neoptolemus feels in his own soul the anguish of Philoctetes; his own emotional condition, like the wound of the afflicted man, intensifies in a kind of sympathetic response: "A kind of compassion, / a terrible compassion, has come upon me / for him. I have felt for him all the time" (965-67). The wound of shame is transformed into compassion, akin to what his father conveys to Nestor and to Agamemnon in the funeral games at the end of the *Iliad*—the spirit of heroic generosity born through loss, shame, grief, and abandonment.

Miguel de Unamuno profoundly develops the conviction that in order to love everything and feel compassion for all that lives, "you must feel everything within yourself, you must personalize everything" (152). He goes on to suggest that "we pity, that is, we love only that which is like us, and thus our compassion grows, and with it our love for things in the measure to which they are discovered to be in our likeness" (153). As our awareness grows, so too may our compassion: "Consciousness... is participated knowledge, and it is co-feeling, and co-feeling is compassion" (153). Sophocles' drama not only engages a poetic exploration of a movement from wounding to healing, but it also

opens a profound vision of how compassion develops in the soul
through a deep witnessing to the suffering of another. Seeing
Philoctetes' suffering bends Neoptolemus from shame to compassion with the same intensity that the wound itself bends
Philoctetes to its literal pain.

Philoctetes knows the inner conflict in Neoptolemus and feels
a growing compassion for him; he then upbraids him for the
"foul lesson" that he hopes he will abandon in choosing once
again to honor his word as Achilles' worthy son. At the very
instant that Neoptolemus, at his most intensely pivotal moment,
is poised to honor Philoctetes' wish to return home, Odysseus
appears. He wrenches the bow from Neoptolemus and leaves
Philoctetes. As the crippled man withdraws once more into the
cave, its opening reminiscent of both a mouth and an open
wound, Odysseus admonishes Neoptolemus to leave with him,
especially worried that Neoptolemus' "generosity / may spoil our
future" (1067-68). The younger man complies, but he also feels
the pity rise in him, knowing in his own shame what honorable
action is needed. The chorus, comprised of the men under Neoptolemus' command, lacks this moral vision. Seeing only
Philoctetes' stubbornness, it blames him for condemning himself:
"It was you who doomed yourself, / man of hard fortune. From
no other, from nothing stronger, came your mischance" (1092-93).

❊   ❊   ❊

As he comes into awareness through his compassionate bending towards Philoctetes' suffering, Neoptolemus knows that he
must return the bow, then bend to the suffering man's will, freely,
out of compassion. He reclaims the bow from Odysseus and takes
it to Philoctetes in his cave, where he confronts a shower of abuse
from the despairing and unbending man. Neoptolemus' response
is curt and decisive: "Do not curse me any more. / Take your
bow. Here I give it to you." Philoctetes answers, "What can you
mean? Is this another trick?" (1282-87). Instead of making himself
the referent, Neoptolemus elevates his action to Olympus and
divinity's presence: "No. That I swear by the holy majesty / of
Zeus on high!" (1288-89). Odysseus, not to be denied, rushes in
at the critical instant when Neoptolemus hands over the bow—and
for a minute this trinity faces off as Philoctetes loads the bow

with an arrow to slay Odysseus, but is deflected by Neoptolemus. The pivotal figure between them, he tells a frustrated Philoctetes, as Odysseus flees: "This is not to our glory, neither yours nor mine" (1305). Killing Odysseus will wound them both in the deeper layers of their being, where true honor dwells. While Odysseus interprets the bow as the signal to victory, and Philoctetes understands the bow as his means to survival and as a token of his past connection with the now deified Heracles, Neoptolemus understands it as the emblem of a heroic tradition that cannot be violated without causing a polluting wound that will fester and suppurate in the Greek soul.

Philoctetes refuses to compromise. He will not bend. Yet when we imagine the bow itself as unbending—that is, unstrung—it is most upright, yet without strength; as a weapon it is virtually worthless. Left stringless, it is not only unyielding but without force. But when the bow bends to the given measure that the string allows, it gains its force in and through the tension of opposition. So the bow gains its strength and even its entelechy in bending to the string. Bent into a curve by the string that the two ends, in bending towards one another, straighten, the strung bow is an archetype. The bow wishes to be upright and straight—that is its desire. But when it gives way to the string's demands, its natural bent consists in wanting release. Yet the string insists that it yield to the state of tension. This is the image of Philoctetes specifically, but it might also serve as one for tragedy generally. Philoctetes must yield, and even though his own mind resists doing so because of his outrage, he does learn to bend, like the bow, in order to follow the instructions of Heracles, give power to the Greeks, heal himself, and win the glory prophesied as both his right and his destiny.

One more step with the bow: the string restrains the bow from yielding up its tension, and herein lies the bow's strength, its use as a weapon, and its accuracy, for the more taut the string, the greater the accuracy and deadliness of the bow. No longer relaxed, but now taut and powerful in its obedience to the string's demands—that is the bow's existential condition. And this, the bow comes to know, *is its true nature*—to yield to the string and, in this taut yielding, to gain its power and its usefulness in the world that it serves. The rigidity of the string is matched by the yielding resistance of the bow—a truly harmonious, proportionate, and

paradoxical tension of opposites. Still another step: in this provocative image lies the archetypal action that comprises tragedy—gaining
possession of power by yielding to the tension of *ananke*. The bow
passes its strength to the string that supports the bow in its obsti-
nate bending or yielding power. When the two work in harmony,
one avoids *hamartia*, a cardinal sin in archery and the fatal mistake in tragedy.

Sophocles imagines the tongue and the bow together, because
both have the capacity to wound deeply. Much the same dynamic
is incorporated into the human tongue, mentioned so frequently
throughout the drama. Lying flat in the mouth, it lacks force;
but when it bends to form words, it gains incredible power either
to wound or to heal. Words are formed only when the tongue
rises up in the mouth, curves, and forms words that may have a
multitude of intentions. I would thus add the tongue to the
other symbols, the wound and the bow, as another way of seeing the bodily genesis of tragedy: myths out of the mouth,
released into the world as story, as memory, and as destiny by
the power of the tongue. For Sophocles, the power of words to
create and shape the world, or change our perception of it, is as
much a part of the plot or mythos of the drama as the deeds
that bear on Philoctetes.

Neoptolemus now replaces the chorus as a voice of wisdom
and moderation and insists that Philoctetes surrender his anger:

> Your anger has made a savage of you. You will not
> accept advice, although the friend advises
> in pure goodheartedness.
> . . . .
> You are sick and the pain of the sickness is of God's sending
> because you approached the Guardian of Chryse,
> the serpent that with secret watch protects
> her roofless shrine to keep it from violation. (1320-24, 1326-29)

Then Neoptolemus not only returns Philoctetes to the origin of
his affliction, but he also pushes him toward the future by pleading with him to accept healing at Troy under the ministering of
"the Asclepiadae, / who will relieve your sickness; then with the
bow / and by my side, you will become Troy's conqueror" (1332-
34). To this admonition, Neoptolemus adds:

> Now since you know this, yield and be gracious.
> It is a glorious heightening of gain.
> First to come into hands that can heal you,
> and then be judged pre-eminent among the Greeks.... (1342-45)

The wound's violent eruptions of pain reveal to us how deep is the inability of Philoctetes to yield, to give up what has sustained him for almost ten years. So the persuasive energy flows, increasing, from the chorus, to Neoptolemus, and finally to Heracles himself.

At the end of the play, the god stands above Philoctetes' cave and announces that he comes from his realm of the dead, not to force Philoctetes to bow to his will but to serve him towards his own healing. It is through Heracles that the heroic tradition is reinstated, given its language again and imaginatively remembered. Heracles informs him that what he himself has suffered "must be your suffering too, / the winning of a life to an end in glory, / out of this suffering" (1421-24). But Philoctetes must go with Neoptolemus, for the two of them together will, "like twin lions hunting together," protect one another. Philoctetes is destined to be healed, then to slay Paris—that other archer—and to return to his own home with great rewards, some of which must be dedicated to the memory of Heracles' funeral pyre and "in memory of my bow" (1432). Reminiscent of the end of *Oedipus at Colonus*, Heracles ends his prophecy with a warning to "keep holy in the sight of God":

> All else our father Zeus thinks of less moment.
> Holiness does not die with the men that die.
> Whether they die or live, it cannot perish. (1441-44)

Heracles returns Philoctetes and Neoptolemus to an invisible source that lies beyond the heroic tradition, one that gives it its particular energy and form. Holiness is what Philoctetes violated and what led to isolation and resentment stemming from his wound; but the same wound, through its paradoxical pollution, takes him back into the presence of divinity. The play's last lines are Philoctetes' affectionate and deeply nostalgic sentiments towards the craggy hard earth that gave him solace and fed him for so long. It is to this spirit of the earth that he prays for a safe voyage. The ending plea is to the "all-conquering / Spirit who has brought this to pass" (1466-67). Completing the circle from wounding to healing, the action ends as the Chorus announces in the last lines that all on the island should leave only after praying to "the nymphs of the sea / to bring us safe to our homes" (1470-71).

Philoctetes lived a life of scarcity, punctuated only by excessive pain and self-disgust. Praising the source of the wound, remembering implicitly the original violation, and receiving the blessing within the pollution—these comprise the reconciliation to which tragedy leads us, if we can bend to its powerful but invisible force deep in the natural order. Perhaps the spirit of tragedy has its home in the chthonic regions below the visible order; the deeper verities that guide the lives of mortals as much as the sky gods on Olympus lie there. *Philoctetes* is Sophocles' encomium to the forces of Nature, to *Physis*, the wounding origin of conscious knowing. With the human body as its most forceful and compelling analogue, it is the source from whence all knowledge emanates. To be wounded, the drama asks us to remember, "is to be opened to the world; it is to be pushed off the straight, fixed, and predictable path of certainty and thrown into ambiguity, or onto the circuitous path, and into the unseen and unforeseen" (*The Wounded Body* 13).

Tragedy is a conspiracy. We may think of it as something in and of the body and the world. Some form of being marked by the world, by divinity, by our own actions, may be its genesis. Through woundedness we are given an opportunity to enter into the essence, the center of the world and of ourselves, with part of the process including a reordering, a restoration of something lost, forgotten, or never possessed. Tragedy's fundamental action is a revelation of the woundedness of the world, something off the mark, blemished, displaced, homeless. Tragic action is restorative: some essential part of our nature is retrieved. Some impulse in us to retrieve it is part of our nature, with direct and powerful affinities with the created order.

7

Through the Unlit Door of Earth:
Sophocles' Transformation of Tragedy

BAINARD COWAN

The value of *Oedipus Rex* as a core text has long been established; it no doubt is one of the first texts to be thought of
as essential to the liberally educated person. But *Oedipus Rex*,
though valuable in itself, is incomplete without *Oedipus at Colonus*,
written some thirty years later but in unbroken succession in
Sophocles' mind and imagination. *Oedipus Rex* establishes the helpless nobility of the magnanimous person in the face of destiny.
Our concept of tragic irony is almost completely derived from its
stunning reversal of fortune. Complete as the play is in itself, and
definitive as it has been since Aristotle as the one most representative Greek tragedy, it is read perhaps erroneously if one considers it to be the whole story. For *Oedipus at Colonus* reveals
something hidden from Oedipus and the audience in the earlier
play—and that is the purpose of the whole enterprise. For, as the
second drama reveals, the noble person is destined to a terrible
fate for a reason. And that reason is to perfect him as a hero.

The tragic abyss is evoked brutally and horrifically in the language of the last third of *Oedipus Rex*, interposing mad self-
destruction and moments of blinding lucidity: "Ah, cloud of
darkness abominable, coming over me unspeakably, irresistible,
sped by an evil wind!... if there is any evil even beyond evil, that
is the portion of Oedipus" (1313-15, 1365-66 LJ).[1] The hero's
carefully plotted steps of rectitude are revealed for what they are:

steps toward a precipice, beneath which yawns a cavernous darkness. Repeatedly in his plays Sophocles sends his heroes there,
though almost nowhere else with the destructive force that he visits on Oedipus. It is all the more remarkable then that Oedipus
returns in Sophocles' last play. First produced by his grandson
after the dramatist's death, *Oedipus at Colonus* might be considered a kind of last will and testament of the author. Through it
his rapt audience could verify the interest gained in his most
painfully accrued account and find no diminished principal. In
this play much has changed from the standard Sophoclean model
of tragedy, yet everywhere what happens touches on that model—
the downward plunge into darkness of the noble human being
who has found something demanding fealty, let the family, the
city, the universe oppose.

The chorus of Aeschylus' *Agamemnon* issues the terse watchword for hope in Greek tragedy: *pathei mathos*—through suffering
comes learning. For Aeschylus what comes of tragedy is of course
something much more profound than simple learning. But for
Sophocles in *Oedipus at Colonus* the hero's encounter with the
abyss issues in a transformation of the entire tragic world. First,
the significance of suffering changes: that it has a meaning at all
emerges slowly but confidently here. Through suffering the law
and the *polis* are transformed. Second, the concept of the hero
is expanded and connected to its roots not only in the *polis* but
in religion. Third, the central *praxis* of tragedy's *mimesis* is now
definitively enlarged to include the offering of mercy and the
granting of blessings. Fourth, the kindly natural world reenters the
polis; fifth, the feminine rejoins the masculine and leads it where
it is blind to go; and finally and ultimately, the passage through
the "unlit door of earth... into a space unseen" (1661-62, 1681-
82 F), as Antigone says—no longer reveals a horror but an opening out into the infinite and the eternal.

This sweeping transformation is most immediately notable in
the figure of the hero. Pierre Vidal-Naquet observes that whereas
in the first play Oedipus begins as hero and protector of the city
and by the end becomes a *pharmakos* to be expelled, in the second play "everything is the other way around": Oedipus is "a suppliant soon to become a hero and a savior" (350). Each entity
described in this crisply formulated reversal is also transformed
significantly. The *pharmakos* headed out of the *polis* in *Oedipus*

Rex becomes the suppliant headed into it in *Oedipus at Colonus*, and in the process the emphasis of the Oedipus story is transferred from retributive justice to mercy. The concept of protector of the city is changed: in *Oedipus Rex* it describes one who would use the explicit political powers of his office as well as his "mother wit" to act on the *polis*' behalf—a role that would better suit a simpler crisis like the Sphinx's holding the city hostage. Like a modern *stratêgos*, the Theban Oedipus is prepared to fight the previous war. At Colonus the protector figure that Oedipus has become will protect the *polis* cosmically, in a spatio-temporal blanket beyond the powers of political action, offering advantages and victory in unseen future wars. The concept of hero in the earlier play meant designated leader, one proven to act decisively for others; in the later play it is a religious designation, the object of cult veneration, a special channel from the world of the dead to the living.

The world of *Oedipus Rex* is flat, an arena of political argument, until it can be flat no more and the dark, repressed forces of the universe burst in terribly upon it. By contrast, from the outset the world of *Oedipus at Colonus* is three- or four- (or perhaps more-) dimensional, not even round but more like the "open universe" of modern cosmology, leading out beyond visibility at both ends. This perspective is made explicit at the end when Oedipus' exit is described ambiguously as an opening out either into the heaven of the gods or the darkness of earth, beyond human ken either way:

> But some attendant from the train of Heaven
> Came for him; or else the underworld
> Opened in love the unlit door of earth.
> For he was taken without lamentation,
> Illness or suffering; indeed his end
> Was wonderful if mortal's ever was. (1660-65 F)

These awe-inspiring dimensions are not revealed as on a map but as an openness to the unlimited, as a uniting of opposites; and it is brought about because of this paradoxical hero, stripped of every bit of strength in his long humiliation, steadfast still in his long submission, who has transmuted submission to love and through this love has had a transcendent power conferred on

him: a power of prophecy, blessing, and curse. He bears with him
a world also extending outward into the temporal dimension,
toward the future, where Oedipus assures King Theseus of Athens
that he will "forever hold this city / Safe from the men of
Thebes, the dragon's sons" (1533-34 F).

Space is transformed into place: the sociopolitical grid of *Oedipus Rex*, together with its definitive rupture in the last scene,
becomes in *Oedipus at Colonus* a complex map of "singularities"
where, like the black holes that deform space-time itself, places
have their own powers and might open into other dimensions of
the unknown universe in which the human is situated. Vidal-
Naquet points to the recurrent motif of frontiers in the play.
When Creon, regent of Thebes, kidnaps Ismene and Antigone,
Theseus is concerned lest they reach the frontier between Thebes
and Athens, whence recovering them would become embarrassing
for him ("run full speed... for the place / Where the two high-
ways come together. / The girls must not be taken past that
point," 899-902 F). Sophocles' frontiers are like the "event horizon" of black holes: if one crosses them a terrible collapse will
ensue. Oedipus evidently has already breached that line: he is
described by the chorus as a promontory lashed by waves that
roll in from all four cardinal points, from the frontiers of the
known world (1248).[2] The gravitational collapse is palpable here.
It is something he has experienced.

And yet this uncanny object seems in appearance no more
than a weak old man, subject as much as any to the normal
political law of frontiers. Creon, ever seeking legitimacy for his
regency, hopes to return Oedipus not to Thebes but to its frontier, where he is to operate somehow not as a curse but only as
a blessing: "To settle you near the land of Thebes, and so / Have
you at hand; but you may not cross the border"; Oedipus' tomb
will not be covered by "Theban dust" because his "father's blood
forbids it" (400-07 F). As Vidal-Naquet puts it, "Oedipus is to
live as a *paraulos*, in the space outside... [as] a Philoctetes whom
his city will nevertheless keep under its thumb" (354-55). One can
identify a logic of the *paraulos*, according to which one is not
permitted to enter the space whose integrity one is considered
indispensable to maintain. This is of course the logic of the slave,
the *–udra* in India, and subalterns everywhere. But in Sophocles'
final vision this lowly status is vindicated and the magnificent

foundations of its support revealed.

Colonus itself is the most notable frontier, "this earth's / Doorsill of Brass, and buttress of great Athens" (56-58 F).[3] In the familiar paradox, a threshold both connects and divides two spaces, in this case Athens and the world below; and yet a threshold is also its own space of singularity, uniting the two entities in a third that is scarcely recognized but indispensable, the place of transformation. In a related spatial paradox, the buttress follows the logic of the *paraulos*: it stands outside the space that it is indispensable in supporting. These two paradoxes define a topology of space that is both familiar and uncanny. They become the defining figures not only for Colonus but for Oedipus himself, whose confrontation with the abyss has made him the uncanny space through which heaven, earth, and the chthonic are catastrophically combined and then redivided in piety. *Paraulos*, neighbor, becomes an accursed status in that it will keep him permanently outside the *polis*, perpetually foregrounding his pollution. From this fate he is defended by Theseus, and yet this role of one who remains outside while supporting what is inside is the very role he embraces, remaining in Colonus outside Athens to his death.

In Colonus Athens is both present and absent: "the towers / That crown the city still seem far away" (14-15 F). A "double vision" of the city reigns here as it does, more violently, in Euripides' *Bacchae* when Pentheus "seems to see two Thebes." The ominous vision of *The Bacchae*, somewhat as in *Oedipus Rex*, bursts in upon a civic mind—Pentheus'—that has stubbornly refused to see beyond the two-dimensional political grid. In *Oedipus at Colonus*, by contrast, the announcement of the towers of Athens appearing both near and far, coming as it does at the very beginning of the play and spoken by the innocent Ismene, suggests a condition that has been accepted rather than resisted. So the second vision of the city, rather than exposing the first as a fraud or illusion, stands as the root, the cause, the true distilled version, of the first. As Vidal-Naquet notes, Colonus in this play "is a miniaturized, condensed Athens" (356). The olive groves, the horses, the oarsmen, all the gods mentioned in the play (virtually the entire pantheon), the hero Kolônos, and the sanctuary devoted to the Eumenides that is the focal point of the play: all present the "sacred and reverent" (287 LJ) aspects of

Athens, the sacred history of its connection to gods and heroes.

The sorting out of earth from chthonic domination is accomplished centrally in Oedipus' reflection on his own crime. When he first encounters the citizens of Colonus, he reveals that he is an exile, *apopolis*, but begs them not to ask further, for "my star was unspeakable" (212 F).[4] The chorus wants to know what "seed" (*spermatos* 214) he came from—who his father's people were; the metonym reinflicts on Oedipus the agony of his tortured life. Strikingly differently from this first mention of his unhappy fortune, Oedipus' next exchange with the chorus provides a new version of the horrible scene of suffering given in *Oedipus Rex*. Oedipus recalls what he now labels as his *thumos*, passion and fury (434), affirming that "nothing so sweet / As death, death by stoning, could have been given me" (434-35 F). This desire for nothingness is recalled not so much emotionally as discursively. His *thumos* was only a moment, though unbearably intense, and it receded with the passage of time; as he now relates, "after a time" (437 LJ) he returned to reason and realized he had gone too far in punishing his *hêmartêmena* (a word that can be translated as failures, errors, or sins, all assignable to an ethical scale rather than invested with unredressable chthonic aura).

This sorting out ultimately rests on the conflict between *themis*, the unshakable sense of what is right and wrong in dealing with blood guilt and other polluting acts, and the sense of morality linked closely to the rise of the *polis*, in which competing claims about justice had to be balanced against one another and resolved by questions of motive and end. Oedipus insists to the chorus who fears his very name that his guilt was acquired by suffering rather than doing (279-80). In the next exchange, Oedipus and chorus seem to be entering into a relation of complete sympathy until the chorus, after saying "you suffered—" adds "you sinned—" (539 F), and he brings them up short with "No, I did not sin!" Then he explains his patricide as an episode of heroic *atē* like that of Heracles or Ajax: caught in *atē*, he insists, he murdered and slaughtered; and again he counterposes the higher ethical law: "but according to the law (*nómô*) I am clean" (547-48 LJ) (*katharós*, "clean, pure," its use here as elsewhere in tragedy perhaps related to Aristotle's choice of the term *katharsis*).

Cedric Whitman observes that the scene of Theseus driving off Creon, the would-be abductor of Oedipus and his daughters, is one of several scenes in Athenian drama "in which a Greek prince prevents the incidence of barbarian outrage, or an Athenian ruler thwarts the highhandedness of an oligarchic authoritarian," all of them implicitly "commentaries on what it was felt Greek civilization was and should be, providing important evidence for the self-consciousness and world-outlook of the Athenians" (197). The routing of Creon, one Greek ruler defeating another, provides no opportunity to express the customary Greek xenophobia but instead is an occasion to sort out ethical priorities. Accounting for human intention is often considered a crucial advance in histories of ethical consciousness, and Theseus makes this distinction, between laws broken knowingly and unknowingly, when arresting Creon for the abduction of Antigone and Ismene: "He shall be subject to the sort of laws / He has himself imported here," for, he tells Creon, "You come to a city-state that practices justice, / A state that rules by law, and by law only" (907-908, 912-13 F). At the same time that he praises the justice of the system of laws, he emphasizes that Thebes has instituted these laws too: "Yet it is not Theban training that made you evil; it is not their way to breed unrighteous men" (919-20 LJ); Creon has had the full panoply of law, including foreign (intercity) relations, in his training, and must be held fully accountable for his failing. In this way the villainy of the Theban regent is connected to his free choice rather than to the mythology of the "dragon's sons" and the recurrent curse in the Theban past. Theseus establishes a tie between the city as an advanced achievement and the accomplishment of justice based on reasonable law.

Nowhere else than in this last play does Sophocles portray a just city. Here he affirms the divine approval of the *polis* based on the human freedom to choose the good, and this almost unexpected note rings out like nowhere else in tragedy outside Aeschylus' *Eumenides*. Whereas Aeschylus could portray the justice of the *polis* as in the process (and it is specifically a judicial process) of being *discovered*, however, Sophocles rather differently grounds it simultaneously in something quite specific—the clarity of ethical consciousness—and something quite vague and universal—the mysterious sacredness of heaven and earth. Whitman observes that "the last two plays, [*Philoctetes* and *Oedipus at Colonus*] where quiet deliverance after pain and true insights of inner value are the aims, have prologues where people enter searching, either on an unfamiliar island or at the fringes of an unknown city" (193). Colonus has something fundamentally unknown about it that leads to a questioning and examining of the nature of the *polis* throughout this play. What is the relation of the city to power—to political power, but also to the powers that reside in or under the land? A religious context is constantly put forward as the more comprehensive framework for the justice of the city.

This duality of the practical and the mystical, the political and the transpolitical, is maintained throughout the play. Oedipus' first speech is formulated in careful opposing pairs of terms (1-13): to what region (*chôros*) or what city (*polis*) have we come? Seat me on unconsecrated or near sacred ground. Antigone replies (14-20): there are towers of the city (*polis*), but they seem far off. Oedipus asks the first citizen he meets what form of government they have—a ruler or rule by the people? This is a practical question, an Attic version of "Take me to your leader," but it furthers the discourse on the *polis* that runs through this play. Whereas the Athens of Sophocles' mythic past is ruled by a king, a *basileus*, Theseus, a deeper manifestation of the common will is asserted by the chorus and is allied more to *themis* as the sense of rightness and piety than to the letter of the law: the chorus declares that they will never allow Oedipus to be taken by force from this place, but they clearly fear for the city's fortune, and they counsel him, "learn to respect what the city (*polis*) holds dear (*philon*) and loathe what it loathes (*aphilon*)." Beyond political processes there persists a life, a "heart," as we might put it, of the city itself, and rather than being an empty cliché this expression serves as a way of saying that the common good of the people must be known intimately, almost instinctively, as love and loathing, by each of its citizens. Ironically, it is precisely Oedipus' presence that forces Thesean Athens to make its defining choice, choosing exactly what it holds dear, a lowly supplicant, over what it loathes, a threatening tyrant.

Throughout the play recurs the implication that the city that simply pursues power is actually unmaking itself as city. Creon's attempt to force Oedipus' hand by having his daughters abducted is punctuated by the chorus exclaiming "The city, my city, is being destroyed by violence!" (841 LJ); if Creon succeeds in his kidnaping, they insist, "then I no longer consider this a city!" (879 LJ). Oedipus' sons, "thrice-unhappy," have entered into "an evil rivalry to grasp at dominion (*archê*) and royal power (*krátos turannikou*)" (373 LJ). The love of power unmakes the blessing of the stranger and turns it into a curse. This operationalizing of the stranger's blessing employs the logic of the *paraulos*, as we have seen: Thebes wants to have Oedipus *near* but not *in* the Theban municipality, so that he may be used by but not included in the community. They want him specifically not to have self-rule (*autou kratos* 405).

Sophocles' heroes are victims; they are carefully mutilated by surgically removing their conditions of freedom from them. As critics have well noted, this is precisely the logic of Philoctetes' treatment, whose wound makes him a pariah to those for whom his divine blessing is essential. In *Colonus* this crisis is brought to bear on the city. The tragic hero becomes a test for the human order, which must decide what it considers supreme: its own order, figured here as cleanliness, or the gods' favor, allied to the stranger. For Sophocles, most intensely in his last two plays, the blessings of the gods are granted only if the outcast is accepted, and the outcast is always to an extent unclean. Early on, and in answer to their speech about loving and loathing, Oedipus humbly reminds the still-wary chorus that the true source of Athens' fame is its reverence for the gods and its protection of *xenoi*, foreigners.

Oedipus is in any case a breaker of ordinary custom, no more showing wise fear and avoidance now than he did in challenging the Sphinx or in the central disaster of his life. The chorus of countrymen at first consider Oedipus "the man most impudent of all... one who shows no reverence," for he has gone straight to the seat of the Dread Goddesses, "whom we are afraid to name," whereas the people's custom is to "pass without looking, without sound, without speech, moving our lips in respectful silence" (120-34 LJ). In dialogue they tell Oedipus "you go too far, too far!" (155-156 LJ). Indeed he has; perhaps, though, it is he who should be dreaded in respectful silence. His boldness has changed in character: it no longer proceeds from his enlightened disregard of the deities but from his solidarity with them.

Whitman maintains that the intent of Sophocles' tragedies "was to raise the god within man to the dignity of a legitimate and recognized universal" (190). It was Knox, however, who first explored the deep relation of the hero cult to Sophocles' poiesis, arising out of the great dramatist's own participation in the cult of Asclepius, which, combined with his civic service and honor, led to Sophocles' own veneration by a hero cult in Athens after his death (*Heroic* 54-56). Colonus was Sophocles' birthplace, and there the tomb of Oedipus was venerated; Sophocles' last play thus examines the playwright's own heroic inheritance.

Knox relates that the figures venerated in the hero cults "were of many different kinds: faded divinities, healing powers, historical figures, founders (real or imagined) of cities, even local goblins or earth spirits"; that what they had in common, celebrated in poetry, was that "by the awesome force of their personality, the greatness of their achievement, their suffering, and in most instances their passionate anger, [they] seemed in life to exceed the proportions of ordinary humanity and even in the grave continued to compel the fear and admiration of mankind." Their graves themselves, therefore, were holy places, "sources of strength and prosperity to the land, or of danger to it if their cult should be neglected" (*Heroic* 55-56). Hence what Thebes and Athens struggle over in their contest for Oedipus is this holy strength and prosperity recognized by the cult.

Knox argues that the one indispensable trait of Greek heroes is "their irreconcilable temper; the greatness of their passion brought them into conflict with men and even with the gods... the cult of the hero was a ceremony which aimed to appease his wrath, and the sacrifices were called *meilígmata* 'propitiatory offerings.'" He quotes Martin Nilsson in his study of Greek religion, who calls the hero cult "apotropaic; it is designed to appease the mighty dead who are by no means slow to wrath." Nilsson insists that the strength of the hero "does not need to be of a beneficent kind... [it has] no relation to moral or higher religious ideas but is an expression of naked power or strength" (Nilsson 194). Further probing the ambivalent religious roots of the hero concept, Knox draws on a study by Angelo Brelich in which the hero is defined as a person with whom death has a special relation; he is connected with combat, contest, prophecy, healing, and initiation into adulthood and the mysteries; he is a founder of cities whose cult has a civic character; yet he is monstrous, theriomorphic or androgynous, sexually abnormal, given to violence, madness, trickery, theft, sacrilege, and in general to that transgression of limits not permitted to mortals (Brelich 174 n. 83).

What was suppressed in *Oedipus Rex*, then, reemerges in *Oedipus at Colonus*. Oedipus in Thebes proudly played the role of hero as it is conventionally defined, one who performs a great service for others. The outbreak of the plague, the oracle's word, and the onset of Oedipus' self-destroying rage all indicate obscurely that this conception of heroism, and consequently of human life and the life of the *polis*, is deeply insufficient. What might be an adequate conception of these matters remains completely and literally out of sight. Sophocles' return to this myth in reflection, however, rediscovers the "primitive" source of heroic power in the cosmos of the gods and chthonic spirits, the world beyond human ken that manifests itself in the human world with ambivalence and paradox: the old, blind, decrepit Oedipus truly embodies the hero in his magical power as the active and accomplished Oedipus of Thebes did not.

Already Aeschylus' *Choephoroe* employs the ritual structure of libation offerings brought to a dead war hero and king. The implacable nature of the dead—their unbreakable tie to their own graves; the sanctification or curse on the land according to their treatment—all suggest another dimension to human life. The land as territory may be socioeconomic and political; as earth and gateway to the dead it is holder of dread powers.[5] Penetrating the *xy* plane (plain) is a *z* dimension of unplumbed, perhaps bottomless, depth. The heroes were ones who faced those powers unafraid; their bodies were thresholds bringing together the clash of the powers of the cosmos in order to keep them safely apart for others. They stand at the foundation of the *polis* but outside it, buttressing it. They are civic yet not. Cities are built in tribute to them; their worship is apotropaic. Tragic drama, then, is also apotropaic, honoring the hero as the dangerous one who has stood against the power of the abyss over human life by entering it, or letting it enter him.

The abyss is that place imagined, feared, dreamed of, where life and hope are snuffed out, where the good is destroyed, where the ordered world is delivered unto chaos. The hero's grave offering emphasizes imagery of the abyss, with gravity and entropy doing their work in the lightless night as the life blood drains from the offered black animal. This was old religion; in fifth-century Athens the hero cult must have seemed unenlightened, a throwback, though still practiced. In drawing on its suggestive power, Sophocles archaized where Aeschylus contemporized. Aeschylus seems in the *Eumenides* to be extending civic order even up to Olympus; Sophocles goes in the opposite direction, placing his heroes in a world with no overarching divine plan, where the gods' motives are unknown, not to be counted on. The curses are old and forgotten until it is too late. In that world a dream of justice is yet conceived by one who is unafraid: Oedipus to find the murderer; Antigone to bury her brother. These cases, the most well known today of Sophocles', point to an idealism of justice that is all the more dramatic for being conceived in the face of a recrudescent dark universe; yet the plan of justice is no less tied to death and cannot keep itself from contamination by the very wound in being that it would clean and dress.

The last episode of Oedipus' life inducts him into the hero cult. First this happens by coincidence or destiny, as he comes unknowingly to the place of a hero-god, the very place he had been told by the oracle would be his final resting place. The local inhabitant he meets informs him that the horseman Kolônos is claimed for founder of this municipality and is honored not in words (*ou lógois*) but rather in their being-together (*xunousía*). The hero cult is founded in a shared belief deeper than words. In his next speech Kolônos is referred to as a *theos*. The meeting between Theseus and Oedipus calls into play several systems: they are hero to hero, aristocrat to aristocrat, suppliant to stateholder (569), and finally allies in war (631-35). In sympathizing with Oedipus, Theseus cites the traits they hold in common, and they are succinct characteristics of the hero:

> For I
> Too was an exile. I grew up abroad,
> And in strange lands I fought as few men have
> With danger and with death. (562-64 F)

For Sophocles, then, to be a hero is also to call on a communion of heroes that subtends the everyday reality of the *polis*. Oedipus's great speech taking Theseus into his confidence proposes a heroic line of descent of the mysteries of wisdom specifically regarding the *polis*: he will tell "what is appointed for you and for your city: / A thing that age will never wear away" (1519 F). This knowledge is sacred, "mysteries, not to be explained," requiring an attitude of reverence by the city in its action, not "arrogance" nor "put[ting] off God and turn[ing] to madness" (1526-27, 1535, 1537 F).[6]

The language of gift, favor, boon, advantage, and blessing in this play is pervasive and searching. To be able to dispense a gift or advantage is a power that the play's action restores to its inner stature, repeatedly juxtaposing it ironically to those in power who have refused to grant kindness and thus robbed themselves of the power of the gift. Oedipus is a suppliant in this world of outer power, but from the beginning he is acutely conscious of his personal ability to reverse that hierarchy. On first arriving in Colonus he sends for the king with the message that "a small favor may gain him much," for, though blind (and the peasant asked to bear this message is properly disbelieving at Oedipus' imperiousness), "All I shall say will be clear-sighted indeed" (72, 74 F). Steadily Oedipus' language converts this oracular power to a practical position of superiority.

Hand in hand with the power of the gift comes the power to curse. Oedipus' prayer in the sacred garden of Colonus rehearses Apollo's oracle, which foretold that the blind exile would become someone "Conferring benefit on those who received me, / A curse (*atê*) on those who have driven me away" (92-93 F). As hero, Oedipus is free to dispense a zero-sum logic: good fortune for Athens, misfortune for its enemies. Sophocles explores the balance of boon and curse throughout his late plays. When Oedipus curses his sons because they want to use him for their own power, he goes on to tell the new story of his exile as unwished for, bitterly remarking that his sons could have stopped the banishment with a very little act of kindness (*smikros charis* 443).

If gift and curse are zero-sum in the ineluctable world of human power, the two may also be combined in an acute act of irony. Thus Oedipus refers to his marriage with Jocasta as a "special gift" from the people of Thebes, a gift he "should never have accepted!" (539-41 LJ). This hidden "poisoning" of the gift— one thinks of the profound English-German pun "gift, *Gift*"—is a constant possibility. Its opposite in genuine kindness is what Oedipus says when he first meets Theseus: "I come to offer you the gift of my miserable body" (577 LJ). This "miserable" gift counterposes the "special gift" of his mother's body that he was given in Thebes and contains the promise of being better rather than worse than it seems, specifically because he brings the blessings of the hero.

A favor may also be a false favor. Oedipus accuses Creon of denying him the true *charis* of casting him out from Thebes when he wanted it, but then exiling him when he had recovered and wanted to live at home—giving "when charity was no charity at all" (*oudèn hê cháris chárin phéroi* 779 F). The perversity of which human beings are capable is indeed unfathomable: "Why is it so delightful to be kind to men against their will?" (775 LJ). Oedipus responds to this disingenuous mockery of charity with an ironic exchange of gifts: "You shall not have that [my return to Thebes], but you shall have this, my vengeful spirit (*alastor*) ever dwelling here" (787-88 LJ). The curse, at least, is open in its hostility; it may poison the receiver but not the very institution of the gift.

The curse also works in reverse as a gift to the giver, conferring strength on him while at the same time blighting the receiver. Oedipus recalls that he cursed Polyneices in the past and now he calls these curses "to come and fight beside me" (1376 LJ). Then he issues a fresh round of curses: not only that Polyneices may die by his brother's hand in killing him, but that "the hateful paternal darkness of Tartarus [will] give you a new home" (1389-90 LJ). Polyneices' name may be translated as "many quarrels" or "much strife"; Whitman, more authoritatively, renders it "man of the heavy curse" (211).

Jocasta as a gift to Oedipus; the gift of exile and homelessness; Creon's gift of Theban *non*-citizenship: these ironic gifts-as-curses expose and explore the dual dimension of the gift poisoned by the tragic stain, in which the circle of exchange darkens into a cycle of retribution and political loyalty becomes treachery. In another play, in *The Women of Trachis*, Sophocles has displayed his most explicit symbol of this poisoned gift: the clotted blood of the centaur Nessus poisoned by the Lernaean hydra, which Nessus gives to Deianeira at his death, deceptively telling her it will charm Heracles from ever loving another woman, whereas actually it is so corrosive to flesh that, once daubed with it, Heracles suffers such agony that he commands his son to build a pyre and throw him on it. "I had an ancient gift from a monster long ago, hidden in a brazen pot," begins Deianeira's speech that introduces this motif in the middle of the play (555-56 LJ). Sophocles strikes his characteristic archaizing note with ominous power: this remarkable speech, unanticipated in the texture of the play and brought out as if dimly remembered, seems to open a door into the abyss where one was expecting firm ground. Here as in *Oedipus Rex* there is no stopping the dark circle of destruction widening outward from an old wound. It is only in the last play, inside the sacred garden at Colonus, that the poison is annulled and the irony flows the other way in the gift of Oedipus' miserable body.

The positive dimension of the gift opens in *Oedipus at Colonus* as the result of a profound reimagining of the human world and the life world. Oedipus' daughters redeem the masculine-feminine relation that had been poisoned in *Oedipus Rex*. Oedipus asks that one of his daughters make the purification ritual that the citizens of Colonus have instructed him to perform in atonement for having entered the garden of the Eumenides. "One soul, I think, often can make atonement / For many others, if it be sincere" (498-99 F). It is Ismene who offers to go and is sent, and this is a significant choice in light of her antiheroic portrayal in the earlier *Antigone*. Ismene's matured portrait in *Oedipus at Colonus* is significant in that it ushers the motifs of patience, sympathy, and healing into Sophoclean drama as attributes of the feminine alongside Antigone's heroic traits.

Antigone and Ismene are Oedipus' constant support: Ismene tells Oedipus, "now the gods are lifting you up" (*orthousi*, setting you upright, 394 LJ), and although Oedipus answers her bitterly, the events of the play bear out her hopeful view. Knox has drawn attention to the Sophoclean hero's frequent rejection of advice by others to listen to reason, to good sense, to moderation, or to authority, as a trait of his solitary steadfastness (*Heroic* 11-18). One of these counselors is Jocasta, whose desperate words "Why should anyone in this world be afraid, / Since Fate rules us and nothing can be foreseen? / A man should live only for the present day" Knox has convincingly seen as encapsulating the rejection of tradition characteristic of the fifth-century Athenian Sophists (*Oedipus* 121 *et passim*). Her daughters move constantly in quite a different direction, countering Oedipus' harsh steadfastness with a steady emphasis on mercy and kindness.

Antigone's and Ismene's view of their brothers' mischief too contains a sympathy for the sufferings of one caught in self-destructive *atē*, even if self-chosen. Oedipus wants to refuse even to hear Polyneices' supplication, for his son's "speech would be more painful for me to hear than any man's" (1173-74 LJ); but he lets himself be dissuaded—a rare event in the Sophoclean canon—by Theseus and Antigone, both of whom counsel him simply to listen (*akouein* 1175, *akousai* 1187). Only in this final play does openness to others and their word succeed in softening the hero's resoluteness; and it does so because here, finally in Sophocles' work, the focal center is no longer the necessity of heroic resistance but rather the new sense of the universe that can open up out of his heroic integrity. Through such opening out to those he loves and trusts, the vision can be revealed to be founded on love. Oedipus prepares for death with the ritual of libation and purification, addressing his daughters as they bathe him: "It was hard, I know, my daughters, but a single word dissolves all these hardships. For from none did you have love (*philein*) more than from this man" (1615-18 LJ).[7]

The grove of Colonus is the gift of kindness, *charis*, surrounding this gift of love in death. From the opening scene, when Antigone first describes the grove as replete with laurel, olive, vine, and nightingales, and calls it sacred (14-20), a lyric of darkness constitutes the setting for the play. The central and most beautiful choral ode (668-719) associates birds, foliage, flowers, melodious sounds, and darkness and the deities of the underworld in compressed images such as the nightingale, "beneath the green glades, living amid the wine-dark ivy and the inviolable leafage of the goddess, rich in fruit, never vexed by the sun," and the narcissus, "ancient crown of the two great goddesses," Demeter and Persephone (683 LJ).

Two qualities are stressed that suggest both Oedipus' character and the ever-present powers of nature. The first is mentioned in connection with the stream that flows through the grove:

> nor are the sleepless streams that flow (wandering, *nomádes* 687) from the waters of Cephisus diminished, but ever each day the river, quick to bring crops to birth, flows over the plains of the broad-breasted earth with moisture free from stain. (685-91 LJ)

Oedipus' sufferings have made him close kin to the life-world that solaces him now. His nomadic wandering is transformed in this image as its quality is transferred to the natural surrounding here, losing its desperate and cursed character and becoming the soothing and purifying motion of a stream, not constrained by channels of custom but free to re-enliven the land where it chooses.

Then comes the paean to the olive, whose relation to the earth is special since it is *acheiroton autopoion* (698), not planted by hand but self-creating. Its self-organization, ever springing forth out of the soil no matter what ruin is wrought on the land, is a touchstone for Sophocles. Modern system theorists, who study the property of autopoiesis or self-organization, would note Sophocles' emphasis on the olive's victory over entropy, like any self-organizing system—that same entropy to which the heroic sacrificial ritual is such a grim concession. Oedipus' unmaking and remaking, his central experience between Thebes and Athens, now allies him with the powers of the ever-springing olive.

The strength of the olive is especially emphasized since it is a particular emblem of Attica that grows neither in Asia nor the Peloponnese but "flourishes most greatly in this land." Whitman notes how remarkable Sophocles' references to Athens are in this play which was presented after Athenian land was already scorched by Spartan forces: "When [Sophocles] speaks of Athens in the play, he never mentions her sufferings. He speaks of her as if she were inviolable, as if the sacred olive trees were not burned stumps and the land ravaged and ruined" (210). The olive of this central ode remains "a terror to the spears of enemies," especially steadfast and hardy in the face of aggression. This line Sophocles wrote in defiance of the spoliation of Attica wrought by Athens' enemies in the last years of the Peloponnesian War; the olive springs eternal in this ode, just as the truly great qualities of Athens, "what the *polis* holds dear," extolled earlier in this play, should persist unspoiled.

The link between olive and Athens was forged earlier than Sophocles' time; how much earlier no one can say, but Herodotus relates that the sacred olive on the Acropolis, burned by the Persians, had put out fresh shoots the next day (*Persian Wars* 8.55). The olive is a balm counter to the ravages of history. It is "gray-green nurturer of children" and so a sustainer and token of ever-renewing life: no one young or old can destroy it and bring it to nothing (702-03). And while self-creating, it is also looked upon by the ever-seeing eye of Zeus Morios and gray-eyed Athena (704-06). The *moriai* was the name for the sacred olives in the Academy, so called because they were from the original olive-stock that grew in the Acropolis. Zeus Morios is the guardian of these sacred olives. Euripides in his *Ion* says Athena first planted the olive in Attica;[8] Sophocles, however, makes the gods not originators but guardians as he mentions their eyes, a sign of recognition. The entity that, having organized itself in arising out of the earth, is recognized by the eyes of the gods, attains the status of boon to the land. Such too is the status of the hero worshipped in cult, who may have various origins, whose actions in life betoken a struggle with order, with the powers of the cosmos as well as the human, but whose death finally seals his divine status.

Oedipus at Colonus reveals what Jacques Derrida has explored about the exemplary nature of the gift—its incomprehensibility from the viewpoint of a metaphysics of presence.[9] Sophocles' play opens onto a blessed space of revelation afforded through tragic suffering, adjacent to the harsh and unforgiving terrain of tragedy but cool and green and welcoming—a spatiality and a temporality intimately familiar with the "pre-ontological" (in Derrida's term) nature of the gift. Insofar as tragedy is conceived as retribution for injustice, it remains within the ring of exchange and sacrifice. The Oedipus of *Oedipus Rex* has to learn the brutal lesson that he thought wrongly when he thought that he could escape his fate, that he could take possession of the royal throne and bed, that he could be the secure bulwark of his people. The Oedipus of some twenty years later is all too conscious of his frailty, but he is also the redoubtable advocate of a few fundamental paradoxes that can discern wrong from right, honor the generous and heroic in the most unpromising of circumstances, and unseat the proud, powerful and threatening though they may be.

The one who witnesses this sufferer steadfastly, Theseus, who plays wedding guest to Oedipus' ancient mariner as the blind seer instructs him for the future, now anchors the human community with secret knowledge brought back from the abyss. "Keep it secret always," he is told by the old seer, "and when you come / To the end of life, then you must hand it on / To your most cherished son, and he in turn / Must teach it to his heir, and so

forever" (1530-33 F). This knowledge is of the nature of the hero,
the centrality of the hero's moral compass for the survival of the
polis, the need for the *polis* to unite in loving the good and hating the bad, the rejection of the worship of power, generosity
toward the outcast; and beyond these features and supporting
them, of a mysterious universe whose outlines are not known,
which extends into darkness in all directions, but which welcomes
the courageous human being with an embrace of love. This is not
a knowledge one can apply to a progressive dialectic of history or
conquest, even in the name of greater freedom (Derrida's critique
of Hegel is apropos here). It is not "standing reserve," in Heidegger's phrase, but rather delight in a being that loves to hide
and reveal itself at will. Like the stream Cephisus running through
the grove of Colonus, it is wandering and yet also ever-flowing for
those who are open to it in love. Beyond the resoluteness and
sober steadfastness that so distinguished the view of citizen Sophocles, this is his ultimate wisdom on Athens and mankind as he
neared—serenely, one likes to think—his own demise.

NOTES

[1] Line number references to Sophocles' plays are to the Greek text
in the Lloyd-Jones edition; the lineation is followed by Fitzgerald
as well. Lloyd-Jones' translations are cited as LJ, Fitzgerald's as F.

[2] See Knox's extended comment on this passage in *Heroic* 9.

[3] Literally "brazen-footed threshold," *chalkopous hodos*. Vidal-Naquet
calls it an allusion to the path to Hades (493n87). Hogan (82)
finds a reference to the brass doorsill at the beginning of *Iliad*
VIII, in which Zeus threatens the other Olympians not to inter-
fere in the siege of Troy or he will throw them

> down to the murk of Tartaros,
> far below, where the uttermost depth of the pit lies under
> earth, where there are gates of iron and a brazen doorstone,
> as far beneath the house of Hades as from earth the sky lies. (13-16)

Note Homer's specific differentiation of Tartarus from Hades. As
a Homeric allusion Colonus' brass doorsill connects the town not
just to heaven and earth but to this terrible "uttermost depth of
the pit," a place of punishment and oblivion proper to the fears
of tragedy, suggesting that the peculiar sacredness and serenity of
Colonus are a stamp of authority won through the emergence
from such an abyss.

[4] Lloyd-Jones has, more literally, "terrible was my birth"; the Greek is *deinà phúsis*, an amazing phrase that sums up much of tragedy in its extended meaning, which can include "terrible is nature." See Heidegger's famous discussion of the "hymn to man" in *Antigone* for implications of *deinon*.

[5] See Charles Segal's distinction between land as *chora* and as *chthon* or *gê*.

[6] Perhaps the closest to a direct criticism of the Athens of Sophocles' time in the whole play.

[7] Fitzgerald completes the implied connection between these two lines: "And yet one word / Frees us of all the weight and pain of life: / That word is love."

[8] I am grateful to Charles Segal for pointing out this reference to me.

[9] In his writings since the middle 1980s and especially in *Given Time* and *The Gift of Death*.

8

Fortune and Freedom:
Euripides' *Medea* and *Bacchae*

VIRGINIA ARBERY

As a tragic action unfolds, it inexorably reveals that misfortune cannot be avoided by the assertion of one's freedom. Tragedy exposes the folly of trying to overcome fortune, a major limit to free choice. In Euripides' two plays *Medea* and *The Bacchae*, the skewed thinking and warped desire to be free from contingency reveal themselves in different but related ways. Jason, for instance, justifies himself to Medea as fulfilling the simple desire to "live well, and not be short of anything" (559-561).[1] In exile in a Greek city with his two young boys and his barbarian wife Medea, Jason argues that it is now politic for him to wed the young Corinthian princess, since otherwise his family's future will be insecure. At one level, Jason's argument seems reasonable: he is choosing a better life for his sons. The attempt to control fortune is hardly unnatural when it is aimed at overcoming the suffering brought by bad fortune. But the attempt to control contingency at the expense of the bonds of gratitude opens up worse vulnerabilities. For a whole culture to do so, as the city of Thebes does in *The Bacchae*, is foolhardy.

Tragedy addresses what any self-satisfied city is most in danger of forgetting—the limits of what the human order can do. As James Redfield writes, the tragic poets use versions of the predicaments of the old legendary heroes to put "this year's universal for this year's city" in front of the Athenians as an antidote to their

own delusions (326). He observes that contemporary journalists
and social scientists *think* that they too awaken the public, but
they fare poorly in comparison to the tragedians, because their
concerns are finally not important enough. "Tragedy was (dare I
say?) stronger than social science in that the interpretations provided by this occasional art were explicitly in and of the moment"
(326). Without tragedy the citizen-spectator inhabits a vulnerable
city, one falsely confident because it is blind to its own assumptions. Redfield makes the point that freedom is one such assumption: "In tragedy man appears in a diminished state, non-free.
And as Aristotle says, the terror of tragedy lies in the recognition
that such a person is like ourselves" (326). The tragic poets can
instill true confidence in what is humanly possible—the resource-
ful resilience, for example, praised in the choral ode to man in
Antigone—because of their exploration of what is not possible.

Like Pentheus, the arrogant young ruler of Thebes, modern
planners have held that life would be tidier if we simply eliminated the unpredictable aspects of it that impede our progress,
tyrannize us, and make us unhappy. The spirit of tragedy, like
Dionysus in Thebes, mocks this rationalism. It shocks us from
the comforts and devices that seek to ward off sickness, imperfect looks, deficient intellects, old age, unfortunate marriages,
imperfect births, poverty, war, and death. The psychological urge
of modernity is to escape from tragedy and the kind of knowledge it yields. Such an urge can only lead to depression and
melancholia, for there is no freedom from all the accidentals of
fortune and the inevitability of death. Tragedy itself, however, is
apotropaic,[2] not toward misfortune per se, but toward the pre-
sumption that misfortune is avoidable. Pragmatic solutions, it
shows, are by no means safe choices. But this tragic knowledge
is more for the audience than for the character in the play receiving the force of retribution. In a real way, the irremediable character of the tragic hero's plight moves the audience to recover
accuracy in human feelings and to remain open to difficult paradoxes. Tragedy's cathartic action rectifies false feeling by healing a
presumptuous, unbalanced view of human freedom.

But *Medea* and *The Bacchae* unquestionably test the limits
of pity and terror. They strain the audience's ability to accept the
action Euripides depicts. Jacqueline de Romilly writes that
in Euripides' tragedies, one's attentions shift away from "divine

significance" and toward "the sufferings and tricks of human life." Citing her in his "Intimations of the Will in Greek Tragedy," Jean-Pierre Vernant calls this the Euripidean shift to the "expression of the pathetic" (83). Romilly herself concludes that Euripides' world "leaves no room for responsible action," and Vernant's response suggests that leaving out the gods to focus on the human choice of the characters results in more loss than gain.

But one could certainly think otherwise. Behind both of these tragedies is a radical openness to the central question posed in Plato's *Laws*: "Do the gods exist, and if they do, do they care about men?" Redfield's suggestion—that in tragedy man is "dignified in his acceptance of responsibility for acts not fully his own, but relatively nonfree"—is more helpful in revealing the tragic vision of Euripides. This playwright blurs the clear lines between human responsibility and divine dispensation. His uncertainty is the poet's attempt to deal unsparingly with the darkness of the tragic abyss. The question of the gods' existence and their care for human things is posed by Euripides experientially: given these circumstances and these characters and their choices, how do the characters experience the divine interaction with man—positively, negatively, or ambiguously?

Departing from those who see Euripides as a skeptic, I would argue that his depiction of the divine order is not a display of indifference. Charles Segal asks that moral praise or blame not be leveled against the god Dionysus in *The Bacchae*, (Segal 20), and I would ask the same for Euripides himself.[3] In these two plays, human willfulness is the primary cause of suffering, but the suffering opens up an abyss of ignorance about the divine. On the one hand, gods should intervene and do not, as in *Medea*, and on the other, they enter into human affairs so completely that they violate the most private things, as in *The Bacchae*. In general, Euripides' characters cannot say, "I am not guilty, but I have learned from my misfortune and am thus more free."[4] Human choice in the realm of unaided freedom lacks the means to attain the good intended. Imagined psychologically, the plays pose the following questions: without good fortune, how free is a human being? Is good fortune a blessing and bad fortune a curse of the gods, or is fortune altogether separate from the divine order? One cannot be sure that there are clear answers.

* * *

If Agamemnon could be said to sacrifice Iphigenia for a religious or political reason—in obedience to the goddess, or so that
his household would not be destroyed, or so that the army could
be unified—Medea by contrast hatches her plan herself, sacrificing
her children for one clear reason: so that she will not be left
alone in the abyss into which Jason's new marriage has plunged
her. Under Medea's edict, Jason will at least be reunited with her
in spiritual annihilation. The real horror of the play ultimately
lies not in the killing of the boys, a deed that we feel with emotional immediacy, but rather in something that emerges only
upon reflection: the fact that, after the killings, Jason recognizes
no difference in the quality of her love for him. He sees nothing about his own culpability or his violation of their sons.
Medea takes to its logical extreme his instrumental treatment of
their sons in order to speak the language of her own passion,
but her costly rhetoric of blood is lost on her husband. Even the
once sympathetic chorus cannot support this revenge. Nevertheless,
as Bernard Knox argues, Medea's revenge is sublime, turning a
human quality into a *theos* (306), and there is no suggestion in
the play that anyone, with the exception of Jason at the end,
regards Medea as a barbarian (Knox 311). To Jason, by killing
their sons, she becomes the other, the "monster" (1342), but
Knox concludes that in her thought, speech, and action, she is
as Greek as Jason, or rather, as Ajax and Achilles (311).

In *Medea* we also see the sublime horror accompanying a love
that is "too thick," as Paul D in *Beloved* describes the love of
child-killing Sethe. Out of Medea's thick love emerges a magnificent, outrageous response to what the Corinthian chorus soberly
states is a common experience for women—a husband's infidelity.
From the beginning, Medea had made her marriage itself the universal. Over and over she mastered impossible fortune for her
beloved.[5] Her jealousy, however, is almost an anomaly, because it
reveals *eros* and marriage at the same time, a pairing that is not
necessarily compatible. Medea is different from Clytemnestra, who,
as we know from Euripides' *Iphigenia in Aulis*, merely accommo-
dates herself to Agamemnon. Agamemnon forcibly took her from
her husband Tantalus, dashed her nursing baby to the ground,
and trod him underfoot—a non-felicitous courtship, to be sure. But

Medea passionately loves Jason; she demonstrates from the very beginning that she is ready to kill for his honor and to restore his kingship. Her violent acts against her own family make it impossible for her to go back to them. The intensity of *eros* has made her a stranger everywhere. Jason is not only the *oikos* but her whole world. Once profoundly grateful to her, he promised his undying troth. She felt herself loved as intensely as she loved. Thus, the crowning insult leveled at her by the wildly-grieving Jason after she kills their sons is this:

> When you were married
> To me, your husband, and had borne children to me,
> For the sake of pleasure in the bed, you killed them.
> (1336-1338)

He adds that he passed over many Greek women for a "monster," and he goes on to complain mournfully that he will "get no pleasure from newly wedded love" and that his life is over (1348-50).[6] Like most tragedies in which a dark outcome follows inexorably from some choice made before the action begins, Euripides' play makes us wonder what so blinded Medea that she wanted a man for whom the murder of her own kin would be the price—murders that could be blandly absorbed into Jason's pragmatic morality.

Medea's retrospective view locates the beginning of her tragic plunge with her mistaken trust: "My mistake was made the time I left behind me / My father's house, and trusted the words of a Greek" (800-1). Apparently, however, she employed her *sophe* (cleverness, with connotations of sophistic aptitude) only to have her devotion reductively interpreted as the pleasure of sex. In the dialogue before the murders, Euripides clearly exposes the character of her spouse. He shamelessly addresses his wife and family as "friends" whom he will not desert after their banishment by Creon. He will make "provisions" for them. But to his wife, this very rhetoric makes him the embodiment of "shamelessness." In the barbaric world the keeping of troth between men is the bond of all relationships, and their marriage bond was unusually marked by the male practice of clasping right hands.[7] He has broken their friendship—friends they were, shipmates on the *Argo*, fellow warriors, and now enemies. Indeed, she asks herself:

O God, you have given to mortals a sure method
Of telling the gold that is pure from the counterfeit;
Why is there no mark engraved upon men's bodies,
By which we could know the true ones from the false ones? (516-519)

Medea reduces all her husband's accomplishments to one: "A distinguished husband I have—for breaking promises" (510-511).

Greeks, as Medea suggests, are known for their perfidy. The historical context of the play gives her comments an additional sting. Produced in 431 B.C., the year recorded by Thucydides as the beginning of the Peloponnesian War, Medea invites the Athenians to examine what distinguishes them as a people—virtue or vice. Perhaps the "universal for the year" is that, as Thucydides later will observe after the plague, words in their ordinary relation to things were broken. In subsequent plays, such as Trojan Woman, Euripides surely has in mind Athenian excesses, such as the massacre of the Melians (Redfield 326). Is Euripides' depiction of Jason, like his own exodus to Macedonia in old age, a commentary on Athenian—indeed Greek—degeneration?

Medea, the stranger and the non-Greek, gains the sympathy of the chorus of Corinthian women in the household. These women come to acknowledge the bitter truth of what it is to be dismissed, to have one's defining reality in the world erased. The fate of all women becomes a major subject of this tragedy. At first the women of Corinth seem to take in stride the predicament she is in:

Suppose your man gives honor
to another woman's bed.
It often happens. Don't be hurt.
God will be your friend in this.
You must not waste away
Grieving too much for him who shared your bed. (154-59)

The emotions of this woman who embodies the full grief of the broken-hearted are trivialized by the worldly-wise women of Corinth, who live lightly, not caring too much. By contrast, Medea's love for Jason reveals a singular tenacity in love that knows no other law. Such a love, dangerous as it is, cannot be dismissed without disservice to an essential feminine expectation.

The women of Corinth—a city also known for its sacred prostitution—have not expected love from marriage. Up until now Medea
has banked her whole existence on what to them is no more than
a business arrangement. Is she a fool, or are they not as com-
pellingly female? When she explains to them, "But on me this
thing has fallen so unexpectedly," she expresses both her naiveté
and the palpable feeling of tragic circumstance. She continues,

> It has broken my heart. I am finished. I let go
> All my life's joy. My friends, I only want to die.
> It was everything to me to think well of one man,
> And he, my own husband, has turned out wholly vile. (225-227)

Medea's ode on the misery of women—a striking contrast to
Sophocles' choric ode to man in *Antigone*—reassesses her life
according to the usual lot of women. She speaks of the ironies
of paying a dowry to acquire a master whose customs and beliefs
she does not even know. Then she contrasts the male situation
in marriage with the female:

> A man, when he's tired of the company in his home,
> Goes out of the house and puts an end to his boredom
> And turns to a friend or companion of his own age.
> But we are forced to keep our eyes on one alone.
> What they say of us is that we have a peaceful time
> Living at home, while they do the fighting in war.
> How wrong they are! I would rather stand
> Three times in the front of battle than bear one child. (244-251)

By the end of the speech, Medea has succeeded in turning the
chorus around so that they now endorse her pending revenge.
After their dismissive urbanity, it is astonishing that they acqui-
esce in the ominous import of her final lines, where she says
that a woman might fear weapons in other contexts, "but, when
once she is wronged in the matter of love, / No other soul can
hold so many thoughts of blood (263-266). She asks them "Just
to keep silent," and they concede; in their tacitness, they sanction her revenge.

How does she do it? What does Medea unlock about the
dark side of female love? In a real sense, the murders are as

communal and female in this play as they are in *The Bacchae*. Acknowledging that she is dominated by *thymos*—"Fury that brings upon mortals the greatest evils"—Medea, unlike Agave, knows she is responsible for the nature of the terrible revenge she has devised (1079-1080). But like the possessed Theban, she also feels herself as lost, repeating it three times, and then claiming it is the gods' fault. She tells the old tutor: "Oh, I am forced to weep, old man. The gods and I, / In a kind of madness, have contrived all this" (1013-1014).[8] There is a terrifying insight here into the power of *thymos*, which is reflected, it seems, in the enduring power of the Furies, Aeschylus' *Eumenides* notwithstanding. Medea's curses upon Jason's fair head have awakened in the chorus a permanent insight also intimated by Sophocles' Deianeira in *The Women of Trachis* and by the painful stories of Philomela and Procne dramatized by Sophocles in his lost *Tereus*. The key insight is this: pragmatic accommodations in marriage are a reflection of pragmatic—and thus non-friendly—arrangements in the body politic.

One should remember that the word "friends," (*philoi*) not husband and wife, is used repeatedly in the play. Since Jason and Medea initially are allies in conflict with her own family, their alliance depends on maintaining mutual agreement about all the important decisions; when Jason breaks their friendship for his public standing, he breaks the troth upon which the private things depend. Public arrangements are at the expense of private honor and are thus effectual in the Machiavellian sense but not honorable or trustworthy. Medea calls Jason a coward who lacks "manliness." His boldness is that of the shameless who can "look friends in the face, friends you have injured" (470-471), and shamelessness is the worst of "human diseases." Deep truths in the play are painfully revealed precisely because of the crassness of Jason, whose base suggestions about the nature of his wife's love for him show that his management of their affairs has really been mere opportunism. Through Medea's speech the chorus comes to recognize how they have demeaned themselves by thinking only of expediency. Their change demonstrates that their resignation to their place as women is really a failure of character. But rejecting their pragmatic accommodation, they now side with Medea:

Flow backward to your sources, sacred rivers,

And let the world's great order be reversed.
It is the thoughts of men that are deceitful,
Their pledges that are loose.
Story shall now turn my condition to a fair one,
Women are paid their due.
No more shall evil-sounding fame be theirs.
Cease now, you muses of the ancient singers,
To tell the tale of my unfaithfulness;
For not on us did Phoebus, lord of music,
Bestow the lyre's divine
Power, for otherwise I should have sung an answer
To the other sex. Long time
Has much to tell of us, and much of them. (410-430)

The chorus concludes their agreement to her revenge by saying that "Good faith has gone, and no more remains / In great Greece a sense of shame" (439-440). Euripides thus makes himself the poet who first pays women their due. But the payment is ironic, to be sure, and it leaves the audience shocked by the extravagant cost.

Bernard Knox considers this passage a tour de force in Greek tragedy, for "all the songs, the stories, the whole literary and artistic tradition of Greece, which had created the lurid figures of the great sinners, Clytemnestra, Helen, and also the desirable figures of faithful Penelope and Andromache—all of it, Hesiod's catalogues of scandalous women, Semonides' rogues' gallery of women compared to animals, is dismissed" (315). I would add that there has been a political reordering when the chorus sings "Story shall now turn my condition to a fair one, / Women are paid their due. / No more shall evil-sounding fame be theirs" (416-420). Conjugal union mirrors the body politic: the marriage bond is the public word that binds the husband and wife to a public relationship without shame in the community. The irony is of course that the chorus heralds a new low in stories of what evil women can execute.

Knox argues that Medea expresses as a barbarian the Greek hero's Greek rage at injustice and dishonor. What she finds galling is that she is being dishonored for the sake of his honorable standing *apart from their partnership*. She regards him as honor-bound to her. According to Medea, this bond is sanctioned by divine order, as she argues in response to his utilitarian arguments:

> Faith in your word is gone. Indeed, I cannot tell
> Whether you think the gods whose names you swore by then
> Have ceased to rule and that new standards have been set up.
>
> (492-494)

Jason will not recognize her argument. He claims that he has made their children's position more secure by elevating his own social position, but he cannot seek his own good by going behind her back.[9] For Jason, love is an obstacle in serious, effectual life. In fact, he had rather be rid of women altogether but for the purpose of child-making. "Then," he concludes, "Life would have been good" (573-575).[10]

But can we sympathize with Medea after she kills her children? I suspect that most viewers, ancient or contemporary, lack the fortitude to keep up their sympathy for Medea. It is hard to affirm her deed, just as it is hard to grant Dionysus his right to revenge himself on Agave and her morally righteous son Pentheus for doubting that Semele was pregnant by Zeus. Unlike *The Oresteia* or the Oedipus plays, *Medea* and *The Bacchae* give no window of hope. Aeschylus' Eumenides and Medea do not dance the same dance. Instead, Medea chooses to stay in the Furies' place where there is "no joy." But then no one—certainly not Jason—can show her any compelling reason to do otherwise. There has been no Athene with sweet persuasion, only Apollonian logical argument.

Nevertheless, all this being said, there is a certain bracing clarity, a disconcerting pleasure, in Euripides' disciplined willingness to keep his play in the abyss. Medea's glorious prospect of emerging as the righter of wrongs for her sex dissolves when she uses the innocent to revenge herself against Jason, yet with this deed she obviates any chance of looking weak or laughable—merely another betrayed woman. The tragic pleasure does not lie in witnessing Creon's daughter withering away in the gorgeous gown, her head wildly on fire, or her father dissolving in poison. How can we tolerate her—or the play—after the triumph of a heroic *thymos* that can be exercised only by overcoming her love for her children? Is her fear of being ridiculed or laughed at so great that it compels her to kill those she loves the most? Is her vengeance on Jason's commensurate with his perfidy? Is *he* worth such a price? No, but apparently her own honor is.

But her elevation also completes the loss of her stance as the defender of women. She says early on that her masculine mind makes her feared and suspected, and the final destruction of her ground is the direct consequence of her planning and cleverness. Moreover, we are left with the terrible irony emerging whenever a thinking being, man or woman, tries to overcome fortune. Medea *is* remembered in fact as non-human, not because she is a goddess, but because her elevation has proceeded through defiance rather than reconciliation and acceptance. It is human to accept. Her desperate boldness proves her early statement to the Chorus that "Of all things which are living and can form a judgment / We women are the most *unfortunate* creatures" (230-231). In *Medea* the attraction of both self-determination and mutual love turn out to be problematic. Medea clearly will not be laughed at for trying to have both; truly she is serious and able to act on her seriousness no matter what the cost. And while she is clearly not happy, neither is she free. Honor-bound to her own logic of mutual pain as the new ground of their marriage, her words rouse her hurt and fire her *thymos*, so that she becomes the slave of her rhetoric and betrays the voice of her heart in the process. She has not acted like a man; neither has she unsexed herself. It is frankly hard to judge her at all. Helene Foley argues that "Medea never elsewhere indulges in such bloodless decision making; indeed, she aims in her revenge precisely to make Jason find the emotions he once rejected" (247).[11] Both sexes look overdetermined, and without the sympathetic Aegeus— duped into helping because he desires children of his own—she would have no escape and neither would the audience, vexed as the outcome is.

The murder of the children in the play is a shocking reminder that neither life nor tragedy culminates in a justice that conforms to rationality. When Euripides places Medea above the house at the end of the play in a chariot drawn by dragons, the children's still-warm corpses with her, Knox argues that he elevates her to a deity's stature because of her dark choice. "Achilles relents," he writes. "Medea does not. Her final words to Jason are full of contempt, hatred, and vindictive triumph; her rage is fiercer than the rage of Achilles, even of Ajax: it has in the end made her something more, and less, than human, something inhuman, a *theos*"

(315). Medea's rage, elevated to a divine plane, frees her from the human consequences of her deed and removes her to another level of meaning. The specter left by this play might be expressed in Dionysian terms. This is the domain of theater that releases citizens from the Apollonian frame of structure, from *nomos* generally, for a non-anarchical purpose. The end is to restore order, but—more than that—it is to give relief, to give pleasure and fulfillment to an intuited desire for unity. I would like to suggest that Medea's flight to Athens under its progenitor Aegeus and his unwitting protection of this murderess is parallel to the protection that tragic poetry affords us from our darkest distortions. Athens itself, then, begins in an attempt to get around the bad fortune of infertility. The final irony is that the cure for Aegeus' sterility comes from the child-murdering mother—an irony worthy of Dionysus.

❁   ❁   ❁

In his last play, Euripides makes the irony still more difficult to bear. Indeed, freedom turns out to be less attractive than it first appears to be in *The Bacchae*. Released from the household, the Asian Bacchants who make up the chorus of foreigners in Thebes are women freed from their children and their husbands, able to participate in a chaste sylvan frolic with beasts and nature. "And let the dance begin" (114), the chorus cries out:

> Follow...
> with a cry of Phrygian cries,
> when the holy flute like honey plays
> the sacred song of those who go
> *to the mountain!*
>   *to the mountain!—*
> —Then, in ecstasy like a colt by its grazing mother,
> the Bacchante runs with flying feet, she leaps! (159-167)

The maenads cry out with joy as they scale the mountain at Dionysus' command: "Blessed, blessed are those who know the mysteries of god," and "Blessed are the dancers and those who are purified, / who dance on the hill in the holy dance of god" (72, 76). It is in this beatitude—one accompanied by dancing—that a woman knows freedom. Everything oppressive seems lifted away in the maenads' leaping worship. Not social constraints, but desire itself governs one's choices. The god's great gift of wine frees memory from its sorrows, bringing an unearned freedom from care. If Asclepius frees the body from its ills and pains, Dionysus does the same for the soul. Paired imaginatively, with their temples in close proximity in Athens, both gods renew life, *zoe*.

There is a problem, however, with this benign picture of Bacchic revelry. We know, from the very beginning of the play, that Dionysus is in earnest about participation in his kind of pleasure. Though a new god, he expects the piety reserved for the Olympians. In his opening lines, he proclaims his purpose—to make Thebes an example to other Greek cities. The Thebans will participate in his rituals, he declares, or else they will be "compelled to wear my orgies' livery" (34). If they do not recognize him and acknowledge his mother Semele and his father—Zeus himself—great grief rather than peaceful primordial unity will result. Ancient spectators came to protest that the relation of the plays to Dionysus grew more and more attenuated. If, as the quip developed, the plays had "nothing to do with Dionysus" (Winkler and Zeitlin 3), we might complain that the tragedy dealing most directly with his myth and cult yields the least clarity about his greatest gift—freedom. Indeed, *The Bacchae* leaves us confused, unable to make clear cause and effect statements about the relation between pleasure and responsibility. It leaves us in the depths of freedom, where freedom itself eludes us. How can we celebrate a divine gift that we cannot hold onto? We might conclude with good reason that in this play reputed to be the last of Greek tragedies, the god of birth and rebirth is shown to be the one most malicious of all. George Steiner writes that Euripides' *Bacchae* "stands in some special proximity to the ancient, no longer discernible springs of tragic feeling." He goes on to discuss the inordinate punitive measures against the house of Cadmus at the end of the play. Dionysus' explanation that Thebes is simply doomed means that "there is no use asking for rational explanation or mercy. Things are as they are, unrelenting and absurd. We are punished far in excess of our guilt" (Steiner 9). Better not to be born—that's the simple truth at the heart of the tragic abyss.

An opposing view of *The Bacchae* is that its disturbing aspects awaken its reader to a new awareness of that primal unity with oneself, with the natural world, with each other, and with the divine order. Intoxication has its benefits. In the experience of seeing double, which is exemplified in Pentheus' seeing two suns and two Thebes, intoxication opens one to many planes of existence at once. On the face of it, Pentheus appears to have flipped over into madness. In fact, Dionysus instructs his Bacchants to "first distract his wits; / bewilder him with madness" (850-851). But this unbalanced state allows him to see for the first time the doubleness that truly abides in things. The gift of Dionysus is analogous to the multivalent vision that poetry allows. The problem is that seeing the paradox and contradiction in things looks like madness to the linear mind. The riddle-laden responses of the stranger Dionysus exasperates Pentheus. Why aren't the meanings of things plain? Why do mysteries and their adherents, who claim that in them abide a complete account of things, have to be so irrational?

In an attempt to identify the different manifestations of irrational but meaningful speech, Plato has Socrates speak in the *Phaedrus* of four kinds of madness and their sources: poetry (the Muses), ritual (Dionysus), prophecy (Apollo) and eros (Aphrodite). All four levels of madness are manifest in the action of *The Bacchae*, and all levels are attributed to Dionysus alone. The category of madness helps draw attention to the nature of Pentheus' problem—one common to "responsible" men of affairs: he cannot submit to mystery because it isn't manageable. He cannot relinquish the position that *he* is fully in charge. It irks him that his domain of political rule has proven vulnerable and that his leadership has been made to look ineffectual. It enrages him that his grandfather and Teiresias thwart his will by donning the Bacchic trappings, but the deepest humiliation for Pentheus is that he has not been able to control the women. "We are disgraced, humiliated in the eyes / of Hellas" (779-780). He feels threatened by the otherness of mystery; it is something outside the normal boundaries of ordered, predictable human affairs.

What shocks and horrifies the contemporary reader is the same kind of thing that horrifies Pentheus, a budding tyrant, as the young ruler of Thebes. Dionysian mysteries that connect the god with women and wine, birth and rebirth, death and resurrection, concealment and revelation, also endanger the natural, moral, and lawful order as Pentheus sees it from the perspective of rational doubt. Pentheus, we might say, has been raised by skeptics, as have most "educated" Athenian young people.[12] Pentheus' mother, Agave, and his aunts refuse to acknowledge their sister's coupling with Zeus and thus refuse to recognize the miraculous birth of Dionysus, itself a triumph over Hera's jealousy. They would rather think the worse of their sister than grant the possibility that their family and their city has been chosen to be blessed.

No evidence is enough for this kind of doubting mind. A house still smoking—the vines wrapping around it, richly growing nonetheless—is not convincing enough as a sign of Semele's privileged union. *The Bacchae*'s particularly lasting power may lie in its unsparing depiction of the perennial human failure to distinguish between honest questioning that leads to wonder and a dishonest skepticism that wards off the power of the holy in order to protect the rational status quo. This tendency is rooted in a false view of freedom that sees humanly made order as order itself. Not free to believe, Pentheus does not even know who he himself is, according to Dionysus. His assurance comes from an ignorance of self. "Do not be so certain that power / is what matters in the life of man; do not mistake / for wisdom the fantasies of your sick mind," Teiresias suggests (310-313). The weight of Pentheus' name, meaning "man of suffering" (Kerenyi 193), increasingly bears upon the spectator, even as Pentheus remains blind and boldly defiant of the divinity of his cousin. And all the time he is disavowing Dionysus' divine sonship, he exposes his prurient interest in spying on what he presumes are the sexual licenses of his mother, aunts, and other Theban maenads. The fragmented character of Pentheus' soul thus is exposed long before the pieces of his dismembered body clutter Mt. Cithaeron.

Pentheus is the double of his cousin Dionysus, the god who presides over the form of tragedy with its characteristic rending of the body. Dionysus is the dismembered god who is reintegrated or remembered. And what is being remembered? Man's essential freedom through the total loss of freedom. Euripides' *Bacchae* is the play about the god of tragedy to whom the Great Dionysia was dedicated every spring, the rites which preceded the competing plays; judgment followed them and a prize was given, with the highest official in democratic Athens, the *archon*, awarding it. Modern scholarship focuses on Dionysus more than on any other god (Goldhill 126). One might say that Dionysus appears where the fragility of freedom is broken by dishonest skepticism, a fundamental mistrust of fortune that leads one to deny that the holy encompasses the everyday. It is this skepticism that is deadly; it kills the possibility of renewal and redemption in people of both sexes, young and old, and in the institutions that should sustain them. In keeping the laws and customs antiseptic, as it were, a city closes out creativity. Such a city is suspicious of play because it is not engaged in the serious things of life—the criticism leveled at both philosophy and poetry. But as Johan Huizinga has shown in *Homo Ludens*, true play is always serious.

What happens when a community refuses to celebrate human freedom, to ritualize pleasure? What happens when it will not risk believing in what naturally pleases? What happens if we only worship work and productivity—when play is not for its own sake but only so that we might be more effectual in our work? We might ask ourselves these questions with some terror after reading this play. There is nothing particularly human about a regime or an education that places conformity above pleasure. Indeed, as Plato's Athenian Stranger says, the first activity of the human being within the womb is leaping, and that pleasure is still expressed in adulthood. The philosopher's life is a dance with wisdom. As Platonic thought exposes the utilitarian motives of the sophists, so the Dionysian spirit disdains those who place their practical lives above the festive celebration of life itself. Dionysus hates "him who scoffs" and "him who mocks his life, / the happiness of those / for whom the day is blessed / but doubly blessed the night" (423-426). The "rich and poor" are indiscriminately given the "simple gift of wine" (421). The chorus praises the common sense of ordinary folk.

Teiresias tries to instruct Pentheus that from Dionysus' gift of wine "comes sleep; with it oblivion of the troubles of the day. There is no other medicine for misery" (281-282). The chorus asks, "When shall I dance once more / with bare feet the all-night dances, / tossing my head for joy?" The chorus longs to be "free from fear of the hunt, free from the circling beaters." They long to be "leaping for joy, to dance for joy in the forest, to dance where the darkness is deepest, where no man is" (862-877). As liberating as these lines are, we must bear in mind the circumscribed range of this kind of freedom. Dionysus is a democratic god, but

as in the eighth book of Plato's *Republic*, *The Bacchae* highlights
the fine line between democracy and tyranny. Dionysus' powers do
bring a surcease to pain. But looking at the androgynous figure
before him, with his soft curls and white skin, Pentheus pinpoints
the sinister side to Dionysian pleasure: his fair skin "comes from
the night when you hunt Aphrodite with your beauty" (457).
Unwittingly acknowledging the god's power in the secrets of desire,
Pentheus suggests the very way his own dark desires will be
exposed. Dionysus has hunted down Pentheus' desire to spy on the
women, a desire so keen that he agrees to disguise himself as a
woman. "He fed on his desires," (618) the god as stranger explains
to the chorus. True, many opportunities are given Pentheus to
change his attitude to his god-cousin; his only risk would be not
to seem to exert total control. Still, *sparagmos* is a high price to
pay for not wanting his women to go off to the woods. Dionysus
is a democratic god, but he is a tyrant god to tyrants.

Why is he so merciless? An unconsoling but absolute explanation is that Dionysus himself is under a natural law that no
man's law exceeds: "Whatever long time has sanctioned, / that is
a law forever; / the law tradition makes / is the law of nature"
(894-895). And then, ironically undercutting the seriousness of
belief, just as Cadmus did in his Pascalian wager, they add
"Small, small is the cost to believe in this" (893). But the cost
of unbelief is unfathomable. Jean-Pierre Vernant writes that

> in no circumstance does [Dionysus] ever come to announce a better
> fate in the beyond. He does not urge men to flee the world nor does
> he claim to offer a soul access to immortality achieved through a life
> of asceticism. On the contrary, men must accept their mortal condi-
> tion, recognize that they are nothing compared with the powers that
> are beyond them on every side and are able to crush them utterly. The
> god has no need to explain himself. He is alien to our norms and
> customs, alien to our preoccupations, beyond good and evil, supremely
> sweet and supremely terrible. His pleasure is to summon up the mul-
> tiple aspects of otherness around us and within us. (Vernant 411)

Given Vernant's assessment, we might legitimately charge that
Euripides' tragedy about the god of tragedy has nothing to do
with freedom. If he does not promise eternal freedom, why
should we bother with him? What is beautiful or desirable about

an inexplicable abyss guaranteed by the nature of human mortality, by the way things are constituted?

Yet there remains the conviction that if the play ended any other way, we would be spared the full effect of the tragedy. Therefore, we would miss the full exploration of the depths of lost freedom, freedom wasted out of fear and mistrust of the unexpected power of divine epiphany. The usual and the traditional stultify without the resources of divine possibility. Like the surprise of poetry, divine epiphany restores wonder. How can life go on if nothing remarkable is still being witnessed to? I am suggesting that Euripides asked himself these questions as he conceived this play, and then he conceived it with this question in mind above all: what will it take imaginatively to bring about a Dionysian catharsis, one that will lead the latent skepticism in each of us to take seriously the pleasure of freedom?

The play comes to an imaginative focus, not on Pentheus, but on Agave. It is in her horror that we experience the tragic abyss. At the very moment she boasts to her father of her hunting victory, just as she exults in leaving the shuttle and loom for the hunt, she is made by Cadmus to look up, away from the lion cub's downy head, only to lower her head then and see it as her own beloved son. Does she become a true believer after this experience? No. Her last words to the chorus are: "Let me go / where I shall never see Cithaeron more, / where that accursed hill may not see me" (1384-1386). Do we blame her for her impious attitude? Leave piety to others, she says. This is the pessimism of which George Steiner writes. But does her final defiance give the meaning of the play its definitive shape? If so, we would go away from the *Bacchae* ironically celebrating the sublime insight into the nature of freedom revealed in a mother unwittingly attacking her own son and then being exiled for being polluted. One can moralize about what Agave should have done, but such a line of resolution seems callous and fruitless.

Tragedy evokes pity and terror—one of the great Aristotelian understatements when it comes to *The Bacchae*. All poses adopted for the sake of *nomos*, including civil religion, fail to hold up. Nothing said to be dependable can withstand the inexorable, downward pull. While the action makes the spectator very aware of human limits—and those limitations are the constant tragic refrain—we awaken from tragedy as if aware of the consequences of freedom for the first time, both privately and socially. We can be free only when we know *how* we are not. While comic action yields a malleable knowledge of the human predicament, tragic knowledge resists taming. It refuses to be domesticated. And, while comic knowledge celebrates the body in all its potential grossness and joy, tragic action tests our capacity to welcome all the painful consequences of having a body. It demands a brutally honest realignment of affective life.

The Athenian tragedians are their city's harshest critics. To be sure they heap their most unsparing criticism on the city of Thebes, but that scapegoating displacement imaginatively allows the Athenians a needed distance from themselves. Athens was known for tremendous cruelty. Thucydides reports, for instance, that the free citizens of Melos begged the Athenian assembly simply to allow them to remain independent in the Peloponnesian War. Athens had nothing to gain except the reputation for power, but in order to assert their superiority, the Athenians killed all the men and enslaved the women, erasing in one stroke 700 years of Melian self-rule. One way to put the most basic and general human nub of truth revealed in Agave's horror is this: we cannot often see the murder we have committed, even when we hold our prey in our own hands. We see it as alien one moment, and in the next, we recognize it as what is dearest to us, though the recognition is too late and ineffectual. The nature of freedom is that its preservation depends on our not being deluded by its intoxications. These two plays open up the abyss anterior to those choices made in the false confidence that fortune can be mastered. The incomplete nature of all human choices seems at the root of all failed ones. Finally, freedom depends upon remembering who we are. It is our good fortune that Euripidean tragedy helps us do so.

NOTES

[1] Parenthetical references to Euripides' texts are to the line numbers in the Warner and Arrowsmith translations.

[2] Kathleen Kelly Marks' work with Toni Morrison's *Beloved*, reflected in her essay later in this volume, first made me aware of this useful term. In his essay on Sophocles, Bainard Cowan points out that hero cults, considered by some the origin of tragic

practice, were apotropaic, meant to stave off the monstrous aspects of the ancestral hero.

3 His view is not as bleak as that articulated by the chorus of *Oedipus at Colonus* when they observe the most unfortunate of all, the wanderer Oedipus. They chant, "Not to be born is best of all." Compare Nietzsche (42) on the "wisdom of Silenus."

4 However, in his *Iphigeneia at Aulis*, Euripides gives us the paradigm of the figure who can say so even as she accepts her status as a sacrificial victim.

5 It is helpful to note that her name means the very parts of the body meant for sex—*medea* means genitals, and in the *Iliad*, *medea* doubles in meaning as the genitals and the plan of Zeus. Medea herself is *a fortiori* the realization of clever planning and erotic attachment.

6 This assessment of his prospects should not be seen as out of character. Earlier in the play, Jason dismisses his wife's affection for him concisely:

> My view is that Cypris was alone responsible
> Of men and gods for the preserving of my life.
> You are clever enough—but really I need not enter
> Into the story of how it was love's inescapable
> Power that compelled you to keep my person safe. (17)

Then, after his dismissal of her love for him, as one being ordained by the goddess, he condescendingly credits his acceptance of it as that which allowed her to be with Greeks who alone value her cleverness.

7 "In the standard marriage the man grasps the woman's wrist in a gesture of domination" (Foley 259).

8 Bernard Knox draws parallels to Procne's ode in Sophocles' lost *Tereus* (Knox 312).

9 Pietro Pucci writes that Medea's views of marriage look to the *diké* of love, rather than to actual marital practices. Her views, he says are "probably upheld both by religious feelings and by epic and mythical representations" (Pucci 63).

10 Without troth-keeping, life would be good. Machiavelli had the same advice for *The Prince*.

11 Foley considers it insufficient to oppose Medea's reason to her spiritedness, as some commentators do, thus making her an example of the Aristotelian divided self. Foley instead points to Euripidean exposure of woman's incapacity to stay within femi-

nine categories and still revenge as a man would, i.e., according to the Greek heroic ideal (243-271).

[12] Aristophanes' play *The Clouds* is the comic version of this scenario.

Part Three

THE CANCELED

BOND

Come, seeling night,
Scarf up the tender eye of pitiful day,
And with thy bloody and invisible hand
Cancel and tear to pieces that great bond
Which keeps me pale!

MACBETH (3.2.46-60)

9

Fathoming "Cliffs of Fall Frightful":
Hamlet's Mappings

JUDITH STEWART SHANK

> O the mind, mind has mountains; cliffs of fall
> Frightful, sheer, no-man-fathomed. Hold them cheap
> May who ne'er hung there. Nor does long our small
> Durance deal with that steep or deep.... (152)
> Gerard Manley Hopkins

It could be said that these lines from one of Hopkins' "Dark Sonnets" embody the experience of Hamlet—with one crucial exception. The evocative word "fathom" has two related meanings: first, to find the bottom or extent of something, to measure its depth and sound it; secondly, to reach or penetrate with the mind, to get to the bottom of something, to comprehend it thoroughly and master it. Hamlet is the exception to Hopkins' vision of the frightful cliffs of fall, because Hamlet fathoms the abyss in both senses of the word: he plummets to its depths, and he fully comprehends and masters its nature. *Hamlet* is Shakespeare's mapping of the tragic abyss, and Hamlet is the mapmaker.

In the archetypal tragic pattern, the protagonist falls into sin, discovers his culpability, and chooses either to accept his guilt and its consequences or to deny his guilt and persist in that evil which leads to despair.[1] Hamlet is unique among tragic protagonists in that the inevitable vision of his own fallenness and original sin occurs *before* the action by which he fears to bring guilt upon himself.[2] Hamlet fathoms the nature of the tragic abyss, not in retrospect, but in prospect. From the time the Ghost issues his commandments, Hamlet explores with increasing horror the paradoxical contours of the vast darkness before him and finds that, being a man, there is no way he can escape guilt through his own actions.

Hamlet's "world-sorrow" is, of course, evident from the beginning of the play: "O God, God, / How weary, stale, flat, and unprofitable / Seem to me all the uses of this world!" (1.2.132-34). What apparently has not been evident to many is the *cause* of this sorrow and overwhelming disgust. Hamlet has been accused of being indecisive, excessively self-reflective, neurotic, genuinely insane, and suicidal, none of which diagnoses a close reading of the play bears out. Hamlet's disgust rises from his ever-increasing vision of the depths of human fallenness—in other words, from coming face to face with the inescapable fact of original sin, that "age-old anvil" on which his cries "wince and sing" (to quote Hopkins once more): for, as Hamlet says to Ophelia, "virtue cannot so inoculate our old stock but we shall relish of it" (3.1.17-19). Hamlet's disgust flows from his realization that man's ontological dwelling is in the house of guilt.

Thus we find Hamlet in his first soliloquy, *before* he has seen the ghost of his murdered father, articulating his dawning awareness that something is terribly, terribly wrong with the postlapsarian world and those fallen men and women who inhabit it, with the "too too sullied flesh" of incarnate man:

> O that this too too sullied flesh would melt,
> Thaw, and resolve itself into a dew,
> Or that the Everlasting had not fixed
> His canon 'gainst self-slaughter. O God, God,
> How weary, stale, flat, and unprofitable
> Seem to me all the uses of this world!
> Fie on't, ah, fie, 'tis an unweeded garden
> That grows to seed. Things rank and gross in nature
> Possess it merely. (1.2.129-37)

What has precipitated this disgust is not only his mother's "o'er-hasty" marriage with his uncle but also his burgeoning doubt that appearances genuinely reflect reality. As he has said to Gertrude, "I know not 'seems' " (1.2.76); yet, faced with the "dexterity" with which Gertrude has posted "to incestuous sheets," Hamlet now doubts whether his mother's love for his father had ever been what it seemed. In his youth, Hamlet saw Gertrude hang upon his father, "As if increase of appetite had grown / By what it fed on," and yet within a month after following King Hamlet's dead body "like Niobe, all tears," Gertrude married Claudius. How then, Hamlet questions, could Gertrude have truly loved his father, as she seemed to? Even a beast, he exclaims, would have mourned longer than one "little month," before the tears dried in her eyes or her funeral shoes grew old. Nor can Hamlet console himself with the idea that Gertrude has merely sought an approximation to her lost husband, since Claudius, Hamlet says, is "no more like my father / Than I to Hercules" (1.2.143-56). The discrepancy between appearance and reality—"seeming" and being, "acting" and acting—is one of the dominant themes of the play.

Worthy of notice also in Hamlet's first soliloquy is his dismissal of suicide as an alternative for a disgusted and world-sorrowing man. Hamlet is a Christian. In his first soliloquy, the acceptance of suicide as a sin and its consequent dismissal from the realm of possible actions is stated in all simplicity: "O that... the Everlasting had not fixed / His canon [law] 'gainst self-slaughter" (1.2.129-32). In his disgust with humankind and the world, does Hamlet, in his first soliloquy, cry that he wishes suicide were an option? Yes. Is it obvious that Hamlet, the Christian, accepts the fact that suicide is *not* an option? Yes. The cry of the tragic protagonist, from Job to Oedipus to Lear, has ever been "Cursed be the day that e'er I was born," but it is one thing—and an altogether human thing—to voice one's despair over living in a fallen world and entirely another thing to act upon that despair by committing suicide. At no time in the play does Hamlet actually contemplate suicide. It is mentioned and dismissed in his first soliloquy, and suicide is not the contemplated action of the "To be, or not to be" soliloquy, despite its being so played by many, though not all, Shakespearean actors.[3]

The "To be, or not to be" soliloquy is about whether the contemplated *action* (Hamlet's execution of Claudius) is "to be"; the question is whether Hamlet is to bring the *action* into being. That is why Hamlet refers, at the end of the soliloquy, to "enterprises of great pitch and moment"; it is high and momentous enterprises which "lose the name of action" because of the possibility of judgment and damnation after death, which is Hamlet's theme in this soliloquy. The Christian Hamlet, who is so very noble and possesses, as do all the greatest Shakespearean characters, a fully developed imagination, would never speak of suicide as an "enterprise of great pitch and moment"; only the most vain and deluded of men could so regard themselves and their own ultimate act of despair, and Hamlet is not among them.

Indeed, it is nobility which Hamlet first ponders in this soliloquy, as a consequence of asking whether the action is to be or not. Is it nobler simply to suffer in the mind, or is it nobler "to take arms against a sea of troubles" and thus end them by active opposition? If he were to act, then what? Being mortal, he knows that at some point, probably as a consequence of acting, he will die. What then? What happens at death? Does death issue only in an eternal sleep? If, when we die, we do *no more* than sleep—"To die, to sleep— / No more" [than sleep]—and all the heartaches "and the thousand natural shocks / That flesh is heir to" are ended in that eternal sleep, then why not act? Why not take arms against the sea of troubles and end them? But, on the other hand, if "in that sleep of death" dreams perchance may come, we must pause before acting and reflect upon the consequences of our actions. The dreams which may come in the sleep of death are an image of divine judgment and its consequent damnation or salvation. These reflections about consequences—about the guilt we may incur for our actions—are why men bear calamity for so long without acting, why they "bear the whips and scorns of time." It is the fear of judgment and damnation—"the dread of something after death"—which "puzzles the will" to action "And makes us rather bear those ills we have, / Than fly to others that we know not of." Death is "The undiscovered country, from whose bourn / No traveler returns." Hamlet cannot be sure that his action will not result in his damnation after death. It is concern about the eternal fate of his soul which causes Hamlet's "native hue of resolution" to be "sicklied o'er with the pale cast of thought." It is the desire not to be damned for his action which "turns awry" the currents of the momentous enterprise of slaying Claudius and makes that enterprise "lose the name of action." It is not insignificant that Hamlet's greeting to the "fair Ophelia," who enters at the end of this soliloquy, is a request that she remember all Hamlet's sins in her prayers (3.1.56-89).

Bertram Joseph has observed that the "To be, or not to be" soliloquy should be regarded as a continuation of Hamlet's previous soliloquy, in which Hamlet, goaded by the passion with which the Player has rendered Hecuba's suffering, examines his own reasons for delay in fulfilling his promise to the Ghost (2.2.560-617). This soliloquy, which closes Act Two in most current editions of *Hamlet*, precedes the "To be, or not to be" soliloquy by no more than fifty-five lines, and Joseph further notes that, according to "the good Quarto and the First Folio," there was no act division at this point in the manuscript. Thus, audiences of Shakespeare's time would have heard, first, the soliloquy in which Hamlet questions his reasons for delay, confirms the necessity of ascertaining that a devil in the form of his father's ghost is not ensnaring him, and plans to acquire "evidence" of Claudius' iniquity, followed almost immediately by Hamlet's further meditations in the "To be, or not to be" soliloquy on the possibility of being damned for slaying Claudius as the cause of his delay (Joseph 110-11). Thus, as has been said, Hamlet's concern in this soliloquy is with the potential consequences of his action in slaying Claudius, not with the consequences of slaying himself.

But with his profound and contemplative soul, Hamlet sees in his own particular situation an instance of universal human experience. Were it not for reflections about guilt and damnation, who would bear "Th' oppressor's wrong, the proud man's contumely, / The pangs of despised love, the law's delay, / The insolence of office... Who would fardels bear, / To grunt and sweat under a weary life...?" Any man who thus suffers, Hamlet sees, could take on himself the making of his own "quietus" "With a bare bodkin [dagger]"—that is, any man could be quit of all that oppresses him by thrusting a dagger into the agent of all which he suffers or, alternatively, into himself (3.1.71-73, 75-77). It is perhaps this passage in Hamlet's soliloquy, especially when taken out of context with those "enterprises of great pitch and moment" toward which the soliloquy moves, which has led interpreters to think that Hamlet is contemplating his own suicide. But in this part of his soliloquy, Hamlet is pondering human anguish and the fear of taking action to end it on a *universal*, not a personal, scale. Moreover, the word "quietus" is a legal term which means a full discharge or release from debt, obligation, or office and therefore conveys a range of possibilities in terms of action.[4] In Hamlet's case, he would be released from his obligation to his father's ghost and the debt of his own promise to avenge his father's murder by executing Claudius; he would be discharged from his heaven-appointed office of "scourge and minister" (3.4.174-76). But, as

Hamlet sees his situation at this point in the play, he would
thereby also put his soul in peril.

For the Christian Hamlet, the possibility of damnation is his
dilemma. How does one, as a Christian, and not in self-defense
or war, kill another human being? More especially, how does a
Christian prince kill his uncle, his mother's husband, and his
king? Hamlet, with all his excellence of forethought, can imagine
the chaos that will afflict Denmark if Claudius is killed. The consequences of the death of kings—even evil kings—permeate Shakespearean drama with particular ominousness, and for all that
Rosencrantz is a sycophant, his speech to Claudius on that subject rings true:

> The cess of majesty
> Dies not alone, but like a gulf doth draw
> What's near it with it; or it is a massy wheel
> Fixed on the summit of the highest mount,
> To whose huge spokes ten thousand lesser things
> Are mortised and adjoined, which when it falls,
> Each small annexment, petty consequence,
> Attends the boist'rous ruin. Never alone
> Did the King sigh, but with a general groan. (3.3.15-23)

Hamlet, however, faces a still more profound question: how does
he know by whom (or what) he has been charged to kill
Claudius? He has nothing to act upon but the word of a ghost,
and Hamlet has ample evidence that words do not always express
the truth. No earthly court mandates him; he has no legal sanction, and—however disordered its current condition—Denmark presumably has its laws and trials to ascertain guilt and render
judgment. In any case, Hamlet is prince of a state, not a state-
appointed executioner. Thus the Christian Hamlet says:

> The spirit that I have seen
> May be a devil, and the devil hath power
> T'assume a pleasing shape, yea, and perhaps
> Out of my weakness and my melancholy,
> As he is very potent with such spirits,
> Abuses me to damn me. (2.2.610-15)

And again, as he lays the plot for the play and asks Horatio to observe Claudius "with the very comment" of his soul, Hamlet says:

> If [Claudius'] occulted guilt
> Do not itself unkennel in one speech,
> It is a damnèd ghost that we have seen,
> And my imaginations are as foul
> As Vulcan's stithy. (3.2.82-86)

Hamlet's instinctive response when he first sees the Ghost is a prayer: "Angels and ministers of grace defend us!" Is the apparition before his eyes a sanctified soul or a devil?

> Be thou a spirit of health or goblin damned,
> Bring with thee airs from heaven or blasts from hell,
> Be thy intents wicked or charitable,
> Thou com'st in such a questionable shape
> That I will speak to thee. (1.4.39-44)

It is unholy that a Christian soul, buried according to the sacraments of the church, should again walk the earth—that it should, as Horatio has already said, "usurp" the night and the form of the dead King Hamlet. Why, Hamlet cries, should his father's "canonized bones" have "burst their cerements"? Why should the sepulcher in which King Hamlet was "quietly interred" have cast him up again? (1.4.47-51) Can such an aberration from all Christian doctrine and belief be anything but demonic?

After the Ghost charges Hamlet with revenging his murder by Claudius and vanishes, Hamlet vows, "thy commandment all alone shall live / Within the book and volume of my brain" (1.5.102-03). But now Hamlet is caught between two commandments: the Ghost's "Revenge his foul and most unnatural murder" and God's "Thou shalt not kill." Hamlet is in the situation we have come to call a "double-bind"; he has fallen into the crevasse of paradox—literally damned if he does and damned if he doesn't. Hamlet's delay in acting, so often attributed to neurotic indecision or some sort of Prufrockian hyper-consciousness, is due to neither of these but to his being caught in a situation in which he can see no way to act without incurring guilt.

Indeed, the first image implanted in Hamlet's mind by the Ghost is that of the tortures—the "sulf'rous and tormenting flames"—not even of hell, but of purgatory. For King Hamlet, as he tells his son, was "Cut off even in the blossoms" of his sin and died unabsolved, "No reck'ning made, but sent to [his] account / With all [his] imperfections on [his] head" (1.5.76, 78-79). The Ghost's term of purgation is finite, but its terrors are such that, were he not forbidden to communicate this revelation of eternity to the living, he could horrify Hamlet:

> I could a tale unfold whose lightest word
> Would harrow up thy soul, freeze thy young blood,
> Make thy two eyes like stars start from their spheres,
> Thy knotted and combinèd locks to part,
> And each particular hair to stand an end
> Like quills upon the fearful porpentine. (1.5.15-20)

If such "fasting in fires," such a "prison house," is the temporal fate of the merely unabsolved, what images of the horror of eternal damnation must invade Hamlet's mind?

And yet Hamlet has fallen even more deeply into the crevasse of paradox than has thus far been conveyed, for the Ghost issues, not one, but *three* commandments, saying, "If thou didst ever thy dear father love—," then: 1. "Revenge his foul and most unnatural murder"; 2. "Let not thy soul contrive / Against thy mother aught"; and 3. "But howsomever thou pursues this act, / Taint not thy mind...." (1.5.23, 25, 84-86). What a commandment is this last, that Hamlet must revenge his father's murder without tainting his own mind! Not only must he not damn his own soul, but he must find a way to revenge the murder that leaves his mind pure, unstained, untroubled, and at peace. And yet revenge, as Hamlet knows, is not a Christian act, even if commanded by a less dubious authority than a ghost. Hamlet's task, then, is, not only to revenge his father's murder, but to do it without damning his soul *or* tainting his mind. The mark of Hamlet's engulfment in the tragic abyss is the profound suffering into which he is plunged by the paradoxical nature of his task.

However, paradox in tragedy teaches. What it teaches Hamlet is that there *is* no way, being human, that he can escape guilt through his own actions or, to put it another way, that he can know with certainty that he will not incur guilt by acting. As Hamlet looks within himself for that spiritual place from which he could act in innocence, he discovers progressively that, because he is human, there is no such place. Hamlet's entrapment by paradox leads him to the insight that man's ontological position in the universe is that of the guilty one—in other words, to the insight that the time has been out of joint ever since the Fall from the Garden. To ascend from the abyss will demand of Hamlet a transformation: a face-to-face encounter with original sin as a reality within the souls of all men, including himself, despite deceptive appearances of virtue.

The themes of appearance-vs.-reality and the fallenness of mankind are intertwined from the beginning of the play. Hamlet's questioning of the reality of his mother's love for his father is verified by the Ghost's contemptuous description of Claudius and his liaison with Gertrude:

> Ay, that incestuous, that adulterate beast,
> With witchcraft of his wits, with traitorous gifts—
> O wicked wit and gifts, that have the power
> So to seduce!—won to his shameful lust
> The will of my most seeming-virtuous queen.
> O Hamlet, what a falling-off was there,
> From me, whose love was of that dignity
> That it went hand in hand even with the vow
> I made to her in marriage, and to decline
> Upon a wretch whose natural gifts were poor
> To those of mine.
> But virtue, as it never will be moved,
> Though lewdness court it in a shape of heaven,
> So lust, though to a radiant angel linked,
> Will sate itself in a celestial bed
> And prey on garbage. (1.5.42-57)

With the Ghost's use of the words "adulterate" and "seeming-virtuous"; his description of Gertrude's having been won over to lust for Claudius; his distinction between the sacramental love of marriage and the "decline" to extra-marital lust, the Ghost simultaneously intensifies Hamlet's distrust of appearances and his perception of the depths of human fallenness—so easily is mankind seduced to "prey on garbage."

As Hamlet, hiding behind his "antic disposition" in the depths of the tragic darkness, struggles to ascertain the reality of the Ghost and to fulfill his commandments, he is further confounded by the "seeming" of Ophelia, who, obeying her shallow and devious father, has presented to Hamlet the appearance of not loving him. What, and whom, in this visible world, can he trust? To his childhood friends, Rosencrantz and Guildenstern, he voices his world-disgust and ever-increasing awareness of human fallenness:

> I have of late, but wherefore I know not, lost all my mirth, forgone all custom of exercises; and indeed, it goes so heavily with my disposition that this goodly frame, the earth, seems to me a sterile promontory; this most excellent canopy, the air, look you, this brave o'erhanging firmament, this majestical roof fretted with golden fire: why, it appeareth nothing to me but a foul and pestilent congregation of vapors. What a piece of work is a man, how noble in reason, how infinite in faculties, in form and moving how express and admirable, in action how like an angel, in apprehension how like a god: the beauty of the world, the paragon of animals; and yet to me, what is this quintessence of dust? (2.2.303-17)

Yet these friends in whom he confides have answered Claudius' and Gertrude's summons, and they will attempt to play upon him as on a pipe, as Hamlet says, to lie to him, snare, and sound him, and "pluck out the heart of [his] mystery" (3.2.372-74).

But it is in Hamlet's well-known "nunnery" scene with Ophelia, which immediately follows the "To be, or not to be" soliloquy, that the agony of Hamlet's deepening vision of man's—and his own—fallenness is most fully articulated (3.1.90-152). Hamlet's behavior toward Ophelia in this scene has been much maligned. His attitude has been interpreted as misogynistic and abusive. But we must first remember that Ophelia, however pathetically, has placed herself among those whom Hamlet cannot trust. Much more importantly, however, we must see the essence of the scene as Hamlet's expression of his disgust with the fallen condition of all humanity, including himself. Because he *loves* Ophelia, he expresses to her the depths of his despair, although she does not understand it and indeed goes beyond filial obedience into the realm of deception in their conversation. In this scene, we see that Hamlet has moved from an initial horror concerning the sins of others toward a profound awareness of his own potential for sin. He says to Ophelia:

> I am myself indifferent honest, but yet I could accuse me of such things that it were better my mother had not borne me: I am very proud, revengeful, ambitious, with more offenses at my beck than I have thoughts to put them in, imagination to give them shape, or time to act them in. What should such fellows as I do crawling between earth and heaven? We are arrant knaves all; believe none of us. (3.1.122-30)

We are not meant to believe from this speech that Hamlet is a bad man. The point is that Hamlet is a *man*, and that he now knows that to be a man means to "relish" of original sin, not to be able to "escape calumny." Having eaten from the tree of good and evil, humans cannot undo their aboriginal choice for self over God, and all now bear in their hearts the knowledge of evil through participation in it, whatever particular sins they may or may not commit. All human beings since the Fall are of the "old stock"; virtue may be grafted upon it, as one grafts young saplings to old trees, but the original unfallen state cannot be regained, and individual sins, in thought and in deed, will issue from the tainted stock (3.1.17-19). It is for this reason that Hamlet tells Ophelia, "get thee to a nunnery," for why would anyone want to "be a breeder of sinners"? Every man and woman born into the world will bear the inescapable taint of original sin and its consequences. As Hamlet says to Ophelia, "be thou as chaste as ice, as pure as snow, thou shalt not escape calumny.... Go to, I'll no more on't; it hath made me mad" (3.1.137-38,148-49). This is not the madness of insanity; this is the agony of a noble and honest mind that is caught in the depths of man's fallenness and the darkness of the abyss.

Not for nothing do images of the original Fall dominate this play. "'Tis given out," the Ghost says, "that, sleeping in my orchard, / A serpent stung me.... But know, thou noble youth, / The serpent that did sting thy father's life / Now wears his crown" (1.5.35-39). With the Fall of Man comes the loss of the Garden in its health, purity, and innocence—the serpent is in the orchard, the weeds in the garden, the canker on the rose, the "leperous distilment" in the blood, the "vicious mole of nature" in mankind. Indeed, *Hamlet* is filled with images of weeds, thorns, and diseased flowers. Hamlet calls the world "an unweeded garden / That grows to seed" in his first soliloquy, conveying the image of a self-propagating infestation. Ophelia dies while "Clamb'ring to hang" "on the pendent boughs her crownet weeds" and "down her weedy trophies and herself / Fell in the weeping brook" (4.7.172-75). The Ghost has told Hamlet to leave his mother "to heaven / And to those thorns that in her bosom lodge / To prick and sting her" (1.5.86-88). However, Hamlet is summoned by Gertrude and, when he confronts her, says:

> Confess yourself to heaven,
> Repent what's past, avoid what is to come,
> And do not spread the compost on the weeds
> To make them ranker. (3.4.150-53)

The Ghost bemoans that he was "Cut off even in the blossoms" of his sin (1.5.76); Laertes uses the image of flower buds galled by cankerworms in his ill-advised speech to Ophelia concerning Hamlet's affection for her (1.3.39-40). Not only the Ghost, but even Claudius sees King Hamlet's murder as the repetition of the curse of Cain when Claudius so abortively tries to pray: "O, my offense is rank, it smells to heaven; / It hath the primal eldest curse upon't, / A brother's murder" (3.3.36-38). And, coming full circle, Claudius' use of the word "rank" again evokes Hamlet's initial image of the world as an unweeded garden possessed by "Things rank and gross in nature," smelling of weeds.

The fallen world is permeated by poison, spreading contagion, premature decay, and seeping corruption. While Hamlet waits with Horatio and Marcellus for the appearance of the Ghost, Horatio asks Hamlet whether King Claudius' drunken revels are a Danish custom. Hamlet answers that, although it is indeed a custom, it would be "More honored in the breach than the observance," since the "heavy-headed revel" soils Denmark's reputation in the eyes of other nations, causing them to ignore genuine Danish achievement and see only drunken Danish orgies (1.4.13-22). As an analogy for the way in which this fault of excessive revelry poisons Denmark's reputation in the eyes of other nations, Hamlet says:

> So oft it chances in particular men
> That for some vicious mole of nature in them,
> As in their birth, wherein they are not guilty,
>
> . . . .
>
>   [that these men]
> Shall in the general censure take corruption
> From that particular fault. (1.4.23-36)

Thus Hamlet introduces the idea of the corruption that spreads from a single but vicious innate blemish of nature—an analogy of the effects of original sin.

The Ghost horridly intensifies this image of spreading corruption as he relates the manner of his poisoning by Claudius. While King Hamlet was sleeping within his orchard, his "custom always of the afternoon," Claudius stole upon him with the juice of a poisonous plant in a vial, "And in the porches of my ears did pour / The leperous distilment" (1.5.60, 63-64). The Ghost recounts in detail the action of the poison, including the "posset" made of his blood, and the "lazarlike" bark, the "vile and loathsome crust" that instantly spread over all his "smooth body" (see 1.5.65-73). In *Hamlet*, as Wolfgang Clemen (crediting Caroline Spurgeon) has written, "the idea of an ulcer dominates the imagery, infecting and fatally eating away the whole body; on every occasion repulsive images of sickness make their appearance" (113). Spreading poison, he writes, "becomes the *leitmotif* of the imagery: the individual occurrence [the poisoning of King Hamlet] is expanded into a symbol for the central problem of the play. The corruption of land and people throughout Denmark is understood as an imperceptible and irresistible process of poisoning" (113).[5] A cancerous mole, a vicious innate blemish, a corruption in the blood, a spreading infection, a seeping poison—these are the images in which *Hamlet* embodies original sin and its consequence: the tendency of man to serve himself rather than God, to make those choices for self which Dante witnessed in the *Inferno*. Although the particular egregious sin in *Hamlet* is fratricide, Hamlet's vision, as a tragic protagonist, is universal: given the fallenness of man, thus must it always be that the corruption of original sin issues in individual sins, be they great or small, actual or potential. The Greek image of the curse upon the house prefigures original sin as the curse upon the house of mankind.

But to return, then, to Hamlet's dilemma. The journey of a tragic protagonist, as Aristotle pointed out, is one from ignorance to knowledge; more than that, however, the odyssey of a tragic protagonist demands a redefining of identity, a new knowledge and image of self. A successful tragic protagonist is one who chooses to accept that new identity. Thus, Hamlet's vision of the depths of iniquity possible within the human soul moves rapidly from a focus on the sins of others to the real and potential sins within himself. He knows that, being a man, he is not free from sin, and he believes that he cannot act without incurring guilt and damnation. He has fathomed the depths and seen that, as a man, he stands in the condemned place, the abode of the guilty. How then to act? How to fulfill the commandments of the Ghost to avenge his father's murder without tainting his mind? Because Hamlet is greater and nobler than Laertes, he cannot say, as Laertes does when he learns that Hamlet has mistakenly slain Polonius,

> Conscience and grace to the profoundest pit!
> I dare damnation. To this point I stand,
> That both the worlds I give to negligence,
> Let come what comes, only I'll be revenged
> Most throughly for my father. (4.5.132-36)

It is not until the events at sea, which he recounts to Horatio, that Hamlet can resolve the Ghost's paradoxical commandments and act with a mind untainted.

The resolution of Hamlet's dilemma, begun at sea, is composed of two elements. First, Hamlet has gained positive proof that Claudius has ordered his execution by England's rulers through the agency of Rosencrantz and Guildenstern, and Hamlet, through his substitution of the execution order, has sent Rosencrantz and Guildenstern to their deaths. Hamlet's reaction to the fact of Rosencrantz's and Guildenstern's presumed execution manifests the first shift in Hamlet's conscience. When Horatio comments, "So Guildenstern and Rosencrantz go to't," Hamlet says, "Why, man, they did make love to this employment. / They are not near my conscience; their defeat / Does by their own insinuation grow" (5.2.56-59). Rosencrantz's and Guildenstern's deaths do not impinge on his conscience; insomuch as Hamlet has acted as the agent in bringing about their deaths, he has done so without tainting his mind.

But more important is the freeing of Hamlet's conscience regarding the execution of Claudius. At Horatio's exclamation, "Why, what a king is this!" Hamlet replies:

> Does it not, think thee, stand me now upon—
> He that hath killed my king, and whored my mother,
> Popped in between th' election and my hopes,
> Thrown out his angle for my proper life,
> And with such coz'nage—is't not perfect conscience
> To quit him with this arm? And is't not to be damned
> To let this canker of our nature come
> In further evil? (5.2.63-70)

In this speech we see the ultimate shift in Hamlet's conscience: from fearing damnation *for* killing Claudius to expecting damnation for *not* killing him. To let such a "canker of our nature" go on living to commit further evil would indeed, Hamlet says, condemn him to damnation for his inaction. And if he can act without fear of damnation, he has made a major step toward acting without tainting his mind.

There is, however, more to the freeing of Hamlet's conscience than the empirical proof of Claudius' treachery, and this second element has fully changed Hamlet and brought him to his final redefinition of self. Hamlet has surrendered himself into the hands of a divinity and fully accepted the shaping of who he is. Further recounting the shipboard events to Horatio, and reviewing his insomnia over his own "deep plots," he renounces self-will and famously concludes: "There's a divinity that shapes our ends, / Rough-hew them how we will" (5.2.10-11). What is in store, Hamlet does not know, but he no longer bewails that heaven has chosen him to be a "scourge and minister" and to set the time right. His role, he now knows, is to wait, to be ready for action, to be guided as heaven dictates, to let his end and his very self be shaped by God. Hamlet has found, to borrow an image from T. S. Eliot, the "still point" of his soul, from which action may flow without tainting his mind.

Nonetheless, like all great tragic protagonists, Hamlet remains human until the end. As the Oedipus of *Oedipus at Colonus* retains the irritability of a humbled and suffering old man, as Lear howls at Cordelia's death, so Hamlet is visited by trepidation. After Hamlet hears of the fencing match arranged by Claudius between Laertes and himself, he has a presentiment—an "augury"— of his imminent death; "thou wouldst not think," he says to Horatio, "how ill all's here about my heart" (5.2.213-14).[6] But, encouraged by Horatio to decline the match, Hamlet says: "Not a whit, we defy augury. There is special providence in the fall of a sparrow. If it be now, 'tis not to come; if it be not to come, it will be now; if it be not now, yet it will come. The readiness is all" (5.2.220-24). Hamlet's "prophetic soul" may retain the human quality of misgiving, but he knows himself to be in the hands of that providence which embraces even the fall of a sparrow.

From this point on in the play, Hamlet is courteous and courtly. More importantly, he acts with a free and untainted mind. In order not to taint his mind, he had to learn to act without evil intention—without "a purposed evil"—and leave the rest to God. Thus, immediately following the "readiness" speech, he asks Laertes' pardon and acknowledges that he has wronged him by slaying Polonius but says also that he did not intend the evil:

> Sir, in this audience,
> Let my disclaiming from a purposed evil
> Free me so far in your most generous thoughts
> That I have shot my arrow o'er the house
> And hurt my brother. (5.2.241-44)

Hamlet's "disclaiming from a purposed evil" in his apology to Laertes may strike some as sophistical. But Hamlet would never have taken it on himself to slay Polonius intentionally, reprehensible as the old man's behavior was. Obviously, he did not intend the "evil" of killing Polonius, although he later seems to see the event as mysteriously woven into the designs of providence:

> For this same lord,
> I do repent; but heaven hath pleased it so,
> To punish me with this, and this with me,
> That I must be their scourge and minister.
> I will bestow him and will answer well
> The death I gave him. (3.4.173-78)

A possible further question, however, is how Hamlet can disclaim a "purposed evil" in general when his intention was to slay Claudius. In his speech to Laertes, Hamlet says that his "madness," his "sore distraction," was the cause of his killing Polonius:

> Was't Hamlet wronged Laertes? Never Hamlet.
> If Hamlet from himself be ta'en away,
> And when he's not himself does wrong Laertes,
> Then Hamlet does it not, Hamlet denies it.
> Who does it then? His madness. If't be so,
> Hamlet is of the faction that is wronged;
> His madness is poor Hamlet's enemy. (5.2.234-40)

He was not himself but caught in the darkness of the abyss. Speaking in the presence of Claudius and the court, he both dissembles and tells the truth in this passage. The fiction of "madness" as insanity must be maintained in front of Claudius. However, it is quite true that, when Hamlet mistakenly slew Polonius, he had not yet come to that "still center" of surrender into the hands of God. Hamlet was at that point still in the throes of his agony over being chosen as Denmark's "scourge and minister"; he was "mad"—not in the sense of insanity—but with the fear of damnation, as we have seen. His intention was not to do evil but to fulfill the role appointed him by heaven through the agency of his father's ghost. In his speech to Laertes, Hamlet speaks from his current vantage, which is that of a purged and surrendered soul.

In the final scene, Hamlet fully manifests his surrender to God and His providence. His actions and his end are indeed shaped elsewhere; he neither intends evil nor contrives; he becomes God's instrument. In this denouement of "purposes mistook / Fall'n on th' inventors' heads," Laertes is, as he admits, caught in his own snare and "justly killed with [his] own treachery" (5.2.385-86, 308). Claudius cannot forestall Gertrude from drinking of the cup he has poisoned for Hamlet. When Gertrude proclaims her poisoning and Hamlet cries that the source of this villainy and treachery be sought out, Laertes answers:

> It is here, Hamlet. Hamlet, thou art slain;

No med'cine in the world can do thee good.
In thee there is not half an hour's life.
The treacherous instrument is in thy hand,
Unbated and envenomed. The foul practice
Hath turned itself on me. Lo, here I lie,
Never to rise again. Thy mother's poisoned.
I can no more. The King, the King's to blame. (5.2.314-21)

Hamlet does not engage in the fencing match with the intention of killing Claudius, although he believes that he would court damnation by letting Claudius live. Hamlet has not manipulated the time and events to this moment; it has come, as he prophesied, of its own accord. Claudius' treachery is now a matter of public record. Hamlet is ready to act with an untainted mind, without contrivance or "a purposed evil," and with the knowledge that he cannot, through his own efforts as a man, free himself from whatever guilt adheres to his actions.

Moreover, as befits the actions of a Christian prince, Hamlet's slaying of Claudius at this point is not so much a matter of private revenge as it is a public execution before the forum of the court, in which Hamlet's attitude has the character of God's righteous wrath and his action that of nemesis. Justice, not revenge, is the theme in the death of Claudius. Laertes has already declared his own death to be just because of his treachery. After Hamlet forces Claudius to drink from the cup by which Gertrude was poisoned, Laertes again evokes the dictates of justice, saying that Claudius "is justly served. / It is a poison tempered by himself" (5.2.328-29). Indeed, it is a poison that Claudius first tempered when he poured the "leperous distilment" of "cursed hebona" into King Hamlet's ears (1.5.61-64). Because he has not repented, Claudius is caught in the net of a strictly retributive justice. As he murdered his brother by poison, so is he slain by poison.

The dying Hamlet and Laertes pray to free each other from guilt. Laertes says, "Exchange forgiveness with me, noble Hamlet. / Mine and my father's death come not upon thee, / Nor thine on me!" And Hamlet replies, "Heaven make thee free of it!" (5.2.330-33). Hamlet knows that only Heaven, the "divinity that shapes our ends," has the power to free man from guilt. Hamlet's faith in that divinity remains true faith, which is, by its nature, blind to things not yet seen. Death is still the "undiscovered country, from whose bourn / No traveler returns," but Hamlet's surrender to the divinity has been complete. Augury is no longer his province. Indeed, augury is not a human concern under the grace of that providence which encompasses even the fall of a sparrow. "The rest is silence" is not an expression of nihilism but an avowal of Hamlet's faith and a testament of his surrender to the providence and purposes of God (5.2.359).

Although there is to be no augury—no words to reveal truly the "undiscovered country" of death and eternity—there will be words from Horatio that express the truth of the events which have corrupted Denmark:

> Of carnal, bloody, and unnatural acts,
> Of accidental judgments, casual slaughters,
> Of deaths put on by cunning and forced cause,
> And, in this upshot, purposes mistook
> Fall'n on th' inventors' heads. (5.2.382-86)

In the world of this play, where words have not expressed the truth of human thoughts and deeds, at the last Horatio's words will truly reflect reality, as Hamlet's would have if that "fell sergeant, Death," had not been so "strict in his arrest" (5.2.335-38).

As Horatio's words articulate reality in the final scene and beyond, Hamlet's journey of insight has embodied the deepest reality of all: the truth of that darkness into which the tragic protagonists are called. Hamlet has seen man's inescapable guilt in its depths. He has seen that it is man's place because it is the home of the guilty—that place where finite fallen man, "this quintessence of dust," meets the "divinity that shapes our ends / Rough-hew them how we will." In fathoming the tragic abyss, Hamlet has answered the question that permeates all tragedy: "What place is this?"—a question given explicit voice by Oedipus after he has discovered his true identity and his guilt, found Jocasta hanged, and blinded himself within the dynastic house. The same question dominates the opening of Oedipus at Colonus, which begins with Oedipus' inquiry to Antigone, "Where, I wonder, have we come to now? What place is this, Antigone?" (Fitzgerald 2-3)

The answer to the tragic protagonist's question, "What place is this?" is consistently embodied throughout tragedies in paradoxical images and specifically in images of the place where earth meets sky: the binding of Prometheus at the horizon; the confrontation of the Furies and Apollo in the *Oresteia*; the mysterious end of Oedipus, who seems simultaneously to ascend into the sky and descend into the earth. The tragic abyss is that metaphysical place where finite man, composed of dust, meets the infinite, whose purposes his reason cannot fully comprehend. This is the meaning of the theophany at the end of the Book of Job, in which God speaks from the whirlwind in the sky and gives Job, not *concepts*, but *images* of Himself as Creator. Job and Hamlet are alike in their choice to surrender completely to the "divinity that shapes our ends" without a conceptual understanding of the mystery of God's intentions.

But in *Hamlet* the answer to the question "What place is this?" is given a more explicit mapping than in other tragedies. Hamlet fathoms man's paradoxical ontological situation: that there is no way, being human, to escape guilt through one's own actions. But in his encounter with the paradox of original sin and unavoidable human guilt, he has also seen that Heaven can make him free of it, if he will allow God to shape his end, to lead him to a new identity, and to remake him into a new self. All tragic protagonists encounter this mystery at the depths of the tragic abyss. After Oedipus' true identity has been disclosed in *Oedipus the King*, the Chorus says, "I see your life finally revealed / your life fused with the god" (Berg and Clay 1518-19). Whether a particular tragic protagonist's god has been Apollo, as in the case of Oedipus and Orestes, or the Christian God, as in the case of Hamlet, there is a sense in which all tragic protagonists encounter Dionysus, the paradoxical dismembered god of tragedy, in the depths of the abyss. The tragic protagonist must let his old identity, his idea of who he is, be torn apart in order that a new self be born—not that self which he thought he was but the person whom the gods intend him to be. The successful tragic protagonist must answer the call of Dionysus to yield and move beyond his old self (*ecstasis*) and join in the mysterious ecstasy of death and rebirth. Thus the self-blinded Oedipus, after he has discovered who he really is and his own unspeakable guilt, proclaims, "Now / I am / Oedipus!" (Berg and Clay 1768-70). Lear, after Cordelia rescues him from his metaphorical descent into infernal regions and the grave, redefines himself as "a very foolish fond old man... old and foolish" (4.7.60, 84). It is only after Hamlet has surrendered himself into the hands of the "divinity that shapes our ends" and consented to that dismemberment of his old identity requisite for the birth of a new self that he can declare "This is I / Hamlet the Dane" (5.1.258-59).

Hamlet maps the depths of the abyss and the parameters of the ascent from it. Although the tragic fall plunges the protagonist into groundlessness, this "yawning into the indeterminate" is, as Glenn Arbery writes, something "out of which ground itself stabilizes, an exposure of depths mysteriously astir with terror and healing, a revelation of the blackness-to-us of the divine" (vi). For a successful tragic protagonist—that is, a tragic *hero*—the ground indeed stabilizes in such a way that an ascent from the abyss is possible and a destination is revealed. Confronted with original sin and the ontological paradox of inescapable guilt, the protagonist must surrender himself to purposes that the mind of man cannot encompass and experience that healing which emerges from the terror. The destination of a successful tragic protagonist is the mystery of a life beyond the vision of mortal men, in which the old self has died and a new self been born. Hamlet, most noble of Christian princes, maps the way.

NOTES

[1] Of course, "sin" is not the concept usually applied to the fall of Greek (or pagan) tragic protagonists. The Oedipus cycle, for instance, speaks of Oedipus and his actions as inexpressibly impious, a pollution and curse upon his house and kingdom. Consequently, one might say the word "sin" is applied only analogically to Greek tragic protagonists, and yet this depends on one's view of creative intuition and the existence of eternal patterns which constitute the very fabric of reality and are Christian. This viewpoint is obviously not a Christian apologetic but rather an insight which, as Hans Urs von Balthasar writes, springs from the foundation of faith. This insight is too intricate to be unfolded fully here, but the basic idea (again from the standpoint of a faith which enables one to *see*) is that the Christian pattern of man's sin and fallenness, redemption, and salvation *is* the very fabric of reality from its beginning and that the Greek tragedians intuited and embodied this pattern in their plays, calling the components

of the pattern (e.g., "sin") by the closest approximation they had prior to Revelation. (See von Balthasar 419-20 and 500-03.)

[2] Although the analogy between Orestes and Hamlet is apparent, I think the assertion of Hamlet's uniqueness is still valid. Orestes understands the commandment of Apollo to revenge Agamemnon's murder and the consequences he will suffer if he does not, but it seems to me he does not clearly anticipate the consequences of following Apollo's commandment. Orestes seems to be shocked by the appearance and pursuit of the Furies roused by Clytemnestra's slaying. Hamlet, on the other hand, foresees the whole dimension of his paradoxical situation, as will be discussed.

[3] In my opinion, Kenneth Branagh is the only actor in the filmed versions of *Hamlet* which I have seen who has interpreted the "To be, or not to be" soliloquy correctly, perceiving the action in question to be the slaying of Claudius, not of himself.

[4] "Quietus est," again in legal terminology, means "he is quit," in the sense of being discharged from the debt, obligation, or office. This meaning of "quietus" is identical with the primary definition of "quittance," as when we say, "He has received his quittance," meaning he is no longer under any obligation, although "quittance" carries the additional meaning of recompense, repayment, and reprisal. When Hamlet says "he himself might his quietus make / With a bare bodkin," he is saying that any man might be "quit" of debt, obligation, or office by violent action, by taking "arms against a sea of troubles, / And by opposing end[ing] them." See also Hamlet's use of the word "quit" in his speech to Horatio (5.2.63-68).

[5] For example, Hamlet understands his mother in this way; he tells Gertrude not to console herself with the idea that he is mad when he confronts her with her sins, lest that idea "skin and film the ulcerous place" in her soul while "rank corruption" spreads underneath the surface, infecting "unseen" and undermining "all within" (3.4.145-150). The corpses "nowadays," comments the gravedigging clown, "scarce hold the laying in" before they rot, because they are so infected with the pox (5.1.166-68). "And, furthermore," adds Clemens, "this poisoning reappears as a *leitmotif* in the action as well—as a poisoning in the 'dumb-show,' and finally, as the poisoning of all the major characters in the last act" (113).

[6] This presentiment of his imminent death is not the first time in the play that Hamlet has revealed a capacity for augury. He has,

of course, suspected Claudius of murdering King Hamlet since his father's death and Claudius' marriage to Gertrude, which is why he cries, "O my prophetic soul!" after the Ghost says he was slain by Claudius (1.5.40).

10

Ritual, Epic, and Tragedy: Notes on Dante's *Commedia* and the Renaissance Tragedy of Time

MARY MUMBACH

Aristotle apparently recognizes two sources for tragedy—the ritual acts of sacrifice enacted by a community and the narratives of heroic deeds recited by bards. He considers tragedy to be, as a matter of fact, a refinement of and improvement upon epic. Following this line of thought, one might discern in Shakespeare's tragedies two parallel sources: medieval drama, originating in the central liturgical celebration of the mass, and the poetic cosmos formed by the central line of epic. Several commentators have noted connections between Shakespearean drama and Ariosto's heroic narratives, and a few have mentioned in particular the relationship between the tragedy of *Othello* and Virgil's *Aeneid*. It would be hard for anyone to miss the more obvious continuity with a later epic, Milton's *Paradise Lost*, for the kinship between Iago and Milton's Satan is anything but obscure. But at least as definite, though much ignored, is another connection. Shakespeare's tragedies are borne to us, at least in part, by the particular epic that, as Erich Auerbach has written, changed the consciousness of the Western world—the *Divina Commedia*.

As Homer provided the cosmos within which Aeschylus and Sophocles could enact their tragedies, so Dante provided for Shakespearean drama a world of amplitude, variety, and dimension sufficient for the habitation of the tragic action. And perhaps more notable, he provided a new conception of the abyss.

Dante the pilgrim found written over the forbidding gates giving
access to the underworld:

> Through me you enter the woeful city,
> Through me you enter eternal grief
> Justice moved my high maker;
> The divine power made me;
> The supreme wisdom and the primal love...
>   (Inf. III, 1-6, Charles Singleton trans.)

Shakespeare's tragedies inherit this world view, recognizing this
ultimate place of abandonment not only as it had appeared
before in classical tragedy, a realm of deformation and infinite
chagrin, but as a necessary corollary of love. Thus, in Shakespeare, the vision of happiness from which the heroic personage
falls is fuller and more poignant than that of earlier portrayals.
It may be viewed in the Earthly Paradise of *Purgatorio*, where the
poet hero is reunited with Beatrice before his "transhumanizing"
entry into the Paradiso. The loss of this bliss in which "the will
is whole" is the subtext of the lamentations uttered by Shakespeare's protagonists. Lear speaks of being "bound upon a wheel
of fire / that mine own tears do scald like molten lead." These
tears represent a new element in tragedy. The bitter regret and
self-recrimination they express constitute an added dimension to
the devastation of the abyss. Indeed, the entire cosmos within
which the Shakespearean tragedy is enacted is Dantean.

❧ ❧ ❧

The main line of epic ancestry for Othello should include
Homer, Virgil, and Dante. Though connections with less important epics such as Ariosto's need not be excluded, they are less
to the point of the central action. Of particular interest in the
connection between Dante and Shakespeare is what might be
called the spatialization of time in the Middle Ages. It might be
said that time was the true place within which man lived. Francois Laroque describes the experience of a year in the Middle
Ages as "so many rites of passage that made the transition from
one season or temporal cycle to the next" (201).

> In the traditional festival view, accordingly, time was not perceived as a system of differences that provided a basis for calculating the movements of men, things, and capital (giving rise to interest); rather, it was seen as a system of prescriptions and prohibitions that provided a code for social behavior (dress, food, and sexual customs). In the popular view, time was not an undifferentiated interval to be used as desired by individuals and groups planning their activities and leisure. Instead, it was a mysterious space in which forces, now benevolent, now malevolent, interacted, the object either of impatient expectation or of anxiety on the part of individuals and groups alike. (201-2)

So prominent was the history of salvation in the experience of eternity in the Middle Ages that it should be no surprise that Dante was deeply concerned with the dimension of time as this "mysterious space." The sense of time redeemed made the Middle Ages a high culture—and rendered it incapable of producing tragedy. The sense of the fullness of the Incarnation brought together time and eternity, with the result that the dramas evolving from medieval liturgy always have a comic bent, so certain is their belief in the *felix culpa*. Coming out of this tradition, playing off of it, and changing it, Shakespeare dramatizes the fall from grace as a fall of time itself in the tragedy of *Othello*.

❉ ❉ ❉

If the Middle Ages could not produce tragedy, it was not because poets writing at that time were incapable of visualizing the possibility of eternal loss. Not only Dante, but lyric poets and the writers of morality plays were deeply concerned with death and final judgment. The plot of the morality play *Everyman*, with its focus on the last things, seems to have the structure of tragedy, but it does not arouse pity and fear or produce the catharsis that is the characteristic response to tragedy. For it is not the prospect of damnation that renders a poem tragic; rather, it is the overwhelming sense of one's responsibility for that loss. Admittedly, comedies can be very dark indeed—Dante's *Commedia* is populated by more damned souls than ever grace the stage during the final act of any tragedy, but the work is openly designated as comedy. In *Everyman*, though the sense of loss is diminished almost beyond possibility, the raw materials for tragedy are nonetheless present. It is as though the whole universe conspires to help Everyman get it right.

A large part of Everyman's aplomb derives from a temporal amplitude, despite the appearance of haste. Suddenly notified that his death-day has arrived, he is refused a delay of that event; nevertheless, he seems to be given all the time he needs. In Marlowe's *Dr. Faustus*, a play written some hundred years later, the protagonist knows the exact hour of his death *twenty-four years in advance*, but, in stark contrast to Everyman, he does not believe he has time to repent. The protagonist of the medieval morality play has available to him time of another order—sacred time. The single day is sufficient for him to make rather elaborate preparations for the final day of judgment. The difference between the two attitudes is a difference in the experience of time. Faustus faces the horror of the abyss that characterizes tragedy. In fact, for Faustus the experience of time irremediably lost is the experience of a kind of vertigo. In tragedy time is always running out. The loss of a sense of the efficacy of any kind of ritual that could stop the flow of linear time opens the possibility for tragedy. The ceremony cannot be found that would prove Faustus' reclaiming. The very success of Marlowe's tragedy heralds the loss of the wholeness of sensibility that characterizes the Middle Ages. Faustus's contract with the devil has split open a gulf between himself and the heavens that seems unbridgeable.

❊   ❊   ❊

Everyman is saved without having had to be tragic. Even more than Statius in the *Commedia*, he enters eternity with his specific work in the world having had little apparent connection to his eternal destiny, except insofar as all men's offices allow them to do good or evil deeds. Everyman goes to the sacrament of confession, to a priest who has the appointed office to forgive him, but his sins are related to his simple humanity, not to his calling in life. One need not be told his own occupation in life; whether king, prelate, farmer, or beggar in his earthly time, he faces the same eternity, has apparently committed the generic sins, and must repent in the same way. Faustus' failure, on the other hand, is a failure in his specific profession. He becomes weary with professing the liberal arts, because they do not give him the worldly success and satisfaction that he seeks. Hence the life of learning is lost, which should provide him with a "second city," in which may be discerned the true value of his and every man's work in the world, imbuing his mind with a sense of the high destiny of the entire cosmos. In his age, he is forsaking a life already diminished, the vision of the *Commedia* already forgotten.

This play is a tragedy, but, unlike Shakespeare's plays of about the same time, it lacks a full Christian sensibility. In fact, it is tragic because it is actually about the loss of a sacred sense of time. In this play, angels may argue that Faustus has the opportunity to renounce his errors through repentance, but their argument is as abstract as Faustus' sins have been. The possibility of such hope applying to him seems unimaginable—it implies no changed imagination about how life should be lived. Rather, it is some solely interior act, a renunciation of his errors that has no manifestation in the world. With no images of efficacious action in the world, Faustus has no model for an interior act. The experience of time redeemed, in particular, does not seem available to him imaginatively. His dilemma reminds us of an episode in the *Commedia*—the damnation of Guido da Montefeltro (Inf. XXX), who was given absolution *before* committing his sin. At his death, the devil argues that it is not possible for one to sin and repent at the same time, taunting him for not knowing that the devil is a logician. One has the sense that, had Faustus been faithful to the spirit of his studies, to their liberal quality, he might have found the means to beat Mephistopheles himself at his own game of logic. He might have argued that his original contract was invalid, for he had not owned his own soul and so had no right to sell it. But never seeing the implications of his own particular high calling, and feeling imprisoned in his own history of past choices and past actions in the world, Faustus is trapped in time from the beginning of the play, not only at the end.

❊ ❊ ❊

But what relation does the Venetian general Othello, marked throughout the text as "the Moor," have to this Dantean comic vision? Many valuable studies have remarked the presence in Shakespearean tragedies of elements normally characteristic of comedies. Whether critics have considered these characteristics to be flaws, diluting the tragic effect of the drama, or foils that intensify it, they recognize the necessity of acknowledging that these shadows of comic celebration, distorted by being placed in the context of actions that evoke pity and fear, produce a particular effect on the rest of the play. Francois Laroque, for instance, concludes his study of the festival origins of both the tragedies and comedies of Shakespeare with particular consideration of *Othello*, where the contrast between the elements of *commedia del arte* and the sharp downward movement of the drama increases the shock and poignancy of the action almost beyond endurance. The exceptional nobility of Othello among Shakespearean tragic heroes, often remarked by critics, is submitted to degrading ridicule that, far from providing comic relief, increases the horror of his downfall. Neither Laroque's study nor others which convincingly link a myriad of details in the plays to corresponding elements in the liturgical calendar proves surprising when we remember that Aristotle traced the probable origins of that earliest age of great tragic and comic drama to sacrifices and feasts of the country life that predated the founding of the City of Athens.

❊   ❊   ❊

An inestimable contribution to our understanding of Shakespeare's plays has been made by the growing recognition among critics that not only Shakespeare's comedies but his tragedies are deeply connected to medieval drama—that they issue from dramatizations of events in the medieval liturgical calendar, the celebration of sacred time. This realization has made us aware of the connection of Shakespeare's plays to Christianity in its ritual and sacramental character and to its allegorical and typological mode of thought. *Othello* has been recognized as the most allegorical of the tragedies, indeed as a version of a morality play, paralleling *Everyman* and, more explicitly, *Dr. Faustus*. Othello is the soul to be saved or lost; Iago is the demonic figure provoking Othello to seal a pact with him in exchange for his soul; and Desdemona is his good angel, inspiring those around her, even the cynical Emilia, to acts of virtue and, further, as Christ Himself did, taking sin upon herself with her dying breath.

These connections to liturgical drama parallel those that

Aristotle attributes to Greek tragedy in his *Poetics*. But for Aristotle the dramas that precede the fullness of form in tragic drama seem to provide an account of the historical development of tragedy rather than a formal one. A more essential connection within the realm of achieved art is his consideration of tragedy as a refinement of Homeric epic. If it was the *Iliad* which, as Louise Cowan has said, "bears to us" the genre of tragedy, embodied in the Greek dramas, then Shakespeare's tragedies have a parallel relation to the *Divine Comedy*.

※　※　※

Although *Othello* begins with a sense of emergency—with indications of a sense of the need for haste in all quarters—one soon sees embedded in the play a possible leisure, a reprieve, a possibility for new chances. Time is passing swiftly for everyone, so that no character has a moment to lose; yet the response of each issues from one of two radically different perspectives on the crisis. When the tragedy opens, Othello and Desdemona are, so to speak, in the Garden at the top of Mount Purgatory. Othello has been moving toward this union, he suggests, throughout his life. At some point, no later than when he recounts his life's story to Desdemona, he has come to see it as his "pilgrimage" (I.3.152). His is not the only such journey to a beloved in Shakespeare, if one remembers Romeo and Juliet's playful first encounter, identifying him as pilgrim and her as saint. Othello's story to Desdemona of the tribulations he has met along the way occurs within a larger, more serious, context. It suggests the catalogue of sufferings enumerated by the Apostle Paul after his conversion from waging war against Christians to leading them, his turn from the Law to love. It suggests the action within the tradition of the life of Augustine, whose spiritual wanderings are revealed actually to have been a pilgrimage: from a practicing merchant of words to a lover of the Word which, long unknown to him, had been guiding him since conception.

The vows of these voyagers in Othello's hard-won earthly paradise have been made in lyric time, and they are the potential instruments of a renewal of the original order of creation through what they have promised to each other. It is by means of such acts of love that all creation may be renewed—marriage itself being an image of word made flesh that indicates the god-like power of human language to say a word in time that is a new creation and that resounds through eternity. Dante recognizes the significance of dedication when he is rebuked in the earthly paradise at the top of Mt. Purgatory for having been unfaithful to Beatrice for the minor reason of her death, as though mere death could have bearing on love. Othello's marriage to Desdemona corresponds to that great turning point in Dante's journey when he visits this *paradiso terrestre*. Dante's encounter with his lady is a reunion after long estrangement, Othello's the completion of a journey to a new life that involves the transformation of his past.

❉ ❉ ❉

Cutting across this lyric time is Iago. The time in which he acts, the framework into which he immediately draws Brabantio and will soon pull Othello, is the sense of time as running out, already lost. In the time dominated by Iago and introduced by him with the opening words of the play, any action taken, however heroic or radical, is *already too late*. This is time as the manifestation of the abyss, tragic time. Even at the beginning of the play, when Iago protests that he has found out about the elopement of Desdemona and Othello too late to warn Roderigo, much less to prevent the unexpected union, his announcement has about it a chilling finality. Then his coarse manner of announcing Desdemona's marriage to her father is calculated to evoke a sense of the futility of his knowledge, for his daughter is already lost. Of course any elopement suggests a motive of haste as well as secrecy.

❉ ❉ ❉

The other characters act within that large view of time that characterizes the epic cosmos, most immediately as it is embodied in the *Commedia*—a time in which even what is counted as the utmost loss by the mundane world may be revealed as actual triumph in the larger scheme of things. Both the marriage of Othello and Desdemona and the Venetian preparations for defense occur in time as experienced in the cosmos created by Dante's *Commedia*. When the Duke calls a nocturnal session of

the Senate in order to sort out conflicting reports of an impend-
ing Turkish attack, everyone but Brabantio—that is, all the other
senators, the Duke, Othello, and Desdemona—respond without
desperation, but with both haste and courtesy, in recognizing the
kairotic moment.

At first the sudden revelation of Othello's and Desdemona's
marriage makes it seem an unconsidered decision, with no time
allotted for a proper courtship (an impression elopements tend to
give). When he discovers the marriage of his daughter to the
Moor, which he is too late to prevent, Brabantio accuses Othello
of witchcraft. But in fact the testimony of both newlyweds reveals
the complex and mutual development of their love. In answer to
Brabantio, he soon assures the senators that their union was a
mutual decision not based at all on magic, mesmerism, or desperate haste. Desdemona strongly seconds him. She accepted Othello's proposal over those of all her other suitors in Venice, not
in spite of his otherness and the danger that attended a partnership with such a warrior, but because of her fascination with
these evidences of the heroic life. What looks at first like a rebellion against parental authority she pleads as a fulfillment of its
teaching: she has chosen a close companion of her father, whom
she first met when (obediently) waiting on him as a guest in her
father's house. Besides, she pleads, far from being impious, she
is following in the footsteps of her mother by devoting herself to
her husband. Later more details of the intricacies of their
courtship emerge: Cassio, the Florentine gentleman, whom Iago
considers over-refined, has been Othello's emissary to Desdemona,
so that their courtship was not entirely private. The apparent
haste of the marriage is itself a deceptive impression.

Othello and Desdemona see the unfolding of their marriage as
an epic task in which Othello's call to Cyprus is the continuation
of his pilgrimage, now transformed and enriched by their partnership. The Duke apologizes for not being able to spare Othello
even for the rest of his wedding night, but all those involved act
competently and speak with grace. Were it not for Iago's success
in controlling the way that time is experienced, Brabantio might
be able to live in comic time, at least as the duke interprets his
situation. The duke recommends that Brabantio make the best of
the situation, suggesting that the match is far from the worst possible and that Brabantio can begin anew from where he stands.

Had he been persuaded, the play might have been a comedy.

❀ ❀ ❀

But time in this play belongs to Iago. If the *Commedia* is characterized by a new vision of the fullness of time, *Othello* is about the possibility of having actually experienced that fullness and then rejected it. Iago's chief tactic is to hurry first Brabantio, then Othello, to the point at which neither can make a considered decision. The only actual haste in the play is the precipitous jumping to conclusions of these two men. By gaining control of time itself, Iago opens a yawning fissure deep as the hellmouth of Marlowe's play.

Glenn Arbery characterizes Iago's actions as arising from his recognition that he is the never-to-be-chosen one (111). Virgil, too, is, by comparison to Dante, the unchosen, but he shows no trace of anxiety or rebellion against his destiny, only gravity and generosity in his treatment of Dante. Virgil's place has to do with time—specifically, with having lived in the time of the "false and lying gods" and just missing the moment of the Incarnation. He is a kind of precursor, much like John the Baptist. Unlike Virgil, Iago claims *seniority*. Who goes first is, with him, the one with the just claim. He becomes the anti-Virgil, Othello's guide away from his new-found innocence and lyric joy in union with Desdemona. Virgil appears when Dante is failing to reach truth by the most direct route and tells him he must go another way, by what is apparently the most circuitous path, full of delay. The code of manners practiced by all the gentlemen in Othello is based on a similar delay. It requires that one not *respond* immediately or impulsively. Unlike Virgil and very much against this code of the gentleman, Iago wants those under his rhetorical spell to act *at once*, before it is too late *again*.

❀ ❀ ❀

Iago accomplishes control initially by undermining, with a well-placed comparison or two, the code of behavior that guards the honor not only of the gentleman but of the lady. Iago's rival Cassio elaborates the code to the point of drawing ridicule (affectionate and otherwise), treating the three ladies he encounters with elaborate courtesy, so refined that it is in danger of losing touch with the reality it mediates. For example, his ornate language and his false protestations of love to Bianca are exaggerations that Iago can use for his own ends. By urging upon Othello an immediate, instinctual response, he implies that the customary forms of courtesy are demeaning, childish, mendacious, and he opposes to such forms his own "honesty."

Iago can use Othello's ignorance of such courtesy to make Othello doubt, first Cassio, then Desdemona herself. Most disastrously, he can lead Othello into using debased and horrific language in his rage against Desdemona and his accusations of her. Othello even strikes her in public before a horrified visiting relative. Such "honesty" necessarily leads to horror and deception rather than an unveiling of truth.

※ ※ ※

The loss of what G. Wilson Knight called the "Othello music" is essentially a loss of a sense of the fullness of time. It is an indulgence in immediate, impulsive responses, without consideration of the context or the consequences. The change in Othello's language under the influence of Iago indicates a precipitousness that suggests the abyss. Iago, however, goes beyond an undermining of courtesy to call into question the efficacy of ritual itself. The traditional connection of ritual with tragedy endures in the Elizabethan era. In the Middle Ages the efficacy of ritual was assured by the theology to the point that the celebration of the Mass did not depend on the faith of the congregation. The principle of *ex opere operato* resided in the resounding certainty that penetrated the sensibility of the culture itself. The abyss lurks not in the possible inefficacy of the sacrament but in the lack within the disposition of the recipient. No matter his disposition, a person receiving communion truly receives it, though, as St. Paul says, if he receives it "unworthily," he receives it "unto his damnation," through committing sacrilege. It is the actuality of the Transubstantiation that makes any act of desecration an even more serious violation.

Yet Iago can play upon Othello's lack of certainty to make him ask profoundly unsettling questions. Was the sacrament of matrimony valid? Was it powerful enough to join these two so

different people? If it was not, then the efficacy of Othello's bap-
tism is also called into question. Perhaps, he surmises, it is not
really possible for an infidel such as him to become a believer,
a Venetian, a husband. How can one know whether the sacrament has "taken"? Iago says one can achieve certainty only
through logic applied to evidence. He leads Othello to a rejection of Desdemona, a figure of Christ, far greater than Pentheus's
rejection of Dionysus. In the end, no expression and no act of
revenge is immediate enough.

❊   ❊   ❊

The last scene is a reversal of the scene of Dante's reunion
with Beatrice. Othello's final journey into jealousy and murder is
an unraveling of the fabric woven by Dante's journey as far as
the *paradiso terrestre*. Dante arrives in that garden under the guidance of his ancient master Virgil, to be handed on to his beloved
lady for the completion of the journey to paradise: *Othello* opens
with the hero having completed his life's pilgrimage to reach a
state of innocence and union with a beloved lady. In this case
the lady will be replaced as guide by a figure claiming to represent reason and virtue, as well as seniority, an anti-Virgil whose
purpose is to turn her virtue into pitch. Whether we are to think
that Iago's urging the lady to beg mercy on behalf of an errant
"Florentine" is an explicit parallel to the relations among Virgil,
Beatrice, and the exiled Florentine Dante, the structure certainly
works as an unraveling of that achievement of cooperation
between the Classical and the Christian world to rescue a sinner.

In the final scenes of this play, Desdemona is the voice of
Beatrice offering reunion if only Othello will accept redemption
and forgiveness. Cassio's sweet new style that makes praise of
ladies possible has been silenced. Iago's wily persuasion, claiming
to be the voice of purity, justice, and morality, is revealed for
what it is: an attempt to deconstruct the Christian vision, to erase
the redemptive view of time and its effects. To demand justice,
as he has been doing, is not simply to return to a noble, more
manly era but to perpetrate an act of de-creation that ends in
the death of good people and the damnation of a noble soul.

※　※　※

Othello's final speech is a culminating rejection of salvation as represented in the *Commedia*. Caught in the fact of his betrayal, accepting responsibility for his actions, he has come to the nadir of tragedy. The depth to which he falls exceeds those into which any of the heroes of classical tragedies descend, for it is a fall from the heights that Dante claims to have reached when he says that words cannot possibly exaggerate what he has experienced. He has moved from having his story celebrated, perhaps even embellished, in his courtship of the leadership of Venice and of Desdemona herself, to asking for this plain telling of the "unlucky deeds" of his betrayal. When Othello, the former hero, says, "Speak of me as I am; nothing extenuate," he renounces the warrior's *kleos*, his reputation as a noble warrior, his "honor" in the sense that the heroes of the *Iliad* would have understood it. And since this was what won Desdemona, it is the equivalent of destroying even their love. Even this—that he was ever loved by Desdemona—is not to be taken into account in the story of his life, but only that he loved "too well" and could therefore be "wrought" to jealousy. Allegorically, he erases his better angel with his tempter. Much has been made by critics, rightly, of his identification with the "base Indian" (or Judaean) who threw a pearl away. At least as telling is the fact that for the man whose epic words about himself wooed the remarkable lady, such a reduction to plainness represents the victory of time as Iago fashions it, in the desperate line of Faustus. It marks the defeat, tragic and prophetic at once, of the temporal amplitude of the Dantean cosmos, where a day, an hour, a single moment truly open to possibility, was time enough.

11

King Lear and the Space of Ritual

GLENN ARBERY

*...how else partake in the psychic revelry of the world
when it celebrates a crossing of the abyss of non-being?*
Wole Soyinka

King Lear is one of a very few plays that have come to seem
definitive of absolute tragedy—*Oedipus Tyrannos, The Bacchae,*
and perhaps *Antigone* being the others. Like the Greek plays, *King
Lear* makes one feel that the "innermost abyss of things spoke to
him perceptibly" as Nietzsche wrote of Dionysian music. It mysteriously conveys "an assured premonition of a highest pleasure
attained through destruction and negation" (Nietzsche 126),
although it lacks the musical and more specifically religious dimensions through which a Greek spectator might experience such a
premonition. Written for a wholly different stage, it nevertheless
seems to engage the kind of intensified theatrical space that Wole
Soyinka calls "the ritual arena of confrontation" that "require[s] a
challenger, a human representative to breach it periodically on
behalf of the well-being of the community" (*Ritual* 2-3). Shakespeare's tragedies often end with symbolic oppositions—Hamlet and
Claudius, Macbeth and Macduff, Othello and Iago, Coriolanus
and Aufidius—but in *King Lear*, Edgar's challenge of Edmund gives
way to Lear's final confrontation with death itself. The loss of
Cordelia takes place on an unprecedented metaphysical plane, and
in its final rending of hope and expectation one feels a strangely
purifying draft from the tragic abyss.

The reasons for this effect, of course, go to the very roots of
art. Coleridge writes in one of his letters on the inspiration of the

Scriptures "that in the Bible there is more that FINDS me than
I have experienced in all other books put together," and one feels
something of the same thing in *King Lear*. It is about the bond
of loving gratitude between children and fathers—spontaneous,
enforced, or feigned—and the inconvertibility of feeling into a kind
of verbal object that can be represented quantitatively and used
instrumentally. The play goes to the very roots of language, beginning with the refusal of it as a currency too easily made counterfeit. It is about what can be represented and said, and what
cannot. For all its noise, it is a play of great silence. At its heart
are the central mysteries of mortality and transition from one generation to the next, as these affect a whole cosmos.

If all power—familial, legislative, juridical, sacerdotal—resides in
the one figure of the king, then to move from the old order to
the new without a ritual of transition is a cosmic unmaking and
remaking. This passage through the destruction of representation
into unmediated feeling and silence and back into form is what
the play most fully embodies. The double plot—the "Gloucester
plot" that echoes the "Lear plot"—is also a single movement from
the kingship of Lear to the kingship of Edgar. In a crossing and
transference of powers, the old man in his grandeur moves
toward death, and the young man—Lear's godson Edgar, to whom
Lear himself gave his name (2.1.91-92)—humbly and unknowingly
moves toward kingship.

Since the world of *King Lear* is one without mediating institutions, such as church or Parliament, and without rituals of transition, the passage from the England of Lear to the England of
Edgar is enacted without symbolic substitutions. The characters
must actually undergo what the anthropologist Victor Turner
describes ritual as ideally miming or re-enacting: "a transformative
self-immolation of order as presently constituted, even sometimes
a voluntary *sparagmos* or self-dismemberment of order, in the subjunctive depths of liminality" (83). Without a ritual of symbols,
they enact the reality of ritual involuntarily: "Actuality takes the
sacrificial plunge into possibility," writes Turner, in what could be
a description of this play, "and emerges as a different kind of
actuality" (83-84).

When Wole Soyinka speaks of the stage as "the ritual arena
of confrontation" requiring a challenger, he is describing Yoruba
culture, where the stage symbolizes the chthonic realm, "the

seething cauldron of the dark world will and psyche, the transitional yet inchoate matrix of death and becoming" (*Stage* 28). If
a human challenger must breach this realm periodically on behalf
of his community, who exactly is the challenger—the actor on the
stage, or the character invoked and made real in the role? Perhaps the question makes no sense in the Yoruba context, but if
Soyinka's terms were transposed to the world of Shakespeare's
plays, it would be entirely the thing to ask. Without ritual forms
to *represent*, Shakespeare's stage itself becomes the site of a ritual
enactment of what would otherwise be formally symbolized and
distanced. This ritual "plunge into possibility" repeatedly brings to
the fore the nature of representation itself—the nature of the
actor—and puts a great deal of emphasis on those who are either
playacting or refusing to playact. Does the real-life *actor* enter the
chthonic realm of creative and destructive essences, or is it rather
that the figure in the role does so? Does the actor, in tracing
out the depths of the role, break afresh into the same realm of
essences that Shakespeare has entered, or is he secondary by
necessity, determined in advance?

> The experience of Shakespeare has been at least as textual as the expe-
> rience of Milton or Joyce for a very long time. Two hundred years ago,
> Charles Lamb spoke for many when he objected to the idea of stag-
> ing Shakespeare's greatest plays at all. The imagination of the reader
> always carries him into the character of the speaker, Lamb thought,
> whereas the play on stage makes the spectator concentrate on the
> "looks, or tones" of the actor. Lamb asserts that Lear cannot be acted:
> The contemptible machinery by which they mimic the storm which he
> goes out in, is not more inadequate to represent the horrors of the
> real elements, than any actor can be to represent Lear: they might more
> easily propose to personate the Satan of Milton upon a stage, or one
> of Michael Angelo's terrible figures. The greatness of Lear is not in cor-
> poral dimension, but in intellectual: the explosions of his passion are
> terrible as a volcano: they are storms turning up and disclosing to the
> bottom that sea his mind, with all its vast riches. (Lamb 298)[1]

One might speak of Gielgud's *performance*, but the measure for it
would lie in *King Lear* and in the scripted words of its title role.
But this answers nothing. To the extent that the theater is itself
a site of "the passion for disclosure of being" (*Metaphysics* 107), as

Heidegger puts it, rather than simply of representation, then the actor makes it possible for the charged existence of that truer world to spring into appearance.

Can this understanding be transposed to Shakespeare? Without question, his stage is a region where a communal agreement to suspend the indicative reality of space and time summons a subjunctive, "as-if" world in its place, in order to allow the disclosure of being in its deepest relation to representation. If we imagine Shakespeare's stage in Soyinka's terms, the actor himself—Gielgud in the role of Lear—is the challenger of the chthonic depths. He risks himself by entering this intensely focused space and undertaking to subsume his own life in the realization of a symbolic role. To be worthy of his part, he has to sustain the common subjunctivity, vulnerable in every instant of its enactment, with absolute seriousness. Unless it becomes *more real* than the ordinary lived world around the stage, he and the other actors have failed. To enter this space at all means to enter a larger configuration of psyche, to move amid a horde of potencies in a place where unrealized essences stir and take on new forms.

Shakespeare himself is always calling for the active participation of the audience in invoking the subjunctive world. So much has been written on plays within plays, on metatheater or metadrama, that Shakespeare's prismatic self-consciousness about the stage is thoroughly cataloged.[2] Even for the reader like Lamb, then, the stage cannot be avoided as part of the imagination of the play. It cannot simply be effaced in the service of a purer fiction from which the stage disappears, as the screen disappears in a movie theater. Shakespeare takes considerable care to establish the trope of the stage: this place of revelation, where things imagined have to come to light in all their truth or falsity, and where "counterfeiting" of every kind undergoes the most severe scrutiny. The stage serves as an *inset* both into nature and into the *saeculum*, a ritual space of cosmic focus and disclosure, and as such it exercises a powerful capacity to impel things to appear.

✼ ✼ ✼

King Lear, then, should be imagined as "on the stage" in this sense, even if one is reading the play. Summoned upon this stage is the world of appearances on which Lear insists from his first

entrance, where Goneril and Regan correctly perform their roles
as loving daughters. Stephen Greenblatt argues that "the theater
itself is already saturated with social significance and hence with
the family as the period's central social institution" (90). In this
respect, there is a continuity between the theater per se, in his
view, and the family as a performance. "Goneril and Regan
understand Lear's demand as an aspect of absolutists theater"
(97). Cordelia, on the other hand, will not perform. She will not
be an actor and thus seem other than what she is, even if she
would be acting what she really feels. The tragedy begins with her
high, rebellious stubbornness about having to *play* her own identity in a way that publicly dramatizes her affection. Playing it
seems to her a betrayal of the truth rather than a revelation of
it, because display can be used to deceive. "Sincerity forbids play-
acting," writes G. Wilson Knight, "and Cordelia cannot subdue
her instinct to any judgment advising tact rather than truth"
(161). Asked what she can say "to draw / A third more opulent
than [her] sisters" (1.1.86),[3] Cordelia allows a momentary hiatus,
as if the actor had forgotten her lines. The subjunctive world of
staged relations is imperiled at the outset, and Cordelia lets it fail
entirely when she finally replies, after a terrible pause, "Nothing,
my lord" (87).

An actor, disappearing into the role, discloses Cordelia in this
devastating refusal. On some palpable level, aided by Cordelia's
asides,[4] the audience understands how dangerously the player
enacts the refusal to act. The metaphysical quality of nothing in
this risk of stage conventions is necessary to the play's internal
awareness that it is a world being played, a "great stage of fools"—
something like "the baseless fabric" in Prospero's speech to Ferdi-
nand. From this point on, the distinction between the ritual stage
action and the play-world of its conventional characters becomes
absolute, with the Cordelia-actor as the first metaphysical challenger. Lear himself, to counter her, peremptorily ratifies the false
play-world where simple honesty is impossible, where Goneril,
Regan, and Edmund are rewarded for hypocrisy, and where irony
and disguise become modes of survival, yet this world that Lear
fashions is not itself analogous to the stage. His play-world of dissimulation is *exposed by* the stage, rather than being identical with
it, because of Cordelia's metaphysical risk, including the sublime
character of Lear.

The problem is that not everything can be impelled to appear. Most importantly in *King Lear*, gods *as gods* (rather than as inferences) cannot be disclosed by any human means. The gods might be the ground and possibility of disclosure, but never what can be disclosed. This problem becomes even more crucial when we recognize that *King Lear* plunges its whole given world into the "abyss of transition," in Soyinka's terms, with more outright boldness than any other Shakespearean tragedy. Lear's enormous ritual power does not come from his centrality, but from the way he bears the meaning of centrality out from its civilized protection into the open. Having abdicated his kingship and estranged his daughters, Lear mounts an increasingly profound metaphysical challenge to *nature* understood as including the "germains" of all things. In doing so, he must take the whole force of destruction onto himself.

The first irony, given the need to reveal the divine, is that the old king has had to be a kind of god himself, and now, with his natural powers failing, he wants to put aside the burden. At the beginning of the play, Lear is trying to forestall what he foresees as a catastrophic struggle for power after his death, given the absence of a male heir. In trying to ward off jealousy about the inheritance, he gives Cornwall and Albany portions of the realm that are as equal as he can make them; then, in an attempt to bestow the advantage on Cordelia, who has least claim to it as his youngest daughter, he insists on the formal display of affection that quickly becomes an unseemly contest of flattery. When Cordelia disastrously refuses, any hope of a peaceful exchange of power disappears. Instead, she must prove her greater love in death rather than in speech. When Cordelia defies him with her "nothing" in the first scene, Lear immediately swears by "the sacred radiance of the sun, / The mysteries of Hecate, and the night" (1.1.109-10) that he disclaims all "Propinquity and property of blood" (114) in her, invoking these divine powers to erase his kinship and make her a stranger to his heart.

It would be a mistake to read this kind of curse simply as evidence of Lear's rash old age, because it is symptomatic of his habitually dramatic self-understanding. Shakespeare's Lear is not a king in any legally circumscribed medieval or Renaissance sense. The Englishmen of Shakespeare's audience were accustomed to "the divine right of kings" and the idea of the king's near-sacramental stature as the analogy to God in a "great chain of being," but Lear has been something more, since all power—political and religious—has rested in him. There are no archbishops with a rival authority; there is certainly no political check on his power. As king, he feels to his marrow a potency both as priest and ruler, and both roles demand a kind of theatricality. From the beginning of the play, his deepest impulse seems to be the desire to put aside his divinity and experience his life, for once, simply as a man, yet he does it, if anything, more theatrically than before, because of the requirements of display in making a transition effective.

Cordelia's refusal of this play-acting means that his evacuation of kingship as a role or a set of responsibilities has two opposing effects: it empties the power of the "coronet" of its real moral authority, exposing those who vie for it to the worst political passions, and it reveals the person of the king as possessing an indomitable majesty that could never have appeared while he himself had actual sway. Yet if Lear removes this real, incarnate authority from its place, the England left behind can be nothing but a "play-world," in which "legitimacy" becomes the thing of scorn that it is for Edmund. Is human order an artificial construct over a moral abyss of the blind struggle for power, or is it grounded in deeper realities out of which the good of power itself arises? The play seems to me unquestionably to affirm these deeper realities and to reject the alternative of a moral abyss, but it does so by uniquely opening the tragic abyss to reveal a grounding depth of suffering beyond all hope of comprehension. What this means, paradoxically, is that the tragic abyss must subsume the moral one in its greater mystery, although the encounter means the destruction of all existing forms.

The obvious failure of Lear's actual cosmic power, at least in protecting *him*, reveals more truthfully his place as the dying protagonist of the old order. Such a descent cannot be undertaken by the king without itself becoming a profoundly symbolic, ritual act—not so much a disburdening as a kenosis. If he is a Jove, he is a mortal one whose storm-summoning does not exempt him from the testing of souls that he urges on: "Let the great gods, / That keep this dreadful pudder o'er our heads, / Find out their enemies now" (3.2.49-51). If he finds himself "more sinn'd against than sinning" (60), though he has certainly injured

Cordelia and Kent, he nevertheless begins to direct his attention to those like him who "feel what wretches feel" (3.4.34). One of those wretches will be the one replacing him as king, though part of Lear's kenosis is that he himself never recognizes his godson and true heir.

* * *

Unlike Lear, Edgar has done no harm at all. Although the removal of clothing, for both Lear and Edgar, signifies a putting-aside of any identity associated with public recognition as they had enjoyed it before, Edgar differs from Lear, whom he encounters and profoundly affects, in that his disrobing is a disguise that allows him some freedom to act when his official identity would leave him none. In his nakedness, he is not most himself, but most hidden from view, like Kent as "Caius."[5] Perhaps because of his innocence, Edgar begins to take on and even to heal Lear's injustice when the two of them meet in the storm. In *Shakespeare: The Invention of the Human*, Harold Bloom argues that Edgar is the real protagonist of *King Lear*, based on his prominent mention in the quarto subtitle of the play and the fact that Edgar replaces Lear as king. (In the Nahum Tate revision, of course, Edgar actually ends up marrying Cordelia.) On one level, Bloom is right that there is something "profoundly disproportionate in Edgar's self-abnegation" (480) and that it is a "voluntary overimmersion in humiliation" (481), but, when one considers that he is actually on the way to kingship, Edgar's reasons seem less unnatural than ritually exact and initiatory. Shakespeare clearly means for Edgar to embody the great resources of comic disguise, but in a more profound tragic context. He becomes almost definitionally liminal, despite the fact that neither Edgar nor anyone else in the play has any suspicion that his descent is also the way toward becoming king. If Edgar had the slightest trace of the calculation that characterizes his brother Edmund—the conscious, skeptical "policy" of the Machiavellian—then none of the ritual's real power would be engaged.

Yet it is revealing to contrast what Edmund does as a play-actor with what Edgar does. Edmund does not enter a ritual space of transition so much as he inhabits a kind of moral no-man's-land. Conceived outside marriage, as his father Gloucester readily admits, Edmund likewise exists just barely outside the structures of legitimacy that might give his abilities adequate scope.[6] Educated as a gentleman, he is ideally positioned to feel the arbitrariness of the law that denies him an inheritance. The world he sees is a play-world. He employs what he has learned in observing it to draw the audience into an appreciation of his finesse in manipulating others with pure fictions and self-referential "scenes."[7]

When Gloucester comes in exclaiming about Kent's banishment and the fact that the king has "subscribed" his power, he asks Edmund for his own news and sees him hastily putting away a letter. Asked what he was reading, Edmund innocently quotes Cordelia:

> Edm. Nothing, my lord.
> Glou. No? What needed then that terrible dispatch of it into your
>   pocket? The quality of nothing hath not such need to hide
>   itself. Let's see. Come, if it be nothing, I shall not need spec-
>   tacles.
> Edm. I beseech you, sir, pardon me. It is a letter from my brother
>   that I have not all o'er-read; and for so much as I have perused,
>   I find it not fit for your o'er-looking.
> Glou. Give me the letter, sir.
> Edm. I shall offend, either to detain or give it: the contents, as in
>   part I understand them, are to blame.
> Glou. Let's see, let's see. (1.2.31-43)

Without the soliloquy about bastardy that precedes it ("Thou, Nature, art my goddess...."), this scene would lack its extra fold of consciousness. The audience is aware that Gloucester's reactions are falsely elicited and that Edmund can finesse this betrayal of his father and his brother with a single gesture. Once the rhetorical frame has been put in place, to see is to be deceived. Edmund's staging reveals an "effectual truth" in Machiavelli's sense—that an audience will believe anything, regardless of its cost to them, if they are convinced that it has been first withheld and then forced out. But Shakespeare takes care to show that this "discovery" is a lie, however rhetorically effective the assumptions underlying it might be: his stage exposes the dissimulation.

Edgar's lack of calculation could easily make him appear as the gull—the Roderigo to Edmund's Iago. But something very different is going on here. At first victimized by Edmund's manipulation of appearances, he can acknowledge that "Edgar I nothing am" (2.4.21), strip off the social identity that would damn him, and, like Lear, instinctively cast himself in liminal symbols. According to Victor Turner, these tend to fall into two characteristic types: "those of effacement and those of ambiguity or paradox. Hence, in many societies the liminal initiands... are stripped of names and clothing, smeared with the common earth, rendered indistinguishable from animals" (Turner 26). When he becomes Tom o' Bedlam, Edgar is literally an initiand with respect to kingship—he is "at once dying from or dead to [his] former status and life, and being born and growing into new ones" (Turner 26). Edgar's very ignorance of the fact of his own transition into kingship makes his ritual transformation all the more complete. He returns to a condition symbolically prior to all social forms where even his language seems to undergo a dissolving immersion. As he takes up the part of "poor Tom," the audience witnesses a miserable madman, possessed by a demon, and *at the same time* a prodigiously inventive imagination extemporaneously using this figure to generate a series of vignettes. The invented Bedlam beggar is as unfree as possible, but Edgar, who invents him, not only retains his physical freedom but discovers a radical creative liberty.

❊   ❊   ❊

The play's crucial scene puts the old king and his successor—one descending into insanity and the other, by feigning it, ironically contributing to the overthrow of his predecessor's reason—in the same hut. "Thou art the thing itself," Lear tells Edgar. "Unaccommodated man is no more but such a poor, bare, forked animal as thou art" (3.4.106-7). One might pause over the implications of Lear, in his transition out of kingship, saying this to Edgar, who will succeed him. What does it mean that the one who will become the body of the realm must first be reduced to the "thing itself"? In the cracked molds and spilled germains of this scene, the "poor, bare, fork'd animal" appears to be man in his primal condition before any cultural addition could falsify his true nature. "Off, off you lendings!" cries Lear, trying to strip off his own clothing and reveal what he is as a mere animal, who "ow'st the worm no silk, the beast no hide, the sheep no wool, the cat no perfume" (3.4.103-5). By all appearances, it is a shattering recognition of man in his fundamental nakedness.

But what makes this scene especially tantalizing is the inaccuracy of Lear's insight. Again, the stage impels things to appear, and the audience remains aware throughout these exchanges that all the other characters are responding to Edgar's *playing* of poor Tom. Edgar has introduced the presence of the conscious actor in ways that differ from Edmund's mere deceit and that require him to fulfill the adopted role, however painful it becomes, for the duration of the scene; he accepts play-acting on the same terms that Cordelia refuses it—according to his bond. Lear looking at "the thing itself" looks at no such thing, but at a profound disguise. "Unaccommodated man" is in fact the high artifice of the imagination. This scene contains the germ of Edgar's later recognition that he can similarly affect Gloucester's real emotion by feigning. He cannot help seeing that his disguise has an entirely unintended effect, simply because he has had to sustain his role once he is in the scene. If Lear can be so moved by this chance encounter, then a conscious use of playing adapted to the requirements of other scenes can be the way of supplying what appears to be lacking in providence. Or to put it another way, this kind of access to the molds and "germains" of identity allows him to enact what would otherwise be lacking in the good: playing *is* providence. Edgar can perform his saving part with Gloucester because of the recognitions that he comes to with Lear. Gloucester can have a profound experience of grace in response to a fiction, and playing can act as the means of transformation in a soul made rigid by long identification with a cultural role.

Another scene even more forcefully foregrounds dramatic invention and its effect on its audience. Many critics have commented on the way that Edgar tricks Gloucester into thinking that he has survived a fall from the cliffs of Dover. When Duncan praises Macbeth's castle or Casca describes the storm on the night before Caesar's assassination, the verbal texture makes one enter an imaginary space that the stage scenery makes only the barest attempt to render.[8] Because Edgar's speech so clearly echoes stage conventions, the audience of *King Lear* always has difficulty not believing that Gloucester is at the "extreme verge" of the cliff when Edgar describes what he sees below him:

Come on, sir, here's the place; stand still. How fearful
And dizzy 'tis, to cast one's eyes so low!
The crows and choughs that wing the midway air
Show scarce so gross as beetles. Half way down
Hangs one that gathers sampire, dreadful trade! (4.6.11-15)

Edgar's presence, like that of Athena in the *Odyssey* or Raphael
in the *Book of Tobit*, keeps one from ever regarding Gloucester's
situation as hopeless. Since Edgar stands in a near-divine relation
to his father in the high irony of his role, the old man's very
real despair can be addressed by this stunning trope.

Edgar has found a way to convert inner absence into a dramatic image—the giddy heights of Dover as the moral abyss into
which the old man gives himself up. What exactly is literal here?
That he falls on his face[9]—or that he intends to commit suicide
but is miraculously saved, leading to a turn in his moral disposition and a new vision of himself with respect to the divine gift
of his life? The cliffs of Dover become the inner site of conversion, and Gloucester's real suicidal intention becomes a sublime
comedy because of Edgar's orchestration of effects—the counterpart
to what Edmund has done with the letter. "Think," says Edgar,
"that the clearest gods, who make them honors / Of men's
impossibilities, have preserved thee" (4.v1.73-74). Is this merely
benign abuse of the old man's credulity? If so, it is difficult to
see what the consolation would be in having Gloucester respond,
"I do remember now. Henceforth I'll bear / Affliction till it do
cry out itself / 'Enough, enough,' and die" (4.v1.75-77). Edgar's
repeated risks—such as the duel he fights with Edmund—rather
have behind them an attempt, not so much to make the gods
show themselves, as to "show the heavens more just" (3.4.36), as
Lear first conceived of doing in the great storm scene.

In his exploration of *King Lear*, Lawrence Danson cites Pascal's
passages about man in the scale of the universe: "seeing himself
suspended in the material form given him by Nature, between the
two abysses of Infinity and Nothingness, he will tremble" (quoted
in Danson 124). Danson ultimately understands these two abysses
as "a modernist nothing or a Jansenist all" (135). I also see two
abysses, but I differ in seeing them as two senses of the same
experiential groundlessness, one moral or tropological, the other

anagogical or metaphysical—tragic in a sense corresponding to the highest completions of comic meaning in Dante's allegory. Lear, to my mind, never experiences the moral abyss as Gloucester does; when he can no longer defy it, his mind fails him. He is reserved for that deeper, more mysterious abyss.

The moral abyss has its affinities, as Danson suggests, with modern nihilism. It bespeaks the absence of any undergirding, natural or metaphysical, for the bonds that Cordelia and Gloucester affirm in the first act, and it is easy to see the presence of such an abyss in Gloucester's lament after his blinding—"As flies to wanton boys are we to th' gods, / They kill us for their sport" (4.1.36-7). Much as Cordelia's adherence to her "bond" enrages him, Lear lovingly recalls the good of such connections when he reminds Regan of "The offices of nature, bond of childhood, / Effects of courtesy, dues of gratitude" (2.4.178-79). Edmund best articulates and embodies the new effectual truth that uses such customs and bonds for its own ends, but Goneril, Regan, Cornwall, and such subsidiary figures as Oswald occupy a world so merely evil in its moral darkness that Edmund looks exceptional among them in at least having principles that arise from his "bastardizing." Because it involves evil, the moral abyss is more profound than the gap between the interpretations of nature that characterize the traditional good and the effectual truth that challenges it. At stake with evil is the despair so evident in Gloucester: not only that there is no hope—that is, that nothing will get better in the future—but that time as the very quality of what is "present" manifests only absence in the most yawning metaphysical sense, so much so that one's own anomalous awareness is experienced as excruciating meaninglessness, and one's very act of being becomes egregious and absurd. This feeling comes, actively or passively, through the experience of real evil, and its sense of gaping absence is what I am calling the moral abyss. But this feeling of unsupportedness or groundlessness is different from the tragic abyss, which penetrates to the causes behind causes—even to the "no cause" of Cordelia—where evil cannot reach. It consumes even hope itself, which Lear exhibits to the end, yet its pitiless absoluteness has the capacity strangely to heal and purify.

By his art, and perhaps as the king to be, Edgar apprehends the moral abyss and saves his father from it—first with the fiction of a miracle, then with the final revelation of his own steadfast identity under his protean guises. But for the departing king who tried to forestall the terrors of transition, that still more terrible abyss is reserved. Old, magnificent Lear meets his successor once more, immediately after Gloucester's supposed fall from the cliffs of Dover. When Lear appears "fantastically dressed with wild flowers," the transition of power is already nearing its completion, and Lear has entered what might be considered entirely a play-world. Now he plays "the king" ("Ay, every inch a king") with an irony of madness quite different from that, say, of the deposed Richard II. Again (as in the hut during the storm scene), the theme is sex, especially the womanizing for which Gloucester was so unrepentant at the beginning of the play. Spotting the blinded old man, Lear proclaims, theatrical as ever,

> I pardon that man's life. What was thy cause?
> Adultery?
> Thou shalt not die. Die for adultery! No,
> The wren goes to 't, and the small gilded fly
> Does lecher in my sight.
> Let copulation thrive; for Gloucester's bastard son
> Was kinder to his father than my daughters
> Got 'tween the lawful sheets. (4.vl.109-16)

Lear's imagination of his daughters and the "lawful sheets" where he begot them leads him to a ferocious condemnation of the dissimulation of women:

> Behold yond simp'ring dame,
> Whose face between her forks presages snow;
> That minces virtue, and does shake the head
> To hear of pleasure's name—
> The fitchew nor the soiled horse goes to't
> With a more riotous appetite. (4.vl.118-23)

The nausea here seems Dionysian, in Nietzsche's sense. For Lear in this mood, the appearance of chastity merely covers the unbridled lust that characterizes all of nature. But it is important to distinguish the "sulphurous pit" (128) of female sexuality from the moral abyss, because the difference here is not between human good and moral evil, but between the lawful human measure and great nature's "riotous appetite" in blindly begetting itself.

This abyss Nietzsche calls the "primal unity," accessible through Dionysian ecstasy, and Lear, like Nietzsche, associates it both with birth out of sex and with a sense of having fallen into an individuated role. After recognizing Gloucester, he says,

> Thou must be patient; we came crying hither:
> Thou know'st, the first time that we smell the air
> We wawl and cry. I will preach to thee. Mark.
>   [*Lear takes off his crown of weeds and flowers.*]
> Glou. Alack, alack the day!
> Lear. When we are born, we cry that we are come
>   To this great stage of fools. (4.6.178-83)

Like Macbeth in extremis or Prospero in his moment of despair, Lear conceives of the whole character of reality as a stage in a disparaging sense. But what exactly does he mean? The "great stage of fools" is the world as that space in which one is forced to appear and act a demeaning part, in which being born at all is a falling-off.[10] Yet this vision of the world as a stage also has a passionate, protean energy, not least in the wawling infant it brings before the imagination—a vital premonition of Cordelia dead in Lear's arms. The carnival sense of the "stage of fools" with its reference back to Lear's "all-licensed fool" and forward to the "poor fool" who is reported hanged in the last scene subtly preludes the character of the tragic abyss toward which Lear is actually moving.

❄   ❄   ❄

Edgar's playacting with his blind father prepares for the truly ritual enactment of *King Lear*, in which the old king and his daughter act out their roles to the end, without evasion or mask, and thus take the audience past all irony and into a ritual experience of the tragic abyss. Both Edgar and Lear enter the space of cosmic challenge. Adopting still another accent and role—a peasant with a Somerset dialect—Edgar first undertakes his new role as a killer by dispatching Oswald when he threatens to kill Gloucester. When he appears, again in disguise, to challenge and defeat Edmund in the last act of the play, he undergoes a ritual

confrontation with the powers of the moral abyss, with evil insofar as his brother embodies it. His victory seems inevitable,
because, unlike his brother, he has a mastery that comes from
having plunged to the source of appearance, where disguise or
deception can become the means of disclosure.

But Lear has no such power. After he wakes from his madness to hear Cordelia tell him quietly that she has "No cause,
no cause" (4.2.74) not to love him, his part is to undergo the
worst. Yet it would be a mistake to say that his successor is
spared it. In a sense, Edgar's encounter with the tragic abyss—like
that of the audience—occurs only when the old king's cosmic,
kingly, and paternal powers fail entirely over Cordelia at the end
of the play and he cannot summon the least breath back into
her body. The effect of Lear's final metaphysical impotence is like
the revelation of Oedipus' spiritual power in *Oedipus at Colonus*.
For the audience increasingly drawn into a ritual enactment, it is
a mysteriously cleansing agony of boundless depth; for Edgar in
the play, it is the mysterious source of moral authority.

Why it should be so relates to the nature of loss. When the
inevitability of death becomes part of consciousness, one also
becomes conscious that love increases the agony of loss. The
depth and gravity of one's bearing in the world stems from the
disposition toward potential loss or, more to the point, toward
the agony that love can cause, the abyss that loss of the beloved
can open. The death of Cordelia at the end of *King Lear* is more
unsparing, in an entirely different way, than the end of *The Bacchae*. The death of the beloved daughter has nothing to mediate
it—no blame or guilt to make it more acceptable, as the deaths
of Goneril and Regan do. Nothing here can shift the emphasis
away from the absoluteness of loss. A Stoic would say that Lear
is at fault because he should never have invested his love so completely in a mortal being; a strict theologian would say that he
should have loved the eternal and unchanging God whom he
could never lose. Both, concerned with the dangers of the moral
abyss, would miss the theological mystery that comes in this pre-
Christian scene from the absence of any consolation or any hope
of resurrection (5.3.16). Samuel Johnson complains that "Shakespeare has suffered the virtue of Cordelia to perish in a just
cause, contrary to the natural ideas of justice, to the hope of the
reader, and, what is yet more strange, to the faith of chronicles"

(224). Perhaps even more than those considerations, however, what shocked him was the chill of the abyss that comes from these lines:

> Why should a dog, a horse, a rat, have life
> And thou no breath at all? Thou'lt come no more,
> Never, never, never, never, never. (5.3.307-9)

Why is it, then, that we can feel Cordelia's innocent death and Lear's great, broken grief over her as infinitely more compelling, in the tragic sense, than what Johnson had hoped to see—"the final triumph of persecuted virtue" (224)? The action plunges, definitively and contrary to all wish, through everything that might ground the imagination in some ordinary or extraordinary satisfaction of justice.

Gloucester's salvation from despair moves us, but in this play, only the most agonized vision can sufficiently immolate the old order to provide the grave metaphysical precondition of a new beginning. But we do not even think in that way during the play itself, though we might recognize it afterward. Gathering toward Cordelia's death, with the word *nothing* running through it from beginning to end, with its themes of old age, parent and child, lust and filial love, nature, bonds, madness, the justice of the gods, the hypocrisy of the powerful, the powers of the weak, the play finally issues in a grief that penetrates the secret cause. In the tragic abyss, the profundity of suffering lies in the experience of death as the absolute unmerited pain of severing the inmost bond of love. The abyss is opened by death, but love is its excruciating medium.

Unlike Kent or Edgar—or Edmund, for that matter—neither Lear nor Cordelia will participate in disguise, but this refusal stems from a kind of absoluteness about who they are. If Lear asks for someone to tell him who he is, the reasons do not lie in something malleable about him, but in his confusion about the actions of his daughters, since they do not seem to be reacting to the man he knows himself to be. Cordelia, for her part, will not seem other than what she is. The tragic action begins with her high, rebellious stubbornness about having to *play* her own identity in a way that foregrounds and dramatizes her affection, even if it is what she actually feels.

Because of this strength of character, however, her final scene in the play has a profound iconic effect. Coming as it does after Edgar's profound play-acting, her death turns the greatest effect of the play outside its own bounds, like the inverse perspective of an icon that locates the vanishing point no longer in the illusory depths of the image but in the spectator. Because Edgar has made us so keenly aware of the way that love can transform playing, Cordelia's integrity precisely here, her final truth to what she is in this scene, makes this play uniquely affecting. "Love, and be silent," she says in an aside at the beginning, when her sisters disgust her with their effusive displays. Now in her silence, her nothing, she completes this tacit word of love. She plays her integrity with an absolute sacrificial power, and in her absence from herself becomes the thing itself, in which the perfect speech of love is her dead body, uttered without breath. Cordelia in this last scene *must* say nothing, do nothing, despite the urgent, heartbreaking pleas of a great father restored to his majestic sanity. The absolute word of love means that the reality of death must not be denied.

But, one asks at the same time, how *could* she deny it? "Cordelia" is nothing but a dead body, a thing. She wills nothing, she means nothing: how can this be a Cordelia with any intentionality at all—except that Lear exercises over her his whole theatrical and hieratic powers of summoning her still to be Cordelia. In this scene, Shakespeare puts an almost unbearable focus on the living body of the actress. An intense irony broods over the lines when Lear holds up the feather to the lips of the breathing actress and says,

> This feather stirs, she lives! if it be so,
> It is a chance which does redeem all sorrows
> That ever I have felt. (5.3.266-68)

Yet the very awareness that the audience has of the scene being *played* enforces rather than undercuts the sense of tragedy. The more Lear protests that she is alive, the more thoroughly the audience, in whom the ritual action takes place, knows—knows beyond doubt, beyond any possibility of palliation—that she is indeed "dead as earth." It knows that there is life in the body, but not Cordelia's life: life plays this absolute death and impels it to appear. Lear himself has passed beyond it, beckoned by the something he can now make of her nothing. But if she were not truly dead, her nothing could not speak as it does; nor could the love in it so ground and right the moral universe.

Cordelia's death contradicts all hope, not so much for temporal justice as for a kind of visible blessing that descends upon the good. Because the extra fold of consciousness that informs scenes of conscious playing, such as those of Edmund and Edgar in their different modes, has been torn away, this final tragedy takes place in that ritual space of appearance for which the stage is ultimately the metaphor. This is a sanctuary of the imagination where one does not merely picture or fantasize an action, but one recognizes there a supreme, transfiguring power, since real spiritual powers become manifest in it. It has reality, beyond any power that illusion has, and on this ritual stage, Samuel Johnson to the contrary, the audience can encounter the absolute mood of loss.

Or call it the power of death, the power to make nothing of something, metaphysically imagined. Milton's allegorization of Death in *Paradise Lost* appears grotesque beside the nothing summoned to appear in this space of confrontation that Shakespeare clears for the imagination of the west. Edgar's challenge of Edmund, whose vision of nature is a veil hiding the power of death, prefigures this last confrontation, beyond disguises. Death cannot appear as nothing, as *what it is*, without the particularity of love that refuses death itself as its limit. Lear's refusal to accept the absence of Cordelia in death "Look on her, look, her lips, / Look there, look there!"— forces the nature of death to show itself by making it appear without disguise through the power of love. Death makes Lear's hope look like illusion, nothing. But death itself is literally the illusion on the stage.

What remains is a sense of grandeur not to be entirely identified with the opinions of the devastated survivors in the play itself. The tragic abyss proves to encompass the moral abyss and paradoxically to ground the transition from one world to another.[12] Within *King Lear*, it is the transition to the new regime of the man who is, in a sense, the recipient of the immolation of the world of Lear, the one on whom the new actuality of kingship will now rest—"The weight of this sad time" (324), as Edgar puts it in the last speech. When one considers the effect of participation in the ritual enactment that is the play itself, it is the transition that Edgar as ritual participant, both player and representative of the audience, enacts on behalf of the poor, bare, forked animal: the acceptance of an excruciating kingship mysteriously prepared and inevitably conferred.

NOTES

[1] More recently, Harold Bloom writes, "I begin sadly to agree with Charles Lamb that we ought to keep rereading *King Lear* and avoid its staged travesties." (476).

[2] Thomas G. Rosenmeyer summarizes the range of explorations following upon Lionel Abel's introduction of the term "metatheater" in 1963:

> Depending on the critic, the emphasis may be... on the play-within-the-play; or on the dramatized awareness of characters that they are characters in a play, i.e., the further 'theatricalization' of what is already theatrical; or on the play as a discourse on playmaking; or on the capacity of characters to act like playwrights; or on the tenuousness of the distinction between character and actor; or on the breakdown of the separation between the stage and audience...." (89).

[3] All citations of Shakespearean texts are from *The Riverside Shakespeare*.

[4] Greenblatt writes of the "odd internal distance" in Cordelia's asides, as if they were being spoken by the playwright himself.

[5] Greenblatt and others have made it fashionable to say that Shakespeare, operating in the power system of Renaissance drama, "subverts authority" while he "recuperates hierarchy" (Spotswood 266). Jerald Spotswood goes on to put the requisite slant on *King Lear*:

> In The Tragedie of King Lear individual characters challenge authority; yet systems of hierarchy are reinscribed performatively, especially in the actions of disguised characters like Kent and Edgar, whose essentialized aristocratic identities are maintained in their performance of an assumed identity. Kent's foray into the lower orders, like Edgar's, demonstrates not an alliance between gentry and commoners but the social distance between them. Banished and threatened with death, each disguises himself by stripping away the outward signs of status. (Spotswood 268)

The insight here into playing or acting would be more accurate if one were talking about good men instead of "essentialized aristocratic identities." One would have to recast the argument, however, to say that the "performances" of Kent and Edgar in the play do not recuperate "hierarchy" so much as they recover what is ultimately authoritative about virtue, because their goodness is ultimately what ennobles them, not their places in the hierarchical system. Spotswood is at some pains to moderate the view that Cornwall's servant, who kills him, is nevertheless made to seem better than his master, though he obviously is. The whole discussion is framed in terms of the successful overcoming of a "peasant rebellion" (275-77).

6 Edmund does not deny that outside causes frame his character in a certain way, but those causes are the social effects of his being begotten as a bastard. When he says, "I should have been that I am, had the maidenliest star in the firmament twinkled on my bastardizing" (1.2.142-44), his thought anticipates—in fact, exhibits—"cultural materialism" in a way that might give contemporary critics pause.

7 Richard III and Iago share this capacity.

8 Harry Levin showed forty years ago that its power stems from the fact that Edgar employs exactly the same verbal techniques to deceive his blind father that Shakespeare uses to create his own scenes.

9 G. Wilson Knight has commented that "the grotesque [is] merged into the ridiculous" in the bathos of this scene (171). But if something is grotesque, it is the disparity between imagination and outer appearances.

10 The mood of this passage approaches that of Nietzsche's Silenus, who tells King Midas, "What is best of all is utterly beyond your reach: not to be born, not to be, to be nothing. But the second best for you is—to die soon" (BT 42).

11 Johnson famously refrained from re-reading it until he was obliged to do so as an editor. It shocked him, not least because he was unable to escape the recognition that the playwright had deliberately changed the story to make the ending what it was. In Raphael Holinshed's well-known historical account, Lear goes into Gallia, reunites with Cordelia, leads the Gallic army against his usurpers, conquers them, and rules for the remaining two years of his life.

12 Terry Eagleton argues that "the play is not about the emergence of new life from this sacrificial self-divestment. It is rather about the fact that if such life is ever to labour through, as it does in

the Last Comedies, it can only be as a result of such drastic self-abandonment" (284-85).

12

Intervals of Risk and the Tragic Action of *Macbeth*

JAMES WALTER

Macbeth is a mystery play in several senses. Questions have arisen, for instance, about the text itself. Passages in its First Folio version are thought to be spurious additions by a hand other than Shakespeare's—but whose? Does this ghostly hand account for the play's odd inconsistencies? In some places the plot precisely follows details of its early sixteenth-century source, Raphael Holinshed's *Chronicles of England, Scotland, and Ireland*, but other episodes freely revise history to change the agency and effect of important actions (Coursen 15-21). Gaps in the plot undermine the dramatic credibility of sequences of events and of characters' movements between particular locales represented in the play's world. Did Shakespeare's attention lapse, or has his unknown editor or collaborator—or censor—warped the internal structure of the play? Some scholars deny that any such gaps or inconsistencies exist, arguing that the play's construction provides sufficient clues for a reasonable account of every cause operating in it (Lowenthal),[1] while others have declared that the play is hopelessly riddled with unaccountable happenings. Far from yielding a satisfying artistic coherence, they claim, *Macbeth* will induce incurable anxiety in readers wanting answers to whys and wherefores.

The mystery of *Macbeth* has been amplified by the fact that it appears to support not so much variations on an accepted reading as diametrically opposed interpretations of character, plot, and

theme. Admired, on the one hand, for its endorsement of a
Machiavellian prudent boldness in wresting political rule from
weaklings (Riebling), it has also been praised, on the other, for
supporting the Christian virtues that legitimate the sovereignty of
good King Duncan and his son Malcolm (Knights). Macbeth himself has been viewed as a butcher-tyrant whose slaughter falls dis-
proportionately on women and children and, quite conversely, as
a capable leader whose tanist claim to Scotland's throne has been
unjustly undermined by Duncan's cunning (Valbuena 110).[2] Analyses have disagreed about what the Macbeths hope to gain by their
daring partnership—whether something obvious and attainable,
such as high position, honor and troops of friends (Lowenthal),
or an ecstatic fulfillment exceeding the earthly reach of their lust-
ful spirits (Calderwood). And many questions have become so
vexed as to seem, four hundred years after the play first appeared,
irresolvable. What, for example, is the nature of the witches or
"weïrd sisters" and their function in the plot? How should one
approach the many associated problems to which they give rise:
the interdependence of good and evil, the efficacy of human will,
and the relation of tragic fate to significant choice? This indeter-
minacy of *Macbeth*, while making it immune to summary explanation, has given its social, psychological, and political themes a
certain usable pliancy, not only for academic special pleading, but
for social causes as diverse as gangster culture and national
restoration movements (Stríbrn´y).

The variety of responses suggests that contradiction and irrec-
oncilability might be the dramatic intent. Crucial to the play's
meaning is the experience of dramatic perplexity, even of aporia,
in readers and audiences. How else could it pull them to a
boundary of life where the most trivial and the most conse-
quential questions gather to a head and await answer—where the
action either reveals life as "a tale / Told by an idiot" or a
glimpse of ultimate truth? This dramatic experience of the unfathomable, the irrevocable, the irremediable, and the incommensurate
is most germane to *Macbeth*'s unique effect as a "mystery
tragedy." Without sufficient cognizance of this experience, textual
studies and theory-laden interpretations amount to what Keats
called an "irritable reaching after fact and reason." Through its
representation of the unknown and unknowable in human life,
Macbeth draws readers to a place we recognize as hauntingly

familiar, one that permits a concentrated perspective on definitively opposed human possibilities.

Since provocation to question the accepted meanings of life and to respect its dark ambiguities seems to be a deep motive behind the play's design, I propose to explore crucial moments in *Macbeth* when the *dramatis personae* find themselves in liminal situations. Understood temporally, these supreme moments are dramatic intervals in which King Duncan, Macbeth and Lady Macbeth, Banquo and his sons, Macduff and his family, and Malcolm consciously exercise a radical freedom. Outside the structures that ordinarily constrain them, they authenticate their identities in relation to the natural world, the human community, and the continuum of time. In these transitory suspensions of plotted time, the characters, by their choices, experience the internal and external impulses bearing on the present from the accumulated past and the desired future. Feeling the immensity of the cosmos, the fleetingness of *chronos*, and a need to conform their human powers and deeds to ultimate origins and possibilities, they either open or close themselves to a *kairos* exceeding their foresight.

The play is designed to draw its readers and audiences to a similar threshold of awareness. Finalities, the play's dramatic structure suggests, show themselves at moments when opportunity and despair, life and death, *now* and eternity intersect. In this interval of imagination, the audience of tragedy is helped to understand motives for feeling pity and terror toward dreadful acts of wayward humanity, whose antagonists are both at large in the visible world and hidden in recesses of the self. The range of vision from this threshold includes not only a glimpse of an abyss that can open beneath us, but also a glancing perspective on a measure that actions of justice and mercy give to the plot of time.

❖ ❖ ❖

In the beginning of *Macbeth*, the rebel MacDonwald has just led a guerrilla revolt with the aid of Irish mercenaries; with Scotland's attention already thus occupied, the Norwegian King Sweno has attacked from a different direction. Such situations are common, and for Scotland to have any future in this political climate of treachery and chronic conflict, King Duncan must swiftly capitalize on his victories to strengthen the social bond that is his only hope for averting future rebellions. Scottish lords have offered their very blood on his behalf to secure his crown, and he has no option but to build his sovereignty on their loyalty, even though past traitors have taught him that "There's no art / To find the mind's construction in the face" (1.4.12-13). In *Macbeth* the political urgency for Duncan to place "An absolute trust" in "gentlem[e]n" who show loyalty is made more dire, unfortunately, by the deep psychological and societal wounds that transgenerational warfare has created in every soul and human relation. As the play begins, beleaguered Duncan works swiftly, with public displays of generosity, to tie to him and his rule the heart of "brave Macbeth," who has been essential to the defeat of both MacDonwald and the Norwegians.

In societies like Duncan's, a king's most effectual means for strengthening the allegiance of his nobles is the bestowal of titles and property, exchanged not simply as payment for services but in an honorable spirit of gift-giving. The climate of inherited war and strategic treachery among the clans in Shakespeare's tragedy is not unlike the terrorist climate that exists among twenty-first century political organizations that do not mutually acknowledge any third party, or higher political unity, presiding over resolution of their differences. Each group wants the right to include and exclude as it sees fit. Where this posture is endemic, fear and the sense of isolation run deep, as does the heady dream of personal conquest to overcome all uncertainties. Subgroups battle for supremacy, and even within families distrust can be so rife as to compel a brother to say to a brother, "The near in blood / The nearer bloody" (2.3.140-41).[3] In this condition of stark options preceding submission to any superior authority, the reciprocity of gifts is an elementary contrivance that wards off the temptation of war, because it creates a social sense of mutual indebtedness.[4]

Duncan's gift-giving, then, has an extraordinary importance in forming bonds of obligation. Both the soundness and the tenuousness of Duncan's tactic in rewarding Macbeth are made apparent later when the hero resists momentarily his wife's entreaties that he be another traitor:

> He hath honor'd me of late, and I have bought
> Golden opinions from all sorts of people,
> Which would be worn now in their newest gloss,

Not cast aside so soon. (1.7.31-34)

Gift-giving has at least a temporary effect. But this apology for not killing the king indirectly expresses both desire for impersonal, unabridged power and a conviction of entitlement to it: the oxymoron of honors "bought" by loyal deeds, but not specifically *political* honors. What profoundly moves Macbeth and his wife is a "greatness" often associated with theatrical spectacle in the metaphorical texture of their language: "greatness" appeals to their capacity to dream. In Macbeth's soul, a vaunting pride in visible accomplishment veils his underlying dread of personal insignificance and nullifies the spirit of gifts.

Macbeth's human coldness and Duncan's sense of it are evident in their first meeting after the defeat of the rebels and invaders. Although the king bestows due honors, he recognizes the impossibility of ever repaying men whose commitment to his cause has been so absolute as to risk their very blood and lives. Acknowledging the "sin of [his] ingratitude" that rests "heavy" on him, since Macbeth's due is "more than all can pay" (1.4.15-21), Duncan promises to speed up slow "recompense." In such circumstances, the giver of titles must hope that these are received as adequate symbols of his gratitude. There is already a tragic potential in the incommensurateness of such exchanges; Duncan hints at it when he resorts to a metaphor of having to hurry to "overtake" Macbeth's deserving. Shortly afterward, Macbeth's man outruns the royal messenger in a horse race to deliver news of the king's progress to Inverness. Hinted here is the possibility that the hero may need to speed himself to a more satisfying recompense.

In this first exchange of Macbeth and Duncan following their victory lurk signs of some deficiency of love and trust. Although the king prefaces his greetings to Macbeth with the words "O worthiest cousin," his first speech to Macbeth seems quite solemn and obligatory, very much unlike his later repartee with Banquo. For his part, Macbeth appeals to the family for his paradigm of social exchange:

The service and the loyalty I owe,
In doing it, pays itself. Your Highness' part
Is to receive our duties; and our duties
Are to your throne and state children and servants;

> Which do but what they should, by doing every thing
> Safe toward your love and honor. (1.4.22-27)

The sinuous syntax of Macbeth's discourse here suggests a contrived quality in his adherence to "duties." Political fatherhood, not being entirely natural, has to be earned by tact, and, knowing the failure of even natural family bonds to end the havoc in Scotland, Duncan broadens the discourse on social order with a more spacious, less problematic metaphor of gardening: "I have begun to plant thee, and will labor / To make thee full of growing." Given the present excess of deserving on Macbeth's side, the king will need time to make his children "full of growing"—but speed is the hallmark of Macbeth's ambition.

Duncan's trace of melancholy as he notes his "sin" of laggard gratitude suggests a philosophic wisdom regarding the inevitable gap or imbalance in all historically contingent exchanges. Rough-hewn outcomes can be shaped to a general fairness only by steadfast good will and mutual dedication among all parties. When men accept gifts graciously and express their willingness to take good intentions for actual deeds, they annul the incommensurateness in their relationships. Only then does something of eternity reach forward to nurture peace in the present. Further evidence of Duncan's philosophical trait is his imaginative transcendence of the familial:

> We will establish our estate upon
> Our eldest, Malcolm, whom we name hereafter
> The Prince of Cumberland; which honor must
> Not unaccompanied invest him only,
> But signs of nobleness, like stars, shall shine
> On all deservers. (37-42)

Conceiving his kingly prerogative as analogous to that of a cosmic artificer who founds, strengthens, enhances, and shares his handiwork, Duncan tries to lift the sights of his hearers to see that the family, ordinarily inward-looking, must find completion of its meaning through outward-directed human work conformed to the majesty of primordial creation. Opposed to this philosophic wisdom is Macbeth's dark ambition. He responds to Duncan's *poiesis* of Scotland's possible future with a private aside of rebellious guttering: "Stars, hide your fires / Let not light see my black and deep desires" (50-51). His Luciferian repudiation uncovers a first glimpse of the impenetrable darkness he harbors within himself.

※   ※   ※

Against the backdrop of first one, then another rebel's descent into a terrible abyss in *Macbeth*, Shakespeare's drama explores and concretizes another possibility of tragic endurance that must be fashioned in the storm, smoke, fog, and darkness covering the human world. Strangely, the characters experience these manifestations of chaos as media of access to "metaphysical aid." The metaphysical anxiety that permeates the world of *Macbeth*, gathered and focused on a "bank and shoal of time" (1.7.6) where different worlds interpenetrate, spurs repeated human attempts to reach beyond the self, the kingdom, and the present for knowledge and remedy. With rhythmic frequency characters in the play whisper their "amens" to forces beyond themselves; they prayerfully petition and try to conjure powers they imagine as either latent or ascendant; and this gesture of the soul, elicited at a boundary where life's last alternatives are posed, functions dramatically as something like a "meme" of this tragedy's morphology.[5] This disposition of human consciousness to couple with invisible powers at a boundary of great risk recurs in the drama as a sign of something easily (and tragically) forgotten in times flush with opportunity: it is the fate of the temporal creature to seek and find all its meaning at a literal deadline, definite yet unpredictable, drawn across all doubts, dependencies, and unfulfillments.

In this respect *Macbeth* is like *Julius Caesar, Hamlet,* and the later romances *Pericles, Cymbeline, The Winter's Tale,* and *The Tempest* in which hints of supernatural agency, within and without the characters' psyches, periodically disturb the world's immanence. Unlike Shakespeare's whole-hearted deniers of metaphysical height and depth such as Iago, Edmund, and Richard III, Macbeth and all the other Scots instinctively depend on an alliance of limited human efforts with more powerful brokers of fate—such as the witches planning their mischief in the play's opening scene—to resolve their personal and political uncertainties. As present contingencies in *Macbeth* await a future realization, the atmosphere of irresolution underlines how fateful are the acts of faith, trust, tenderness, and loyalty, as well as treachery, that in time's interstices bond human realization and meaning.

Closely examining this recourse to "fate and metaphysical aid" (1.5.29), as Lady Macbeth calls it, can assist our understanding of the tragic darkness that threatens all the inhabitants of the world of *Macbeth*. Lady Macbeth's first appearance in the play extends the theme of equivocation already begun with the witches' "Fair is foul, and foul is fair" insofar as she is, in a sense, alone with her husband though he is not with her.[6] She is privately reading a letter from her husband (1.5.1-14) announcing King Duncan's approach to Inverness, and its ending plays on metaphors of conception and childbearing: "'This have I thought good to deliver thee, my dearest partner of greatness, that thou mightst not lose the dues of rejoicing, by being ignorant of what greatness is promised thee. Lay it to thy heart, and farewell.'" The written words of the letter, removed from the directive force of Macbeth's overriding presence, are free to provoke thoughts, evoke imaginings, and instigate explorations of possibilities in ways peculiar to language set free of its author. The boredom of his "dearest partner in greatness" at Inverness has whetted her desire to conceive and give birth to a more substantial life (1.5.57).[7]

The letter appears in what Kay Stockholder describes as a "desire-laden atmosphere, producing a world so pervaded by compelling emotion that the protagonists seem to have little control over the forces that move them" (86). After reading her husband's letter, Lady Macbeth's soliloquy is actually a prayer—another instance of a call for "metaphysical aid." She interprets the news as proof that chance is conspiring to make their dream possible:

> Come, you spirits
>   That tend on mortal thoughts, unsex me here,
> And fill me from the crown to the toe topful
> Of direst cruelty! Make thick my blood,
> Stop up th' access and passage to remorse,
> That no compunctious visitings of nature
> Shake my fell purpose, nor keep peace between
> Th' effect and it. Come to my woman's breasts
> And take my milk for gall, you murth'ring ministers,
> Wherever in your sightless substances
> You wait on nature's mischief! (1.5.40-50)

In effect, as the word-figures free up—by expressing them—motives that had been inarticulate in Macbeth and Lady Macbeth, they also serve to focus their thoughts on performance of the script that gradually becomes legible. Lady Macbeth's interpretation of the letter channels her inner desires and takes on a magisterial authority that will quickly enthrall her, then her husband through her.[8] She imagines here that, although "heaven" watches the deeds of earth, its view will be blocked when her compact with murderous spirits causes a "blanket of the dark" to rise and deprive heaven of either its power or will to "peep through... To cry / Hold, Hold!" (1.5.54) The phrases of her prayer move from the more personal to the impersonal (from "you spirits" to "thick night"), from heaven to earth, from the life-giving to the death-dealing—all in the name of seeking a new lease on life. Her imagination never really transcends a chance-dependent universe. The "murdering ministers" who will allow her to forestall the "compunctious visitings of nature" are the same sightless substances she calls to help her kill the king. The "spirits / That tend on mortal thoughts" are identical with her conviction that nature's process is entropic at all its levels. Ironically she would kill something in herself to abet her part in a murder.

In effect, as the full course of dramatic action she instigates here will show, Lady Macbeth has appealed directly (and naively) to instruments of the abyss to facilitate her and her husband's life-renewal. Almost immediately, new aspects of their "partnership in greatness" reveal themselves. The division of labor allows each to contribute the major share of an aptitude in which the other is weak. If one of them reneges on the letter of their agreement, as Macbeth does when he hesitates to murder Duncan, then the other can issue a demand for performance: Lady Macbeth will later bring up the difference between hotly broaching his "enterprise" with her and his subsequent lame delay. The genius of their peculiar relationship is in its facilitation of a division between his judgment regarding final causes of actions ("toward what end?") and her calculation of efficient causality ("by what means?"). If *his* understanding pertains more to being and having, while *hers* concerns planning, urging, and directing, then their *modus operandi* has already abandoned the order of gender cooperation that cultures have traditionally held to be natural.

Consequently, the wife's rejection of this order in her "unsex me here" soliloquy is not surprising. If, as Stockholder maintains, "Macbeth and Lady Macbeth are the most intimate of Shakespeare's lovers" (88), their intimacy has not included honestly sharing their deepest desires and fears. Rather, their partnership makes them usefully collaborate in action even though they are not intersubjective in their existence. Thus, the deepest longing of each entails a peculiar displacement of their sexual energies from the conjugal bed (that yields "no children" [4.3.216]) to an eroticized sphere of risk-taking in which they strive to acquire immortality. Their arrangement, oddly, takes them out of integral and loving participation in present life; it makes them spectators of deeds that their unexamined desires propel them to perform in a theater where the dénouement is already foreseen as "the future in the instant" (1.5.58).

The principal lesson Macbeth takes from his wife's coaching is how to face the mysterious contingency that surrounds cruxes of decision. Macbeth's schooling in his wife's hard lesson is evident in the prayer he makes after hers: when he moves in the dark towards Duncan's chamber, he imagines an interregnum in nature's living course. His prayer as he goes to commit the murder begs "sure and firm-set earth" to "Hear not my steps... And take the present horror from the time, / Which now suits with it" (2.2.57-60).[9] In asking "earth" to pall and deaden both sensation and sense while he performs an unanswerable deed, he barters away all his natural feeling of the horror of the act by which he will create himself at once King of Scotland and a dark monstrous thing. From this point, his tragic fate, like a cancer, riots in its own declension. Opening the abyss created by his inward sacrifice of native human powers, he renders the outer world prey to what is most bestial in all of nature—irrational humanity. This self-willed lack escalates its havoc all along the fateful progress of Macbeth and his wife, as their lust of spirit mounts their judgment, corrals the "firstlings" of their hearts into a mechanism of retaliation, and rides down sympathy and fear. Ultimately, the deepest human emotion they truly know will be savage hatred of life—hated because it gives up those who have lost natural feeling to a bottomless lack that mysteriously exceeds nature.

* * *

Macbeth's definitive creation of unnatural darkness within himself completes the moral devolution that began with his impulsive "Stars, hide your fires." Reflecting this devolution, the play's visible action moves from nature's daylight to full dark. If Macbeth's darkness is a direct effect of nature's own transition to darkness and thus a darkening of nature, or, on the contrary, a function of Macbeth's conjuring—in either case, as the play suggests, a determinism cements human action to natural process. The responses of other characters to natural qualities of light suggest, however, a more finely graded awareness. In the scene in which Duncan and his retinue arrive at Inverness, the stage directions calling for "torches" indicate evening's vespertinal light. Since "evening" in Patristic theology symbolically represents, in Patricia Parker's words, a "pendant moment" before the onslaught of full dark, an "interval of decision or choice" regarding ultimate things, the darkness of this scene contrasts importantly with the deeper darkness about to descend on Inverness (44-53). The fragility of this interlude is underscored by the immediate entrance in the scene of the "Lady" who has recently turned herself into a witch devoid of all gentle feminine qualities. In light of the "unnatural" deeds soon to begin, this twilight evocation of human possibility serves as a backward-looking remembrance of blessings of daylight, which will be absent or obscured through the entire middle of the play before it dawns again in the final scenes.

This twilight scene at Inverness plays significantly against another scene a few hours later. In the first scene of Act Two, as Banquo and Fleance prepare for sleep after attending the Macbeths' entertainment of the King, their conversation pegs the time as shortly after midnight. Although readers have debated how to interpret Banquo's observation that "There's husbandry in heaven, / Their candles are all out" (2.1.4-5), David-Everett Blythe's contention that "all out" must mean, not extinguished, but "lit up and in view.... wide-awake" makes eminent dramatic sense, particularly since stars would be especially visible in the moonless sky remarked by Fleance (773). Despite Macbeth's collusion with powers of darkness, this scene would suggest that demonic forces never have absolute sway as long as some men conserve effects of light in their thoughts and feelings. Banquo's witness, in his son's presence, to the constancy of heavenly "husbandry," so different from the impulse counter to creation in Macbeth's "Stars, hide your fires," expresses a profound sympathy with nature. This trust is implied, also, in a following prayer that Banquo addresses to nature's conservator:

> A heavy summons lies like lead upon me,
> And yet I would not sleep. Merciful powers,
> Restrain in me the cursed thoughts that nature
> Gives way to in repose! (6-9)[10]

Evidently Banquo's thoughts resist nature's summons to sleep at this interval because the dynastic prospect shown him by the witches has stirred his thoughts of taking initiative in his own hands. Acknowledging the appeal to his vanity and lust in the witches' prophecy, Banquo petitions "Merciful powers" that are sovereign over nature (including human nature) to protect him from the inner darkness of his "cursed thoughts." In the short view, this prayer may appear feckless, even ironic. In the long view, however, time's own production, evident in the tragedy's denouement, will unite the proleptic vision of the witches, Banquo's dynastic desire, his husbandry of justice, and the substance of his prayer.

When Banquo, in this troubled moment, reconfirms the valence of the metaphysical aid that orients his life, he is interrupted by an intruder—Macbeth making his rounds of the sleepers' rooms. Banquo's sudden reaching for his sword reveals how fragile is the balance he holds in faith. "I dreamt last night of the three weird sisters," he tells Macbeth, indicating his willingness to talk openly about possible consequences of the witches' apparition. But Macbeth dismissively responds, "I think not of them"— most true at a level he does not recognize. The lonely anguish that increasingly sears Macbeth's soul comes to a head of self-awareness, not in the act of killing the king (which is not represented in the play), but in regret immediately provoked by the murderer's sense of exclusion from the fellowship of human prayer. With Duncan's blood on his hands, Macbeth meets his wife beyond the sleeping chambers to make a report and probe a worry: "I have done the deed. Didst thou hear a voice?" He wants to know if she also heard sounds coming from the "second chamber" where Donalbain rested with another unidentified boarder:

> There's one did laugh in 's sleep, and one cried, "Murther!"
> That they did wake each other. I stood and heard them;
> But they did say their prayers, and address'd them
> Again to sleep. (2.2.19-22)

When "One cried, 'God bless us!' and 'Amen!' the other," Macbeth, muzzled by fear and guilt, "could not... pronounce 'Amen',," although he acutely felt "most need of blessing." He desired to answer, but his "Amen," he says, "Stuck in [his] throat." This spiritual incapacitation experienced as an obstruction of actual breath spells the end for Macbeth of "Sleep that knits up the ravell'd sleave of care." It begins the chronic wakefulness of incessantly patching together his defenses against every danger, real and imagined.

The inclusion of this episode in *Macbeth* does more than illustrate the uselessness of prayer for humanity threatened with horrors. The two different dreams suggest that there are many different things to see in that region of memory and future-seeing from which dreams mysteriously rise. Macbeth's report of the incident fixes on the singular power of the dreamers' joint prayer. Since trust in divine providence can free souls from the worry of having to battle horrors alone, Macbeth envies the dreamers' freedom from anxiety, their existential hope. Compared with Macbeth's new world of absolute wakefulness, the natural "sleep" to which they return, in this case a corollary of their faith in divine aid, is a blessing. When Macbeth habitually makes "the firstlings of [his] heart... / The firstlings of [his] hand" for protection against the horrors that haunt him, he will bring into every social and intimate relation in Scotland the war he had once heroically helped to end. Such fretful servitude to mere stimuli, the mark of an exile from divine aid, leaves no time or space for human feeling, reflecting, or ordering.

Moments later, immediately following the wry comical interlude of the Porter imagining Inverness as Hell's mouth, the discovery of the king's murder confirms the literal hellishness of the newly created kingdom. Macbeth's first publicly expressed thought after the murder represents perfectly the irrevocable bind in which he has put himself:

> Had I but died an hour before this chance,

I had liv'd a blessed time; for from this instant
There's nothing serious in mortality:
All is but toys: renown and grace is dead,
The wine of life is drawn, and the mere lees
Is left this vault to brag of. (2.3.91-96)

Following upon his earlier recognition of his loss of grace and
sleep, these words clearly evince genuine knowledge tragically
acquired. The deep irony is that the tragic hero's habitual reaction to events now forces him consciously to speak his truest feelings in a fiction staged for sake of appearance. Just after the
horror of his deed has touched the quick of his sentient heart,
he must mask his heart in an outward lie. His outer and inner
aspects are already so divorced that never again will they meet in
peace. Moreover, the once charming relation he had with his Lady
Macbeth, as Kay Stockholder has observed, from this time begins
to conform to merely conventional roles from which all the first
excitement of the "partnership in greatness" quickly fades (98).

❊   ❊   ❊

In a thought-provoking essay, Henri Suhamy questions "the traditional view of *Macbeth* as based on a tragic process, the self-
destroying trajectory of an exceptional being" (287). To grant the
common assumption that the dramatic main-spring of the play is
"a tragedy of damnation from the beginning to end" only underlines, Suhamy argues, how "tediously repetitive and accumulative"
its action is. Seiko Aoyama argues that "in *Macbeth* the dramatist is concerned with more than the problem of the hero's character or choice of action" (97), since these are basically settled
very early in the play and what comes to the fore in the latter
scenes is a "painful but poetical probing of [Macbeth's] identity,
and of the relationship between the human and the superhuman,
between the physical and metaphysical" (104). Aoyama's look
beyond "character" can serve as a needed corrective to Harold
Bloom's narrower preoccupation with "Macbeth's phantasmagoric
and proleptic imagination" (524), a preoccupation so marked that
Bloom passes over important elements of Shakespeare's plot that
reveal the fuller terms and dimensions of Macbeth's tragic fate.[11]
    At the core of *Macbeth*, argues Suhamy, deeper than the fanat-

ical drive of a hubristic individual to embrace his fate, is "all the metaphysical, political, historical, and human—insofar as *human* also implies the belonging of the individual to a community—contents of Shakespeare's Scottish tragedy [reminding us that] *sheer evil* (emphasis added) is a powerful mainspring in the history of humankind" (287). The mainspring of the drama, then, is not just the aim of Hecate and her hag-sisters "to entice one particular individual to his own ruin, but to put Scotland to fire and sword, to drive humanity to despair, to shatter its faith in Providence, to make confusion reign" (285). In Suhamy's view, even though Hecate "cannot alter the course of destiny and the restoration of order that the seeds of time contain," she can exploit the abyss created by Macbeth's sacrifice of his "eternal jewel" (3.1.67).

As important as Macbeth's visit with the witches is a preoccupation of his that temporally straddles it. Before going to meet them the second time, he had worried to his wife, "How say'st thou, that Macduff denies his person / At our bidding?" After the meeting, he resolves to do something about his most troubling fear following Fleance's escape: "The castle of Macduff I will surprise" (4.1.150). At the heart of the visitation itself are portentous images that equivocally prophesy Macduff's role in the vengeance that mysterious powers are about to launch against Macbeth, yet these are designed to induce in their gull the sense of "security [that] Is mortal's chiefest enemy."

Dramatically, Macbeth's visit to the witches must take place at the same time as Macduff's visit to Malcolm in England, even though the latter follows in the text, separated by a scene in which Macbeth's henchmen murder Macduff's wife and son. In a savage irony, Macduff does not know how intimately Macbeth's terror already touches his own dearest relations when he describes for Malcolm the general condition of their country:

> Each new morn
> New widows howl, new orphans cry, new sorrows
> Strike heaven on the face, that it resounds
> As if it felt with Scotland and yell'd out
> Like syllable of dolor. (4.3.4-8)

Yet this ironic coincidence that displays to the audience the extreme hopelessness of Scotland is not without latent redemptive overtones: it echoes the sufferings of Deutero-Isaiah and Christ, the records of which are retrospectively read as precursors of Heavenly restoration.[12]

* * *

Behind the four visions shown to Macbeth—an armed head, a bloody child, a crowned child with a tree in hand, and eight kings descended from Banquo—the main instrument of Hecate's justice will be Macduff the Thane of Fife. To the extent that the witches are subject to more knowing masters, Shakespeare's play, like Sophocles' *Oedipus at Colonus*, shows that tragedy in its full sweep reaches beyond despair and nihilism. In fact, tragedy has as one of its deepest motives the discernment of powerful, hidden creative sources that can work through human suffering, familial and social interindebtedness, acknowledgment of divine aid, and acceptance of distinctively human fate.

While Macbeth's actions follow the universal course of lust—his powers dissipating in a "waste of shame" that makes visible an "expense of spirit," as Shakespeare puts it in Sonnet 129—Macduff's actions, likewise costly, will produce a real abundance for Scotland because they are rooted in genuine love. "Spirit" thrives in the interval of risk, and Macduff's generous labors will show a different inclination of spirit: to trust the interval to unveil the chance of a new condition of life, even a new state of being. But in such risky ventures to set right the times, the margin of error is inevitably wide and potentially fatal. Choices are clouded by finitude, and the will's fearful hesitancy often deforms judgment.

To understand the tragedy of Macduff that devolves from the devastating career of Macbeth, it helps to see how the Thane of Fife, in conformity to the play's genetic code, takes a self-defining step in a supreme moment of choice that propagates tremendous and irrevocable consequences. His moment of risk—like that of Duncan announcing the succession, Macbeth murdering the King, and Banquo renouncing temptation—reveals how tragically fraught with mortal danger is any human undertaking that aims at decisively transforming a people's future. History and story commonly distinguish among the purposes that those who act have tried to serve. Although Duncan may have been imprudent to place his night's rest at Inverness in the protection of two foolish groomsmen, his people nevertheless venerate him for striving to secure Scotland's peace and freedom. Macbeth and Lady Macbeth, in contrast, earn their people's abhorrence by making their pursuit of their own absolute "greatness" the mainspring of their deeds. Banquo, for holding to the integrity of personal honor, is generally respected as a worthy progenitor of a royal dynasty. And Macduff, although he left the "precious motives" of his wife and children exposed to a tyrant, is generally embraced as an epitome of compassionate innocence; his forgetfulness of his own family resulted in part from his devotion to the larger family of his people.

Of primary interest to each man when Macduff and Malcolm meet is the perdurance of innocence real enough to bridle equivocation. Macduff has come to England, an unidentified Lord reports, "to pray the holy king," the miraculous healer Edward the Confessor. More specifically he comes to find whether there are still "good men" who have feeling enough of Scotland's suffering to rise to its defense. Malcolm, not wanting to be "a weak, poor, innocent lamb" added to the general carnage, withholds trust in Macduff until he can be sure that falsified motives have not brought him to England. He obviously has doubts about any political operative who would sacrifice guardianship of his family to considerations of state, no matter how abstractly noble. While allowing that Macduff *may* be an "angel" whose goodness has been accidentally obscured by the fall of the "brightest," Malcolm clearly believes that the only political ambitions to be trusted are those purified by emotions of the heart nurtured in family affections.

As Malcolm leads Macduff along by pretending to be a cesspool of every vice, lacking any of "the king-becoming graces," his probing finally touches home when Macduff indignantly condemns the Prince: "Fit to govern? / No, not to live. O nation miserable!" (102-03). This "noble passion," unselfconsciously exhibiting Macduff to Malcolm as a "Child of integrity," inspires the latter's prompt declaration of his own innocence before God: "I am yet / Unknown to woman, never was forsworn, / Scarcely have coveted what was mine own, / At no time broke my faith" (125-128). His oath that he has not even engaged in the heart's glib equivocation that men use for sexual conquest confirms Malcolm's freedom and worthiness, in effect, to marry himself honestly to the good of his country.

Still Macduff's innocence does not excuse him from the high cost he must pay for abandoning his family to Macbeth. Shortly Ross enters the scene to bring the report of Macduff's "wife, and babes, / Savagely slaughtered" (205). On hearing this, the husband and father's first impulse is to lash out ferociously, "Did heaven look on, / And would not take their part?" Yet immediately he confesses a personal responsibility: "Sinful Macduff, / They were all strook for thee!... Not for their own demerits" (223-26). So fatuous would it be to try to fathom Macduff's psychology at this juncture that interpreters should probably refrain from recourse to logical explanation. Macduff's response to his misfortune is less a feature of his individuality than the action of his profound ontological faith. After instinctively blaming "heaven," he almost immediately acknowledges that humans share responsibility for the progress of evil in the world, and therefore they should not presume to expect Divine Providence to counter darkness according to their lights. "Let's make us med'cines of our great revenge... Dispute it like a man," Malcolm urges. Macduff replies, "I shall do so, but I must feel it like a man."

Macduff's enormous suffering undeniably attests to some irreparable gap between desert and reward in the world's justice, a gap that widens as Macbeth's rule straitens the resources of mercy. Oddly, this incommensurateness near the play's end echoes the quandary of Duncan at the play's beginning, when he felt he could not reward Macbeth enough for his military valor. Macduff's prayer for Macbeth before chasing him to earth—"If he 'scape, / Heaven forgive him too!"—heightens the effect of incommensurability, since not a thousand murders Macduff might inflict on Macbeth could ever duly repay him for his cruelty. Still, the scales of justice do seem mercifully to turn toward a balance when, in the fateful showdown between the two sinners, the Thane of Fife fits his killing wrath to an end larger than that of his own family. Taught by his "wife and children's ghosts" that his enemy is a "bloodier villain / Than terms can give [him] out!" (5.7.7-9), he finds again the "natural touch" against which he had sinned (4.2.9). When Macbeth tries to stage the final performance of a theatrical heart, Macduff's relatively understated fury rehabilitates both himself and Scotland.

❊   ❊   ❊

Preoccupation with the unknown in its many variants, I have argued, makes *Macbeth* a tragedy more than commonly mysterious in its construction, its plot, and its outcome. Further contributing to this effect is the play's obvious strategy of turning its audience's deepest sympathies away from the tragic protagonist and toward the victims of the evil his anointing in blood lets loose in the world. Macbeth's belittling irony stems from his taking too literally a chance to act in a theatrical interlude free of time's unstopping laws. He makes of himself an artifact so lacking the human touch that, finally, his only world is theater-as-all: "Life's but a walking shadow, a poor player, / That struts and frets his hour upon the stage.... Signifying nothing" (5.5.24-28). If Henri Suhamy is correct in questioning whether Macbeth's damnation can "create among the audience the impact, the idea of a paradox, the terror, the pity, and the lesson" that tragedies usually provoke, then for the roots of *Macbeth*'s undoubted tragic effect we must look in another quarter.

Of greater interest and significance in this tragedy, with its themes of human finitude measured against the dark of metaphysical mystery, is its emphasis on the necessity of the temporal creature faced by ravages of sheer evil either to capitulate or defy them. Even if they have recourse to miracles, men are not exempt from venturing themselves. Says Caithness, a Scot going into war knowing he cannot be faithful to a shadow king,

> Well, march we on
> To give obedience where 'tis truly ow'd.
> Meet we the med'cine of the sickly weal,
> And with him pour we, in our country's purge,
> Each drop of us. (5.2.25-29)

And indeed, the blood to be poured out to purge Scotland soon becomes actual. Young Siward, for example, overwhelmed by events of historical consequence beyond his scope of experience, enters imaginative memory as a sign of hope. His father mourns him—"They say he parted well, and paid his score, / And so God be with him" (5.9.13-18)—and the audience mourns him as well. Macbeth, on the other hand, finally expends all his action against life itself, to enter human memory as a tragic sign of "nothing."

These grand gestures of the soul evoke some apocalyptic struggle that every human person and society must wage. They awaken pity and terror for every mortal who enters the fray, unmistakably linked with others—vulnerable, unknowing, and typically weighted down with the wrong resources for any facile and clear-cut moral victory. In such representations there is an uplifting majesty, sustained from the least expected sources. Such unspeakable temporal ironies as Macduff's wife calling "Now God help thee, poor monkey!" just before the executioner approaches to kill her son, allow only fatuous explications. They force us to stare at connections the more hidden the more they show themselves. In the metaphoric texture of this remarkable tragedy, it is shocking to see that Macduff's innocent son is, in truth, the "naked new-born babe" (1.7.21) Macbeth had fatefully foreseen. The sacrifice of this innocent child will play its part in finally stirring pity enough in the suffering country to make its terror a positive resource toward the rout of its evil enemies.[13] If we resort to Aristotelian terms, catharsis is surely more a function of purifying those fundamental emotions and thus making them aids to purposeful action than of simply discharging them.

The complete action of *Macbeth* is artfully constructed to reveal the verity that murder will out. But deeper than this grim motive is the play's impulse to argue that so, too, good will out through the full sweep of tragic action—good mysteriously inspirited through knowledge of life's tragic depth. A unique achievement of this last of Shakespeare's great tragedies is its showing us with such resonance of experience, within its plot, how pity and terror bring knowledge that can bear fruit. In the hearts and minds of characters in the play who observe interlinked tragic careers—Macbeth's and Macduff's taken together—the enlivening of the tragic emotions of pity and terror works to clarify human capacities to see, to feel, and to care about human life and to risk something for it. The affinity we feel has more to do with our recognizing the truth contained in its dramatic action than with our identification with an enthralling character. Although we see ourselves reflected in Macbeth's "expense of spirit in a waste of shame," we learn more about the tragic dimension of our human state from recognizing the synthesis of *all* the elements that make the plotted action of *The Tragedy of Macbeth*. We learn more, in particular, of tragic truth as it bears on human action—its necessity, its risks, its openness to powers exceeding it, its costs, and their redeeming potential.

NOTES

[1] In analyzing Macbeth David Lowenthal develops the idea of a "mystery play" as one in which a persistent detective can finally get to the bottom of a most important question by uncovering facts hidden in the text. My idea of mystery as applied to Macbeth borrows from the pre-Shakespearean tradition of mystery plays that dramatically represented conditions of human life in which seeing the facts was just the beginning of encountering the mystery of it.

[2] According to Olga Valbuena, "tanistry" means that "the incumbent king should nominate as his successor a member of the dominant collateral and competing royal line—and not his own son—as tanist ('the expected one') to be ratified by vote of the high clansmen" (109).

[3] A "segmented society," in Marcel Mauss's terminology, is "an anarchy of group poised against group with a will to contend by battle that is sufficiently known, and a disposition thereto during all the time that there is not assurance to the contrary" (Sahlins 174). My analysis of Macbeth assumes the applicability of this description to the world Shakespeare presents in the play.

[4] Marcel Mauss, in his classic study of social exchange entitled The Gift, maintains that "Societies have progressed in the measure in which they, their subgroups and their members, have been able to stabilize their contracts and to give, receive, and repay" (80). In "The Spirit of the Gift," Marshall Sahlins shows that the reciprocity of gift-giving, insofar as it provides an assurance against the habitual belief that only war can resolve differences, is "the primitive way of achieving peace that in civil society is secured by the State" (169).

[5] Richard Dawkins elaborates the notion of "memes" in *The Selfish Gene* and *Unweaving the Rainbow*. A meme is a unit of cultural material that shapes and replicates larger forms analogously to the function of genes in organic life.

[6] A reversal of this situation occurs when Lady Macbeth walks in her sleep near the play's end. When her sick thoughts become fixated on the hand-bloodied moments that had immediately followed the murder of Duncan, she will go through motions of writing a letter to her husband and then comforting his presence that she imagines is with her, although by that time her husband's bondage to

action will have carried him irretrievably far away from her. Again she will be with her husband, although he will not be with her, except as a smothering memory she can't see around or beyond.

[7] In a study of the significance of scenes of letter-reading throughout Shakespeare, Mark Taylor concludes that they are "a way of revealing something about the motives and proclivities of the people who read them, of exploring how these readers, in interpreting documents, in fact read themselves" (31).

[8] See Mark Taylor for a summary of what Lady Macbeth ignores in the letter as she interprets its contents (35).

[9] Henri Suhamy aptly describes the Macbeths as not actually dedicating themselves body and soul to evil spirits, but using "magniloquent incantations and creaking phrases that sound painstakingly rehearsed, like words in a foreign language learned for a formal occasion" (286).

[10] For a model of Banquo's petition to "Merciful powers" for peaceful rest see the prayer of St. Ambrose quoted by St. Augustine in his Confessions: "bid the night / in quietness serve the gracious sway / of sleep, that weary limbs, restored / to labor's use, may rise again, / and jaded minds abate their fret" (9.12). Also pertinent to this volume's focus on the "tragic abyss," see Augustine's correspondent account of "a region of unlikeness" (7.10), the spiritual place of the exile who wanders at the farthest distance from the creative source of life.

[11] Bloom's interpretive chapter on Macbeth focuses much more on the psychological qualities of individual characters in the play than on Shakespeare's construction of a plot. The approach of my study aims to be more ontological, following Aristotle's original insight: "Tragedy is an imitation, not of men, but of an action and of life, and life consists in action, and its end is a mode of action, not a quality" (VI, 10).

[12] See Isaiah 50:6-7 and Mark 15:18-20.

[13] See Psalms 8: "Out of the mouths of babes and sucklings / You have fashioned praise because of your foes, / To silence the hostile and the vengeful."

Part Four

TRAGEDY AND

MODERNITY

How cold the vacancy
When the phantoms are gone and the shaken
    realist
First sees reality. The mortal no
Has its emptiness and tragic expirations.
The tragedy, however, may have begun,
Again, in the imagination's new beginning,
In the yes of the realist spoken because he must
Say yes....

WALLACE STEVENS, "ESTHÉTIQUE DU MAL"

13

Alternative Destinies:
The Conundrum of Modern Tragedy

ROBERT S. DUPREE

In an early poem entitled "Opera" and apparently inspired by a performance of *Tristan and Isolde* he attended around 1912, T.S. Eliot describes the music as depicting "love torturing itself" and "Flinging itself at the last / Limits of expression," only to conclude:

> We have the tragic? Oh no!
> Life departs with a feeble smile
> Into the indifferent. (Eliot 17)

Evidently, Eliot had read *The Birth of Tragedy* and was aware of the claims made there for Wagner's music drama as the harbinger of a modern tragic theater. While the young Eliot was apparently very much moved by what he heard on that occasion (as he indicated later in life to Igor Stravinsky), his disappointment suggests a disjunction between the affective power of modern art and the failure of the modern artist to offer a meaningful vision of human existence.

Nietzsche's and Eliot's reactions, separated by some forty years, mark the boundaries of an intense period of activity among playwrights anxious to recover the spirit of ancient Greek tragedy. Succeeding writers were eager to take up the challenge launched in 1872 by a young academic whose treatise was intended to be both a scholarly dissertation (albeit an unconventional one) and a cele-bration of the tragic potential of Wagnerian music. *The Birth of Tragedy* was a novice's bravura piece, marked by the emergence of the new German state and spurred by the possibility that tragedy might once more find expression in the modern world in a sort of Dionysian second coming. Under the spell of Schopenhauer's concepts of representation (or appearance) and will (or perception), Nietzsche saw in this new form of Germanic drama the impetus for a break with a theater and music that had become mere enter-tainment. His enemy was the nineteenth-century bourgeoisie that supported this kind of art, and his target in Section Nineteen of his treatise was the theatrical art that was most characteristic of it, what he called "the culture of the opera."

Nietzsche's critique of opera begins with the emergence of this new art form at the beginning of the seventeenth century, which he compares unfavorably with the "ineffably sublime and sacred music of Palestine" (Nietzsche 114). As he had earlier accused Euripides of bringing the great era of tragedy to a close, allow-ing in its wake an "Alexandrian cheerfulness," so he saw in the genesis of opera "the sweetishly seductive column of vapor from the depth of the Socratic world view" (118) that he viewed as the great antagonist of true tragedy. He discerned that the origins of opera were not Greek tragedy, as the intellectuals pretended, but the pastoral interlude, with its golden age of innocent shepherds and happy lovers. Indeed, the first operatic versions of that sav-age story of the descent of Orpheus to the underworld were given happy endings, since the tragic seemed out of place in both the courtly environment where opera began and the commercial theater where it ended.

For Nietzsche it was German rather than Italian music that was the "only genuine pure and purifying fire spirit in contem-porary culture" (12). Wagner's *Tristan* was a particularly suggestive point of reference, since it embodied three aspects central to the attempt at a modern recreation of tragic art: a reassessment of the main sources of European culture, a personalization of the concept of destiny, and an emphasis in the theater on the affec-tive as opposed to the objectively dramatic.

Nietzsche's glorification of things Germanic came in the wake of a major shift from Italian influence on European music from 1600 to 1750 to its domination by the great Austrian and

German composers from the Mannheim school to Beethoven and, later, Wagner himself. The generation of thinkers that included Madame de Staël, Schlegel, and Coleridge marked a change in European self-awareness in the 1790s and early 1800s. In his *Lectures on Dramatic Art and Literature*, Schlegel proposed an opposition between two styles and two geographies of art: classical vs. romantic, Mediterranean vs. Northern European. He was echoed by de Staël and Coleridge, who introduced this idea to the French- and English-speaking publics. The medieval or the gothic was brought positively into discourse as a worthy successor and alternative to the Renaissance concept of the classical. Shakespeare was put forward as an example of greatness in a modern and northern author. This discovery of the worth and dignity of Northern art, which was to become the new model for modernity, engaged more than a mere historical shift. It was about an alternative state of the Western soul.

But Nietzsche's enthusiasm for Wagner was soon to be dampened by the thoroughly bourgeois climate of Bayreuth, which offered a haven for secular rituals designed for the very middle class he despised. Fifteen years later, in the "Attempt at a Self-Criticism," added to a re-edition of *The Birth of Tragedy*, he recognized that he had mistaken incipient romanticism for Dionysian wisdom. For all that, he did not renounce his original sense of a life-affirming vision, even if his earlier enthusiasm now seemed faintly embarrassing to him, for tragedy was very much in the air.

In England, Matthew Arnold, Nietzsche's older contemporary, composed a poetic narrative on the Tristan and Isolde motif, "Dover Beach," but his sober account of the obligation to love in a world without feeling rings truer to the modern situation and to the lyric genre than to tragedy. In a bleak and forbidding world, the lovers of whom Arnold writes have only one another and the integrity of their bond. He draws a parallel between the climate from which ancient tragedy sprang and his own, less hospitable North:

> Sophocles long ago
> Heard it on the Aegean, and it brought
> Into his mind the turbid ebb and flow
> Of human misery; we
> Find also in the sound a thought,

Hearing it by this distant northern sea. ("Dover Beach," 15-20)

The poem goes on to detail an instance of the life force that is sure to be crushed, not by the hostile and mysterious divinities of ancient tragedy but by the impersonal and indifferent modern universe. One might imagine that, in the mid-nineteenth century when Arnold was writing, a confrontation with the murkiness and downright hostility of nature as experienced in the North could be salutary as a counter to the facile optimism retailed under the rallying cry of inevitable material and spiritual progress.

The affirmation of life that Nietzsche heard in Wagner's music was doubtless anchored in its powerful representation of desire. By the nineteenth century, the love between man and woman had become the highest force for good, an assertion that is part of the lyric tradition from the troubadours to John Donne, but one that becomes problematic in tragedy. Eliot's ironic pessimism in his poem "Opera" is as much a rebuff to Matthew Arnold as to Nietzsche.

Thus the bleak physical and psychological landscape of Northern Europe and the modern dependence on eros as a source of meaning in a senseless cosmos combined to find in music a possibility for tragedy. Yet even as dramatists were discovering new inspiration in the ancient Greek theater, numerous critics after Nietzsche declared the spirit of ancient tragedy to be irrecoverable.[1] In an essay on the "tragedy of passion," Henri Peyre comments on the numerous accounts given for the death of tragedy: the rise of the novel, the modern democratic public, the myth of progress.[2] Yet as he points out, tragedy has abounded in the twentieth century and a "keener awareness of recent psychology has made many of us readier to admit that there is another kind of fatality, no less implacable, at work within ourselves, made up of evil biological, psycho-physiological or hereditary forces" (Peyre 78). Absent the Greek gods or personified forces of fortune and fate, the modern dramatist tries, as Peyre points out, to make use of contemporary substitutes, alternative destinies that will seem convincing to his audience. To give them weight, he can appeal to theories of evolution (Darwin), of economic and class structures (Marx), or of "psycho-physiological or hereditary forces" (Freud) as proof.

It would be a mistake, however, to think that Darwin, Marx, and Freud were simply the Atropos, Clotho, and Lachesis of the modern theater. Alternative destinies appeared on the stage centuries in advance of the trio of modern thinkers sometimes evoked as the new Parcae. It is instructive to note that the context of Peyre's remarks is an analysis of Racine's *Phèdre*, which draws on Euripides rather than Freud, and that Wagner based his music dramas on medieval literature. The poetry of romantic love that emerged in the Middle Ages, for instance, was a far greater influence on the drama than any current of nineteenth or twentieth-century thought. It represents a unique turn in European culture with enormous consequences for the Western imagination, though, of course, unthinkable without the backdrop of Christian doctrine. For as one scholar has argued, *philia* (that is, the body of obligations created by blood-ties) is central to tragedy in Aristotle's understanding, but love between man and woman has no place in it (Belfiore 72). *Antigone* is about the titular heroine's obligations towards her brother, not her feelings for her husband-to-be. But in the story of Tristan and Isolde, we see the beginnings of a new motif: tragic love.

The Tristan story was given its first incisive modern interpretation by Denis de Rougemont, in an influential, if exceedingly controversial, book called *Love in the Western World.*[3] De Rougemont begins his analysis by noting:

> Passion means suffering, something undergone, the mastery of fate over a free and responsible person.... Passionate love, the longing for what sears us and annihilates us in its triumph—there is the secret which Europe has never allowed to be given away; a secret it has always repressed—and preserved! Hardly anything could be more tragic; and the way passion has persisted through the centuries should cause us to look to the future with deep despondency. (41)

He goes on to ask:

> Why is it that we delight most of all in some tale of impossible love? Because we long for the branding; because we long to grow aware of what is on fire inside us. Suffering and understanding are deeply connected; death and self-awareness are in league; and European romanticism may be compared to a man for whom sufferings, and especially the sufferings of love, are a privileged mode of understanding. (42)

He claims that this myth of passion "lives upon the lives of people who think that love is their fate (and as unavoidable as the effect of the love-potion is in the Romance); that it swoops upon powerless and ravished men and women in order to consume them in a pure flame; or that it is stronger and more real than happiness, society, or morality" (11).

In setting up this opposition between passion and marriage in the history of Western society, de Rougemont puts his finger on the structure of the Tristan myth. It expresses a conflict between individual (and essentially private) relationships and public or familial ones. Romantic love is now a calling, now a destiny. Most important, it privileges personal love over *philia*, seeing in the conflict between one's social obligations and erotic desire not only a source of suffering but also a mode of self-exaltation and greater understanding. This understanding is not simply the Aeschylean "understanding through suffering" which is at the heart of his tragic vision. What the ancient Greek understood was the limitation of human nature, the vast difference between man and god; what Tristan and his fellows learned was that God is love and that, as God showed his love for man by suffering in the person of Jesus Christ, so man comes to understand the nature of that love through sacrifice for another.

De Rougemont, however, sees in the Tristan story as archetypical tale of passion the earmarks of a vast and long-lived Christian heresy that is responsible for most of the woes of modern life, from a skyrocketing divorce rate to total war. Wagner's opera was the means through which "the myth was completed" (239) seven centuries later. It brought to a climax a dream that was to undergo a rapid decline from the heights of its imaginative ecstasy. One may well feel that De Rougemont's account fails to acknowledge the positive side of Tristan and Isolde's love, which is at its core a story of constancy and fidelity despite all that would separate them or forbid their pursuing it actively. Nevertheless, he is surely correct in seeing it as representative, perhaps even generative, of a vast literature to follow. In particular, there emerges during the time of Shakespeare a new kind of play that has been given the name of "love tragedy," and the theme of passion brings a different dimension to the genre as well as a new version of that fatality so central to Greek tragedy. The major difference, however, is in an emphasis on the individual and the psychological rather than on the collective and communal as the source of moral value.

Love tragedies have a long lineage, tales of ill-fated lovers were everywhere throughout the Middle Ages and on well into the eighteenth century: Hero and Leander, Pyramus and Thisbe, Eloise and Abelard. Shakespeare contributed two outstanding instances in *Romeo and Juliet* and *Antony and Cleopatra*. Racine's best-known plays are of this type. Christopher Marlowe, that fertile innovator, wrote one on the death of Dido, and John Webster's *The Duchess of Malfi* is in some degree classifiable among them. The theater of love in the sixteenth century was a public display of emotions on a larger scale than ever before. Unlike the prose and verse romances of earlier centuries, it brought private matters into public space. The entry into the world of personal feelings and individual character—corresponding at least in part to what Aristotle called *"ethos"*—was made possible by a thoroughly commercial enterprise: the modern theater.

Elizabethan theater was organized around a number of motifs combined or reformulated in various ways. The most familiar of these is revenge, which pits an individual against social forces more powerful than himself. The revenger's point of departure is a code of honor or of blood-ties akin to Aristotle's *philia*, a social force in its own right that drives the hero to seek redress. The revenge tragedy, then, is not so much a conflict of individual and collectivity as it is a clash between a corrupt society, incapable for whatever reason of enforcing its own laws, and an individual who champions them, though at the cost of his own existence. It concerns forces of society divided against themselves, the individual but a representative of the principles that allow a given society to cohere. Its source is, clearly enough, the plays of Seneca, but one can see in it the same pattern that characterizes Sophocles' *Antigone*. Revenge has an archaic ring to it in plays written for audiences shaped by Christian belief, and its popularity among dramatists as a motif is evidence that it provided the equivalent of a terrible shaping destiny such as is presupposed by Greek tragedy ("O cursed spite / That ever I was born to set it right," as Hamlet says). Despite their seeming modernity, however, these plays evince a social order that is, like the institution of the monarchy that heads it, ultimately guaranteed by divinity. The hero who upholds a blood-for-blood morality justifies his actions in terms of some transcendent order.

Renaissance love tragedies follow much the same pattern, but they are complicated by the high value accorded in Christianity to love of one's fellow man. This love is also sanctioned by divine order, and the love of man and woman is given pride of place because it is the ultimate source of social order through the intimate organization of marriage. Yet marriage as a social institution, absorbed into the divine order in Christian practice through its sacramentalization, can be corrupted, misused, or misappropriated in the name of secular power. All love tragedies are eventually about the value of the human person. When a human being is reduced to a mere cog in the social machine, as is often the case in societies concerned with dynastic continuity and expansion of tribal power, the love poet protests in the name of the individual soul. What de Rougemont saw as adultery, the creators of the Tristan story saw as a protest against a social mechanism that had lost sight of the very values that made it possible.

Leonora Brodwin offers an extensive survey of the varieties of love tragedy in English Renaissance drama, seeing all of them as emanating from a basic situation: "The force obstructing the union of the lovers, whether it be the husband, family, society or their combination, provides the apex of the eternal triangle" (340). Thus, though Brodwin never quite manages to say that love tragedy is about a conflict between the two elements essential for any society—between the love that generates and sustains a people and the laws that guarantee its continuing orderliness—she does offer a useful schema for understanding the variations on this theme among the different plays of the period in dividing the plays into groups concerned with Courtly Love, False Romantic Love, and Worldly Love:

> The classic pattern of Courtly Love tragedy places its emphasis upon the relationship of the lovers, which develops in a condition of obstruction whose validity they never question; and the actual source of the obstruction is not as highly lighted. The whole impetus of such a tragedy is toward the mutual, transfigured deaths of the lovers, deaths which prove redemptive not only for the lovers but also for the individuals and society whose hostility had led to the lovers' destruction. (340-41)

The lovers, therefore, are sacrificial victims whose death becomes necessary in order to restore to a society its fundamental values.

The tragic dilemma results from the clash of two forces seeking the good. The lovers are aware that their love represents some sort of transgression, but they are equally aware that their attraction to one another is of a higher order than the forces that would keep them apart. In yielding to this fatal attraction, they agree to be the "star-crossed" victims of contending powers that they can reconcile only at the cost of their own destruction. Romeo and Juliet are never conscious of their sacrificial status; they make every attempt to escape the consequences of their challenge to a society gone awry.

But Antony and Cleopatra are aware, in seeking to find new heaven and new earth, that the transformative power of love can affect their world, built upon the drive for absolute power, only if they are willing to execute themselves in its name. Caesar recognizes both that Cleopatra's actions were directed against the imposition of universal political rule:

> Brauest at the last,
> She leuell'd at our purposes, and being Royall
> Tooke her owne way (5.2.339-41)

and that they deserve the highest recognition:

> She shall be buried by her *Anthony*,
> No Graue vpon the earth shall clip in it
> A payre so famous: high euents as these
> Strike those that make them: and their Story is
> No less in pitty, then his Glory which
> Brought them to be lamented. (5.2.361-66)

Even Caesar recognizes that love is a worthy adversary of political power and that he owes his triumph directly to them: his glory has been achieved at their cost. Though unlike Romeo and Juliet, these more ancient lovers fail to change the course of history, they at least achieve monumental—even exemplary—status in the minds of those who triumph over them. True to his pre-Christian setting, however, Shakespeare sees their tragedy not so much as redemptive of society as a moving indictment of it. In the classical universe, love is not yet what makes the world go round.

The motif of tragic love, which might be extended to cover

even such plays as *Othello* and *King Lear*, was a fresh contribution of the medieval world to literature. It reveals a shift in sensibility from the exclusively public domain of classical tragedy to an awareness of the relationship between personal and public. With Marlowe and Shakespeare it is abundantly evident that Aristotle's focus on action to the near-exclusion of character will no longer hold. Whether they be Christians or not, his characters are defined by their individuality and personal characteristics rather than simply by the roles they play in society. The innermost thoughts of Hamlet, Macbeth, Othello, or Lear are indispensable to an understanding of their respective tragedies.

The birth of opera (c. 1600) is exactly contemporary with Shakespeare's mature tragedies. The first attempts at *dramma per musica* were based on the Orpheus and Eurydice story, re-examined through the lens of medieval love themes and provided with an exalted ending suggesting the elevation of the protagonist as a result of his risking all for a woman. More than one critic has observed of *Othello* that it has affinities with Italian opera. At the same moment as the Elizabethan tragedians were enriching the genre by giving it an interior as well as a mask-based exterior, they were moving it in a direction that would prove fatal to the delicate balance Aristotle found characteristic of the best (though not necessarily essential to all) tragic plots. The movement inward of the tragic action made possible by the Christian understanding of the soul (not simply a principle of animation or of unity, as Aristotle understood it, but of immortality) brought new complexity and power to tragedy while opening the genre to the possibility of sweeping oversimplification.

For the next four centuries, the emergence of opera changed the nature of the theater by focusing on the affective consequences of the tragic plot. While the spoken drama had become increasingly dominated by the formulae of the so-called "unities," the sung play underwent further, more drastic changes as it entered the public and popular domain. The scholarly attempts to revive ancient tragedy were soon forgotten, as were the courtly origins of the theatrical entertainments that were the real basis of this new form. Instead, opera found a new environment in the commercial republic of Venice, where the first public opera houses were built in the 1630s; and the first paying audiences filled their seats, attracted by the increasing emphasis on spectacular scenery, stage effects and star soloists (essentially the opera of today).

Meanwhile, the traditional theater had to compete. In France, under the guidance of Jean-Baptiste Lully, the French created their own version of opera, adapting dance and music to the newly emerging neoclassical plays. A dynamic interchange ensued, one that eventuated in a theater combining elements of Aristotle, Greco-Roman themes, operatic passion, and current dramatic proprieties. The great plays of Racine, for all their power, are not quite tragic in either the Greek or Shakespearean sense. They have been repeatedly and rightly praised for the strength of their psychological characterizations; but the cosmos they depict, while set in classical times, is distinctly restricted to a narrow, interior space reminiscent of the tradition of love tragedy. One need only compare *Andromaque* or *Bérénice* with *Romeo and Juliet* or *Antony and Cleopatra* to see what has happened. The universe has shrunken to a drawing room; the conflicts are between love and duty, but the focus is no wider than the very stage on which the players stand. Racine took advantage of the pseudo-Aristotelian unities in a manner superior to any other dramatist: he made them work to his purpose and produced just that kind of concentration of effect that led the author of the *Poetics* to prefer tragedy to all other genres.

In his influential book *The Idea of a Theater*,[4] Francis Fergusson pointed out that the major innovation in Racine's plays is the device of creating suspense in the audience at the end of each act. What is described as tragic in Racine's art is on the level of the affective, both in the way the characters confront their dilemmas and the audience reacts to them. Racine may have rescued the theater one more time from the spirit of music, but he could do so only by concentrating on emotion rather than on the greater action that pits man against a hostile universe. After him, the operatic emphasis on projecting the inner states of the characters onstage dominates all serious theater. The theater becomes rhetorical in seeking a certain effect or affect; the point of a play is to convey to an audience what Orpheus is feeling as he sings his way to the underworld. The affective power of music and its companion, the drama, is ideally depicted in the figure of Orpheus, hence his popularity among operatic composers. The purpose of the unities is simply to get the burden of constructing a properly tragic plot out of the way so that the playwright

can concentrate on his true mission: to move the audience. The
notion of catharsis, misunderstood when mentioned at all, is
invoked to justify this emphasis.

It was a major theorist of French neo-classicism and friend of
Racine, Nicolas Boileau, who first drew attention to another element by translating the treatise of pseudo Longinus into French.
Interest in "Longinus" grew in Europe during the last decades of
the seventeenth century and the first half of the eighteenth, to
be given its most substantial boost by the young Edmund Burke's
treatise in the 1750s. Because Longinus offered, along with Aristotle, the sanction of ancient authority for pursuing an essentially
modern specialization in the affective powers of art, neo-classicism
throughout Europe, far from being an affair of dry rationalism,
was increasingly concerned with the feelings. Northrop Frye has
justly proposed labeling the second part of the eighteenth century
an "Age of Sensibility."

This shift in emphasis did not occur overnight, however. It
was the necessary consequence of the tragic divide that, gaining
momentum throughout the preceding century and a half, propa-
gated in European schools a rhetorical training that taught every
pupil how to move an audience. As Donald M. Lowe points out,

> In the Renaissance, "passion" had been any kind of feeling by which
> one was powerfully affected or moved; and "temperament" was a com-
> bination of the four humors which determined the physical and men-
> tal constitution of a person (OED). Human "character" possessed no
> internal coherence, but was open to outside forces displaying conflict-
> ing passions (OED). Renaissance passion was spontaneous and violent,
> made possible by the reflexive connection between the macrocosm of
> the universe and the microcosm of the person. But "emotion" was a
> new word... to describe an agitation or disturbance of the mind, feel-
> ing, or passion (OED). It was a vehement state of feeling. The per-
> son had become more detached in the spatialized world... than
> previously, and began to have more of an inside as opposed to the
> outside. Emotion, unlike passion, resulted from the new opposition
> between inside and outside, between mental and physical. It was a
> state of feeling cooped inside a person, not coming out spontaneously
> like passion. Emotion, being mental and on the inside, resulted from
> sense perception of the physical, of outside. (Lowe 99)

The link between what we perceive as opposing attitudes, rationalism and sensibility, is provided in the turn towards sensationalism. Greek tragedy was about the external, public world of the *polis*; modern drama, beginning especially with opera, is interested in giving us access to the innermost emotions of the individual. But how are those emotions to be conveyed? How can we know what somewhat else is feeling, since on the stage everything has to be acted out in some physical manner? Though masks were no longer used to convey the fundamental character of the actor, those on the stage still had to project their fictional personalities through certain accepted conventions of representation. New modes of expression came into play, and fortunately, guidelines for their development lay ready to hand in René Descartes's 1649 treatise on *The Passions of the Soul*.

Lowe sees this seventeenth- and eighteenth-century transition to emotion and sentiment from Renaissance feeling as a movement away from a spontaneous connection with the world. In the nineteenth century it joined not only with sensationalism but also with individualism.

> Bourgeois society consolidated the new emotion and sentiment of estate society. On the basis of this emotion and sentiment, "personality" in the late eighteenth century acquired a new prospect, i.e., the quality or assemblage of qualities in a person as distinct from other persons (OED). By the early nineteenth century, the ideology of "individualism" supplemented that new personality. As the person possessed more of an inside, emotion rather than objective reason accounted for his or her individuality. This emotion was disconnected from the visual, rational world. In bourgeois society, "sensitivity" and "sentimentalism" were new concepts, while "sensitive" and "sentiment" acquired new meaning, to indicate emotion as the *ressentiment* of a more autonomous, pent-up being. (99)

Shakespeare's plays, even his love tragedies, still remained within the world of Renaissance passion. The dark, murky realm of internalized passion and personalized emotion becomes the new concern of drama in the nineteenth century; it is celebrated by the Romantics and reaches its climax in Nietzsche's Dionysus, along with its exemplary expression in Wagner's music. It was a brilliant stroke on Nietzsche's part to connect these changes with the emergence and triumph of opera in the theater.

However limited it may now appear, the radical drama of the later 1800s was at least a protest, in the name of a serious return to the tragic dimensions of human experience, against a shallow theater given over almost entirely to spectacle, intellectually empty entertainment, and audience gratification. A new breed of playwrights, some inspired by the Sophoclean standard, reacted by attempting a kind of drama in which the problematic nature of modern life was displayed in all its depressing reality. To write a tragedy, then, meant to embrace modern values while denying them, to use science (or pseudo-scientific themes, at least) to draw attention to the limits of human understanding and power. Audiences found their provocative plays at once repulsive and yet curiously fascinating. Before long, they had become the new orthodoxy which later writers, in turn, felt compelled to imitate and then, inevitably, to reject. Though the plays of Ibsen and Strindberg, to name two of the most influential of these problem dramatists, have continued to be performed for well over a hundred years now, they have long been assigned to the hallowed ranks of those "classic" plays that are safe, because patently out-of-date, to be put on from time to time in the name of culture and respectability.

Ibsen claimed to have learned a great deal from his study of Greek theater, but he never attempted to imitate it. If a play like *Ghosts, A Doll's House, Hedda Gabler* or *Brand* is sometimes called tragic (Oscar Wilde, after attending the third of these, claimed to have experienced a kind of pity and terror akin to that induced by the Greeks), if George Bernard Shaw considered Ibsen a modern Shakespeare, the fact remains that Ibsen himself was not trying to be Greek or tragic in the classical sense. His plays are about an individual pitted against the false values of a false society that substitutes respectability for community. If Brand is crushed by an avalanche, it is not because he has offended against the gods but because he cannot possibly become part of an inauthentic world. His enemy is not a blind force or some malevolent deity but himself: he is a victim of his own refusal to compromise with an impersonal and empty human realm that he does not have the power to transcend. One can speak of Ibsen, as does Raymond Williams, as the creator of a species of "liberal tragedy," but the playwright himself seems to have had a notion of theater that was neither classical nor Shakespearean in its aims.

August Strindberg, Ibsen's younger contemporary, is a different matter. In two of his best-known plays, *The Father* and *Miss Julie*, his intention to write in the tragic mode is explicit. He calls the first "a tragedy in three acts" and the second "a naturalistic tragedy in one act." In the preface to the second play he offers a defense of his attempts to reflect "the ideas of modern times within the framework of the old forms" (Strindberg 62).

> When I chose this theme from real life—as I heard it related a number of years ago, at which time I was greatly moved by the story—I saw in it the ingredients of a tragic drama. To see an individual on whom fortune has heaped an abundance of gifts go to her ruin and destruction, leaves us with a tragic feeling; to see a whole line die out is still more tragic....
>
> The fact that the heroine in this play arouses our pity and compassion is due solely to our weakness and inability to resist such a feeling for fear that we ourselves may meet with the self-same fate. And the over-sensitive spectator may still not be content with feeling pity and compassion; the man with faith in the future may demand some sort of positive action or suggestion for doing away with the evil—in short, some stroke of policy. But, first of all, there is nothing absolutely evil; for the extinction of one family is nothing short of luck for another family that gets a chance to rise in the world. And the succession of rise and fall is one of life's greatest fascinations as luck is only relative. (63)

Strindberg's notion of fate seems more akin to the medieval wheel of fortune than to the inscrutable Greco-Roman goddesses.

An admirer of and even correspondent with Nietzsche, he echoes his mentor in the same preface in which he evokes ancient tragedy and Aristotelian language:

> Not long ago I was upbraided by someone who thought my tragedy *The Father* was too sad. As if a tragedy were meant to be amusing! People are constantly clamoring pretentiously for *the joy of life*, and play producers keep demanding farces—as if the joy of life consisted in being ludicrous and in depicting all human beings as if they were suffering from St. Vitus' dance or idiocy. For my part, I find the joy of

life in the hard and cruel battles of life; and to be able to add to
my store of knowledge, to learn something, is enjoyment to me. (64)

Raymond Williams has called the plays of Strindberg, O'Neill,
and Tennessee Williams "private tragedy." They are, in fact, the
next stage after Racine's claustrophobic court tragedies, where the
disaster affects individuals rather than whole cities, where no
innocent victims are dragged down along with the tragic protagonist, and where the concerns are passion and society rather than
individual and abyss. *The Father* strikes one as ludicrous in its
depiction of a man driven to his death by a willful woman, and
Miss Julie as rather too calculated in its combination of Darwin-
ian and Nietzschean conflicts. The latter is not a love tragedy;
the brief affair between Jean and Julie is the cynical seduction of
a confused and naïve girl, not an exaltation of love that transcends the narrow limitations of society. It is, rather, an illustra-
tion (as is Ibsen's *Ghosts*) of biological forces that operate just as
blindly in the human as in the animal world. Of Julie's suicide-
murder, one can say not simply that the butler did it but also
that the guilt lies with an inexorable and cruel society in which
an effete upper class is being replaced by a vulgar and amoral
lower class. What is left may be pity and terror, but the catharsis so clearly central to Aristotle's understanding of the tragic
effect will have to wait for millennia of evolutionary change
before it can occur.

The spirit of modern music—understood as a monumental shift
that occurred around 1600—robbed the theater of its power over
the community. The Northern turn, marked by Wagner's *Tristan*
and continued in the gloomy world of serious theater to follow,
was addressed to a rather narrow audience that could be moved
personally but not collectively. In its attempt to recapture the soul
of ancient tragedy, the theater lost its own. Shakespearean tragedy
was not simply a later version of Greek tragedy. It was a Nordic
phenomenon that found a fresh way to present human fragility
in the face of an abyss different from that confronted by the
Mediterranean tragedians. Macbeth has his Weird Sisters and Lear
(or, at least, Gloucester) his wanton gods who kill for sport, and
they are not merely latter-day versions of the fates. Iago in *Othello* is not comparable to, say, Creon in Sophocles' *Antigone*, a
man too stubborn to acknowledge his own pride who brings

about the death of a person of great value. The new dimension that enters with Marlowe and Shakespeare is evil, though it retains an ambiguity in the sixteenth century very unlike the medieval face of the devil. In *Hamlet*, this ambiguity of evil is given its definitive stamp: Hamlet is the victim not of procrastination but of an evil that he cannot extirpate without destroying himself and others. After Shakespeare, the Nordic imagination was never again to attain this perfect balance between malevolence and ambiguity. The subsequent darkness that threatens human life and happiness is something internalized and therefore a matter of individual feelings. If the audience feels pity or terror, it is only in recognition that to feel intensely is to suffer terribly and in relief that the abyss of the passions is visited only upon others.

Opera, which emerged from the world of kings and dukes that Shakespeare knew, became a genuinely popular art form at the expense of being a serious one. Wagner attempted to recapture it for the serious theater, but his revolution was readily assimilated by the same middle class for whom it represented prestigious entertainment. Today, it exists as a kind of museum piece in which the union of music and drama guarantees its irrelevance or frivolity. Opera buffs bear an uncanny resemblance to sports buffs, tracking the exploits of tenors and sopranos with the same fervor devoted to batting averages. The power of music to move people to action was demonstrated during the time—the very sixties and seventies—when speculations about modern tragedy were at their height and theatrical experimentation was rife. Music and theater, for a brief time, became politically charged. But whether the modern theater attempted to move its audiences to action or to tears and laughter, it did so in an institutional atmosphere more interested in our private feelings than how we fit into the whole scheme of things. Doing "your own thing" resulted in tragedy for the Greeks but was promoted as the natural course of action for mid- and late-twentieth-century Americans.

The desire to create a modern version of tragedy onstage now seems faintly old-fashioned, a misplaced faith in the theater as an institution that could save us from ourselves. The spirit of music, as Nietzsche understood it in his pejorative sense, is now everywhere. We have lived for half a century in an atmosphere that could be mistaken for a Dionysian one, where the ability to record and reproduce sound has created a kind of omnipresence of music. Used as a tool for setting a mood in public as well as private places, it has become a global commercial power. The impact of the theater is as nothing in comparison with the influence of this pervasive ether at every turn.

Tragedy is about the unforeseen consequences of a human action that, though seemingly slight in significance and impact, leads to a catastrophic outcome, thus revealing the uncertainty of human self-understanding and the inability of man to control his own ultimate end in a cosmos more complex and more powerful than his mind can grasp or his ingenuity can address. It has always stood as a sobering reminder that man can and will go wrong, no matter how hard he tries to avoid error. I suspect that few people today would find such a view of human fate unreasonable or unrealistic, since past and present have given us too many instances of such tragic outcomes for us to ignore their likelihood. Tragedy is the persuasive presentation of such a probable result of man's efforts to overcome his acknowledged limitations. However, the consequence of the tragic vision is—in accord with its own paradoxical structure—not to persuade us to give up on improving our lot, as one might expect, but to admire our own persistence in trying to realize our vision of a better existence for ourselves. Tragedy is not simply about our failure to learn its lesson of our inevitable failure; it is, rather, about our awareness that we will probably fail and will nevertheless still make the attempt. This may have been what Albert Camus was trying to say in his *Myth of Sisyphus*: that man attempts the impossible, knowing that it is impossible but also knowing that there is an infinitesimally tiny chance that he might slip through the iron-bound laws of inevitable failure and, for once, succeed. It is this "blind hope," as Prometheus called his gift to man, that makes us fully human; and for this reason, tragedy is our most important imaginative product. Or so we seem to think.

Our own failure to articulate this vision in the modern theater in an emotionally and intellectually convincing manner must seem, therefore, an abandonment of our own irrational but persistent hope—the same hope that causes one to buy a lottery ticket despite the overwhelming statistical evidence that it will not bear fruit. In the end, we are willing to throw our caution and skepticism to the winds and cast our lot with Dame Fortune or just plain luck. But luck is an element of the comic genre, and tragedy is about inevitability. Ancient and Shakespearean tragedy were about the human dignity that comes from a refusal to submit even to one's own intellectual certainties. It is that irrational hope that the modern world has been too timid to admit, except in the domain of the comic, where it need not be taken seriously, or in the realm of the affective, where it is only subjective and need not be elevated to the level of a universal principle.

The rise and impact on post-Renaissance theater of opera, which from the outset was about the power of music to make us empathize with the sufferings of others, shifted our attention away from the objective and collective human will to survive and prevail to the subjective and individualistic reaction of the victim. Music, which once put us into intimate communion with the same rhythms and harmonies that structure the cosmos, has become merely a mode for representing our feelings about it. In our heart of hearts, we secretly assume that mankind will somehow survive and even change the cosmos in some way; but we are lacking in the means to represent that conviction. That is because the spirit of music, understood in the narrow sense I have given it here, is no longer that powerful force that the Greeks—and Nietzsche—understood it to be. It no longer represents the Big Bang but only our whimpers.

NOTES

[1] Some ninety years after Friedrich Nietzsche wrote of the birth of tragedy, George Steiner proclaimed its demise, taking for granted that the theater had produced nothing in the way of a real tragedy since the seventeenth century. His contentions were by no means startling, but they marked a new conviction in critical attitude that was to usher in a whole series of similar studies during the 1960s, which in retrospect seems to have been the last intensely active period of criticism devoted to the problem. Not to be capable of achieving tragedy—a kind of cultural Everest—was a sign of cultural failure. To scale those heights and reach the summit of artistic greatness seemed to require a heroic imagination capable of overcoming the banality and smugness of a society too preoccupied with itself to confront the outer darkness. Tragedy became an emblem of historical and visionary grandeur; the effort to recover it for the modern world became an epic quest in itself. The pres-

tige of tragedy remained unquestioned by most critics writing in the 1960s (such as Lionel Abel and Raymond Williams). It was a reassuring prestige, one that argued for the continuity of Western literature from the Greeks to the present—an assurance that tragic awareness was universal, not confined to one time or place, and the questions it raises not answered by modern doctrines of science or human progress.

This critical complacency was disturbed by the assaults of Michel Foucault and his contemporaries, who began in the 1970s to assert a radical disjunction between the world-pictures of the past and those of the present. The words and concepts we hold in common with the Greeks (or, for that matter, Enlightenment thinkers) are deceptive; they meant entirely different things because they were supported by altogether different sources of power, political and social. In other words, our understanding of the tragic is often subject to what in philosophy would be called a "category error." The paradox, then, is that a tragic age, as Williams characterizes it, is incapable of attaining the kind of detachment that allows tragedy in the theater to flourish, though it may be evident in the novel, film, philosophy, psychology, or literary criticism and theory. It does not matter that Ibsen was inspired by Greek tragedy or that Strindberg gave a new twist to the love tragedy or that their successors saw equivalents of ancient fatalism in modern theories of social, psychological, biological, political, and economic forces. We are incapable of replicating the tragic on the modern stage because the theater itself no longer has the same meaning in our society.

[2] See Peyre 77. The essay was originally delivered as a lecture in 1951.

[3] The original French version, L'Amour et l'Occident, was published in 1939, followed in the next year by the Belgion translation in its first edition (NY: Harcourt, Brace and Company, 1940).

[4] Fergusson's book offers, to my mind, a more incisive account of the reasons for the lack of tragedy in the modern world than does Steiner's, published more than a decade later.

14

The Strange Upward Draft in the Novel:
Flaubert and Dostoevsky

PAUL CONNELL

As both a manifestation and cause of the spiritual state of Europe in the sixteenth century, the figure of Martin Luther foreshadows what subsequently occurs in both tragedy and the novel. For when Luther declares grace to be external to the person and unable to produce any vital act, a tremendous shift in sensibility is taking place. As Lewis Hyde remarks, "What Luther feels on all sides are disgrace and scarcity…. Now Christians are rare, grace is unusual, and moral conscience is private and without worldly weight" (127-128). In effect, God withdraws to his judgment seat and with him a vast cosmos recedes from view as a new economy of "disgrace" is inaugurated. When grace is common, the world is familiar, and human action is durable and significant. In the absence of the support that grace provides for the human endeavor, the world becomes alien, nature a mere object for manipulation, and knowing itself beset by anxiety. It may be said that modernity begins with this retraction of grace—which I am using as a type of metaphor to describe a basic confidence, or even yearning, that underpins mind and action. With this retraction comes the subsequent eclipse of the divine.

The crisis of grace has the parallel effect of renewing and deepening the tragic dimension. The possibility of a desacralized cosmos opens up, giving a new dimension of horror for the tragic poet. Shakespeare chronicles heroic action that is rendered tragic in the face of divine neglect. The play about that other Wittenberg man, *Hamlet*, can be read as an allegory of the epistemological and metaphysical problem of mediation posed by Luther; *King Lear*, *Othello*, and *Macbeth* would not be imaginable without the groundlessness that already opens up when human action is robbed of the value given to it by the assurance of grace. And the dark, shadowy worlds created by Middleton and Webster are prepared for onstage by what is already unhallowed in the world.

At the same time, however, there is a certain advance with the compensations that the novel provides to this crisis. The novel acts as a counterweight for the world's lost mediating character. Milan Kundera in *The Art of the Novel* considers the novel an ironic force that works against the tendencies of reductionism and the quest for certitude. What he sees as "the depreciated legacy of Cervantes" in the novel, as opposed to the dominant, misguided line of thought inherited from Descartes, may be recast as the retrieval of lost grace. Opposing a body of opinion that sees the novel as coextensive with and virtually congruent to the modern predicament, Kundera shows that the novel instead counters the anomie initiated in the sixteenth century and takes on a certain redemptive power.

"Modernity," Louis Dupre claims, "is an event that has transformed the relation between the cosmos, its transcendent source, and its human interpreter" (249). The novel is the primary medium for this transformation. The medium, as Marshall McLuhan has said, is an area that usually eludes attention, yet it has significant if not decisive effect on the way content is engaged. For McLuhan, the medium is related to content in the same way that ground is related to figure. Change the ground and the figure is altered; change the medium and the content is altered. Such is the relationship between novel and tragedy, and it is with this interplay that the dynamic forces of the novel chronicle the modern period. As a register of the modern "event" where values are measured and tested, the novel creates a cosmos where grace still abides. It is a cosmos not in competition with but in refutation of the very dream of perfection—religion in Luther, philosophy in Descartes, and morality in Rousseau—by which the western imagination has been led astray. Yet it may have been precisely because of this nostalgic passion about its own origins that the western mind was forced to counter the possibility of its own destruction—the possibility it faced in tragedy—as it announced itself at the beginning of modernity. For whatever reason, the novel retains hope and bestows a power that enables the world to reclaim its instrumental and mediatory character.

* * *

The novel arises, as many critics have noted, out of the onset of print culture, and it embodies many of the aftereffects of the technological shift into print initiated by Gutenberg. But at the same time, as Kundera suggests, it often resists the tendencies of the linear culture that occasioned its emergence. It provides new avenues to grace. The novel is nothing if not a highly mediated way of conveying a truth about life, even if its mediatory character, according to McLuhan, passes largely unnoticed. This mediation is manifested in a number of ways. The intention of novelists towards their actions is embedded as a type of inner tendency or attitude in the narrative. Their mastery of technique functions not only as a means of conveying the central action but also as a moral critique on the action itself. And through the enveloping action, they create a cosmos with access to avenues of grace through symbols that inform the consciousness of the protagonist.

The need for these redemptive capacities of the novel increased in the centuries after Luther. With the retreat of metaphysics in the seventeenth century, the narrowing of the epistemological field in the eighteenth, and the collapse of theology into personal devotion by the nineteenth century, the person had become "philosophized" and "theologized" outside of the real human experience. During this same period, however, the novel was maturing in its form. Flaubert, Dostoevsky, and the other master technicians of the genre create worlds of spiritual implication and significance, setting up hypothetical structures where characters make choices and, in so doing, articulate a spiritual content—and not merely a vague sense of transcendence or a quality generally diffused in the work. Rather, the life of the spirit traces definite patterns, and in novels where elements of tragedy shape the action, two clearly defined realities emerge, paralleling Augustine's formulation of two cities: one city of self that ends in hatred of God; and one of God that ends in hatred of self. Novel after novel sets into motion an action that places in bold relief these two states of being.

In this respect, the novel might best be seen as the direct heir of the *Divine Comedy*. While modern in spirit, it arises as a result of the change in literature that was initiated much earlier by Dante. Its roots in worldly comedy can be deduced by many of the works that have set the foundations of the genre: *Don Quixote*, *Lazarillo de Tormes*, *Tom Jones*, *Tristram Shandy*, novels of the picaresque, comedies of manners, Menippean satires, and so on. Yet to locate the comedic aspect within the *Divine Comedy* itself shifts emphasis away from conventional examples—which when taken together form a confusing and perhaps misleading set of tendencies—to uncover instead aspects within Dante's work itself that set the novelistic paradigm. Jacques Maritain writes that

> the *Divine Comedy* is also, indeed, a Tale, or better, a Novel, of the beyond and the here below. It is a continuous and complex narrative, in which the particular adventures of the two protagonists serve to put into existence and motion a world of adventures and destinies, so as to make each human being involved a center of interest, looked at by the poet in its own singular ineffable reality. Though their fates are now sealed, and their lives have become only an object of memory, all these characters have life and existential interiority, because their author knows them, as every novelist does, from the inside, that is, through himself, or through connaturality. (280)

Maritain speculates further that while traces of the novel appear everywhere in the *Divine Comedy*, it is perhaps in the *Inferno* that the spirit of the novel is essentially embodied. This observation is relevant to the novel's relation to tragedy because the sensibility of the poet that produces the *Inferno* is one that is conditioned by generosity and love, as Maritain says, even though it may look upon damnation.

Such an attitude, where the essential compassion of the poet merges into the act of narration and description, is inherited as the viewpoint of the greatest novelists. Moreover, as Maritain points out, the knowledge between poet (or novelist) and character is not merely cognitive but connatural: the poet knows through a kinship with nature, living and suffering through the knowledge of his own creation. Josef Pieper explains the distinction between cognitive and connatural knowledge:

There are two basic forms of knowing; on the one hand knowing on the basis of a kinship with nature, *per connaturalitatem*, as a man recognizes his beloved or what is his own. The stranger does not understand, or misunderstands, but one who is allied with another in love and congeniality knows immediately, and with absolute certainty, what is meant in a fragment of a letter or a dimly heard call. And on the other hand, says Thomas [Aquinas], there is the *cognoscere per cognitionem*, a knowing of what is alien, an abstract, conceptional, mediate knowing of the mere object. (56)

Often the narrators themselves are the primary carriers of the wisdom that connaturality bestows. Whether it be Anton G–v in Dostoevsky's *The Possessed*, Ishmael in *Moby-Dick*, or Nick Carraway in *The Great Gatsby*, this narratorial interpretation of characters and events tends toward benevolence wherever the narrator's perspective assumes prominence and there is a poet-pilgrim relationship (as derived from the *Divine Comedy*)—that is, the narrator is both present to the event and the recounter of it. This pattern holds even if the characters and events he interprets point toward a tragic destiny. As Nick Carraway remarks at the outset of *The Great Gatsby* regarding his own narratorial sensibility, "Reserving judgments is a matter of infinite hope."

William Butler Yeats, in his essay "At Stratford-on-Avon," referring to the way a character is described in Balzac's *La Peau de Chagrin*, makes a similar observation about the compassionate and empathetic portrayal that lies at the heart of the narration of the great poets:

> [Balzac] would have us understand that behind the momentary self, which acts and lives in the world, there is that which cannot be called before any mortal judgment seat, even though a great poet, or novelist, or philosopher be sitting upon it. Great literature has always been written in a like spirit, and is, indeed, the Forgiveness of Sin, and when we find it becoming the Accusation of Sin, as in George Eliot, who plucks her Tito in pieces with as much assurance as if he had been clockwork, literature has begun to change into something else. (102)

What literature changes into when it becomes the "Accusation of Sin" is not tragedy but something more akin to rhetoric. The crux of the distinction is that great literature is capable of rendering a moral level without being moralistic. Moreover, great literature recognizes that human beings have a center to their being—a soul—from which all their actions emanate. Such is Dante's method and logic of character placement in the *Divine Comedy*. Lesser literature does precisely the reverse, taking deeds in isolation and then rendering a judgment of soul, resulting in an approach invariably moralistic that culminates in either empty accusation or hollow praise.

Yet Maritain's connection between the novel and the *Divine Comedy* has further implications. The strong identification between novelist, narrator, and character (using the *Divine Comedy* as paradigm) stands in contrast to the somewhat weaker identification that is made between author and character in tragedy. This change in relation seems to have less to do with a fundamental change in empathy than with the way that empathy can be conveyed in novels as opposed to drama. For it can be no coincidence that most tragedies are dramas. The playwright, in rendering the action, has fewer resources available to assert a level of critique to the action. Yet this weak relation between playwright and character in tragedy is in turn counterbalanced by the strong connatural relation between character and audience in the arousal of pity, which in turn is neutralized by fear. Tragedy's reliance on effect depends on a level of directness and immediacy that is more difficult to achieve in the novel. Novels, then, work against tragedy both in their inception and in their effect.

❊   ❊   ❊

It was perhaps in a spirit of novelistic identification that Flaubert is credited as having said, "*Madame Bovary*, c'est moi!" The passage is telling because it points to one of the paradoxes of the narration of the novel generally—and *Madame Bovary* in particular. The narration is simultaneously impersonal and intimate, with Flaubert's hand in every gesture of Emma Bovary. In this paradox lies the genius of Flaubert: his subtle insertion of himself into the novel through the use of technique as a means of moral evaluation. As a result, *Madame Bovary*, which has the earmarks of tragedy, is transformed into a dark comedy through Flaubert's own narrative approach. Through manipulation of point of view and the ironic juxtaposition of scenes, Flaubert enacts his own interpretation of the very reality that he is rendering intelligible. Reality for Flaubert is something acted upon, something rendered, not merely something to be described. Flaubert, therefore, is not really a "realist" in the pure sense, as he himself said: "For it was out of hatred for realism that I undertook this novel." Rather, he creates a moral universe, a system of values which operates as an intensifier and critique to the action. Thus the highly-mediated—almost satirical—character of the narrative accounts, in part, for the "strange upward draft" in the novel.

A number of scenes serve to point out this effect of moral evaluation. When Charles first courts Emma, he pays a visit to her at Les Bertaux, and she insists, overcoming his first shy refusal, that he take a liqueur with her:

> She brought a bottle of curaçao from the cupboard, reached to a high shelf for two liqueur glasses, filled one to the brim and poured a few drops in the other. She touched her glass to his and raised it to her mouth. Because it was almost empty she had to bend backwards to be able to drink; and with her head tilted back, her neck and lips outstretched, she began to laugh at tasting nothing; and then the tip of her tongue came out from between her small teeth and began daintily to lick the bottom of the glass. (26)

Here it is not so much Emma Bovary who acts, but the detail that acts through her, the tongue daintily licking the bottom of the glass, which in turn becomes a synecdoche of her soul's yearnings. Straining after those last drops becomes the image of her whole life.

With the same technical finesse, Flaubert describes the "steady current" of Charles's happiness after Charles and Emma marry and take up residence in Tostes—his delight upon waking and lying alongside Emma, his morning departure for his rounds, and Emma's fond farewell:

> From the saddle Charles would send her a kiss; she would respond with a wave; then she would close the window and he was off. And on the endless dusty ribbon of the highway, on sunken roads vaulted over by branches, on paths between strands of grain that rose to his knees—the sun on his shoulders and the morning air in his nostrils, his heart full of the night's bliss, his spirit at peace and his flesh content—he would ride on his way ruminating his happiness, like

someone who keeps savoring, hours later, the fragrance of the truffles
he has eaten for dinner. (39-40)

By a carefully-worked technique, images of seeming delight are
transformed—with a point of view now in the consciousness of
Charles—to an image of repulsion, of "someone who keeps savoring, hours later, the fragrance of the truffles he has eaten for
dinner." Charles is a type of noble savage, brought up by a
Romantic coddling mother and a cynical father, "a disciple of
Rousseau"; Charles is variously a "namby-pamby" (according to
Emma's down-to-earth father, Monsieur Rouault), a dullard, an
angel, a "booby" (according to Emma), and an egoist. The moral
critique which Flaubert absorbs in the narration has an overall
effect that is analogous to Dante's elaborate structure and placement in the *Inferno*, *Purgatorio*, and *Paradiso*, with characters
unconsciously enacting their own moral definition.

Flaubert's *Madame Bovary*, then, signals the transition effected
so often in the novel from apparent tragedy to black comedy. The
genre of black comedy which emerges out of the *Inferno* is a displacement from tragic cause to comic effect through the genius
of a highly-mediated narrative; in a similar way, *Madame Bovary*
metamorphoses from a tragedy of passion in inception to a morality play in result. It is the mediation in the narrative, the technological imagination of the novel, working over all the action,
that effects this change.

This is not to say, however, that *Madame Bovary* lacks many
of the hallmarks of the tragic genre. In many ways Emma Bovary
is the emblematic tragic heroine placed in a world of inauthentic values, a culture where no one actually thinks. She is a con-
duit for *idées reçues* in a culture defined by kitsch—"the translation
of the stupidity of received ideas into the language of beauty and
feeling" (Kundera 163). Such a milieu constitutes the enveloping
action of the novel. It is a world determined by fashions in reading and the ready parroting of ideas, opinion, and taste. Ortega
y Gasset chronicles the same movement in *Revolt of the Masses*: the
ascendancy of the mediocre, the vulgar, and the dull, with the
accompanying lack of standards, the aggressiveness of the com-
monplace, and the debasement of the noble.

Charles Bovary himself is the very symbol of the diminishment
of French culture at mid-century. The novel begins with his awk-

ward entrance into study hall, taking his place with the other schoolboys, his outrageous composite cap—"containing elements of an ordinary hat, a hussar's busby, a lancer's cap, a sealskin cap and a nightcap"—placed in his lap. Flaubert describes it as "one of those wretched things whose mute hideousness suggests unplumbed depths, like an idiot's face." Impressions aside, the technique at last focuses on pure description:

> Ovoid and stiffened with whalebone, it began with three convex strips; then followed alternating lozenges of velvet and rabbit's fur, separated by a red band; then came a kind of bag, terminating in a cardboard-lined polygon intricately decorated with braid. From this hung a long, excessively thin cord ending in a kind of tassel of gold netting. The cap was new, its peak was shiny. (4)

The cap is a hybrid crafted without regard for form or integrity, a patchwork from various professions, implicitly making light of the different callings it contains. Above all the cap is a sexual object, ovoid and phallic, but the sexuality that it symbolizes is trivialized, like the culture as a whole—akin to pornography, without rules or codes to govern its power.

❖ ❖ ❖

As someone who yearns for something beyond her circumstances, Emma Bovary is unique in her society. Flaubert means for her to be taken seriously. She is a high figure, a woman spirited enough to be capable of a tragic demise; she should be a redemptive presence for the community, the beautiful woman that society does not sufficiently value. Her being embodies, then, a type of paradox: on one hand she is a type of victimized woman, unvalued and unprotected, like an Anna Karenina or a the pure-hearted Sonya in Dostoevsky's *Crime and Punishment*; on the other hand she is an adulteress, a predator, a sensualist. The point of intersection of these conflicting aspects of Emma lies in the education of her imagination. After she marries Charles and discovers that the happiness she expected does not occur, she thinks she must have been mistaken: "And Emma tried to imagine just what was meant, in life, by the words 'bliss,' 'passion,' and 'rapture'—words that had seemed so beautiful to her in books" (40). The intensity of her yearnings is tainted from an early age, her imagination having been conditioned from the double thrust of the sentimental religion of the nuns on the one hand and the romantic pocket novels of the resident spinster at school.

As the novel progresses, Emma's imagination becomes increasingly fantastic; she develops a debilitating incapacity to interpret and understand her own experience. When Monsieur Rouault sends her a turkey with an accompanying letter—an opportunity to check her diseased Romanticism and to draw her back into an incarnate existence—the way Emma responds to the letter pointedly indicates the pathology in her imagination. Emma's father is one of her few images of ordinary, earth-bound existence. His letter arrives on "coarse paper," "thick with spelling mistakes" and is an occasion for her to have a real memory and therefore to have access to a vision of wholeness and ultimately to salvation. After she reads it she remembers her father with affection, and her mind is cast back to her youth:

> How happy she had been in those days! How free! How full of hope! How rich in illusions! There were no illusions left now! She had to part with some each time she ventured on a new path, in each of her successive conditions—as virgin, as wife, as mistress; all along the course of her life she had been losing them, like a traveler leaving a bit of his fortune in every inn along the road. (201)

First, she falsifies the memory; then, she turns the memory into an illusion, relapsing into an introspection that romanticizes her own diminishment.

Madame Bovary chronicles the fearful effects of a malformed imagination. Her education has given her the wrong order of the human heart, misplaced affections, unrealistic expectations, a set of passions set adrift. Early enchantment turns to disenchantment and subsequent dissatisfaction with her husband, her child, her house, and her town. In her despair after the love affairs with Rodolphe and Leon and her financial entanglements with Lheureux, she slides ever closer to an abyss. When Rodolphe sends her his letter in the basket of apricots to end his affair with her, her nature's pure physicality and sentiment intensify. Going up to the attic to read the letter and leaning against the window frame, she sneers angrily as she reads; she tries to concentrate, imagines holding Rodolphe in her arms, feels her heart beating faster and faster, "like great blows from a battering ram":

> She cast her eyes about her, longing for the earth to open up. Why not end it all? What was holding her back? She was free to act. And she moved forward. 'Do it! Do it!' she ordered herself, peering down at the pavement.
>
> The rays of bright light reflected directly up to her from below were pulling the weight of her body toward the abyss. The surface of the village square seemed to be sliding dizzily up the wall of her house; the floor she was standing on seemed to be tipped up on end, like a pitching ship. Now she was at the very edge, almost hanging out, a great emptiness all around her. The blue of the sky was flooding her; her head felt hollow and filled with the rushing of the wind: all she had to do now was surrender, yield to the onrush. (240-241)

Again Emma is revealed in a moment of interpretation. But she refuses the remaking of herself and, overtaken by a vertigo of the spirit, nudges further "toward the abyss." Her reactions become entirely sensual; she becomes all feeling, all hearing, all touching, with each sense taking on its dark edge, its threat of violence.

Yet with each setback Emma rises to a type of transcendence. With "brain fever" she takes to bed and her feeling for religion is rekindled. When the priest, Monsieur Bournisien, arrives to give her the sacrament, her rooms have become her own temple: "Emma felt something pass over her that rid her of all pain, all perception, all feeling. Her flesh had been relieved of its burdens, even the burden of thought; another life was beginning; it seemed to her that her spirit, ascending to God, was about to find annihilation in this love, like burning incense dissolving in smoke" (249). This eroticized religious annihilation has its darker counterpart later in the novel, when her financial troubles come to a head. In Rodolphe's final rejection of Emma, fantasy and self-destruction coalesce. At this point all her avenues have been exhausted as youth has given way to illusion, marriage to boredom, adultery to banality, and debt to humiliation. When she leaves Rodolphe, who is unwilling to give her the money she desperately wants,

> [i]t suddenly seemed to her that fiery particles were bursting in the

air, like bullets exploding as they fell, and spinning and spinning and
finally melting in the snow among the tree branches. In the center of
each of them appeared Rodolphe's face. They multiplied; they came
together; they penetrated her; everything vanished. She recognized the
lights of houses far off in the mist.

Suddenly her plight loomed before her, like an abyss. (369)

Emma's perceptions become increasingly more idiosyncratic and
interiorized as the action progresses, with fantasy itself turning
into hallucination and phantasmagoria. If it is true as Ortega y
Gasset says that "the hero is one who wants to be himself," (152)
the tragic hero is someone who wants, ultimately, to be nothing.
Emma's imagination moves ineluctably toward the tragic desire for
annihilation: she wants to be blotted out, to have her existence
erased. At this point she succumbs to the tragic desire for non-
being that every tragic hero in some way voices: as Everyman says
in response to his predicament, "I would to God I had never
been get!" (1.189); Dr. Faustus: "Cursed be the parents that engendered me!" (5.2.184); and Hamlet: "O cursed spite, / That ever
I was born to set it right!" (1.5.188-189). So too Oedipus, King
Lear, Othello: at some point all invoke a desire for oblivion.

The song of the blind beggar sounds the terrible irony of
Emma's own decaying relationship to the flesh. When the beggar
rides alongside the carriage at his post on the hill at Bois-Guil-
laume, his wail resounds in Emma's soul: "The sound spiraled
down into the very depths of her own soul, like a whirlwind in
an abyss" (316). Then when she hears the beggar's song in her
dying moments, her tragic fate is sealed in another fateful act of
misinterpretation. For despite her "passionate love-kiss" on the
crucifix on her death bed, she has consistently scorned the image
of Christ in the beggar, a negation that is cemented into her
dying moment. Emma's ultimate failure, despite her fantasies and
hallucinations, is a victory of literalization, with her banal religious pieties and dreams of love planting the seeds of death in
all of her desires.

Emma's death-bed scene is essential to understanding the overall form of the work because it averts the final tragic effect.
Flaubert reports the death, and the reader sees it, but does not
witness to it. The witnessing function would implicate the reader
in the action, which seems to be so central in the communal

and political character of tragedy. Even in the way in which Flaubert takes pains to describe her final communion, emptied of significance, illustrates the centrality of the sacrificial and immolative aspect of the death of the tragic hero—the death the reader is *not* seeing. These tragic elements are absent but not merely because Flaubert seems to wish it to be so, but because the mediating character of the novel makes it difficult to stage. In a novel, the reader is rarely more than a reader; the form does not require anything more. In tragedy, on the other hand, witnesses proximate enough to feel pity and fear seem central to the effect.

The overall mediating form of the novel—as expressed through authorial intention, narrative technique, the enveloping action, and the ascendancy of the symbolic—has the cumulative power to blunt the final tragic effect, transforming the action into a parable, a cautionary tale, a morality play. When Emma laughs her final "horrible, frantic, desperate, laugh," prompted by the beggar's song, the object of her horror and desperation is that ironic dark side of what she has been pursuing all of her life. Fixed in her mind's eye is the face of the beggar, her own ironic mirror-image in death: blinded, corrupted flesh begging for money in abjection. But what this vision bodes is for Emma alone to see; the reader understands the action but does not participate in it. Like Dante into Hell, the reader goes into Yonville-l'Abbaye with a guide—Flaubert himself, the revealer of provincial life, the moral evaluator who diverts the reader's gaze away from the internal dynamics of the tragic abyss. The reader sees that by the end of the novel the society is devastated and there is little hope in the future since the future belongs to the positivist pharmacist Homais, who has "public opinion... on his side." The infernal aspect of the novel has now come full circle with the stewardship of the community in the hands of a petty devil.

Emma's incremental spiritual isolation defines the condition that the modern novel so often works to redress. Like Ishmael in *Moby-Dick* or Raskolnikov in *Crime and Punishment*, the alienated person is placed in a culture in decay and a civilization turned against itself. Out of these societies—the circumambient universe that the novel creates in its enveloping action—emerges a figure of alienation whose destiny is to be the hero. But it is only by renunciation of the right to self-determination in spiritual activity—indeed, a renunciation of spiritual isolation itself—that the hero is made. The enveloping action in the novel is not only a guarantor of verisimilitude, but a cosmos, a full order of reality that is accessible to the hero, even if that order is debased. Implied in this observation is the fact that every human order has its avenues of grace. For Emma Bovary there are always examples given to her of rootedness in the earth, first in the figure of her father, and subsequently, though to a lesser degree, in the peasant woman at the Agricultural Show, Catherine Leroux, both presences that serve as occasions for turning around, opportunities of grace and transformation. In the novelistic cosmos there are not only the "cosmocrats of the dark aeon," as St. Paul describes them in his letter to the Ephesians (6:12), but the unexpected presences of benevolence as well, always some form of a Queequeg, always some version of a Sonya.

Tragedy, by contrast to the novel, is the most highly fictionalized of all genres. It depends upon a high degree of condensation and abstraction, and in defining a boundary and isolating a certain state of affairs over and against the ebb and flow of the world, it also withdraws the instruments of grace embedded in the enveloping action. Time is conditioned against tragic necessity because there is always something in time which is unrealized. As Walter Benjamin asserts in one of his "Theses on the Philosophy of History": "For every second of time [is] the strait gate through which the Messiah might enter" (264). Tragedy cuts off the possibility of the redemptive moment in time and thus excludes that quality of yearning toward which the novel consistently rises.

* * *

Perhaps more than any other novel, Dostoevsky's *The Possessed* marks a frontier where the potentialities of tragedy and the resources of the novel meet. As a novel about what has occurred in late-nineteenth-century Russia, what is occurring at present, and what may still be averted, the action pierces in a prophetic way the nature of time. To be prophetic in this sense is not to predict the future, but to present an action in its full implications. This quality in the greatest novelists—the prophetic dimension that is so clear in Dostoevsky, Melville, and Faulkner—mitigates most forcefully against tragedy, since any glimpse into the nature of time contains in its very structure a point of hope. As Mikhail

Bakhtin observes, the world depicted in the novel is an "unfinalized" world, its action an unfinalized action.

Thus, in *The Possessed*, the world described is dark, groaning under the weight of its own ideas, but buried in the action is the yearning for redemption in time. Both Shatov with his love of the earth and Kirillov with his household pieties have access to avenues of grace; at the end of the novel, we know that despite the fact that both die miserably, a redemptive force is present. Despite the downward movement in the novel, with a city left in flames, murders, suicides, the birth of a child into a hopeless situation, the seeming destruction of everything of value, *The Possessed* is not a tragedy. Like *Madame Bovary*, it is infernal comedy in a cosmos populated by devils and epigones, but unlike Flaubert's novel, it contains a simultaneous upward movement in the rebirth of a teacher, exorcised of his demons, and in the end "sitting at the feet of Jesus," like the man in the novel's epigraph from the Gospel of Luke. In this action lies the novel's painful truth: that a weak, sentimental man who does untold damage to a whole generation of students can undergo a change of heart and be redeemed. The luminosity of the comic action of Stepan counters the otherwise darkened claustrophobia of the revolutionary cell and its misdeeds. At the end, with the central tragic action closed, Stepan's story—his spiritual education—is the over-arching and open-ended action. Even though Stepan dies, his story constitutes the after-life of the work.

Much of the power of *The Possessed*, like that of *Madame Bovary*, comes from its mode of narration. In the compassionate and self-effacing narrator, Anton G–v, a confidant of Stepan and member of the coterie of friends, Dostoevsky creates a shared intimacy with the situation and with the reader. The narrator does not merely recount events, but renders literary opinions, makes philosophical judgments, takes sides, and falls in love. The narration is plotted on two planes, one with the upward movement of Stepan and the other downward movement of the princely Stavrogin. Anton G–v as narrator maintains a steady presence in the downward plot, but when Stepan undergoes his own self-realization, undertaking his own pilgrimage and striking out on the "open road," Stepan abandons not only his past life, but his narrator as well. Far from being a weakness in the novel, this unique narratorial strategy allows a certain freedom in the hero's own evolution. Further, the reader gains a greater connaturality with the hero at the end of the novel than would have been possible otherwise. Without Anton's insistence on the "extreme kindness of [Stepan's] gentle and unresentful heart" throughout the novel, the reader would be less inclined to see the paradoxical nature of Stepan, at once "a most excellent man," as Anton tells us, and one also capable of considerable (though unwitting) harm. Anton mediates the relationship between the reader and the unlikely hero, and the narratorial structure imitates the form of the *Divine Comedy*'s spiritual pilgrimage: just as Dante parts company with Virgil to continue his journey with Beatrice, so Stepan leaves Anton behind to discover on his own the great Mother Russia that becomes his fortunate destiny.

The tragic trajectory of Nikolay Stavrogin begins when he is under Stepan's tutelage. Stepan Trofimovitch is hired as a tutor by Varvara Petrovna to undertake the education of her only son. Anton G–v recounts the nature of Stepan's teaching:

> To do Stepan Trofimovitch justice, he knew how to win his pupil's heart. The whole secret of this lay in the fact that he was a child himself. I was not there in those days and he continually felt the want of a real friend…. More than once he awakened his ten- or eleven-year-old friend at night, simply to pour out his wounded feelings and weep before him, or to tell him some family secret, without realizing that this was an outrageous proceeding. They threw themselves into each others arms and wept… When at sixteen he was taken to a lyceum he was frail looking and pale, strangely quiet and dreamy. (Later on he was distinguished by great physical strength.) One must assume that the friends went on weeping at night, throwing themselves in each other's arms, though their tears were not always due to domestic difficulties. Stepan Trofimovitch succeeded in reaching the deepest chords of his pupil's heart, and had aroused in him a first vague sensation of that eternal, sacred yearning, which some elect souls can never give up for some cheap gratification when once they have tasted and known it. (37-38)

Stavrogin's education bears similarities to Emma Bovary's in its stimulation of desire. In Stavrogin it is the "the vague sensation of that eternal, sacred yearning" that Stepan plants in his student that in its development is so toxic to the imagination. This sacred yearning comes to fruition in the ethos that governs the revolutionary association. What Stavrogin experiences as dream and yearning, Shigalov formulates as theory, and Pyotr as tactic, with Kirillov and Shatov laboring through the contradictions of their own ideas in a war of abstraction against intuition.

The danger of the dream of perfection, the over-idealization of reality that is initiated by Stepan, is condensed in the dream of Stavrogin recounted as part of the confession he reads to Tihon. In the dream of the Golden Age myth mankind hatches one of the most dangerous ideas ever unleashed upon itself: the idea that there can be a state of perfection contrary to the divine order of the cosmos. In his confession to Tihon, after he describes a scene of earthly human bliss—"the most improbable of all visions, to which mankind throughout his existence has given its best energies, for which it has sacrificed everything, for which it has pined and been tormented, for which its prophets were crucified and killed"—Stavrogin elaborates:

> I do not know exactly what I dreamed about, my dream was only of sensation, but the cliffs, and the sea, and the slanting rays of the setting sun, all that I still seemed to see when I woke up and opened my eyes, for the first time in my life literally wet with tears. I remember these tears, I remember that I was glad of them, that I was not ashamed of them. A feeling of happiness, hitherto unknown to me, pierced my heart till it ached. (715-716)

In the opinion of Anton, Stavrogin's confession is "the work of the devil" that has taken possession of him. This "lofty illusion" after he sends Matryosha to her death and secretly marries Marya Lebyadkin—both actions undertaken for their sheer monstrous effect—offers the reader a glimpse into the psychopathology of the devil that has gone out of Stepan into Stavrogin. Here, as in *Madame Bovary*, the destructive archetype takes on the dream of perfection as its beautiful illusion.

The illusion is not a mere idea, however, but a world set up in perfect antagonism to the divine. In other words, the dream of utopian perfection is not a conceptual error correctable by instruction; it is a passageway into a type of anti-cosmos. As Vyacheslav Ivanov remarks in his treatment of the tragic nature of Dostoevsky's work,

> Eavesdropping on destiny, Dostoevsky learnt the deepest secrets of human unity and human freedom: That life is basically tragic, because man is not what he is;.... that the sinfulness of an evil deed may be cleaned away because all must take it upon themselves—but not the sinfulness of an evil dream of the world, because the dreamer holds a mirror to himself in solitude, and must therefore continue his dream; that faith in god and denial of god are not simply two different conceptions of the world, but two different worlds of the spirit, existing side by side, like an Earth and a counter-Earth, each fully living for itself in its own orbit of activity. (5)

The creation of this "counter-Earth" goes to the heart of the tragic genre. Every tragic figure at a certain point defects to the other side, journeying past a great divide where, as Macbeth says, "returning were as tedious as go o'er." The tragic action creates a force field that draws the tragic hero to this counter-Earth. Even the struggles of the unstable characters such as Shatov and Kirillov are explicable when seen as the traversing of the boundary between Earth and counter-Earth, these two "different worlds of the spirit" that Ivanov describes.

Once conceived in dream, the spiritual "counter-Earth" wants to be populated in reality. In Stavrogin's encounter with Matryosha, he reveals the core of a new idea that comes to him: the terrible thought that he can put someone in a state of spiritual death. In recounting the Matryosha episode to Tihon, he traces clearly the progress of his own evil. At first he imagines "killing and defiling her." But then the "new thought" comes to him, "...a new and terrible thought, terrible because I was so conscious of my feelings. When I came home I lay down in a fever. But I was so overcome by fear that I even stopped hating the little girl. I no longer wanted to kill her, and that was the new thought that occurred to me on Fontanka" (708). The fearful new idea is that he can take an active part in bringing someone to a death of the spirit, that he can be a psychopomp to nonbeing, a demi-god in his anti-cosmos.

The action of The Possessed illustrates the Augustinian basis that lies at the heart of the novel's engagement of tragedy. In Augustine's cosmology, the two cities built on two different types of loves are mixed in the world, but in the novel they are capable of being drawn out and separated. And in tragedy the reader is shown the outer limits of that city of self which is a type of nonbeing. Dostoevsky traverses the divide between these two realms. In such an order of things there can be a Fedka—runaway convict, arsonist, murderer of the Lebyadkins—who can yet be scandalized at Pyotr Verkovensky's blasphemy in putting a mouse in an icon's receptacle. Despite his criminality, Fedka inhabits God's cosmos: the unbelief, the desecration of the holy, and the positive evil of Pyotr horrify him. On the other hand there is Ensign Erkel, the taciturn young man who gives half his "scant pay" to his invalid mother but who becomes corrupted as the pupil of Pyotr and caught up in the anti-cosmos. Where Fedka's evil is probably not enough to damn him, Erkel's goodness is not enough to save him, one fears, so that by the end of the novel the reader shares Anton's sorrow over Erkel's fate. With Stavrogin himself there is less ambivalence, though he remains to the end full of the noble impulses that are a part of his character. The report of his suicide is like a telegram from the other side. Beyond our capacity to know it connaturally, it participates in nothing—the implosion and disappearance of meaningful reference. As miserable as it is, his death in the attic at Skvoreshniki, hanging from a greased rope, lacks the final tragic effect in large part because the reader is not taken to the necessary brink of vision, because there is ultimately nothing to see.

Unlike Stepan, Stavrogin cannot open himself to the presence of a woman like Sofya Matveyevna, the "gospel-woman" whom Stepan meets in his wanderings. Indeed, he seems to know quite well what always seems to be the case in Dostoevsky—that the spiritual principle lies not so much in the institutional religious representatives as in the feminine presences that intervene as witnesses to the Earth and its sacramental power. Stavrogin deliberately debases such presences and cuts off any possibility of finding his way back from the horror of his counter-Earth. Where the motherhood of the Madonna merges with the love of Mother Earth as it does in the Russian myth, the salvific power of "Holy Mother Earth" acts as vehicle of grace whose expansive effect transforms tragic elements—death, loss, suffering—making them into thresholds, openings into a cosmos where grace abides.

As a document that traces spiritual crises and passages, the novel is weighted on the side of redemption. The anagogical level, the highest and most elusive tracing of the spirit's ascent, will struggle to counter and supersede the other tendencies elicited by tragic elements. That such a highly mediated genre arises at a point when mediated knowledge in image, ritual, and sensation is so contested seems both remarkable and inevitable. The rise of the novel gives a feminine presence to the spirit when religion begins a radical masculinization, losing its life-giving connections to the earth and its larger cosmic relevance. It emerges as a consequence of individualism, and yet affirms over and over again the value of human community. It contains its own metaphysics at a time when metaphysics in philosophy is either absent, as it is in the American and Russian traditions, or in retreat, as it is in Europe. Seemingly so democratic and secular in its tendencies, the novel can be a medium that formulates a new aristocracy of the spirit. In correcting the one-sided tendencies that have come to characterize the modern era, it will be its great posterity for the ages. The great technicians of the novel, Flaubert and Dostoevsky, articulate the tendencies for the whole medium, with its increasingly global range. Distilled to its essential feature, the novel stands as affirmation of Being itself, and in so doing serves to lighten, as through the leaven of its own yearning, the tragic vision.

15

Blood in a Topaz Shrine:
Lorca and the Tribal Imperative

GREGORY MARKS

Federico García Lorca is that rarity in the modern world, a gen-uinely tragic dramatist, for his work gives us a true intimation of the tragic rift in being. His most successful tragedy is *Blood Wedding* (1933), the first part of the cycle that includes *Yerma* (1934) and *The House of Bernarda Alba* (1945). Together they form the so-called rural trilogy, and this name gives some indication of the force that lies behind them. For though Lorca knew such modernist/surrealist artists as Luis Buñuel and Salvador Dali, and therefore was conversant in the avant-garde idiom, he, like much of Spain in the early 20th century, was ambivalent regarding European traditions of modernism. Indeed, Lorca was born in 1898, the year Spain suffered what it saw as a humiliating defeat at the hands of the Americans. One might speak thereafter of a turn inward in Spanish cultural life, an inwardness that finds par-allel in the politics of the day.

Lorca's contemporary Miguel de Unamuno writes that Spain's reticence toward the larger currents of European thought can be traced back even further. In *Tragic Sense of Life*, Unamuno notes that while the rest of Europe was marked by "the Renaissance, the Reformation and the Revolution," Spain managed (or even labored) to keep its identity separate from these "de-essentializing" forces (298). What Unamuno writes of Cervantes' hero Don Quixote has broad application: "he fights against the Modern age that began with Machiavelli and that will end comically. He fights against the rationalism inherited from the eighteenth century. Peace of mind, reconciliation between reason and faith—this, thanks to the providence of God, is no longer possible. The world must be as Don Quixote wishes it to be" (327). For Unamuno, Spain's Quixotism redresses Enlightenment rationalism. Lorca came of age in this quixotic atmosphere of inwardness, and it is typical not only of his character but also of his artistic priorities that he never learned either French or English. Rather, he looked inward for his inspiration, not only to the Spanish Golden Age of the 17th century, but to the folk culture of his native Andalusia in southern Spain. Lorca consciously appropriated that Andalusian idiom, especially the gypsy "deep song"—poems sung to melodies, songs that speak of love and death, songs that he says "occur always in the night" (*Duende* 11). There too he found the force he called *duende*, the creative force native to Andalusia. Knowledgeable of yet segregated from the larger streams of European life, Lorca stood by his own culture.

It might be said without diminishing Lorca's universal appeal that his tragedy was sheltered from whatever in modernity drained off the tragic spirit. Thus while European drama of the time is urban and naturalistic, Lorca's theatre tends to the folk and symbolic; such a culture and such a method ground Lorcan tragedy. Andalusians are "close to the soil... [and] attuned to the world around them" (Edwards 134);[1] their cosmos is mediated by the rhythms and vicissitudes of agricultural life. Socially, the culture operates on the imperatives of shame and honor. Lorca's engagement with this folk culture was not that of a tourist, but rather that of a critical and sympathetic cosmopolitan writer who had visited New York City and had written poems in response. He was familiar with the "the loss of faith, the groundlessness of value, the violence of war, and a nameless, faceless anxiety" (Levenson 5) characteristic of much of modernity. A larger pattern in the creation of tragedy is perhaps visible here: the critical evaluation and articulation of an older folk tradition by an urban consciousness, which also happened in the Greek *polis*, Walter Nestle argues. Ancient Greek tragedy was born "when myth [started] to be considered from the point of view of a citizen" (Vernant 33). It is as if the creation of tragedy required an element of evaluation, a judgment called on oneself, a citizen's thinking through an abyss most present to an older culture.[2]

Situated thus between rural agriculture and urban modernism, Lorca could think through his Andalusian inheritance. How he did so is the object of much speculation; a reading of recent criticism shows a distinctly historicizing tendency. The prevailing critical mode of approaching *Blood Wedding* is socio-political, and it usually argues that Lorca's work both instantiates and unmasks social or cosmic oppression. The plot of *Blood Wedding* can certainly support such an approach: two former lovers, Leonardo and the Bride (as she is called throughout the play), flee moments after the Bride marries; the Groom pursues to avenge this dishonor, and he and Leonardo (whose relatives have killed the Groom's father and brother) stab and kill each other; the play ends with the remaining women lamenting their losses. The sociological strain of criticism sees Lorca's tragedies as essentially realistic, displaying a dialectic between individual eros and societal code. Great-souled figures come up against restrictions with tragic results. As Reed Anderson has it, Lorcan tragedy exposes category errors, as the characters come to realize "human institutions" (such as codes of honor) are not "metaphysical constants" ("Idea" 186).[3] *Blood Wedding* deals with "problems of a social nature"; Leonardo and the Bride feel "doomed to defeat by the superior strength that enforces the culture's moral law, and they will suffer severely for their act" (183). The theme of C. B. Morris' excellent study is best summarized in his chapter title "People as Prisoners"; he concludes that *Blood Wedding* "is a play without hope" (90). Similarly, Gwynne Edwards argues that the play suggests that human life is similarly bounded by fate and death, with humans "enclosed and dwarfed in their smallness and ignorance by forces which control them" (153).

This sociological approach to Lorcan tragedy reflects a broad, general shift over the last few decades towards the historicizing of literary texts. By liberating texts from formal boundaries into the events that generated them, this school of thought maintains, we come to understand the artist's motivations and pressures, conscious or unconscious. But as admirable and necessary as such study is—and as justifiable, considering the turbulence of Lorca's life and times—it cannot pretend to be exhaustive, and it hardly accounts for *Blood Wedding*'s power. Yet neither do accounts based simply on the universality of mortality and unforgiving social constraints. These constants do not in themselves explain the phosphorescence of character or the pleasure in seeing its destruction that successful tragedy entails. It is rather the case in *Blood Wedding* that Lorca meditates on those human ties studied by sociology to reveal a further boundary of loss, articulated and enshrined in lamentation. *Blood Wedding*'s success as a tragedy depends less on the realization of the relative artificiality and shallowness of social constraints than on a gauging of their depth.[4]

※ ※ ※

Tragedy is indeed, as Hegel intimates, about division, contradiction and negation, about severance, being cut off from the flow of life, about the end of hope. Certainly we see this oppositional structure in *Blood Wedding*. For example, at the height of the wedding festivities, it is discovered that Leonardo and the Bride have ridden off together. The suddenness of the peripeteia shows Lorca's overall economy. Within just two or three lines the Mother and the Groom's family decide on pursuit, and the Mother makes the tragic dialectic explicit: "There are two groups here... You with yours and I with mine" (78). The starkness of the opposition sets into motion a seemingly fated division. Yet this oppositional patterning also contains a depth of relation, and *Blood Wedding* shows us that tragedy is as much about binding as about dividing.

Lorca's tragedies recover a folk tradition that can ground this binding in a way that a disconnected culture—such as that exemplified by modernism's Ur-text, *The Waste Land*—cannot. His appropriation of a folk idiom allows him to set up a series of relations among the characters. With the exception of Leonardo, they have relational role-names (e.g., "Mother," "Groom") rather than proper names, and these ties of kinship and of love ground a depth of feeling that cannot be found in an urbanized, secular setting. The Groom and the Mother are particularly bound in these relations. His is a noble dream: that he and the Bride will marry; that they will have children; that the hot, dry wasteland that surrounds them can be cultivated. His aspiration is to get on with the business of living, yet we see an agon in the opening scene with his mother as he tries to make his mother forget old injustices and she insists on remembering them. Getting on with the business of life demands that he keep the past and the dead at bay. His cultivation of the earth requires the covering up of the dead, the burial of the past.

Over against these aspirations looms his mother's grief. She has lost both a son and a husband to Leonardo's family, the Felix clan, and she has become a repository of memory, a guardian of the dead: she protects their gravesites from incursion and has a deep piety for those lying there. We are told that she visits her dead men every morning. She remembers them as they lived and she recalls their suffering. Memory then becomes the site of this blood bond, and for the Groom the play will become a drama of remembering. Through the early part of the play he is future-oriented, but the sexual insult he suffers—his new wife eloping with an old love—forces him to remember his father's and his brother's deaths. Immediately, he is cast backwards. His efforts at forgetfulness fail, and by the third act, the hope of the opening scene is gone, and he is all remembrance.

Not once in the play has he made mention of the bloodshed in his family; not once has he shown any emotional range other than a muddled, cheerful practicality and a sheepish pride in his marriage. Yet soon after discovering that his wife and Leonardo have fled, he pursues them savagely. He asks a fellow-searcher: "Do you see this arm? Well, it's not my arm. It's my brother's arm, and my father's and that of all the dead ones in my family. And it has so much strength that it can pull up this tree by the roots, if it wants to. And let's move on, because here I feel the clenched teeth of all my people in me so that I can't breathe easily" (84). The play has prepared us for this speech: it is not quite true, as is often said, that Leonardo is the only named character in the play. In Act One, a Neighbor enters with news that an acquaintance, Rafael, has had "both arms sliced off by the machine" (38). It is as if those severed arms are now endowed with the strength of the dead to seek revenge. The Groom's arm becomes one with the underworld forces. He speaks not of his own slight—losing his wife to Leonardo—but of all the distilled fury of the dead. Time compacts into the presence of the past. There is an immediacy of action, a simultaneity.

Much of *Blood Wedding* is about being animated by forces outside of oneself that are nevertheless articulated from within. Here the binding strength of the blood, the pull of the dead, bears down on the Groom, as if the dead take the occasion of the sexual wound to have revenge for their own injustices. One hesitates to say that the Groom even seeks personal revenge for the deaths. Rather, these images of blood-bondedness come over the Groom as he becomes the instrument of an imperative both greater than himself and yet his own. Tragedy here meditates on the inevitability and justice of being bound by relation. Why the Groom feels this imperative, this bondedness with the dead, precisely at this time may appear odd at first. Certainly he suffers a violation when his new wife runs away with his family's enemy. But is the present violation not of a different order than the old? Is a sexual offense really like murder? Referring to Oedipus' moment of anagnorisis, H. A. Mason writes that at such times of deep awareness of familial horror, there is an elemental connection to a normally hidden blood consciousness. Taken to extremity, tragic characters engage in an instinctual "blood-thinking" (187). The Groom's immediate and deep connection between his violation by Leonardo and the murder of his kinsmen is made by a deep rationality of the blood. Undeniably, the dead do indeed somehow care about what the Groom suffers. The coincidence of their vengeance and the sexual insult is by no means coincidental. The Groom's humiliation opens up a more general woundedness that involves the whole community. Just as weddings and funerals are public festivities that attempt to parcel out and mediate the earthly forces of sexuality and death, so the violations of those forces require an answer with one communal voice, and the cosmos becomes a circle closing around the illicit lovers.

＊　＊　＊

To explain the process of artistic creation, Lorca appropriated the Spanish notion of a household spirit, *duen de casa*, and re-imagined it as a principle that parries with the artist: *duende*. In his essay "Play and the Theory of *Duende*," he distinguishes *duende* from the more familiar and tame "angel" and "muse." Like these two, the *duende* is an element in artistic creation, and like the Dionysian, touches on death, the irrational, and the earth. Yet its mode is less interior inspiration than agon: "With idea, sound or gesture, the *duende* enjoys fighting the creator on the very rim of the well. Angel and muse escape with violin, meter and compass; the *duende* wounds. In the healing of that wound, which never closes, live the strange, invented qualities of man's work" (*Duende* 58). The human agent must contend with the *duende* in an engagement that draws blood. In this agonized meeting lies a creative knowledge of extremity and of a certain "woundedness" in being that at first only a few see—the Mother, for example—but that becomes general and precipitous.

The Groom's sexual "wound" reconnects him with the *duende* and the realm of the dead through the deeply ambiguous role of blood, especially of spilled blood. Blood is mentioned a number of times in the play, and it takes on a variety of meanings, including evidence of sexual purity and the tribal blood of kinship. But the main instance of it obviously concerns violence—the murderous penetrations of flesh that the father and older brother have suffered, the spilled blood.[5] In the very beginning of the play, the Mother describes her approach to the son's body: "When I got to my son, he lay fallen in the middle of the street. I wet my hands with his blood and licked them with my tongue— because it was my blood. You don't know what it's like. In a glass and topaz shrine I'd put the earth moistened by his blood" (70). This startling image displays a specific connection between blood, language, and the physical tongue, *la lengua*. The Mother's tasting of blood and earth is highly allusive. The scene finds parallels in other images from European literatures, such as Abel's blood crying from the earth in Genesis, but two epics of the underworld—the *Odyssey* and the *Inferno*—are of special interest. In Odysseus' account of his trip to the underworld in *Odyssey* XI, Odysseus tells his audience:

> But I sat still
> until my mother came to drink the blood
> dark as a cloud. And she knew who I was
> at once; I saw her tears, heard her winged words. (217)

Once Odysseus' mother has drunk, she can speak. Blood has not only a revitalizing power, but also a linguistic power. In Dante's *Inferno*, the suicide Pier delle Vigne, embodied in a shrub or tree, speaks only when one of his limbs is broken, so that the dripping blood itself makes possible his speech.[6]

Both instances show a relation between blood and speech

reflected in *Blood Wedding*. Drinking of the spilled blood has opened the Mother's mouth to the expression of the tragic spirit, and her own family blood press to formulation not merely her grief but a meditated "blood-thinking." She thinks on and through the blood; the play's last words belong to her, as she describes the knife that killed the men:

> ...it barely fits the hand
> but it slides in clean
> through the astonished flesh
> and stops there, at the place
> Where trembles enmeshed
> The dark root of a scream. (99)

The Mother is pointing backwards to "roots," to origins.[7] The mention of the knife recalls the very first words of the play. Christopher Soufas argues that by mentioning the "dark root of a scream," the Mother "posits... the definitive origin of tragedy" (44). For Soufas' deconstructive reading, this original point is a pre-linguistic condition for viewing the tragedy, a place perhaps beyond the "astonished flesh."

More broadly, it can be said that the blood has been taken in by the Mother, internalized, and thought upon. The Mother's *lengua* provides the central image of the play. Indeed, with the image of "a glass and topaz shrine" in which she would "put the earth moistened by his blood," she gives the audience an image of tragedy itself: the enshrinement of the horrible, the exaltation of the deadly, the bringing to vision of what should be contained—blood. Bringing to beautiful expression what is prior even to a scream, the scream's "dark root," is the function of tragic theatre. As John Sallis says about Nietzsche, tragedy lets "the horrible turn into the sublime" (95). Taking the merely horrible of this world and sheltering it, taking custody of it ("shrine" in the original Spanish text is *custodia*), and making it overwhelmingly beautiful is precisely the role of tragedy. The shrine becomes a sheltering place, a place of reserve where the evidence of the horrible has been placed. That clotted earth—like that caused by the first fratricide Cain—is evidence of some primal rupture or wound. The Mother would bear that evidence and make of it a public ornament, a sacred thing to be contemplated.[8]

❉ ❉ ❉

This sanctification of the blood-clotted earth foregrounds the strong theme of death in the play. Andrew Anderson argues that in *Blood Wedding*, "The fundamental tragedy is none other than human mortality, which creates and defines the 'tragic' human condition or predicament." (28). For Lorca, Spain is uniquely situated to engage the question of death; he comments that "Spain is the only country where death is a national spectacle" ("Play" 60). And as Geoffrey Ribbans notes, death bears on many Spanish writers of the time. For Unamuno and others, "Death and its consequences—whether or not there is any survival after death—is the fundamental human question" (12). And yet, as Ribbans goes on to argue, Lorca engages death in a fashion, neither philosophic nor oppressive, that does not overwhelm the dynamism of the tragedy. Lorca certainly realized the centrality of death for the cultural life of Spain, but for this playwright, the tragic vision goes beyond a "tragic view of life" framed by mortality.

The third act of *Blood Wedding* represents a shift from realism to a "poetic fantasy," punctuated by two very different instances of lifting up: the dance of the two lovers, and the lifting up of the two dead men. It is here that the attempt to historicize the play falls especially short. The images of death, the moon, the beggar-woman, the knives that dominate the final act are seen as eroticized; above all, they want union. Thus Lorca's tragic vision is not merely that death encircles all things as the ultimate reality. Rather, death is connected to human desires, especially love, such that at the limit of life is both the end and the beginning of human emotion and mourning. Lorca emphasizes not death's reality, but its "consequences for the emotional life of the living" (Ribbans 15). For example, even the deathly moon that exposes the lovers to the hunting party wants an erotically charged union:

Let me come in! I come freezing
Down to walls and windows!
Open roofs, open breasts
Where I can warm myself! (81)

This eroticizing of death in the play—from the mention of the wounding, phallic knife in the beginning to the "dark root of a scream" at the very end—helps explain the rare mention of feminine beauty. Though the plot is structured around a love triangle, there is a surprisingly narrow aesthetic vocabulary. When beauty is marked, it is not the beauty of the play's ostensible object of desire, the Bride. Her strength, goodness, fertility, and husbandry are noted, but her beauty only once, and never by the Groom or Leonardo. Rather, the aesthetic is reserved for another class—the dead men: the father was a "handsome man" (34), Leonardo was a "beautiful horseman" (97), and both are compared to beautiful flowers. The play finds its axis and drive less in feminine beauty than in a further sublimation of the horrible: the expended beauty of the men.

Death and dishonor, the two injustices that overshadow the play, are rearticulated, not only erotically, but also in a religious context. Some readings find in *Blood Wedding* and the rural trilogy generally Lorca's animosity towards and criticism of religion as a domineering force which effaces individualism. John Gilmour, for example, argues that "In their painful search for individual fulfillment, Lorca's tragic heroines in the rural plays reflect this bitter struggle to throw off the shackles of an ideologically dominant social institution" (152). Yet such a reading obscures or ignores what can only be described as a "liturgical" movement in the play as the Bride and Leonardo flee and find their way to a moist forest.[9] The two lovers step beyond, into the forest—a sort of anti-green world. Occupied by the cold moon and death, it is a place of *ekstasis*—of stepping out of oneself in the play of love and death that *duende* describes. They remove themselves from the community and step beyond it, giving their bodies not *to* each other, but *over to* the *duende* in an ecstatic liturgy of immediacy performed at the precipice of death.[10]

> But wherever you go, I go.
> You're the same. Take a step. Try.
> Nails of moonlight have fused
> my waist to your chains. (89)

Just as the Groom feels himself bound by the dead, so the lovers feel chained by passion. The two step together, waists locked, and as the stage directions indicate, "This whole scene is violent, full of great sensuality" (89). Yet despite what the chorus of

Woodcutters and the two clans think, the two lovers do not exchange their bodies; they demand the cold preservation of purity in each other. There is a "fierce insistence on virginity" (Gaskell 110). The lovers' flight ought not therefore be viewed as an escape from the constraints of societal constrictions on passion, but as a prelude to the irruption of *duende*, a contest with death, a creative work that lifts them up in a contested drive to unity. The title of the play indicates its overall tendency—there is a hunger for unity: of living with dead, of Groom with Bride, of lover with beloved, of farm with farm, of knife with breast. The lovers' dance effects this unity by oppositional violence: by repelling each other, they are united; by fleeing, they are chained; by burning, they germinate; by calling down death, they live.[11]

Therefore, just as Greek tragedy occurred in the context of a religious festival, there is something liturgical or ritualistic in the action of *Blood Wedding*. Lorca expressed a concern to develop his own genealogy of Spain's cultural history. In the short essay or prose poem, "The Poem of the Bull," he implies that sacrifice is bound up with Spain, even with its geography: "Spain stretches out like a bull's hide. Spain is not an anaconda, like Chile, but an animal's hide, a sacrificial animal at that. In this geographical symbol lies the deepest, most dazzling and complex part of the Spanish character" (*Duende* 82). Yet this recognition does not require one to see *Blood Wedding* as the portrayal of a sacrificial crisis. Robert Lima's otherwise fine reading sometimes overemphasizes the sacrificial element, so that the mens' spilt blood is part of a "propitiatory" rite, a "libation to appease the powers that be" (257). If a sacrificial element comes to the fore as the two lovers flee, there is a restrained, formal quality to their flight that belies mad escape. Before coming to the forest, the two walked down the stairway of the Bride's house and outfitted the horse with a new bridle. The Bride strapped spurs on Leonardo's boots willfully and slowly. Theirs will not be merely a passion spent outside of the confines of society. Indeed, the Bride and Leonardo recognize the economy of shame and honor in which they find themselves, and alone in the woods, they reject a future of mere illicit coupling:

Bride: (*Sarcastically*)
Carry me with you from fair to fair,

a shame to clean women
so that people will see me
with my wedding sheets
on the breeze like banners.
Leonardo: I, too, would want to leave you
if I thought as men should. (89)

Theirs is a liturgical action, and their destruction has meaning and weight beyond what the avengers can do.

Leonardo and the Bride make their separate deaths their own by envisioning their deaths as given to each other. The death of the lover is pointed to, first in violent tearing, as the Bride's hands would "break the blue branches / and sunder the purl of your veins." Then instead of this sparagmos, their two deaths are imagined as one holocaust:

Fire is stirred by fire.
The same tiny flame
Will kill two wheat heads together. (88)

The "two wheat heads" echoes the Mother's words from the first scene of the play: "That's what I like. Men, men; wheat wheat" (36). Leonardo and the Bride's movement is not only a literal fleeing from pursuers, but a movement of spirit to a place of contemplation, where, as Leonardo says to the Bride, "I can look at you" (88). The desire is essentially lyric, to look upon the lover in a suspended state of immolation, not quite frozen, but as a shimmering flame, violently burning yet not consumed, the Bride dying "lost and virgin" (89). The Bride remains in an in-between state, neither bride, nor wife, nor virgin, immobile.[12] Nevertheless, they both intuit that their movement, over against the rough justice of the pursuers, has an essential rightness to it: "It is fitting," ("*Es justo*") the Bride says. The short scene ends with the mutual declarations, "If they separate us, it will be / because I am dead," and "And I dead too" (90). Like the wheat heads, they are bound for immolation.

Leonardo and the Bride have set themselves apart from the community and lifted themselves out of the sexual economy as if in oblation. Of course, it is not the Bride who dies, but the Groom and Leonardo. The remainder of Act Three shows the reaction and lamentation of the community of women. This final scene is required to formalize but not redress these losses. The previous image of burning wheat foreshadows the bearing up of the two dead lovers. Leonardo and the Groom are now brought in:

Wife: Ayyy, four gallant boys
    come with tired shoulders!
Bride: Ayyy, four gallant boys
    carry death on high! (98)

The two men are lifted up only to be plunged down into the grave as the Mother, Bride, and Neighbors chant in antiphonal mourning. The effort which Leonardo and the Bride started but were incapable of—the re-articulation of their dishonorable love into a visible spectacle—is now completed in the final scene. Thus the male lovers are exalted in a way that Leonardo and the Bride could not be. The Mother, Wife, and Bride, who have lost son, husband, and groom, here unite in a stylized lyric lamentation that perhaps falls just short of tragic exultation.

If this final scene lacks the "metaphysical consolation" Nietzsche speaks of, it nevertheless bears a resemblance to the endings of both Synge's *Riders to the Sea* and Euripides' *The Trojan Women*.[13] Both those tragedies end with a chorus of women in lamentation. The men have been killed in war or by the sea, the masculine principle has been vacated, the destruction of the vital is complete. The women are left to acknowledge, accept, and lament that loss. Like Maurya, the mother in *Riders to the Sea*, the Mother in *Blood Wedding* expresses relief that a limit has been reached and that there are no more men to lose: this is the satisfaction in the last scene. The Mother speaks of peace and calm, and the Beggar talks of the deaths of the men as "fitting" ("*Era lo justo*"), words the Bride has already used to describe death. Thus both the symbolic deaths of the Bride and Leonardo and the actual deaths of the Groom and Leonardo are labeled fitting, upright, or just. Death is lifted on high, but it is put immediately in the context of love as the women set out an antiphony that resounds with the lyrical depth of the *Stabat Mater*, the song of the women at the foot of the cross. The Mother intones, "It's always the same thing. / The cross, the cross." To which the Neighbors respond:

> Sweet nails,
> cross adored,
> sweet name
> of Christ our lord. (98)

The centrality of love in its relation to the dishonor of suffering and death is a paradox not only of Lorca's Spanish Christianity but of life itself. The Mother's final words, almost an encomium to the knife, that which brought about the deaths, reflects the liturgical drive of the third act, as malediction becomes commemoration:

> Neighbors: with a knife,
> with a little knife,
> on their appointed day, between two and three,
> these two men killed each other for love. (98)

She addresses the gathered community of women, formalizes the deaths, and gives them a meaning by connecting them with love. Yet all four main characters have participated in this fitting action. The Bride has avoided the fate of her own Mother, a woman consigned to a loveless marriage. Leonardo lifted the Bride up out of the sexual economy, an economy he had participated in and knew the limits of. The Bride herself has been set apart, and indeed she tries to make such a setting permanent by offering her throat to the Mother.[14] The Groom too has been lifted up, sacrificed for the Bride to a degree he may never have done in life. Finally, the Mother has articulated the tragic situation in the play's central image of blood in a topaz shrine.

Human action finds its rightness in relation to the divine, and she who began the play by cursing ("*Maldite...*") now ends the play with blessings ("*Benedite...*"): "Blesséd be the wheat stalks, because my sons are under them; blesséd be the rain, because it wets the face of the dead. Blesséd be God who stretches us out together to rest" (97). At the beginning of the play she curses the "scoundrel" who makes knives, but the curse is balanced by her blessing at the end, a benediction that extends to all the land that covers the dead. This final image of the cross represents a re-stabilizing emphasis on refounding the meaning of suffering.

The image of *nails* driven into flesh puts the action of the knife plunged into the flesh into a larger narrative. And yet the end also staves off the remainder of any consoling narrative. The loss is irredeemable, incapable of being incorporated—for now, for this community, for this cosmos—into some larger comic action. It is tragic.

It is significant that Christianity is mentioned only at the end. Lorca's rejection of the resolutions that religion offers has perhaps less to do with his own criticism of a "dominant social institution" than it does with the requirements of the tragic genre. At the end of this play, the women know that a boundary to loss has been reached; that in itself is a consolation. The end of some historical process has been reached, and the masculine has been emptied out: therefore there will be no more passing on of the violence. It will go no further. Most importantly, the final scene represents a regrounding of the emotions. The horrible and the unimaginable have been displayed and taken custody of by the human emotional life in the final lamentation of the women.

❊   ❊   ❊

Blood Wedding is the first play in the unnamed "rural" trilogy that Lorca had long intended. *Yerma* was produced in 1934, and *The House of Bernarda Alba* was first staged nine years after Lorca's death, in 1945. Taken as one action the trilogy traces the possible losses that three modes of feminine relation—bride, wife, and widow—can incur. The plot of *Yerma* traces the increasing estrangement and isolation of a woman denied motherhood. The heroine Yerma—her name a variation of *yermo*, "barren"—at first merely laments the absence of children and the dryness of her breasts: "Oh, what a field of sorrow! / Oh, this is a door to beauty closed / [...] / Oh, breasts, blind beneath my clothes!" (131). This static sense of loss reaches towards dynamism with her growing realization that her husband Juan does not share her disappointment—indeed, does not want children at all. In some sense he denies them to her, whether he is impotent, sterile, or merely abstemious. This knowledge of her husband's implicit rejection of her femininity drives Yerma close to madness, to the point where she dreams of auto-regeneration: "Oh, if only I could have them by myself!" (140). Restraining her is the code of honor that denies her extramarital sexual encounters for the sake of procreation; she says of her husband "I don't love him, and yet he's my only salvation. By honor and by blood" (140). And when she discovers that the pilgrimage for barren women in which she participates is less about spiritual intercession and more about a bacchanalia with single men, she is disgusted. Her conception of "honor" becomes nearly identical with pride: "Do you imagine that I could know another man? Where would that leave my honor?" (151). Thus what begins as a sadness at unfulfilled potential ends in Yerma's spiraling into a bodiless outrage at a dispossession which puts her at war with the matrix of both love and generation, the body: "It's one thing to wish with one's head and another for the body—cursed be the body!—not to respond" (143). The materialistic Juan can say, "What matters to me is what I can hold in my hands. What my eyes can see" (152), but there is such a deep estrangement from the body in this play that he is strangled in the final scene by a despairing Yerma, who weeps and exalts: "I have killed my son!" (153).

In *The House of Bernarda Alba*, the field of feminine activity is limited even further and the alienation of the sexes sharpened. Bernarda, a recently widowed "domineering old tyrant" with five daughters, is so concerned with the honor and uprightness of her house that she confines her senile mother and restrains her daughters from any relationship she deems beneath their status. The curse on her "house" is thus a kind of spiritual incest, a closeness that fears and mistrusts any outside force represented by the masculine principle. She grudgingly allows her eldest daughter Angustias to be courted by Pepe Romano. Yet even this minimal masculine presence—no man is ever on stage in the play— causes disorder in the house, because Adela, the youngest, turns out to be the true object of Pepe's attention. Bernarda ignores her servant's advice to allow her daughters more freedom, as whole ranges of play and action are closed to them. All masculine company—for example that of the chorus of farmhands ("Throw wide your doors and windows, / you girls who live in the town")—is denied them, and each act ends with images of brutality: Act One with the violent imprisonment of Bernarda's mother; Act Two with the beating of an unmarried woman who killed her child to hide her shame; Act Three with Adela hanging herself. The play ends with Bernarda Alba's assertion that

Adela died a virgin, and her icy demand for "Silence!"

In tracing out the attenuation of the concept of honor and the diminishment of the feminine, Lorca's vision in these latter plays sinks from the liturgical to the merely societal. The plays' color scheme—a shift from "*sangre*" to "*alba*," red to white—implies a draining away of passion and life, and it coincides with an increased sundering of the sexes. The two lovers fighting over one woman in *Blood Wedding* give way in *Yerma* to the emotionally absent husband, whose waning masculine force dwindles into the complete effacement of the men from the stage in *The House of Bernarda Alba*, where the only masculine presence is the sound of a stallion's hoof knocking against the house.

Just as the plays trace out the diminishment of color, of passion, of blood, they follow three figures of women in the economy of honor. Honor in its public aspect, increasingly superficial, demands the progressive constraint of women. Instead of indicating the deep, sacrificial gift-giving of the body, honor folds into mere reputation and good name. Thus, Juan in *Yerma* does not want his wife to go out, while in *The House of Bernarda Alba*, Bernarda's constrictive circle tightens until it kills one daughter and ends in the lie that she died a virgin. The economy of shame and honor, the ambiguity of which is successfully explored in *Blood Wedding*, is here diminished, criticized, and rejected. Indeed, it might be said that the entire trilogy enacts this draining off of the tragic spirit as crucial understandings of the dead, the feminine, and the notion of honor, along with the imperatives they ground, become less persuasive. The desires that Yerma or the characters in *The House of Bernarda Alba* feel are opaque; they seem not to point beyond themselves, as the felt desires in *Blood Wedding* clearly do.

Felicity Rosslyn writes that while modernism is undoubtedly incompatible with tragedy, the transition to modernism (such as Spain underwent in the 1930s) offers a historical moment ripe for tragedy, for tragedy itself records a transition. "And in this light it may be easier to understand why tragic plots should have so much in common, if they essentially record the same transition: the movement from blood-thinking to thinking, and from family bonds to citizenship, in the evolution of human equality before the law." (217).[15] If Rosslyn is correct and tragedy represents a shift from "blood thinking" to "thinking," then perhaps Lorca's trilogy displays the erasure of the conditions of tragedy. It is as if, after *Blood Wedding*, he had already thought through the modernist idiom and tried, with less success, to incorporate it into his tragic vision. *Blood Wedding*, which sustains and makes sublime the ties to abysmal blood-thinking, therefore remains as Lorca's fullest contribution to the possibility of tragedy in the modern world.

NOTES

[1] Lorca himself shared this closeness to the earth. "As a boy, Lorca once watched a plow unearth a fragment of Roman mosaic from one of his father's fields. He later recalled "how the huge steel plowshare cut gashes into the earth, and then drew forth roots instead of blood.... So the first artistic wonder I ever felt was connected with the earth" (Stainton 17).

[2] At least one critic finds this distinction between urban and folk in regard to Lorca a "cliché" (Smith 52).

[3] In addition to the realist readings, there are biographical, archetypal, deconstructive, gay, and Freudian readings.

[4] Writes H. A. Mason in his *The Tragic Plane*: "It is easy for us, especially if we are inclined to think that Tragedy concerns individuals, to fall into confusion here. Because it so often happens in the best plays that by the time that tragedy gets under way that tragic person seems to stand out as an isolated figure, we forget that there would be no tragedy if there were not tragic circumstances involving a whole society" (41). While admitting that Lorca did not leave us with a developed theory of the tragic, Sumner Greenfield notes that "freedom, in a fundamental, apolitical and non-ideological sense, is his basic theme" (2). A non-ideological, apolitical meditation of freedom is significant, for *Blood Wedding* is about the deep and terrible humanity of finding oneself bound.

[5] With such an image it is perhaps tempting to have recourse to a theory of tragedy as a culture's scapegoating of a sacrificial other. Yet the calm at the end of a tragedy is different from appeasement; as J. P. Vernant notes when disputing the sacrificial origins of tragedy, tragedy is about the death of men, not sacrificial animals. See Rene Girard's *Violence and the Sacred*, and J. P. Vernant, 16-17.

[6] Christopher Soufas finds other parallels between *Blood Wedding* and *Inferno* cantos 15 and 16 ("Geography").

[7] The Mother has done this throughout the play, most obviously though her memory, but also literally, as when she directs her family to pursue the escaped couple: as Soufas points out, she yells "Atras!", which means "after them," but also "back" or "backwards."

[8] This aestheticizing of the ghastly is an especially strong figure against a ground usually devoid of beauty. With the exception of the "moist woods" to which the lovers escape, the native landscape of Blood Wedding is harsh and wasted, arable and productive only by violence.

[9] As Stainton notes, Lorca himself spoke of theo-drama: "In 1932 Lorca told Barraca audiences that through Calderón's mystical theater one could arrive at 'the great drama, the best drama, which is performed thousands of times every day, the best theatrical tragedy in the world. I am referring to the Holy Sacrifice of the Mass'" (287).

[10] Terrence McMullen writes of this liturgical drive: the two "celebrate [...] a liturgy of desire" showing "the sacramental power of instinct"; it is not a literal cuckolding, but a "ritualistic synthesis of their reciprocal passion" (69).

[11] In an article that helps account for this willed destruction, Carolyn Lukens-Olson argues that the play centers around the destruction of the Dionysian life in Leonardo. See her "The Mask of Dionysus."

[12] Mary Douglas writes of this in-between state in *Purity and Danger*: "Danger lies in transitional states, simply because transition is neither one state nor the next, it is undefinable" (96).

[13] Gaskell 106.

[14] Other deaths have also been imagined for the Bride: suicide by drowning (78) and suicide by shooting (86). See Nicole Loraux, in *Tragic Ways of Killing a Woman*.

[15] Rosslyn appropriates Mason's terms here.

16

The Tragedy of Inheritance in
Faulkner's Yoknapatawpha Novels

J. LARRY ALLUMS

Since the 1960s, the "historical method," as Allen Tate called it (552), has cultivated a social awareness in criticism that resists reading the contingent issues of our lives—race, class, gender—as metaphors. The literalism that marks our liberal democracy is instrumental in advancing social and political causes, but is at the same time intolerant of the kind of non-literal, analogical approaches to literature that not so long ago were common in the West. Literature of the Southern Renascence has especially suffered from the loss of analogy as a legitimate way of reading, and William Faulkner's novels most of all. Faulkner's tragic vision in particular has remained largely misunderstood or unexamined because it is in his most important tragic novels—*The Sound and the Fury*, *Absalom, Absalom!*, and *Light in August*—that the offensive aspects of Southern culture are most visible. The best political and social readings of Faulkner are necessarily limited in their emphasis on the South's obvious flaws and his supposed failure to address them responsibly: as a representative of the Negro race, for instance, Dilsey is abject before the Compson abuse; as a representative of women, Lena Grove is passive and rather dumb; as a representative of white Southern males, Quentin Compson is totally inadequate in his response to past and present injustices.

Doubtless the proper focus of history, those flaws take on a different role in analogical readings of literature—readings that relieve us at least temporarily of history's exacting realities, detach us from the necessity of immediate action, and allow us the contemplative distance that even our most pressing social problems ought to include. Addressing the current intellectual conflict between analogy and history, the Caribbean writer Edouard Glissant said in 1996 that William Faulkner's "oeuvre will be complete when it is revisited and made vital by African-Americans" (55), which suggests that those affected most personally by the literal level of Faulkner's work must find a way to approach it that transcends mere history to retrieve the promise that Glissant intuits.

Presently in the U.S., however, the subject matter of Faulkner's tragedies still feels too close and too raw for most people's sensibilities, and in public arenas, dealing with Faulkner at all continues to be a low-yield risk.[1] Its linguistic difficulties aside, his work is chosen for the secondary classrooms of America—when it is included at all—with an eye toward what is least offensive. Thus, the high school teacher who regards Faulkner as important will settle for As I Lay Dying, a powerful novel in its own right, over The Sound and the Fury, Absalom, Absalom!, Light in August, or Go Down, Moses, texts more central to Faulkner's penetration into the American myth. This is understandable, but as long as social and political interests dictate what of Faulkner is read and how, we will continue to miss the full depth of a tragic vision that reveals with unequalled completeness and clarity the shadow cast by the very light of the American dream.

A major consequence of the historical method's dominance in Faulkner studies is that the nearness of his tragic vision to that of his Greek predecessors is greatly underestimated. Many critics have observed the parallels between Aeschylus' house of Atreus and Faulkner's houses of Sartoris, Compson, and Sutpen, or between Joe Christmas and Oedipus, but it has not been noted enough how immediately and profoundly Faulkner appropriated for his own use what might be called, following Aristotle in the Poetics, the "soul" of tragedy as the Greeks understood it. In fact, Faulkner seems to have appropriated it with far less cultural dilution than Shakespeare did in his great tragedies, as if Faulkner's attention to the "old verities" allowed him to glimpse some deeply imbedded correspondence—both ominous and promising—between the West's first emergence in ancient Greece and its much later, much-heralded incarnation as the New World. Faulkner saw that the brief, compact history of America, where the failures of the old order were to be corrected, contained in dramatic potential the fundamental plot of tragedy.

❈ ❈ ❈

During his tragic phase, Faulkner was most concerned with how the burden of inherited guilt could not be simply left behind in what Cass Edmonds and Ike McCaslin call the "old world's worthless twilight" in Go Down, Moses (247); instead, that burden followed the settlers and builders of the New World, much as the Furies pursued Orestes to Athens. Although it appeared as "new," the New World's fruits could be realized only by being possessed, as Canaan was by the children of Israel, but this possession—of both land and other human beings—ultimately revealed itself as the tragic catastrophe and the source of the New World's tragic guilt. Hidden at first under the illusion of ownership, the old, immutable laws of the universe reasserted themselves in the chaos of the American Civil War and yielded the real fruits of tragic inheritance, this time not in ancient Greece but in modern America.

In her introduction to this collection of essays, Louise Cowan indicates that tragic poets discern in human experience a strain that seems to indicate a catastrophic contradiction at the heart of being. In Faulkner's tragic novels, the originary aspect of this contradiction always has to do with inheritance. The individual soul, born into a world not of its own choosing or making, clearly is not responsible for the pattern of events that has determined its cultural milieu. And yet the "sins of the fathers" must be assumed—that is, the injustice of history and the merciless continuity of time. The soul that does not rail against this injustice, but accepts it, assumes responsibility for the cultural inheritance, whatever its appointment in the always emerging "master narrative" may be—to be born into privilege or poverty, to be part of the dominant elite or the disenfranchised.

Ancient or modern, what tragedy opens us to, first and foremost, is the abyss that holds the darkness of our inheritance. To

look into the abyss and acknowledge the truth of what is there—
what one inherits—is to approach the realm of the tragic. In
tragedy's most direct, unmediated form among the Greeks, the
tragic hero—Oedipus par excellence—is both agent and victim, the
unsuspecting inheritor of a dark past that he himself has
extended by his re-enactment of it. The form undergoes revision,
of course, in the trajectory of tragedy in the West. Hamlet's
inheritance—the mission of revenge—continues the Greek tradition,
but his story of introspection constitutes a decisive point in what
Raymond Williams calls the "transformation of the tragic hero
into the tragic victim" (87). Faulkner's most piercing enactments
of the genre seem to illustrate Williams' point: they involve Cas-
sandra-like witnesses rather than instigators and perpetrators of
tragic crimes who endure the whole range of active and passive
stages in the primal plot. In contrast to bold Oedipus, Faulkner
gives us Quentin Compson, Gail Hightower, Isaac McCaslin, and
Joe Christmas, who are overwhelmed upon discovering injustices
and horrors that they themselves have not committed.

But even as it reflects modern tragedy's emphasis on the sort
of introspection foreshadowed in the character of Hamlet,
Faulknerian tragedy avoids the democratic dilution of the tragic
protagonist from agent-victim to victim, in part by exploiting the
capacity of the novel to uncover in vivid detail the origins of the
tragic curse. Quentin Compson in *Absalom, Absalom!*, for
instance, at first glance seems to be simply another character who
exemplifies yet again the Prufrockian deficiencies of the modern
pretender to the classical sequence—"act, suffer, learn." But in
what seems to be his obsession with the Thomas Sutpen saga,
Quentin emerges from the chorus of other self-appointed story-
tellers who elevate Sutpen's story from history to myth and
inherit some portion of his legacy by virtue of their narrations—
Miss Rosa Coldfield, his father and grandfather, and his Harvard
roommate Shreve McCannon. Quentin assumes a different role:
intuiting more, seeing more, and suffering more than either his
father or Shreve. He becomes the reluctant, inactive protagonist,
with the vision of both Cassandra before and Oedipus after the
fall. For different reasons, Shreve and Mr. Compson, Quentin's
main collaborators, can disengage from the story they have helped
put together, but Quentin, perhaps because he alone has been a
"co-author" from inception to conclusion, cannot return from the

"willing suspension of disbelief" that the Sutpen narrative requires.

At the beginning of the novel, Quentin listens to the "impotent and static rage" (3) of Rosa Coldfield and becomes "two separate Quentins now—the Quentin Compson preparing for Harvard in the South, the deep South dead since 1865 and peopled with garrulous outraged baffled ghosts,... and the Quentin Compson who was still too young to deserve yet to be a ghost but nevertheless having to be one for all that, since he was born and bred in the deep South the same as she was" (4). From this point on, Quentin becomes more and more divided: even as he continues outwardly to plot his escape to Harvard, Miss Rosa as unwitting Sibyl initiates his interior descent into the caverns of the Southern past in search of Thomas Sutpen, a search that ends with his face-to-face confrontation with Sutpen's son Henry. Quentin descends into the abyss of tragedy as a witness. As he goes more and more deeply after Sutpen, first with Miss Rosa, then with his father, finally with his roommate Shreve, he sheds a former shared identity with other Southern heirs—"He was a barracks filled with stubborn back-looking ghosts" (7)—and takes on the particularities of the Sutpen lineage. Those old, unnamed ghosts, all wearing butternut and claiming the nobility of the lost cause, are relatively benign and stubbornly evoke only pathos for their fate. Sutpen, by contrast, scatters those other ghosts with their sentimental claims and introduces Quentin into the interior reality of tragedy, an active reality that relegates the common debates about the Old South to the status of enveloping perspective.

The Civil War, in Quentin's imaginings, becomes the background, the historical circumstance, against which a far more fundamental, far more damning story is enacted. Though he never names it, Quentin sees emerging from the "rag-tags and bob-ends of old tales and talking" (243) the infernal landscape of tragedy and finds himself, helplessly and rather suddenly, in the abyss that tragedy opens up. His passage from Miss Rosa's grim house to his father's front porch to the deep cold of his Harvard dorm room occurs almost imperceptibly. It is his imaginative journey that absorbs him and ends with his full comprehension of the human potential for tragic action personified in Thomas Sutpen, of whom Faulkner himself once remarked that "the old Greek concept of tragedy" was at work in his destruction (Gwynn 35).

The structural brilliance of *Absalom, Absalom!* illuminates our

difficulty with notions of the tragic hero since Hamlet unpacked
his heart with words and substituted the "pale cast of thought"
for the "name of action." In his assumptions of power and right,
Sutpen resembles the tragic hero of the ancient Greeks and
makes a strong claim on the reader's imagination as the protagonist of the novel. But perhaps what Raymond Williams suggests
about the thrust of the Greek tragic action—that it "came, not
from the personality of an individual but from a man's inheritance and relationships, within a world that ultimately tran-
scended him" (87-8)—is also true of this action. Sutpen's status
depends on details imagined by Quentin and the others, through
whose "choric energy," as David Lenson says, "Sutpen achieves
heroic stature" (108, 114). To reconstruct Sutpen is to reassemble
the whole of what one has inherited, and, ultimately, Sutpen
depends in this respect most of all upon Quentin, the grandson
of his only friend.

At the end of the novel, Quentin is more haunted than ever,
because what has existed for him as a kind of omnipresent but
vague legendary presence—his common heritage with other young
Southern men trying to understand "why God let us lose the
War" (6)—becomes transformed through imagination into a far
more powerful, more particularized reality. As long as his "twenty
years' heritage of breathing the same air and hearing his father
talk about" Sutpen remains only generally oppressive, Quentin is
"safe." But when he is summoned by Rosa Coldfield actually to
enter the remnants of that history, he must confront—take on or
deny—his heritage as a Southerner in a new way, like Orestes pursued by the Furies or Hamlet commanded by the ghost. As a
result of his unsought vision of the abyss, he becomes guilty of
and responsible for what issues out of it. Small wonder then that
his only commentary on the story he, his father, and Shreve have
constructed is a denial of what seems the logical answer to
Shreve's question "Why do you hate the South?"—"I don't hate it!
I don't hate it!" (303)

Quentin's burden of vision is immense, including in its scope
the history not only of the South but of the entire West, a vast
culmination through time of the accumulated victims appearing to
Cassandra before the palace gates of the House of Atreus—"echoing womb of guilt, kinsmen torturing kinsmen, severed heads,
slaughterhouse of heroes, soil streaming blood" (*Agamemnon* 1088-

91). Lurking behind his vehement denial at the end is the question "what now?" that has always attended recognition of the tragic. Quentin Compson shows himself to be more impotent even than Hamlet, and therefore farther removed from the springs of action, in implicitly but continually asking the question throughout the long interval of his storytelling, especially with his friend and roommate Shreve. The vast differences in the ways the question "What shall I do?" is asked and answered from Orestes to Hamlet to Quentin involve modernity's gradual progress from doubt to irony to skepticism to unbelief, which makes both depiction and recognition of the tragic event *as it occurs* increasingly difficult. As the question "Is what we are witnessing really tragedy?" becomes less certain of answer over time, the suppressed burden of inheritance that has always attended the tragic action gains greater and greater prominence.

❊ ❊ ❊

Allen Tate remarked in 1945 that with "the war of 1914-1918, the South re-entered the world—but gave a backward glance as it stepped over the border: that backward glance gave us the Southern renascence, a literature conscious of the past in the present" (545). The backward glance of Faulkner's imagination went, seemingly without effort and virtually without mediation, all the way to the origins of tragic drama in 5th century B.C. Athens in a similar moment of transition. In Jean-Pierre Vernant's view, tragedy appears in Greece at the moment when "man himself is beginning to experiment as an agent who is more or less autonomous in relation to the religious forces that govern the universe, more or less master of his own actions and, through his *gnome*, his *phronesis*, more or less in control of his political and personal destiny" (46). In both circumstances, Southern and Greek, the possibility of autonomy rests upon the nature of inheritance. The tragic potential of man's circumstance in the flow of time lies precisely in the fact that he is not self-born and therefore not free of inheritance, of the *daimon*, according to Vernant, that integrally affects his *ethos*—the *daimon* which in Greek tragedy "is identified with the malignant power of defilement that, once engendered by ancient crimes, is transmitted from one generation to the next..." (35). Furthermore, it is "a power of misfortune that encompasses not only the criminal but the crime itself, its most distant antecedents, its psychological motivations, its consequences, the defilement it brings in its wake and the punishment it lays in store for the guilty one and all his descendents" (36). Thus Vernant emphasizes that for the Greeks, a "tragic sense of responsibility" (46) for crimes of which one is not personally guilty is at the heart of the tragic action.

This tension between guilt and responsibility is felt most heavily where house and city meet—where the *oikos*, whose most heinous acts must be acknowledged "mine," meets the *polis*, where what is "not mine" by blood is acknowledged and accepted so that the ongoing work of culture can be done. Wherever house and city mingle and merge, the best and the worst of human potential are revealed. Aristotle says in the *Poetics* that "the best tragedies are founded on the story of a few houses" (76): the doors of those "few houses" are thrown open to reveal terrible familial crimes—but reveal them to whom? Both to the chorus outside the doors and to the audience in the theater, an audience possible only in the city. Opening such doors is opening the tragic depths. One might say that the city—that is, the cultural space outside the house—can pursue its proper destiny only by coming somehow to understand, without either assimilating or vanquishing, the terrible realities of the abyss. Since the city's future depends on this understanding, one might also say that the city is built on a relationship with the tragic. But since the city as a whole cannot make the descent into the abyss, it is left to the tragic hero, who is of the house but "represents" the city and its people, to give himself or herself up to the demands of the "dark presences" of the earth. In this sense the tragic hero is also an involuntary victim, a sacrifice who reminds us of what we would rather forget—and *will* forget, if left to our own mechanisms of oblivion. As Tate writes in his novel about the Old South, *The Fathers*, "is not civilization the agreement, slowly arrived at, to let the abyss alone?" (185-6).

If a sacrificial descent into tragedy is indeed a necessity of cultural wholeness, then one can more easily understand Quentin Compson's anguish and inaction. The true witness of the opening up of the abyss becomes, by virtue of his recognition, the candidate for sacrifice on culture's behalf, the *pharmakos* of tragedy. That is why the question of action, central to tragedy from the beginning, becomes more and more problematic as time passes and culture develops. The darkness of both *The Sound and the Fury* and *Absalom, Absalom!* derives from Quentin's impotence in the face of the question "What shall I do?" once he recognizes himself as the latest—and possibly last—heir of the Southern legacy. His fights with Dalton Ames and Spoade in *The Sound and the Fury* are especially pitiable attempts to protect something already past or passing, and the raising of his stature in the later *Absalom, Absalom!* is perhaps a measure of Faulkner's progressive understanding of the Compson tragedy. In neither novel, however, is there a representative of the Compson dynasty capable of acting in such a way that the tragic inheritance is brought efficaciously into the realm outside the house itself, into culture. In *The Sound and the Fury*, that role is finally assumed, for the reader at least, by Dilsey, who gives the largest of all perspectives to the tragedy of the Compsons—*her* family, one may say ironically—with her eschatalogical vision of the first and the last: "I seed de beginning, en now I sees de endin" (297). At the conclusion of *Absalom, Absalom!*, with the Sutpen mansion on fire and Clytie and Henry inside, the far less articulate survivor of Thomas Sutpen's tragic course is the howling idiot Jim Bond, "the scion, the last of his race" (300).

From one point of view, Faulkner presents the very different Dilsey and Jim Bond as, respectively, evidence and consequence of dynastic impotence. Both are culturally disqualified either to act on their family's behalf or to assume the role of sacrifice that would inculcate the hard, cleansing wisdom of tragedy into the white ruling class who dominate the social superstructure. Thus Faulkner's two tragedies involving the Compsons are left without the scapegoat figure necessary to move the tragic pattern to closure, and the resulting sense of cultural stasis is almost overwhelming. In *The Sound and the Fury* and *Absalom, Absalom!* Faulkner simultaneously returns to the classical vision of tragedy and announces a definite alteration of its message for the Christian, democratic West of the modern age. Aristocracy no longer produces the hero capable of taking on the sins of his people; the people themselves, the *demos*, those whose lives were previously circumscribed and defined by the *aristoi*, harbor the figure who must emerge and assume the tragic burden of past crimes, like Christ the lowly carpenter from Judea, so that their chain of endless repetitions may be broken. In between his two novels about the Compson house, Faulkner wrote *Light in August,* his most astounding appropriation for twentieth century culture of the Greek world view. It is also his most completely realized tragedy, containing his purest tragic figure, Joe Christmas, who is attached to no family at all.

Joe Christmas' lack of attachment to a Southern house actually underscores his tragic circumstance. Dilsey, who endures, and Jim Bond, who howls, may in some sense be members of the Compson and Sutpen families, but they are outsiders in terms of being able to effect any change within the dynastic structure. Joe Christmas, by contrast, is a completely liminal figure, having a place in neither the white nor the black world and yet belonging to both.[2] Even he does not know his origins. His in-betweenness dramatically reveals the social or political circumstance that begets the tragic possibility in the South and America, where aristocratic hierarchies are replaced by class distinctions and democratic prejudices regarding race and class. As has often been pointed out, in his state of not-knowing he is like Oedipus, who comes to believe he might be the son of either a king or a slave. And as Faulkner's novel more directly suggests, Joe Christmas also resembles Christ, not only in name and age but in being, like Christ, the Son of Man who "hath not where to lay his head" (Matt. 8:20).

In his total liminality, Joe Christmas seems at once to have more and fewer choices of action than Quentin Compson. It appears that he could "pass" as either white or black, yet he shares with Oedipus a determination to know the truth about himself. For Joe, however, this is more difficult because there is no possibility, or so he believes, that he will discover an eyewitness informant as Oedipus does. So he assumes his Negro blood while at the same time refusing to enter the flow of the master narrative; in not knowing his own origins and therefore remaining betwixt-and-between, he alone can testify to the cultural costs of the fiction that that narrative demands. While alive, he is forever yearning—"*all I wanted was peace*" (112)—and defiant—"I aint hungry. Keep your muck" (35). It is in such details scattered throughout the novel that Joe Christmas most resembles Oedipus, except that Oedipus dwells in his own liminal state of knowing he doesn't know for only part of a day—from Jocasta's mention of a place where three roads meet to the old shepherd's forced answer to Oedipus' final, damning question. Joe Christmas, however, lives almost his entire life with the sense of being in-between, from his time in the orphanage as a child until the private conference with his grandmother Mrs. Hines just before he is killed by Percy Grimm. The suffering of Oedipus' years after his self-blinding is real, irreducible, and conceivably as long as Joe Christmas', but of a different kind. Joe Christmas does not know, but he is not ignorant, as Oedipus was before the plague; in fact, Joe's life from first consciousness has been a progressive awakening to the reality of the dark depths over which Southern society still hovers in spite of what should have been the cleansing of the Civil War some three generations earlier.

Light in August defines the tragic circumstance of the South more completely than *The Sound and the Fury* and *Absalom, Absalom!* by presenting the consequences of its inherited guilt so intimately from the other, non-aristocratic side of the social structure. Joe Christmas represents the inevitable re-assertion of an inheritance that all of America wanted to reject in the twentieth century. But in the same way that Greek and Shakespearean tragedy proceeded from "cultural problems" (succession, legitimacy, lineage, class), Faulknerian tragedy depicts the tragic event as issuing from a troubled heritage of inhumanities. From his Caribbean perspective, Edouard Glissant in *Faulkner, Mississippi* sees this aspect of Faulkner's tragic vision more clearly than most other critics:

> Certainly, when established traditions—races—come into clashing contact, there is a great temptation to get beyond nettlesome cross-breeding by retreating to a primordial unity. We seek truth in Being, trying to insure ourselves against the risks in Becoming. That is, we try to return to a source that would legitimize everything. And we strive to pass down this legitimacy without error or interruption. (78)

According to Glissant, Faulkner shows that such attempts always risk tragedy when a vision of the good is held paramount, as in America's very founding: "Through their vague coming together in a vague corner of the earth—Indians, Whites, and Blacks—tragedy unfolded" (79).

Glissant contrasts the "tragic disclosure" in Sophocles and Shakespeare, on the one hand, and in Faulkner, on the other.

In *Oedipus* and *Hamlet*, the tragic sacrifice is necessary "for equilibrium to be restored at the site of the word" (97), and the sacrifice is efficacious. But this is not the case in Faulkner's vision of the South and the Civil War, Glissant maintains. When Faulkner asks, 'What war is this that presents every aspect of epic struggle, yet has no redemptive effect?" he is really asking, "Can we correct the original sin of the South?" (97) The critical problem, Glissant suggests, is that "tragic disclosure" has traditionally had as its purpose "a restoration of a lost unity," but Faulkner's tragedy "accepts the impossibility of a return to equilibrium." Faulkner's characters are "extreme and monstrous" because "in his life as in his work, it is not study, knowledge, or psychological attention that interests him. In the work at least, it is the abyss" (98). Glissant traces Faulkner's poeticized "path of damnation" for the South as beginning with his attempt to "signify an original abyss which he senses in advance" (99) and from which there is no true escape.

Glissant's analysis recalls Faulkner's great metaphor in *Absalom, Absalom!* in which Quentin's

> stubborn back-looking ghosts [are] still recovering, even forty-three years afterward, from the fever which had cured the disease, waking from the fever without even knowing that it had been the fever itself which they had fought against and not the sickness, looking with stubborn recalcitrance backward beyond the fever and into the disease with actual regret, weak from the fever yet free of the disease and not even aware that the freedom was that of impotence. (7)

This difficult metaphor has important implications for Faulkner's overall tragic vision. Its orthodox interpretation is that the civil war was the fever whose purgative, cathartic effect ought to have been the necessary prelude to the restorative from the disease, slavery, whatever that restorative was to be. The troubling term in the metaphor is the "impotence" of "freedom" from the disease. Does Faulkner's omniscient narrator—one of his few appearances in the novel—mean that the impotence is a natural consequence of the fever, as it often is physically, and that it is therefore a permanent, irreversible condition, the just punishment of past sins? This would be a dark view, indeed, one that Glissant seems to assume from reading *Absalom, Absalom!* Or is the impotence to be taken as an unavoidable condition—but only the impotence of just retribution inflicted upon those who promulgated the old order, even if they did so in ignorance? True, as Glissant says, there is nothing such representatives of the old order can do to "resolve the disturbance" (99), not if they persist in their recalcitrance. But it may be that the impotent, while incapable of action themselves, are awaiting deliverance, though they may not know it, though they may resist it, and though it may bring further violence.

※　※　※

The fate of the Compsons, one of the "great houses" in Faulkner's depiction of the ruined South, makes Glissant's argument seem compelling, because his conclusions offer an explanation for the unrelieved darkness one feels. Certainly at the heart of the Compson saga is the inability of the witness of the tragic past—Quentin, the South, America—to act. Yet in his reading of the tragedies Glissant does not go far enough in tracing the "path of damnation" that leads Faulkner's imagination into the abyss. For the peculiar arc of *Light in August* that carries it beyond the "tragic disclosure" of either *The Sound and the Fury* or *Absalom, Absalom!* lies in the fact that as tragic hero Joe Christmas, born out of the abyss, eclipses the aristocratic heir Quentin Compson. Whereas Quentin can only suffer, Joe completes the ancient pattern of tragedy by acting, suffering, and learning. At the same time, he becomes the sacrifice whose death reflects the efficaciousness of Christ's: Faulkner casts him as an Oedipal figure in his "path of damnation" and simultaneously displaces the King of Thebes as the model of the tragic hero. For a democratic, Christian epoch, the lowly Joe Christmas achieves an apotheosis possible only under the dispensation of a New World capable of producing its own horrors while holding forth great promise even for those cast out to die.

Again in *Light in August* Faulkner utilizes the flexibility and capaciousness of the novel to present Joe Christmas' story. First, he wraps Joe's tragedy within the comic movement of Lena Grove that begins and ends the novel, and then he establishes a character, Gail Hightower, who mediates between the two plots whose trajectories cross but whose respective protagonists never meet. Finally, and most decisively for the novel's tragic movement,

Faulkner presents Joe as a Dionysian epiphany whose sudden appearance and just as sudden "disappearance" become frames for the long middle introspection during which he descends into the abyss of his consciousness and summons its dark presences into the life of Jefferson, a typical small town of the twentieth century South.

Walter Otto calls Dionysus "the god who comes, the god of epiphany, whose appearance is far more urgent, far more compelling than that of any other god" (79). He emphasizes Dionysus' "duality," his characteristic bringing of both death and life into a world that "has become sterile" and "totters to meet its end" (137). In Euripides' *Bacchae* especially, Dionysus is presented as the god whom the city most vehemently denies and most desperately needs; he is the rejected, dangerous god whom Thebes must recognize and acknowledge as its own—at great cost to the rigid, apparently tranquil social surface that covers over the abyss from which Dionysus comes with his unsparing remedy. Jim Bond's idiotic howling in *Absalom, Absalom!* foreshadows a Dionysian madness, but it has no efficacy for the completion of the tragic movement in that novel. Joe Christmas, on the other hand, brings an articulate madness to Jefferson, a town resembling Thebes in its rigidly ordered class structure: it is peopled with "good citizens" yet incapable of responding with genuine generosity to outsiders, whether a pregnant white woman searching for a husband or a white Protestant minister obsessed with his Civil War ancestry.

But whereas Lena Grove goes from town to town within a nimbus of divine protection—"I think she was just traveling" (506), the furniture dealer says at the end—Joe Christmas arrives as the living distillation of accumulated wrongs, like a figure from Cassandra's vision in the *Agamemnon*. In her passage through Jefferson, Lena Grove reveals the comic indestructibility of life that neither Thebes nor Jefferson can affect. Joe Christmas brings with him his story and the necessity of a reckoning, a settling of scores, a purgation of past crimes. Joe is the outsider who is also Jefferson's (and the South's) own and whose epiphany becomes what Hegel in his analysis of tragedy calls the "unavoidable conflict" between contradictory yet separately justifiable claims to legitimacy (Corrigan 332).

Faulkner explicitly enacts the conflict between Joe Christmas, outcast heir of Southern crimes, and Jefferson, bulwark of social order, against the backdrop of the tragic abyss. As Gail Hightower sits in his dark window listening to the church organ and pondering Joe Christmas' capture in Mottstown, he hears the music "pleading, asking, for not love, not life, forbidding it to others, demanding in sonorous tones death as though death were the boon, like all Protestant music" (367). His reverie intensifies until it

> seems to him that the past week has rushed like a torrent and that the week to come, which will begin tomorrow, is the abyss, and that now on the brink of cataract the stream has raised a single blended and sonorous and austere cry, not for justification but as a dying salute before its own plunge, and not to any god but to the doomed man in the barred cell within hearing of them and of two other churches, and in whose crucifixion they too will raise a cross. (368)

Jefferson will discover the abyss the next day in the lynching; Joe Christmas has been dwelling in it, or moving toward complete consciousness of it, for thirty years, as the structure of the narrative suggests.[3] Chapter 5 begins after midnight and takes Joe through just under twenty-four hours, the only day during which we are really "with" him in a narrative sense—an interesting adaptation of the Greek unities. He acts randomly and sometimes viciously, beating the drunken Brown in the little cabin on Joanna Burden's place and then exposing himself to white people in their passing car's headlights before ending up in Jefferson the following night. Yet we also hear in this early chapter the underlying theme of Joe's coming advent as the Dionysian outsider: *"Something is going to happen to me. I am going to do something"* (104) and *"All I wanted was peace"* (112).

Faulkner, then, presents Joe Christmas as both active and passive, agent and victim—a self-contained, fiercely independent figure nevertheless moved by forces greater than himself. Walking at night through the empty streets of Jefferson, Joe appears incredibly isolated, "like a phantom, a spirit, strayed out of its own world, and lost"; during his walk he finds himself "in Freedman Town, surrounded by the summer smell and the summer voices of invisible Negroes. They [seem] to enclose him like bodiless voices murmuring talking laughing in a language not his" (114).

Typically, in the Jim Crow South, this part of town is rigidly segregated from the white section, but Joe does not feel it typically.
It exposes him in his liminal state—a legitimate part of neither.
In fact, Freedman Town poses a greater threat to him because it
is a pocket of comic vitality within the sterile confines of Jefferson and represents to him the easy solution, the inauthentic
escape. Giving in would not only be a lie to himself, but an
abetment of established racist codes, both a social fiction and a
real plague largely defined by denials of those infected by it.

Joe's escape from Freedman Town, the beguiling domain of
"the lightless hot wet primogenitive Female," to "the cold hard
air of white people" (115) marks his course of tragic inevitability.
Once he gains the crest of a hill outside town, he can look back
and see juxtaposed the two realms between which his life has
been poised: "the far bright rampart of the town itself" and "the
black pit" that "just lay there, black, impenetrable, in its garland
of Augusttremulous lights. It might have been the original quarry,
abyss itself" (116). But his escape is temporary, in some sense only
a rehearsal for what he faces in the coming days after he kills
Joanna Burden. By the time he gets to Mottstown, where he will
allow himself to be captured, Joe is aware of being "still inside
the circle" of his 30-year search for peace, but now "the black
shoes smelling of negro"— a black woman's brogans that he wears
to throw off his pursuers— symbolize "the black abyss which had
been waiting, trying, for thirty years to drown him and into
which now and at last he had actually entered, bearing now upon
his ankles the ineradicable gauge of its upward moving" (331).
They have become an emblem of his submission to something at
work in the cosmos larger than himself, more encompassing than
his personal struggle. His yielding at the end is not a sign of
weakness or exhaustion but his acknowledgment of inscrutable
powers that transcend black vs. white in the New World. As
expressions of justice in its age-old natural and political forms,
these powers bespeak simultaneously the importance of his particular circumstance in the human drama and of the larger
unfolding that his own lived experience perpetuates and enlarges.
The woman's shoes that allow him a temporary escape from his
white pursuers are also the final instrument of his long journey
toward the tragic climax, and Faulkner intensifies the moment by
repeating, but adding an explicit fatality to, the image of the

boots as marking "on his ankles the gauge definite and ineradicable of the black tide creeping up his legs, moving from his feet upward as death moves" (339).

Joe's confession to himself that "'I have never broken out of the ring of what I have already done and cannot ever undo'" (339) echoes the classical tragic protagonists' acceptance of responsibility for their misdeeds and at the same time their indicting of the gods for their undeserved fate. Faulkner is careful to portray Joe Christmas as both an innocent victim and a guilty agent, thereby elevating him beyond the typical protagonist of modern tragedy and into the company of classical tragic protagonists who are not spared the severities of descent into the tragic abyss. Max Scheler has written that "'tragic guilt' is of a kind for which no one can be blamed and for which no conceivable 'judge' can be found"; the tragic hero "must necessarily appear 'guilty' even before the fairest judge, when he is in fact guiltless and is so seen by God alone" (Corrigan 14-16). This kind of guilt characterizes Joe Christmas, though Faulkner denies us any further intimacy with Joe after he prepares to enter Mottstown. We are left to speculate with Gavin Stevens about his final hours, including his private conversation with his grandmother Mrs. Hines and the reason why he subsequently runs, as though to his certain death.

Faulkner registers, rather, the impact of Joe's fate on the community of Jefferson, by analogy a microcosm of the twentieth century South, and he does so by changing point of view again after our long acquaintance with Joe. This is the interval during which Gail Hightower listens to the Sunday night organ music and says to himself that tomorrow the townspeople will exact the justice they must have for Joanna Burden's murder. He knows that "'they will do it gladly'.... 'Since to pity him would be to admit selfdoubt and to hope for and need pity themselves. They will do it gladly, gladly. That's why it is so terrible, terrible, terrible'" (368). As always in tragedy, however, the actual impact of the death is far different than anticipated in the remarkable scene of Joe's death and castration by Percy Grimm:

> For a long moment he looked up at them with peaceful and unfathomable and unbearable eyes. Then his face, body, all, seemed to collapse, to fall in upon itself, and from out the slashed garments about his hips and loins the pent black blood seemed to rush like a released

breath. It seemed to rush out of his pale body like the rush of sparks
from a rising rocket; upon that black blast the man seemed to rise
soaring into their memories forever and ever. (464-5)

He unexpectedly becomes both the *pharmakos*, or scapegoat, and
the victim of *sparagmos*, or Dionysian dismemberment.

Joe's advent has been terrifying to Jefferson, although the
reader has come to know him otherwise in details such as his
tortured days at the orphanage and his rigorous upbringing in the
Puritan hands of McEachern. Joanna Burden's murder confirms
the worst fears of Jeffersonians: tainted by Negro blood, Joe can
nevertheless pass for white, and his deceptive appearance, which
fools the eye as only evil can, allows him to violate the most
fiercely held taboos of a racist society. Yet in his death he mysteriously transcends all social constructions and assumes a place
in Jefferson's consciousness that bears witness both to its racial
guilt and to his innocence as a victim and inheritor of those constructions. At the moment of his death, in fact, Joe and his
killers, represented by the inconsequential Percy Grimm, are
revealed as joint-heirs of the monstrous crimes that began with
the middle passage and accumulated over the following two centuries. Jefferson in 1930 is harsh proof that the Civil War failed
to be the "fever" capable of curing the "disease." War is an abyss
of its own kind, but not the tragic abyss into which a people
are led by the individual, the tragic hero, who is a mirror image
that they are furious to deny. In tragic action, the "elemental
depths gape open and out of them a monstrous creature raises
its head before which all the limits that the normal day has set
must disappear" (Otto 140). Not opposing sides in a war—Greek
or Trojan, North or South—but individuals on whom the whole
burden of a historical epoch descends must enact the necessary
catharsis. And as Louise Cowan suggests in the introduction to
this volume, that catharsis exists in its purity only as poetic
image. The tragic purgation occurs only in terms of poetic form
in the communal imagination, whether of the theater or of the
novel, so that a Joe Christmas can appear against the backdrop
of the entire Western tradition as both Dionysus and Christ.

What distinguishes Joe Christmas in Faulkner's tragic canon is
that he both knows and acts; he is neither pathetically inactive,
as Quentin Compson is, nor blindly active—innocent—as Thomas

Sutpen is. Joe progresses toward death with a curious consciousness of his passive-active situation in the world, as if bound by Fate: "*Something is going to happen to me. I am going to do something*" (104). Faulkner's depiction of Percy Grimm as pursuing Joe "with that lean, swift, blind obedience to whatever Player moved him on the Board" (462) is radically different from Joe's introspective search for the meaning of his life, but in their coming together in the climactic chase, Faulkner projects Joe's story onto a level that is at once particular and cosmic—the death of a single light-colored black man as a sacrifice and the instrument of purgation. Joe's part of the novel is a kind of testing ground on which the unalterable boundaries of classical Fate and the limitless hope of Christian Providence are in contention. Authorial choices, most notably the depiction of Joe's brutal killing as an apotheosis of imagination, swing the balance in favor of the latter.

❖ ❖ ❖

The presentation in *Go Down, Moses* (1940) of Isaac McCaslin, whose response to the crimes of the ancestors is singular in modern fiction in the West, is Faulkner's last and greatest meditation on inheritance. Educated at the hands of Sam Fathers in the wilderness, Isaac fully comprehends from the commissary ledgers the sins of his grandfather Carothers McCaslin, yet he is not destroyed by the vision, unlike Kurtz in glimpsing "the horror" or Ahab in assaulting the inscrutability of brute nature. As vicarious participant in the South's and America's "horror," the destructive dream of ownership, Isaac relinquishes his legal patrimony but not the spiritual inheritance of the tragic vision he received after his initiation in the big woods. We see Isaac as we see Sophocles' Oedipus in *Oedipus the King* and *Oedipus at Colonus*, as a youth at the height of his powers and as an old man at the end of his journey. Yet the movement of this novel enacts the distinctive, definitive, and much-misunderstood turn in Faulkner's oeuvre from tragedy to comedy, and as such, it falls outside the purview of this volume. Faulkner denies his Isaac the literal apotheosis that Oedipus experiences, yet in another way he grants his protagonist an extension of influence, if not life, which was Isaac's real hope in choosing as he did. For the novel goes on beyond his last appearance in *Delta Autumn*, figuratively carrying him forward into the culminating action of *Go Down, Moses*. There, Gavin Stevens embodies the figure Faulkner seems to have been artistically striving toward during his tragic phase: the unconscious, self-effacing, often bumbling "hero" who is in but not completely of the world. The lack of a textually explicit connection between Isaac and Gavin is certainly a deliberate strategy on Faulkner's part. The connection is, rather, interior, invisible, operating like a leaven that is never attributable—precisely the influence of the dedicated life and of the witness-bearer.

The canon of Faulkner's work in tragedy is impressive by any standard. It begins with the discovery of his "postage stamp of native soil" and the publication of *Flags in the Dust*, and ends with Isaac's commissary vision. Afterward, in the final two novels of the Snopes trilogy, the Gavin Stevens of *Go Down, Moses* will inherit the mandate to Motion to which Faulkner habitually testified. In this new Gavin's hands, however, the torch will illuminate not the tragic abyss of history but the comic terrain that leads us haltingly upward, into the future. And yet the abyss is always there, existing with either the "shadowy docility" of Sutpen's ghost (4) or the "not particularly threatful" serenity of Joe Christmas' blood (463), or both. Faulkner's own bequest to the tradition of tragedy in the modern West is an extension of commensurate achievement from Shakespeare into our era and also a pure connection back to the ancient Greeks.

NOTES

[1] It remains to be seen whether the recent publication of Randall Kennedy's *Nigger: The Strange Career of a Troublesome Word* heralds a loosening of social and even legal restrictions against racial elements in literature that have largely limited the presence of Faulkner, Twain, O'Connor, and other writers in school curricula. If indeed we are entering a period of more open consideration of cultural taboos such as Kennedy's title word, it still seems clear that the great writers of the Southern Renascence will for many years to come be judged adversely by not only their racial realism but also what political and social readers consider their nearly irredeemable provincialism. In an August 4, 2002, *New York Times* Op-Ed piece under the catchy headline "What the Bard of Oxford Can Teach Critics of the New World Order," Adam Cohen

remarks that somewhere underneath Faulkner's "distinctly Southern tales of lost innocence and declining fortunes is a universal, and remarkably timely, theme: how important it is for localities to stand up to the disruptive force of progress." As it turns out in Cohen's view, however, this salutary aspect of Faulkner's fiction exists in spite of the fact that "he is the ultimate 'pale male,' a writer obsessed with the fate of his own out-of-fashion demographic, the well-born Southern white man" obsessed "tragic mulattoes, embittered small-town spinsters and Confederate colonels clattering around decaying antebellum homes." Thus for Cohen, who like so many contemporary readers focuses exclusively on the social urgencies of the present moment, Faulkner's "intense localism" makes his work surprisingly but very narrowly useful—and otherwise irrelevant.

[2] Joe Christmas never escapes his in-between-ness, "the street which ran for thirty years" and which to him seems also an endless "circle" (*Light in August*, 339). Insofar as his journey and quest are defined psychically and spiritually, however, he does negotiate his passage and effectively transcends his liminality at the very end—coincidentally at the moment when Percy Grimm assumes his grimly ironic role of presiding over Joe Christmas' "reaggregation"—according to Victor Turner, the third and final phase of rites de passage: "separation, margin (or limen...), and reaggregation." For a distinction between "marginal" and "liminal," see Turner (Dramas 231-71).

[3] Faulkner prefaces Joe's long, nighttime reflection spanning chapters 6-12 with the first chapter narrated from Joe's point of view. After Lena's introduction in Chapter 1, Faulkner establishes Joe's presence through Byron Bunch's eyes: "Byron Bunch knows this," Chapter 2 begins. Faulkner then follows this impersonal first glance at Joe with two chapters on Gail Hightower and Byron before returning to Joe in Chapter 5, presented now from Joe's perspective.

17

Resisting the Tragic Self:
The Apotropaics of Toni Morrison's *Beloved*

KATHLEEN MARKS

A t first glance, Toni Morrison's *Beloved* appears to have most of the elements of tragedy. The plot—so positively Greek that an early reviewer of the novel dismissed Morrison as "Aunt Medea"[1]— involves a mother's murdering her child, and the woman who does it, Sethe, is a noble character who might be characterized by her *hamartia*. Structurally, as in tragedy, there is a preexisting problem, a slow accretion of detail, a complication, and a resolution of sorts. Add violent family dynamics, the dead that demand to be remembered, a community plagued by a cursed past, and it seems it is impossible to resist the pull toward tragedy.

Yet *Beloved* precisely does. The novel is at odds with its material, at some variance with its own tragic trajectory. Its resistance to tragedy contradicts even Morrison's more general understanding of her writing: "I write [in] what I suppose could be called the tragic mode in which there is some catharsis and revelation. There's a whole lot of space in between, but my inclination is in the tragic direction."[2] *Beloved* is ostensibly in keeping with this tragic inclination. In itself, the story of Sethe, the slave woman who slays her daughter in order to protect her from slavery, might be melodrama; but the arrival of the ghostly figure Beloved—who carries spiteful traces of the dead daughter and bears death to an entire community—confirms the opening of an otherworldly realm ripe for tragedy. Just as Athenian tragedy "stages humanity's need to defend itself against the nonhuman," and the hope of tragedy is that "something will survive nonhuman attacks" (Padel 5), *Beloved* depicts an entire community protecting itself from a haunting past that includes the inhuman history of slavery.[3]

But the community of *Beloved* averts and survives the tragic devastation that the confrontation with its past might bring precisely because it resists rejecting its own damaged, ensouled self in rejecting Beloved. Paradoxically, Sethe's murderous act instigates a process of distinction-making. While drawing on the idiom of ancient tragedy, *Beloved* interiorizes the struggle: the tension between men and gods is translated into one between a self that is divided over its own boundaries. Sethe's lover Paul D says that "Sethe didn't know where the world stopped and she began" (164). The novel portrays the pain that ensues in any indwelling of the spirit, any attempt to name and keep tragic forces at a distance, actions which involve "keeping the past at bay," to borrow Sethe's phrase (42).

Keeping at bay is the action denoted by the Greek word *apotropaic*, which predates the rise of tragedy, and it is this action that accounts for the tensions in *Beloved*—the offering, deferring dynamic; the inviting yet avoiding of the past; the damaged self opposing the tragic self; the killing that initiates love; in sum, the resistance that is ambiguous in its capacity to both hurt and redeem.[4] The apotropaic is the archetype for resistance, specifically for those actions that attempt to ward off dangers. "Apotropaic" (from *apo-+ trepein*) literally means "to turn away," and this ancient gesture makes an uncanny appearance in Morrison's work, surfacing in *Beloved* as a fundamental trope of history, a manner of taking up a past of suffering. The apotropaic lends its long history to account for Sethe's avoidance of both the past and the self—an avoidance that creates the spectral Beloved. It also explains the final casting out necessary for communal survival. The apotropaic is a fruitful mode of envisioning the past and restructuring a future: thus the touchstone for *Beloved* is indeed Greek—yet its action is not tragic, but apotropaic.

The Apotropaic

Jane Harrison, in her *Prolegomena to the Study of Greek Religion*, distinguishes two quite different types of Greek rituals: those that are therapeutic and those that are apotropaic. The later therapeutic rituals, marked by tendance and service, are those that appease, placate, and invoke the Olympians. A worshipper offers burnt sacrifice, for instance, in order to secure the aid and presence of the gods. The much earlier apotropaic rituals, however, are quite different; they are marked by gloom and fear. These rituals did not summon the divine, but rather put at arm's length those less placid underworld forces. There is a whole realm of the gods that is dreadful for humans. For these divinities, then, the apotropaic (expressed concisely in the common notion of the "evil eye") is appropriate. Pouring libations at the sites of tombs to keep gods at bay, sacrificing scraps of food at crossroads at regular intervals to ward off the underworld goddess Hecate—these are apotropaic rituals.

The apotropaic is not strictly opposed to tragedy, and in fact was early on connected to tragedy through the cult of the heroes, the largely forgotten pre-Homeric and pre-Olympian heroes who roamed the earth "over a space of time beginning about 1500 B.C. and lasting for at least two thousand years" (Kerenyi xxi). Though the myths of the early heroes do not in themselves constitute tragedy, as Jean-Pierre Vernant notes, they "certainly incorporate any number of those *transgressions* that are the very stuff of tragedy: incest, patricide, matricide, the eating of one's children" (306). Indeed, as Kerenyi writes, "the cult and the myth of the hero contain tragedy in germ" (14). The hero-cults were particularly important in being apotropaic, because the rituals performed at the tombs of heroes were said to provide protection to the living: thus the word's current meaning describing the "intent to ward off evil" as by means of magic or charm.

The term undergoes a certain cultural dormancy until taken up by Sigmund Freud to inform his theories of castration. In *Medusa's Head*, Freud supposes that the severed head of Medusa—with its snakes for hair and its potential to turn men who look at it to stone—may in fact be used as an apotropaic defense. The head, he thinks, symbolizes the female genitals, whose horrifying power reminds men of woman as castrated and more emphatically, man as always potentially castrated ("Medusa" 274). The decapitated head produces a fear of decapitation, or castration, mirrored by an actual image of that event. Because it re-situates oppositional terms, the apotropaic attracts Jacques Derrida, who comments on its contradictory nature:

> The paradoxical logic of the apotropaic: to castrate oneself already, in order to be able to castrate and repress the menace of castration, to renounce life and mastery in order to assure oneself of them; to put into play by ruse, simulacrum, and violence, the very thing that one wishes to conserve; to lose in advance that which one wishes to erect; to suspend that which one raises. (46)

The apotropaic then is a method of losing oneself by violence in order to save oneself. By negotiating the interior boundaries between self-destruction and self-protection, it puts identity and otherness into play, and it enacts a violent fiction, mirroring in advance the feared deed. The apotropaic acts as Perseus' mirror does—it affords protection against the Medusa's look.

Prior to tragedy and one of its primary sites of origin, the apotropaic can therefore be said to be a way of avoiding an underworld, a petrifying horror. In *Beloved* the apotropaic becomes a mechanism for both confronting tragedy and turning away the kind of destruction it can bring. Thus while the immediate background is slavery and Sethe's resistance to it, Sethe herself is a kind of cult heroine: her actions have a pre-history, and her resistance cuts into a world much prior to her own stance.[5] Through a series of textual gestures—the staring head of Beloved, rememory, the failure of community, infanticide, and exorcism— the novel enacts this religious trope from early Greek religion to summon, appropriate, and resist the tragic. Though Morrison, of course, never refers explicitly to the term "apotropaic," it is the primordial grounding that lends depth and poetic ambiguity to the action of resistance found in *Beloved*.

A Head to Frighten

Beloved's central action involves a mother's slitting her child's throat.[6] Taken by itself, the act has sacrificial resonance, and taps into what Nicole Loraux describes as an ancient point of women's "glorious sacrifice." The throat is vulnerable, and "death lurks in the throats of women" (52). Moreover, by nearly severing her baby's head, Sethe effectively sabotages herself, for she believes that

the child is the best part of her, her "best thing" (251). This violence directed at the self saturates the ground with the black
blood that, like the sacrifice of Aeschylus' Iphigenia, initiates a certain freedom, but it also summons the guilt and punishment that
accompany dangerously free acts. Like Iphigenia's sacrifice, Sethe's
act too calls into being its own kind of furious consequences.

The baby's killing is not, however, the first textual incidence
of the apotropaic. The apotropaic begins at the graves of the
heroes, and *Beloved*'s first gesture takes place against a tombstone
as Sethe prostitutes herself with an engraver, "her knees wide
open as any grave," to have the word "Beloved" chiseled on the
headstone of her dead daughter:

> Pink as a fingernail it was, and sprinkled with glittering chips. Ten
> minutes, he said You got ten minutes I'll do it for free. Ten minutes
> for seven letters. With another ten could she have gotten "Dearly" too?
> She had not thought to ask him and it bothered her still that it
> might have been possible—that for twenty minutes, a half hour, say,
> she could have had the whole thing, every word she heard the
> preacher say at the funeral (and all there was to say, surely) engraved
> on her baby's headstone: Dearly Beloved. But what she got, settled for,
> was the one word that mattered. (5)

Sethe is proud of what she calls the "perfect death" that she provides for the baby. She loves her baby and even more her own
violent action. With this self-sabotaging act of prostitution, Sethe
reifies and doubles her act of infanticide. She performs what she
later calls in a different context a "fixing ceremony" (86). With
the engraver, she has engendered a new thing, a new head for
her baby, another staring head of stone—this one a permanent
and constant reminder of her complicated love and desire to
Beloved. She thus engages in a kind of objectification of her
child, and further, an objectification wherein she projects her own
failures onto her child. Her prostitution is a way of memorializ-
ing and keeping, yet forgetting and warding off, her own sins:

> Not only did she have to live out her years in a house palsied by the
> baby's fury at having its throat cut, but those ten minutes she spent
> pressed up against dawn-colored stone studded with star chips, her
> knees wide open as any grave, were longer than life, more alive, more

pulsating than the baby blood that soaked her fingers with oil. (5)

As Louise Cowan sees, the figure Beloved arises as an incarnation of this "false word" etched into a tombstone by Sethe's epitaphic love (296). The stone, with its "dawn" color and "star" chips is the still point of a cosmic process. It is a naming that sets apart, consecrates, and literally inscribes Sethe's loss of honor as Beloved.

The gravesite scene is also the first instance in the text of what Sethe calls her "rememory." Though many critics believe Morrison coined this word, it has a relevant, if obsolete, past. The *Oxford English Dictionary* indicates that from its earliest use "rememory" has been connected with writing and engraving, and goes on to quote a fifteenth-century historian, John Harding, by way of example: "He made theim wryten, for long rememory, To rule the Isle by theim perpetually" (qtd. in *OED* 425). While Sethe keeps a long history of past events in her memory, those events become frozen and inaccessible to revision after the murder and her reification of her act with the engraver. Sethe focuses on the inscribed tomb of her dead baby as the object of her remembrance, upon which she has written the word "Beloved" for her "long rememory." As Larry Allums writes, "Sethe has inscribed 'Beloved' on the memory of her terrible act of love, for in that way she can remain convinced that her gesture was not only the right but the only one" (272). Sethe has taken her murderous act and "placed it, frozen and intact, into her memory, simultaneously, we believe, with the baby's being placed into the grave" (Allums 270).

For eighteen years after the murder, Sethe goes about her "work of beating back the past" (73), making a conscious effort not to erase it, but to keep it locked, chiseled, and immobile. The very word "rememory" has about it the suggestion of a cyclical memory that repeats past horrors. As Philip Page argues, "For [Sethe], memory is both an actual repetition of the real events and a repetition of a memory, a circling back in her mind what was previously there both in reality and in its recall" (150). Sethe's mind labors to keep the past at bay, so that what has been done in the past, though burdensome to recall, might not actually harm her. By suspending the dead baby, and thereby the dead past, Sethe willfully forgets to live, and therefore "nothing ever dies" (36). Sethe's rememory is thus at odds with Morrison's own definition of memory as the "deliberate act of remembering" that "is a form of willed creation" ("Memory" 385). Rememory is rather a deliberate de-creative strategy.

That Sethe is deeply meditative about memory is an indication of its centrality to the novel, and by implication, to the African-American experience. In response to her daughter Denver's question about what she is praying for, Sethe denies that she is praying at all:

> I was talking about time. It's so hard for me to believe in it. Some things go. Pass on. Some things just stay. I used to think it was my rememory. You know. Some things you forget. Other things you never do. But it's not. Places, places are still there. If a house burns down, it's gone, but the place—the picture of it—stays, and not just in my rememory, but out there, in the world. (35)

Not prayer, it is nevertheless a longing for some kind of relief from even the act of remembering. Rememory externalizes desire, time, and place. In rememory, things of the mind—psychic experiences—are really out there in the world, and the outside is the same as the inside. When Denver asks whether other people can see the "picture" of things, Sethe responds, "Oh, yes. Oh, yes, yes, yes. Someday you be walking down the road and you hear something or see something going on. So clear. And you think it's you thinking it up. A thought picture. But no. It's when you bump into a rememory that belongs to somebody else" (36). A person can walk by a place (in the given world of this novel) and somehow enter its soul, as she explains to Denver: "Where I was before I came here, that place is real... and what's more, if you go there—you who never was there—if you go there and stand in the place where it was, it will happen again; it will be there for you, waiting for you" (36).

Rememory might be, as Mae Henderson writes, "something that possesses (or haunts) one, rather than something that one possesses" (86). But rememory for Sethe is an apotropaic strategy to ward off evil, a manner of reorganizing an overwhelming past by renaming it as beloved, and a way of preserving it while keeping it at a distance. While the distance affords Sethe an opportunity to reshape her past, that which is awry in her memory keeps her focused on her murderous action, and for much of the novel, she dwells in a fraudulent world of her own creation.

So intent is Sethe on keeping the past at bay that she believes she will remain untouched by her prostitution. But here is precisely where the conflict of the novel starts: something new appears. Within her rememory is a visible crack that exposes a demand for a broader kind of memory. In *this* rememory, Sethe remembers something that she did not before think she knew. She had thought of her act with the engraver as a way of preserving the love she had for her baby. She wants more of what the preacher said at the funeral put on the headstone: "Dearly Beloved." But she settles for the "one word that mattered," the word "Beloved," and "She thought it would be enough shame, rutting among the headstones with the engraver, his young son looking on" to answer the town's disgust (5). Sethe's rememory of the headstone occurs when the baby's ghost pushes a "sideboard" to assert her presence. Denver says, "For a baby she throws a powerful spell" (4). Sethe responds, "'No more powerful than the way I loved her'... and there it was again. The welcoming cool of unchiseled headstones" (4). Past the very fixity of rememory comes the new recognition: "Counting on the stillness of her own soul, she had forgotten the other one: the soul of her baby girl. Who would have thought that a little baby could harbor so much rage? Rutting among the stones under the eyes of the engraver's son was not enough" (5).

Sethe could count on the "stillness of her own soul," but by remembering the "soul of her baby girl," she is beginning to see that something exists apart from her. This moment of self-awareness comes to her through a slip in her rememory that allows her to have a new thought about someone other than herself. If Sethe's furious baby has a soul, then the possibility also exists that this separate being may have preferred to live even an enslaved life, anything but this half-life in her mother's tomb of a mind. The recognition that there is a separation between herself and her best part—a separation that she had not conceived of—begins Sethe's slow process of coming to see the possibility of a new life with Paul D and Denver. Prior to this memory, Sethe has been circling through an endless apotropaic repetition.

The Spilt Blood of Murder

Sethe's shameful recognition of her daughter's otherness eventually leads to a confrontation with the killing itself, though even the description of this scene is veiled. The event lends itself to a variety of readings. The slave-holder called schoolteacher (a word which functions as a proper name, but which Morrison does not capitalize) misreads it because of his own brand of inability to distinguish between self and other. He and his men have come to remand Sethe and her family to slavery; they cross into Baby Suggs' yard and corner her like an animal they regard as property. After freely trespassing 124 Bluestone Road and witnessing a wild Sethe—who by now has retreated with her children to the shed, holding her dead baby with its almost severed head—schoolteacher realizes "that there was nothing there to claim" (149); he has no need for a crazy woman or her children back at Sweet Home. Mae G. Henderson notes that the description of the scene in the shed comes from a white male perspective, thereby narratively reinforcing schoolteacher's mistaken reading: "Inside, two boys bled in the sawdust and dirt at the feet of a nigger woman holding a blood-soaked child to her chest with one hand and an infant by the heels with the other" (149). By this account, Sethe merely confirms "the dominant metaphors of the master('s) narrative—wildness, cannibalism, animality, destructiveness," as Henderson puts it. "In radical opposition to these constructions is Sethe's reconceptualized metaphor of self based on motherhood, motherliness, and mother-love" (97). The murder is motivated by love, albeit a complicated "thick" love, as Paul D calls it (164).

The glaring success of the infanticide in warding off schoolteacher is seductive to Sethe. It is her supreme apotropaic gesture, and Sethe's reading of the event could not be more different from his, for "when she saw them coming and recognized schoolteacher's hat,"

> she heard wings. Little hummingbirds stuck their needle beaks right through her headcloth into her hair and beat their wings. And if she thought anything, it was No. No. Nono. Nonono. Simple. She just flew. Collected every bit of life she had made, all the parts of her that were precious and fine and beautiful, and carried, pushed, dragged them through the veil, out, away, over there where no one could hurt them. (163)

Her killing of the child is not an end in itself; it is a way of placing the child on the other side of the "veil" of death, into safety. In Morrison's terrain the other side of the veil is the realm of psyche, the inner world of interiority and soul that must at all costs be protected even if damaged. Yet the veil is also the ideological way that a society protects itself; Morrison writes that her literary task is to "rip that veil" from "proceedings too terrible to relate" ("Site" 110). Specifically, she is referring to the horrors of black enslavement and to the tendency of societies to mystify the horrible and put veils over unspeakable events. In dragging her daughter "through the veil," Sethe also draws more firmly into place the veil that has been placed over slavery by whites: she plays into the assumption that blacks are animals that, as schoolteacher says, "are in their care," by seeming to act in a manner that accords with the master narrative. In her own inner dialogue, Sethe wants to drag her children to safety, but she can do so only by leaving the veil of ideology intact, thereby warding off her attackers, who leave safe in the knowledge that they simply broke her—the ultimate effect of her apotropaic sacrifice.

Afterwards, as we have seen, Sethe falls victim to a mystification and reification of the baby's murder, believing her own story so much that she thinks the dead child is safer than had it lived even a life of slavery. But in the course of the novel, the figure of Beloved comes back from beyond the veil to dominate both Sethe's life and the action of the work itself until Sethe is in danger of choosing her over her true self. Much is at stake then in describing what this figure is, and much critical effort has been expended to determine precisely this.[7] Neither simply the revenant of the murdered "crawling-already?" baby (93), nor the return of the venomous spirit driven away by Paul D upon his arrival at 124, Beloved is the product of Sethe's avoiding her killing action. She comes from an underwater, underworld place, but she is not merely the dead. Indeed, Louise Cowan argues that she comes from "a place not simply of the dead but of those spirits who have ranged themselves on the side of negation" (295). Moreover, writes Cowan:

> If we posit a kind of *nekros*, a realm of the dead into which the negative flows, we might say that into it goes any guilty event, any dark and intolerable human experience, pain, outrage, injury, wrongs, the

need for vengeance, remorse, shame—all things that speak of annihilation and nothingness. (302)

Beloved is a kind of dark projection of the dead who tries to make her very darkness the condition of existence. She is a being formed first by the separation of Sethe from her precious part, a separation initiated when she killed her child and made her deed legible by her act with the engraver. She finds flesh in the world through a fissure of shame in Sethe's psyche—the illegitimate word that finds flesh in the figure Beloved, a spiteful return of the dead who wants to make the uncanny *join*, as she calls it, with the living (213).

Coming from such a *nekros*, it might be said that Beloved is "a group psychosis" (Cowan 295). Although she bears traces of Sethe's murdered baby, the partitioned and precious part that has become deadened by abstraction, by being in fact partitioned, is no longer Sethe's alone. Beloved belongs to a graceless place where all the unburied and nameless dead dwell: "Nothing to breathe down there and no room to move" (75). It is a kind of breathlessness that links Beloved to the unnamed baby's ghost. Indeed, Paul D's exorcism of the dead baby's ghost from 124 is complete when its "breathing [is] tired" (19). It might be said that Beloved bears traces of the baby because down there in that breathless place, a plan has been enacted—a negative conspiracy (conspire, literally to breathe together)—among the dead. The dead send a conspirator into the world—through the aperture created by Sethe's beloved guilt—to "cry shame" (274). Beloved comes, then, not from a place of the vital dead, of ancestry and memory, but from a realm of beings to whom life and name have been denied.

Beloved is a figural interpretation of the word from the preacher's speech at the baby's funeral, etched into stone by Sethe's prostitution. "Dearly Beloved." As such, she is a metonymy that is without context and meaning except in relation to something other. As a product of objectification, an incarnation of the apotropaic, Beloved is always the object and never the agent of action. Even her name, the imperative "be loved," gestures towards passive rather than active engagement. A Medusa-like figure, manipulative, lost and gorgonish, "with fish for hair" (267), she mimics Sethe's need to be loved, but while Sethe as black and female represents the outermost circumference of a community, Beloved represents an even more set-apart entity. Sethe remains part of a society that can welcome in or turn away, but Beloved blurs the distinctions between self and other; she is merely a product. She is essentially a return, not of the warded-off, but of the warding-off itself, so loved that the gesture has taken flesh. She is what I shall call an "apotrope." As apotrope, the embodiment of complex negation, she depends on the other characters and cannot be a viable part of the final created story.

Beloved, then, means nothing by herself; totally dependent, she is parasitical, drawing the life out of Sethe while pushing away her competition, Sethe's daughter Denver. In the "lyric" section of the novel, the three women enact a love triangle, a hermeneutic circle, and Morrison herself describes in an interview how Beloved's, Sethe's, and Denver's discourses sift together: "[Beloved] speaks a language, a traumatized language, of her own experience, which blends beautifully in her questions and answers, her preoccupations, with the desires of Denver and Sethe" (Darling 247). Yet if Beloved's meaning is ultimately derived, she herself is looming and dominant. Her voice soon quells Sethe's and Denver's, rendering them incoherent. Philip Page stresses the elliptical discourse of the oft-cited lyrical sections, emphasizing the destructive elements and dangers that possession engenders, signaled by the repeated "mine": "Being 'mine' and 'yours' is both loving and controlling. The three characters' insistence on possessing each other underscores the destructive rivalries for affection that plague the various attempted families within 124 Bluestone" (139). The shared intimacy of the family circle becomes too much and easily slips into dependency, tyranny, and infantilism.

As the apotrope, Beloved leads only to exclusion and eccentricity and must herself be completed in being turned away or warded off. She cannot make the *join* because it is essentially a "hot thing," essentially shameful and private, unrelated to the destiny of the larger circle of the community, incommunicable and not realizable. Beloved has no being unto herself; she cannot make love or judgments. She is one of the dwellers in the *nekros* that cannot be a part of the living. As only a fragment of a call to community—indeed "Dearly Beloved" is presumably followed by the more inclusive, "we are gathered here today"—Beloved must be fretted back into an undertone of a larger choral score.

The Clearing

Commenting on resistance to the overwhelming past, Toni Morrison observes that *Beloved* is about "something the characters don't want to remember, I don't want to remember, black people don't want to remember, white people don't want to remember. I mean, it's national amnesia" (Angelo 257). Not only Sethe but also the entire community needs to ward off the terrific horror of the past. In fact, Sethe's apotropaic actions have been a response to the community's lapse in keeping tragic forces at bay. The community's collective failure opens up the need for Sethe's heroism. At the moment Sethe is about to be enslaved again, the community does not warn her of schoolteacher's arrival out of resentment against Sethe and Baby Suggs for hosting a joyous and abundant fest it perceives to be excessive. But it is Sethe who, through her apotropaic gestures, has reversed the community's failure, preserved what it means to be beloved, and provided access to the community's damaged heart.

The community's willful refusal to warn the Suggs family of schoolteacher's arrival is an act of self-sabotage that invites tragedy yet has no mechanism of defense against tragedy. Its act is single; it has no resonance; it is done out of fear and anger rather than love. Throughout the course of the novel, Sethe counterbalances the community. She preserves, at times literally and extremely, the message of self-love that Baby Suggs delivers in the Clearing, the central gathering place of the community. Sethe initiates the figurative clearing that takes place when the women of the community come to redress their previous failure and succeed in warding off the figure Beloved. Thirty women strong, they come not for Sethe so much as to see what Beloved is. Calling the women a "chorus," Lillian Corti writes that "their participation in Sethe's 'liberation' from the past lends to the conclusion of the novel a mellow, comic quality that contrasts markedly with the stark outlines of the tragic denouement" (73). With music that is prior to text, the women begin to pray until Ella lets out the signal for "a step back to the beginning. In the beginning there were no words. In the beginning was the sound, and they all knew what that sound sounded like" (259). In this passage the "Word of the father and even of the biblical God is re-written by the singing women" (Rigney 139). Yet the women's version does not so much contradict as prefigure the Father's Word. There can only be a new testament, a new Word, when what comes prior to words and text is recognized: that is, the primal, mythic, and feminine utterance recalls itself as prior by taking a step back and seeing the limits and boundaries of the Word.

The women make possible a return to origins. If Sethe's backward reach to the apotropaic protects the entire community from a hateful life, now in turn the community shields Sethe by allowing her to glimpse a time prior to her terrible text on a tombstone. The women's sound becomes a music that summons Sethe and Beloved to the doorway. In a liminal moment "it is as though the Clearing had come to her [Sethe] with all its heat and simmering leaves, where the voices of women searched for the right combination, the key, the code, the sound that broke the back of words" (261). The women sing, "Building voice upon voice until they found it, and when they did it was a wave of sound wide enough to sound deep water and knock the pods off chestnut trees. It broke over Sethe and she trembled in its wash" (261). Unlike the "wave of grief" that Paul D encounters upon his entrance to 124, this is a wave of sound that enforces Baby Suggs' message of love that knocked "the pods off chestnuts" (164). It counters the disconnected and fragmented discourse of Beloved. It breaks the back of words by being prior to the Word, by remembering that before there were discrete words, there was only sound—a great continuum of thought that finds expression in an audible formation of a wave. The "wave of sound" is the ritual transition between the negative and positive elements of the apotropaic. It cleanses and clears Sethe of her sin in its baptismal wash as it also marks the women who perform the ritual.[8] It becomes a benediction that initiates the exorcism of Beloved, that breaks the back of "Beloved" as a false word, and restores wholeness to what it means to be beloved.

"Breaking the back of words" plays on two senses of "back": as pointing to the past, and as the recipient of a burden. In a reverse action to Denver's stepping off the porch into the future and into the community to save her mother from the clutches of Beloved, the women also step *back* to experience exclusion; they step back from what they cannot know and from that for which they are yet responsible. The aboriginal backward step hearkens back to a painful past, one that has been forgotten and is yet shared, and it enables a vision of the delineated whole. The "wave of sound" clarifies and initiates the wresting-free of the truly beloved. The step back recalls to mind all that is significant from the past, all that is gathered in the image of what is referred to as the "chokecherry tree" to describe Sethe's beaten, scarred, and ignored back, revisiting and seeing the whole of that past. The singing women's backward step and their formation of the "wave of sound" do not immediately exorcise Beloved, though they do break her hold. The women are surprised by the absence of fear when they see the "devil-child," in "the shape of a pregnant woman," beautiful and "thunderblack" with "vines of hair twisted all over her head" (265). The women of the community help Sethe "choose for the living; despite all mourning and guilt, the ghosts of the past must not usurp life" (Matus 119).

Beloved's gorgonish stature does not, then, turn the women to stone, and Sethe will not complete the deadly cycle of repeating the past, but will re-imagine it. Kimberly Chabot Davis writes of this re-making: "One way to free oneself from the horrors of the past is to reenact and re-configure the past in the present, as Sethe does with an icepick [near] the end of the novel, attacking not her own children this time but the white man Bodwin, whom she perceives as a reincarnation of her slave master schoolteacher" (251). Bodwin, unlike schoolteacher, is a benign white man and Denver's new boss; he comes to pick up his charge at the childhood home he now owns. But seeing him, Sethe's mind reverts to an earlier time and she mistakes him for one who might come to take her family back into slavery. Chopping ice with a pick on this hot day, Sethe sees Bodwin and thinks that "He is coming into her yard and he is coming for her best thing" (262). The "needle beaks" that stick into her hair after schoolteacher's violation at Sweet Home return, "And if she thinks anything, it is no. No. No. Nonono. She flies. The ice pick is not in her hand; it is her hand" (262). This time, however, the community does not fail her and she does not kill again. The communal lyric interlude undercuts the tragic, and the sound of the women summons Sethe unto them instead of Bodwin. Beloved, though she assumes Sethe will kill again for her, witnesses Sethe resist such a repetition. Not only is a tragedy spared, but the action is later translated to comedy by the nervous hilarity of the question that comes up in a conversation between Paul D and Stamp Paid: "Every time a whiteman come to the door she got to kill somebody?" (265).

Now baptized, Sethe is no longer excluded. No longer using Beloved as a weapon, she "is running away from her, and [Beloved] feels the emptiness in the hand she has been holding" (262). Sethe and the women "make a hill. A hill of black people" that in a reversal of Sethe's earlier exclusion now protects her with the warding-off power that they were incapable of understanding until now. This hill now excludes both Beloved and Mr. Bodwin, who rises "with a whip in his hand" to look at Beloved (262). This cairn-like hill of women deflects the stare of the white man so that he faces the gorgonish Beloved—a confrontation that renders him harmless. Though the women of the community come together with several motivations, they act finally in unison and in both proper self-interest and charity. What has been awry in Sethe's memory is awry in the entire community of women, and Beloved represents the limit of what they can take. The cairn of people becomes the new limit. The cairn marks the land;[9] it cuts a boundary between the edge of 124 (a locus of white ownership and the source of psychic trauma) and its own re-created space.

The exclusion of Beloved and Bodwin together connects the false word to the white world forever. Together they are "other." By herself, however, Beloved may be an ambiguous gorgon, forever recalling the community's failings and yet warding off outside attack. While the creation of Beloved has largely originated from within the black community, the "wave of sound" reveals both an overwhelming debt, for which the community is unaccountable, as well as the limits of its own accountability. The hill of black people breaks and heals the word, uniting black and white, mother and daughter, earthly city and underworldly one, parts and story, false word and true Word—uniting them, and yet forever keeping them distinct.

Both Beloved and Sethe are, like the ancient Furies, rearticulated: Beloved is given a place that is not primary, but is defined and subordinate. It might be said that when Sethe names her most precious part *beloved*, she is articulating a reality she wishes existed. Though Beloved is a false articulation, it is, as Sethe knows, the most beautiful word the preacher said, and Sethe has saved it, and now Sethe herself is called the beloved "which was not beloved." A.D. Nuttall writes of this kind of transformation:

We are dealing with a kind of euphemism, but not the kind we employ simply to avoid an undesired image (as in 'passed away' for 'died'). Rather, this euphemism is *put to work* (presumably in the hope of inducing the hearer to conform to the flattering description) with the design of *turning away* hostility. It is therefore an apotropaic euphemism. (Nuttall 54)

In a reversal of the ordinary scapegoat process, then, the sins of the people are not merely placed on Beloved "as a site onto which each member... can project her particular unresolved emotional problems" (Matus 115). Rather, each woman takes ownership of herself, filtering out what it means to *be loved*, and relocating Beloved's negative power where it can be protective. Thus, Beloved becomes something more akin to a *pharmakos*, or a figure of enchantment who both sickens and cures, not because of what she is, but because of what the community makes of her.

The apotropaic, then, is both therapeutic and pharmaceutical. In his discussion of the pharmacosmic process, Theophus Smith writes of toxic/curative elements in the black American community:

A double-sided view allows us to see a convergence here between the curative, healing interests of black culture and its negative tasks. Its negations can become antidotal in the same way that homeopathic medicines are curative. The uses of a toxin to cure its own poisonous effects offers an intriguing trope for the kind of negation that distinguishes the tradition. (218)

Redemption for this community comes from within, from remembering the psychological effects of the original trauma and discovering their antidotal properties. But an antidote can also be dangerous if too much is ingested, and the community must carry within it only that which truly belongs to it as beloved. Thereby, the community can maintain access to the underworld of soul while yet warding off the underworld's negative power. Thus, it can avoid again becoming stoic, unable to distinguish what truly is and is not beloved.

The expulsion of Beloved is enacted, finally, not in fear but in service. Although the effects of the social ill of slavery have not been erased and an investigation into past causes of trauma will continue, Baby Suggs' message of love has managed to sustain this community. The word beloved has been restored to its "original meaning" and now refers to those whose hearts have become dear to themselves (Tate 165).[10] Beloved, as an extreme underside example of what it means to be loved, serves as a catalyst for the living to take some joy in the privilege of life. When the Odyssean Paul D returns to 124, he reminds Sethe, who mourns the absent Beloved, that she, and not Beloved, has been her own "best thing." In the end, the self is paradoxically defined against and in service to other.

The Echo of Tragedy

It may be that tragedy itself is an apotropaic genre. Camille Paglia writes, "Art and religion come from the same part of the mind. Great cult symbols transfer smoothly into artistic experience. Solitary or highly original artists often make apotropaic art" (49). In *Beloved*, as in the myths of the heroes, can be found the raw materials of tragedy with which is forged not tragedy *per se* but an alternative form. A reign of terror comes to an end so that the present community can flourish. The novel develops its own defining word "Beloved" by a kind of *via negativa* whereby we see the word's transformation from fury to talisman. Reaching back to the foundation of the Christian story, as the epigraph of the novel does, is already a way to tap into the origins of cult and heroes, because it is, like the story of Israel, always being "torn from its cultural identity [...] The faith of Israel brings with it a continuous surpassing of its own culture in the openness and breadth of the common truth" (19), as Joseph Ratzinger points out. The word *beloved* develops in the same way that the word of God develops: "through a process of encounters with man in search of the ultimate questions; it did not simply 'fall from heaven' but is a synthesis of cultures" (19). As things change, all that belongs still belongs, and the new word is all-embracing in its ability to gather and welcome and to reform itself as required.

The apotropaic, then, serves to both ward off and welcome in. It offers and defers; it sickens and cures; but most significantly, it exposes the cultural self by a surpassing of self, a stretching of one's own boundaries, a confusing and subsequent defining of limits. If tragedy tends to the destruction of a character or a community through the clash of two opposing moral demands, then *Beloved* shows the extension and attenuation of that opposition through a series of apotropaic gestures. Looking back at the novel as a whole, we see that the word first written in stone—Beloved—has gone out and come back as a choral word of riddance. The novel is a word gone out and returned. It is not a tragedy, but paradoxically both tragedy's source and its echo. Sethe's actions expose the tragic contradictions integral to the human condition, but the entire community's final resistance to the hostile and nonhuman figure, Beloved, avoids and survives tragic devastation. Tragic resolutions tend to focus on the delimiting of character—the tragic figure set apart—but at the end of *Beloved*, there is not a contraction, but an extension of character, beyond division. The community surpasses its own expectations of love. The novel, then, avoids tragedy because it resists the tragic self that Beloved ultimately represents. Sethe's action is one that calls into being and yet pushes away tragic forces. She is the one who "keeps the past at bay" and evokes the hope for a future.

The true afterlife of Morrison's novel lies in its reverberations of myth, in its power to craft a whole story that is not superficial but significant and shaped from below. *Beloved* reenacts cult. The novel is broad enough in Morrison's hands to provide in itself an arena for myth-making rather than for mere allusion. As such, the novel goes beneath tragedy. It goes beneath all generic form to that place of raw materials in order to create a space of transition—a place where the difference between the past and the present is made clear, a place where the desire for the present and for life can be imagined and engendered both in and out of the mind, as Ruth Padel might say. The great force of *Beloved* is that it articulates a paradigm for expressing a new order, which can include mythic elements hitherto excluded. *Beloved* is less a novel than a ritual enacted in language: its visionary power is visited upon late twentieth-century America as an apotropaic meditation on its past and future.

NOTES

[1] Stanley Crouch's "Aunt Medea" is a scathing article that labels *Beloved* not tragic but melodramatic.

[2] Morrison herself has on several occasions noted her reliance on

the Greeks. For example: "Greek tragedy... seems to me extremely sympathetic to Black culture and in some ways to African culture" (Otten 286).

[3] Morrison's first novel, *The Bluest Eye*, speaks in a different context to this meeting: "where was the life to counter the encroaching nonlife?" (135).

[4] Apotropaic gestures are evident in other of Morrison's novels, most obviously in *Sula*, when Sula cuts herself to ward off the threat of a group of white boys. See 54.

[5] For Carole Ann Taylor, *Beloved* broadens the genre of tragedy by representing the horror of slavery while discarding elements she considers unjustifiably exclusive: nobility, high discourse, and catharsis, for example. Taylor's concern with "resistance" is, however, exclusively political and social.

[6] The novel, however, is not about the criminal consequences of this act but about the psychological ones. Thanks to local abolitionists, Sethe spends little time in jail for her deed, and the emphasis in the novel is on the tension between what Morrison says was the right thing to do and the fact that she had no right to do it.

[7] Beloved is a dark manifestation of Medusa, who can be, as Erich Neumann says, the "negative elementary character of the feminine," the "womb of death," or "the night sun" (Barnes 20). As Trudier Harris writes of Beloved, "We can describe the title character as a witch, a ghost, a devil, or a succubus; in her manipulation of those around her, she exerts a power not of this world" (*Fiction* 153). Beloved is a "Fury" (Otten 288). As a "fatal lady without grace, a demon, a double, a projection" (Cowan 295), Beloved is "part ghost, zombie, devil, and memory" (Heinze 205).

[8] In this liminal and ritual moment, the community achieves true *communitas*: Victor Turner describes the movement of community to *communitas*, as one from an "area of common living" to a "social relationship." He writes,

> It is as though there are two major "models" for human interrelatedness... The first is society as a structured, differentiated, and often hierarchical system... separating men in terms of "more" or "less." The second, which arises recognizably in the liminal period, is of society as an unstructured or rudimentarily structured and relatively undifferentiated comitatus, community, or even communion of equal individuals who submit together to the general authority of the ritual elders. (Ritual 96).

[9] "Early Hermes was indistinguishable from the piles of stones and

phallic monuments called 'herms' that marked Greek boundary lines" (Paglia 88).

[10] Morrison says, "I try to clean the language up and give words back their original meaning, not the one that's sabotaged... If you work very carefully, you can clean up ordinary words and repolish them, make parabolic language seem alive again" (Tate 165).

Works Cited

Aeschylus. *The Oresteia*. Trans. and Intro. Robert Fagles. New York: Penguin, 1977.

Allums, Larry. "Beloved: Remembering the Past." Classic Texts and the Nature of Authority. Ed. Donald and Louise Cowan. Dallas: Dallas Institute Publications, 1993. 268-282.

Alter, Robert and Frank Kermode, eds. *The Literary Guide to the Bible*. Cambridge: The Belknap Press of Harvard UP, 1987.

Anaximander. *The Presocratic Philosophers*. Ed. G. S. Kirk and J. E. Raven. Cambridge, Eng.: Cambridge UP, 1957.

Anderson, Andrew. "Lorca's *Bodas de Sangre*: The Logic and Necessity of Act Three." Hispanofila. (1987 May) 21-37.

Anderson, Reed. "The Idea of Tragedy in Lorca's *Bodas de Sangre*." Revista Hispanica Moderna (1974-1975) 174-188.

Angelo, Bonnie. "The Pain of Being Black: An Interview with Toni Morrison." Conversations with Toni Morrison. Ed. Danille Taylor-Guthrie. Jackson: UP of Mississippi, 1994. 255-261.

Aoyama, Seiko. "The Metaphysics of Poetry in *Macbeth*." Poetry and Faith in the English Renaissance. Ed. Peter Milward. Renaissance Institute Monograph 13. Tokyo: Sophia U, 1987. 97-194.

Arbery, Glenn. "Editor's Preface." *The Tragic Abyss*. Ed. Glenn Arbery. Dallas: Dallas Institute of Humanities and Culture, 2003.

———. *Why Literature Matters: Permanence and the Politics of Reputation*. Wilmington, DE: ISI Books, 2001.

Aristotle. *La poétique: texte, traduction, notes*. Eds. Roselyn Dupont-Roc and Jean Lallot. Paris: Editions du Seuil, 1980.

———. *Poetics*. Trans. H. S. Butcher. Ed. and Intro. Francis Fergusson. New York: Hill and Wang, 1961.

———. *Poetics*. Trans. M. E. Hubbard. Ancient Literary Criticism: The Principal Texts in New Translations. Eds. D. A. Russell and M. Winterbottom. Oxford & New York: Oxford UP, 1972. 85-132.

Augustine. *The Confessions.* Trans. Maria Boulding, O.S.B. New York: New City Press, 1997.

Balthasar, Hans Urs von. *Seeing the Form.* Vol. I of *The Glory of the Lord: A Theological Aesthetics.* Trans. Erasmo Leiva-Merikakis. Eds. Joseph Fessio, S. J., and John Riches. San Francisco: Ignatius Press, 1982.

Barnes, Helen. *The Meddling Gods.* Lincoln: U of Nebraska P, 1974.

Bataille, Georges. *Eroticism.* Trans. Mary Dalwood. London: J. Calder, 1962.

Belfiore, Elizabeth S. *Tragic Pleasures: Aristotle on Plot and Emotion* (Princeton: Princeton U P, 1992), 72.

Benhabib, Seyla. "On Hegel, Women, and Irony." *Feminist Interpretations of G. W. F. Hegel.* Ed. Patricia Jagentowicz Mills. University Park: Pennsylvania State UP, 1996: –.

Benjamin, Walter. *Illuminations.* Trans. Harry Zohn. New York: Schocken, 1968.

Berg, Stephen, and Diskin Clay, trans. *Oedipus the King.* By Sophocles. New York: Oxford UP, 1978.

Berman, Morris. *Coming to Our Senses: Body and Spirit in the Hidden History of the West.* New York: Simon and Schuster, 1989.

Berry, Jake. "Mythopoeic Site Origin: Rediscovering the Genius Loci." *Mythosphere: A Journal for Image, Myth, and Symbol.* Vol. 1, Issue 4, 1999. Ed. William G. Doty. New York: Gordon and Breach. 417-28.

Bloom, Harold. *Shakespeare: The Invention of the Human.* New York: Riverhead Books, 1998.

Blythe, David-Everett. "Banquo's Candles." ELH 58 (1991): 773-778.

Breitwieser, Mitchell. "Early American Antigone." *Theorizing American Literature: Hegel, the Sign, and History.* Ed. Bainard Cowan and Joseph G. Kronick. Baton Rouge: Louisiana State UP, 1991: 125-61.

Brelich, Angelo. *Gli Eroi greci: un problema storico-religioso.* Rome: Edizioni dell'Ateneo, 1958.

Brooks, Cleanth. *William Faulkner: The Yoknapatawpha Country.* New Haven: Yale UP, 1963.

Brueggemann, Walter. *The Prophetic Imagination.* Philadelphia:

Fortress Press, 1978.

Burke, Victoria I. "Antigone's Transgression: Hegel and Bataille on the Divine and the Human." Dialogue 38 (1999): 535-45.

Calasso, Roberto. *The Marriage of Cadmus and Harmony.* Trans. Tim Parks. New York: Knopf, 1993.

Calderwood, James L. "'More Than What You Were': Augmentation and Increase in Macbeth." English Literary Renaissance 14 (1984): 70-82.

Calvin, John. *Institutes of the Christian Religion.* Trans. Ford Lewis Battles. Ed. John T. McNeill. The Library of Christian Classics. Volume XX. Philadelphia: The Westminster Press, 1960.

Campbell, Joseph. *The Flight of the Wild Gander: Explorations in the Mythological Dimensions of Fairy Tales, Legends, and Symbols.* New York: Harper Perennial, 1990.

——. *The Power of Myth.* Ed. Betty Sue Flowers. New York: Doubleday, 1988.

Chanter, Tina. *Ethics of Eros: Irigaray's Rewriting of the Philosophers.* New York: Routledge, 1995.

Chiurazzi, Gaetano. "Il 'ponte sull'abisso' come metafora dell'essere artificiale." *Rivista di Estetica* 34-35 (1994-95): 15-25.

Cixous, Hélène, and Catherine Clément. *The Newly Born Woman.* Trans. Betsy Wing. Minneapolis: U of Minnesota P, 1986.

Clemen, Wolfgang H. *The Development of Shakespeare's Imagery.* London: Methuen, 1951.

Corrigan, Robert W., Ed. *Tragedy: Vision and Form.* San Francisco: Chandler, 1965.

Corti, Lillian. "*Medea* and *Beloved*: Self-Definition and Abortive Nurturing in Literary Treatments of Infanticidal Mothers." *Disorderly Eaters: Texts in Self-Empowerment.* Lilian R. Furst and Peter W. Graham. University Park: Pennsylvania UP, 1992. 61-78.

Coursen, H. R. "*Macbeth*": A Guide to the Play. Westport, CT: Greenwood, 1997.

Cowan, Louise. "*Beloved* and the Transforming Power of the Word." *Classic Texts and the Nature of Authority.* Ed. Donald and Louise Cowan. Dallas: Dallas Institute Publications, 1993. 291-303.

Critchley, Simon. "Derrida's Reading of Hegel in Glas." *Ethics–Politics–Subjectivity: Essays on Derrida, Levinas and Contemporary French Thought.* London: Verso, 1999: 1-29.

Crouch, Stanley. "Aunt Medea." *The New Republic*. 19 October 1987. 38-43.

Danson, Lawrence. "*King Lear* and the Two Abysses" in *On King Lear*. Ed. Lawrence Danson. Princeton: Princeton UP, 1981.

Davis, Kimberly Chabot. "Postmodern Blackness: Toni Morrison's *Beloved* and the End of History." *Twentieth Century Literature*. 44.2 (1998): 242-260.

Dawkins, Richard. *The Selfish Gene*. New York: Oxford UP, 1989.

——. *Unweaving the Rainbow: Science, Delusion and the Appetite for Wonder*. Boston: Houghton Mifflin, 1998.

De Rougemont, Denis. *Love in the Western World*. Revised & Augmented Edition, Trans. Montgomery Belgion. Garden City: Doubleday Anchor Books, 1957.

Derrida, Jacques. "From Restricted to General Economy: A Hegelianism Without Reserve." *Writing and Difference*. Trans. Alan Bass. Chicago: U of Chicago P, 1978: 251-77.

——. *The Gift of Death*. Trans. David Wills. Chicago: U of Chicago P, 1995.

——. *Given Time I: Counterfeit Money*. Trans. Peggy Kamuf. Chicago: U of Chicago P, 1992.

——. *Glas*. Trans. John P. Leavey, Jr., and Richard Rand. Lincoln: U of Nebraska P, 1986.

Dodds, E. R. *The Greeks and the Irrational*. Berkeley: U of California P, 1951.

Dostoevsky, Fyodor. *The Brothers Karamazov*. Trans. Constance Garnett. Norton Critical Edition. Ed. Ralph E. Matlaw. New York: W. W. Norton, 1976.

——. *Crime and Punishment*. Trans. Jessie Coulson. New York: Norton, 1975.

——. "The Dream of a Ridiculous Man: A Fantastic Story." *The Best Short Stories of Dostoevsky*. Trans. David Magarshack. New York: Modern Library, 1955: 297-322.

——. *The Possessed*. Trans. Constance Garnett. New York: Modern Library, 1963.

Douglas, Mary. *Purity and Danger: An Analysis of the Concepts of Pollution and Taboo*. London: Ark Paperbacks, 1984.

Dupré, Louis. *Passage to Modernity: An Essay on the Hermeneutics of Nature and Culture*. New Haven: Yale UP, 1993.

Eagleton, Terry. *Sweet Violence: The Idea of the Tragic*. Malden, MA: Blackwell Publishing, 2003.

Edwards, Gwynne. "The Way Things Are: Towards a Definition of Lorcan Tragedy." *Anales de la Literatura Espanla Contemporanea.* (1996) 271-290.

Eliot, T. S., *Inventions of the March Hare*. Ed. Christopher Ricks. San Diego, New York, London: Harcourt Brace & Co., 1996.

Euripides. *Bacchae.* Trans. William Arrowsmith. *The Complete Greek Tragedies.* Volume IV. Euripides. Eds. David Grene and Richmond Lattimore. Chicago: U of Chicago P, 1992.

——. *Medea.* Trans. Rex Warner. *The Complete Greek Tragedies.* Volume III. Euripides. Eds. David Grene and Richmond Lattimore. Chicago: U of Chicago P, 1992.

Evans, G. Blakemore, ed. *The Riverside Shakespeare.* Boston: Houghton Mifflin, 1974.

Faulkner, William. *Absalom, Absalom!* New York: Vintage International, 1990.

——. *Go Down, Moses.* New York: Vintage International, 1990.

——. *Light in August.* New York: Vintage International, 1990.

——. *The Sound and the Fury.* New York: Vintage International, 1990.

Fergusson, Francis. "Introduction." Aristotle, *Poetics.* Trans. S. H. Butcher.

——. *The Idea of a Theater.* Princeton: Princeton U P, 1949.

Fitzgerald, Robert, Trans. *Oedipus at Colonus.* By Sophocles. In *Greek Tragedies. Vol. 3.* Ed. David Grene and Richmond Lattimore. Chicago: U of Chicago P, 1960.

Flaubert, Gustave. *Madame Bovary.* Trans. Francis Steegmuller. New York: Vintage Books, 1992.

Foley, Helene P. *Female Acts in Greek Tragedy.* Princeton: Princeton UP, 2001.

Foucault, Michel. "A Preface to Transgression." *Language, Counter-Memory, Practice: Selected Essays and Interviews.* By Foucault. Trans. Donald F. Bouchard and Sherry Simon. Ithaca, N.Y.: Cornell UP, 1977: 29-52.

——. *Power/Knowledge: Selected Interviews and Other Writings, 1972-1977.* Ed. Colin Gordon. Trans. Colin Gordon et al. Brighton, Eng.: Harvester Press, 1980.

Fraser, Russell, Ed. *King Lear.* New York: Signet, 1987.

Freud, Sigmund. "The Ego and the Id." *The Standard Edition of the Complete Psychological Works of Sigmund Freud.* Trans. James Strachey. Vol. 19. London: Hogarth Press, 1953-74.

——. "Mourning and Melancholia." *Standard Edition*. Vol. 14.

——. "The Medusa Head." *Standard Edition*. Vol. 18.

Frye, Northrop. *Anatomy of Criticism: Four Essays*. Princeton: Princeton UP, 1990.

Gaskell, Ronald. *Drama and Reality: the European Theatre Since Ibsen*. London: Routledge & Kegan Paul, 1972.

Gellrich, Michelle. *Tragedy and Theory: The Problem of Conflict Since Aristotle*. Princeton, NJ: Princeton UP, 1988.

Gilmour, John. "Religion in the Rural Tragedies." *Lorca: Poet and Playwright*. Ed. Robert Havard. New York: St. Martin's Press, 1992. 133-155.

Glissant, Edouard. *Faulkner, Mississippi*. Trans. Barbara Lewis and Thomas C. Spear. New York: Farrar, Straus and Giroux, 1999.

Goethe, Johann Wolfgang von. *Faust, Part One*. Trans. Philip Wayne. Harmondsworth, Eng.: Penguin, 1949.

Goldhill, Simon. "The Great Dionysia and Civic Theology," in *Nothing to Do With Dionysus? Athenian Drama in Its Social Context*. Eds. John J. Winkler and Froma I. Zeitlin. Princeton: Princeton UP: 1990.

Goldmann, Lucien. *The Hidden God: A Study of Tragic Vision in the Pensées of Pascal and the Tragedies of Racine*. Trans. Philip Thody. New York: Humanities, 1964.

Greenblatt, Stephen. *Learning to Curse: Essays in Early Modern Culture*. New York: Routledge, 1990.

——. *Renaissance Self-Fashioning: From More to Shakespeare*. Chicago: Chicago U P, 1980.

Greenfield, Sumner. "Lorca's Tragedies: Practice Without Theory." *Siglo XX/20th Century*. (1986-1987) 1-5.

Grene, David. "Introduction to Philoctetes." *Greek Tragedies: Volume 3*. Ed. David Grene and Richmond Lattimore. Chicago: U Chicago P, 1968. 44-45.

Gwynn, Frederick L. and Joseph L. Blotner, Eds. *Faulkner in the University*. Charlottesville, VA: U of Virginia P, 1959.

Hamilton, Edith. The Greek Way. New York: Norton, 1964.

Harris, Trudier. *Fiction and Folklore: The Novels of Toni Morrison*. Knoxville: U of Tennessee P, 1991.

Harrison, Jane. *Prolegomena to the Study of Greek Religion*. New York: Meridian Books, 1955.

——. Themis. Cambridge: Cambridge U P, 1913.

Hays, Peter. *The Limping Hero: Grotesques in Literature.* New York: New York UP, 1971.

Hegel, G. W. F. *Hegel's Aesthetics.* Trans. T. M. Knox. 2 vols. Oxford: Oxford UP, 1975.

——. *Phenomenology of Spirit.* Trans. A. V. Miller. Oxford: Oxford UP, 1977.

——. *The Philosophy of History.* Trans. J. Sibree. New York: Dover, 1956.

——. *Werke. Theorie-Werkausgabe.* 20 vols. Frankfurt a. M.: Suhrkamp, 1969-71.

Heidegger, Martin. *An Introduction to Metaphysics.* Tr. Ralph Manheim. New Haven: Yale UP, 1986.

——. *Hölderlin's Hymn "The Ister."* Trans. William McNeil and Julia Davis. Bloomington: Indiana UP, 1996.

——. *Poetry, Language, Thought.* Trans. Albert Hofstadter. New York: Harper Colophon, 1971.

Heinze, Denise. "*Beloved* and the Tyranny of the Double." *Critical Essays on Toni Morrison's Beloved.* Ed. Barbara Solomon. New York: G. K. Hall and Company, 1998. 205-210.

Henderson, Mae G. "Toni Morrison's *Beloved*: Remembering the Body as Historical Text." *Toni Morrison's Beloved: A Casebook.* Ed. William L. Andrews and Nellie McKay. New York: Oxford UP, 1999. 79-106.

Herington, C.J. *Aeschylus.* New Haven: Yale UP, 1986.

Hillman. James. *Revisioning Psychology.* New York: Harper Perennial, 1992.

——. "Culture and the Animal Soul." Spring 62. Fall/Winter 1997. Woodstock, Connecticut. 11-37.

Hogan, James C. *A Commentary on the Plays of Sophocles.* Carbondale, Ill.: Southern Illinois UP, 1991.

Homer. *The Iliad of Homer.* Trans. Richmond Lattimore. Chicago: U of Chicago P, 1951.

Hopkins, Gerard Manley. *Selected Poetry.* Ed. Catherine Phillips. Oxford: Oxford UP, 1998.

House, Elizabeth B. "Toni Morrison's Ghost: The Beloved Who is Not Beloved." *Critical Essays on Toni Morrison's Beloved.* Ed. Barbara Solomon. New York: G. K. Hall and Company, 1998. 117-126.

Huizinga, Johan. *Homo Ludens.* Boston: The Beacon Press: 1955.

Hyde, Lewis. *The Gift: Imagination and the Erotic Life of Property.*

New York: Vintage Books, 1979.

Ingarden, Roman. *The Literary Work of Art.* Evanston: Northwestern U P, 1973.

Irigaray, Luce. *Speculum of the Other Woman.* Trans. Gillian C. Gill. Ithaca, N.Y.: Cornell UP, 1985.

——. *This Sex Which Is Not One.* Trans. Catherine Porter. Ithaca, N.Y.: Cornell UP, 1985.

Ivanov, Vyacheslav. *Freedom and the Tragic Life: A Study in Dostoevsky.* Trans. Norman Cameron. New York: Noonday Press, 1957.

Johnson, Samuel. "King Lear." In *Fraser, King Lear.* 222-24.

Joseph, Bertram. *Conscience and the King: A Study of Hamlet.* London: Chatto and Windus, 1953.

Jung, C. G. "Answer to Job." *The Portable Jung.* Ed. Joseph Campbell. New York: The Viking Press, 1971.

——. *The Archetypes and the Collective Unconscious.* 2nd. edition. Vol. 9, 1. The Collected Works of C. G. Jung. Bollingen Series XX. Ed. Sir Herbert Read. Princeton: Princeton UP, 1971.

——. *The Vision Seminars.* Vol. 2. Dallas: Spring, 1976.

Kaufmann, Walter. *Tragedy and Philosophy.* 1968; rpr. Princeton UP, 1979.

Keats, John. "Letter to Benjamin Bailey, 22 November 1817." *John Keats. The Oxford Authors.* Ed. Elizabeth Cook. Oxford: Oxford UP, 1990.

Keil, C.F. and Franz Delitzsch. *Commentary on the Old Testament: Volume IV, Job.* Grand Rapids: William B. Eerdmans Publishing Company, 1973.

Kelly, Henry Ansgar. *Ideas and Forms of Tragedy from Aristotle to the Middle Ages.* London: Cambridge U P, 1993.

Kennedy, Randall. *Nigger: The Strange Career of a Troublesome Word.* NY: Pantheon, 2002.

Kerenyi, C. *Dionysus: Archetypal Image of Indestructible Life.* Princeton: Princeton UP, 1976.

Kerenyi, Karl. *The Heroes of the Greeks.* London: Thames and Hudson, 1959.

Kierkegaard, Søren. *Works of Love: Some Christian Reflections in the Form of Discourses.* Trans. Howard and Edna Long. New York: Harper & Row, 1964.

Kirk, G. S., J. E. Raven, and M. Schofield. *The Presocratic Philosophers: A Critical History with a Selection of Texts.* 2nd ed. New York: Cambridge UP, 1983.

Knight, G. Wilson. *The Wheel of Fire: Interpretations of Shakespeare's Tragedy*. London: Methuen, 1930.

Knights, L. C. *How Many Children Had Lady Macbeth*. New York: New York UP, 1964. 15-54.

Knox, Bernard M. W. *The Heroic Temper: Studies in Sophoclean Tragedy*. Sather Classical Lectures 35. Berkeley: U of California P, 1964, 1983.

——. *Oedipus at Thebes*. New Haven: Yale UP, 1957.

——. *Word and Action: Essays on the Ancient Theater*. Baltimore: The Johns Hopkins UP, 1979.

Knox, Sir T. M. "The Puzzle of Hegel's *Aesthetics*." *Art and Logic in Hegel's Philosophy*. Ed. Warren E. Steinkraus. Atlantic Highlands, N. J.: Humanities, 1980: 1-10.

Kristeva, Julia. "Bataille, Experience, and Practice." *On Bataille: Critical Essays*. Ed. and trans. Leslie Anne Boldt-Irons. Albany: State U of New York P, 1995.

Krutch, Joseph Wood. *The Modern Temper from A Krutch Omnibus: Forty Years of Social and Literary Criticism*. New York: Morrow Quill Paperbacks, 1980.

Kundera, Milan. *The Art of the Novel*. Trans. Linda Asher. New York: Perennial Library, 1988.

Lacan, Jacques. *The Ethics of Psychoanalysis*. Trans. Dennis Porter. New York: Routledge, 1992.

Lamb, Charles. "On the Tragedies of Shakspeare" in *The Complete Works and Letters of Charles Lamb*. New York: The Modern Library, 1935.

Lazer, Hank. "Poetry and Myth: The Scene of Writing, Thinking, as Such." *Mythosphere: A Journal for Image, Myth, and Symbol*. Vol. 1, Issue 4. Ed. William G. Doty. New York: Gordon and Breach, Spring 1999. 403-416.

Lenson, David. *Achilles' Choice: Examples of Modern Tragedy*. Princeton: Princeton UP, 1975.

Levenson, Michael, Ed. *The Cambridge Companion to Modernism*. Cambridge: Cambridge UP, 1999.

Lima, Robert. "Blood Spilt and Unspilt. Primal Sacrifice in Lorca's Bodas de Sangre." *Letras Peninsulares* (Fall 1995) 255-259.

Loewenstein, Werner. *The Touchstone of Life: Molecular Information, Cell Communication, and the Foundations of Life*. New York: Oxford UP, 1999.

Loraux, Nicole. *Tragic Ways of Killing a Woman*. Trans. Anthony Forster. Cambridge: Harvard UP, 1987.

Lorca, Federico García. *In Search of Duende*. Trans. Christopher Maurer. New York: New Directions, 1998.

——. *Three Tragedies of Federico Lorca*. Trans. James Graham-Lujan and Richard Lowe, Donald M. History of Bourgeois Perception. Chicago: U of Chicago P, 1982.

Lowenthal, David. "*Macbeth*: Shakespeare Mystery Play." *Interpretation* 16 (1989): 311-57.

Lukens-Olson, Carolyn. "The Mask of Dionysus: A Nietzschean Reading of Lorca's *Blood Wedding*." *Romance Language Annual*. (1993) 460-464.

Lynch, William F. *Christ and Apollo: The Dimensions of the Literary Imagination*. Notre Dame: U of Notre Dame P, 1975.

Maguin, J.-M. "Rise and Fall of the King of Darkness." *French Essays on Shakespeare and His Contemporaries*. Ed. Jean-Marie Maguin and Michèle Willems. Newark: U of Delaware P. 247-270.

Mann, Thomas. *Death in Venice*. Trans. Clayton Koelb. New York: Norton Critical Edition, 1994.

Maritain, Jacques. *Creative Intuition in Art and Poetry*. New York: Meridian, 1955.

Mason, H. A. *The Tragic Plane*. Oxford: Clarendon, 1985.

Matus, Jill. *Toni Morrison*. Manchester: Manchester UP, 1996.

Mauss, Marcel. *The Gift: Forms and Functions of Exchange in Archaic Societies*. Trans. Ian Cunnison. Glencoe, IL: Free Press. 1954.

May, Rollo. *The Cry for Myth*. New York: Norton, 1991.

McMullen, Terence. "Federico Lorca's Critique of Marriage in *Bodas de Sangre*." *Neophilologus* (1993) 61-73.

Millgate, Michael. *The Achievement of William Faulkner*. New York: Vintage, 1971.

Miola, Robert S. *Shakespeare and Classical Tragedy: The Influence of Seneca*. Oxford: Clarendon, 1992.

Morris, C. B. *Lorca: Bodas de Sangre*. London: Grant & Cutler, 1980.

Morrison, Toni. *Beloved*. New York: Alfred A. Knopf, 1990.

——. *The Bluest Eye*. New York. Holt, Rinehart and Winston, 1970.

——. "The Site of Memory." *Inventing the Truth: The Art and Craft of Memoir*. Ed. William Zinsser. Boston: Houghton Mifflin, 1987. 101-124.

Moss, Leonard. *The Excess of Heroism in Tragic Drama.* Gainesville: UP of Florida, 2000.

Muller, Herbert J. *The Spirit of Tragedy.* New York: Knopf, 1956.

Naylor, Gloria. "A Conversation: Gloria Naylor and Toni Morrison." *Conversations with Toni Morrison.* Ed. Danille Taylor-Guthrie. Jackson: UP of Mississippi, 1994. 188-217.

Nietzsche, Friedrich. *The Birth of Tragedy and The Case of Wagner.* Trans. Walter Kaufmann. New York: Vintage Books, 1967.

—— *The Birth of Tragedy. Basic Writings of Nietzsche.* Trans. Walter Kaufmann. New York: The Modern Library, 1968.

—— *The Gay Science.* Trans. Walter Kaufmann. New York: Vintage Books, 1974.

—— *The Portable Nietzsche.* Trans. Walter Kaufmann. New York: Viking Press, 1977.

Nilsson, Martin P. *A History of Greek Religion.* Trans. F. J. Fielden. Oxford: Clarendon, 1949.

Nuttall, A. D. "*A Midsummer Night's Dream:* Comedy as the Apotrope of Myth." *Shakespeare Survey* 53. Peter Holland. Cambridge: Cambridge UP, 2000. 49-59.

Ortega y Gasset, José. *Meditations on Quixote.* Trans. Evelyn Rugg and Diego Marín. New York: Norton, 1961.

Otten, Terry. "Transfiguring the Narrative: *Beloved*—from Melodrama to Tragedy." *Critical Essays on Toni Morrison's Beloved.* Barbara H. Solomon. New York: G. K. Hall and Co. 1998.

Otto, Walter. *Dionysus: Myth and Cult.* Bloomington, IN: Indiana UP, 1965.

Padel, Ruth. *In and Out of the Mind: Greek Images of the Tragic Self.* Princeton: Princeton UP, 1992.

Page, Philip. *Dangerous Freedom: Fusion and Fragmentation in Morrison's Novels.* Jackson: UP of Mississippi, 1995.

Paglia, Camille. *Sexual Personae: Art and Decadence from Nefertiti to Emily Dickinson.* New Haven: Yale UP, 1990.

Paolucci, Anne and Henry. "Introduction." *Hegel on Tragedy.* Ed. Anne and Henry Paolucci. New York: Harper, 1962: xi-xxxi.

Paolucci, Henry. "Introduction." *Hegel: On the Arts.* Ed. and trans. Henry Paolucci. New York: Ungar, 1979.

Parada, Carlos. "Lemnos." *Greek Mythology Link,* 2003. http://homepage.mac.com/cparada/GML/Lemnos.html.

—— "Mnemosyne." *Greek Mythology Link,* 2003. http://homepage.mac.com/cparada/GML/Mnemosyne.html.

—— "Nymphs." *Greek Mythology Link,* 2003. http://homepage.mac.com/cparada/GML/NYMPHS.html.

—— "Philoctetes." *Greek Mythology Link,* 2003. http://homepage.mac.com/cparada/GML/Philoctetes.html

Parker, Patricia. "Eve, Evening, and the Labor of Reading in *Paradise Lost.*" *John Milton's "Paradise Lost."* Ed. Harold Bloom. New York: Chelsea, 1987.

Peyre, Henri. "The Tragedy of Passion: Racine's Phèdre." *Tragic Themes in Western Literature.* Ed. Cleanth Brooks. New Haven: Yale UP, 1955.

Pieper, Josef. *Guide to Thomas Aquinas.* Trans. Richard and Clara Winston. New York: Mentor-Omega Books, 1964.

Pucci, Pietro. *The Violence of Pity in Euripides' Medea.* Ithaca, New York: Cornell UP, 1980.

Raphael, D. D. *The Paradox of Tragedy.* Bloomington: Indiana UP, 1960.

Redfield, James. "Drama and Community: Aristophanes and Some of His Rivals." *Nothing to Do With Dionysus? Athenian Drama in Its Social Context.* Ed. John J. Winkler and Froma I. Zeitlin. Princeton: Princeton UP: 1990.

Reibling, Barbara. "Virtue's Sacrifice: A Machiavellian Reading of *Macbeth.*" *Studies in English Literature* 31 (1991): 273-286.

Ribbans, Geoffrey. "Tragic vision in Unamuno, Valle-Inclan and Lorca." *Selected Proceedings of the Singularidad y Transcendencia Conference.* Boulder: Society of Spanish and Spanish-American Studies, 1990. 11-25.

Rosenmeyer, Thomas G. "'Metatheater': An Essay on Overload." *Arion* 10.2 (Fall 2002). 87-119.

Rosslyn, Felicity. *Tragic Plots: A New Reading from Aeschylus to Lorca.* Aldershot: Ashgate, 2000.

Ryken, Leland. *The Literature of the Bible.* Grand Rapids: William B. Eerdmans Publishing Company, 1974.

Sahlins, Marshall. "The Spirit of the Gift." *Stone Age Economics.* Chicago: Aldine-Atherton, Inc., 1972. 149-83.

Sallis, John. *Crossings: Nietzsche and the Space of Tragedy.* Chicago: Chicago UP, 1991.

Sanders, Paul S., ed. *Twentieth Century Interpretations of the Book of Job.* Englewood Cliffs: Prentice-Hall, Inc., 1968.

Scheler, Max. "On the Tragic." Trans. Bernard Stambler. *Moderns on Tragedy.* Ed. Lionel Abel. Greenwich, Conn.: Fawcett, 1967.

Segal, Charles. "Earth in *Oedipus Tyrannus.*" *Sophocles' Tragic World: Divinity, Nature, Society.* Cambridge, Mass.: Harvard UP, 1995: 199-212.

Segal, Charles. *Dionysiac Poetics and Euripides' Bacchae.* Princeton: Princeton UP, 1982.

Segal, Charles. *Interpreting Greek Tragedy: Myth, Poetry, Text.* Ithaca: Cornell UP, 1986.

Shakespeare, William. *Hamlet: Prince of Denmark.* Ed. Edward Hubler. New York: Signet, 1963.

—— *King Lear.* Ed. Russell Fraser. New York: Signet, 1963.

Shay, Jonathan. *Achilles in Vietnam: Combat Trauma and the Undoing of Character.* New York: Touchstone Books, 1995.

Silk, M. S., and J. P. Stern. *Nietzsche on Tragedy.* New York: Cambridge UP, 1981.

Slattery, Dennis Patrick. "Of Corpses and Kings: Antigone and the Body Politic." *Lit: Literature, Interpretation, Theory.* Vol. 5, No. 2. New York: Gordon and Breach, 1994. 155-67.

——. *The Wounded Body: Remembering the Markings of Flesh.* Albany: SUNY Press, 2000.

Smith, Paul Julian. *The Theatre of Lorca: Text, Performance, Psychoanalysis.* Cambridge: Cambridge UP, 1998.

Smith, Theophus. *Conjuring Culture: Biblical Formations of Black America.* Oxford: Oxford UP, 1994.

Sophocles. *Antigone.* Sophocles Vol. 2. Trans. Hugh Lloyd-Jones. Loeb Classical Library 21. Cambridge, Mass.: Harvard UP, 1994: 1-127.

——. *Oedipus at Colonus.* Sophocles 2: 409-599.

——. *Oedipus Tyrannus.* Sophocles 1: 323-483.

——. *The Women of Trachis.* Sophocles 2: 129-251.

——. *Oedipus at Colonus.* Trans. Robert Fitzgerald. *Greek Tragedies.* Ed. David Grene and Richmond Lattimore. Chicago: U of Chicago P, 1960. 3: 107-87.

——. *Oedipus the King. The Three Theban Plays.* Trans. Robert Fagles. New York: Viking, 1984. 168-251.

——. *Philoctetes. Greek Tragedies,* Vol. 3. Eds. David Grene and Richmond Lattimore. Chicago: U Chicago P, 1968. 43-106.

——. *Sophocles.* Ed. and trans. Hugh Lloyd-Jones. 2 vols. Loeb Classical Library 20-21. Cambridge: Harvard UP, 1994.

Soufas, C. Christopher. "*Bodas de Sangre* and the Problematics of Representation." *Revista de Estudios Hispanicos.* (Enero 1987) 29-48.

——. "Dante and the Geography of Lorcas's *Bodas de Sangre*." *Romance Notes* (Winter 1997) 175-181.

Soyinka, Wole. *Myth, Literature, and the African World*. Cambridge: Cambridge UP, 1976.

——. "The Fourth Stage: Through the Mysteries of Ogun to the Origin of Yoruba Tragedy." *Art, Dialogue, and Outrage: Essays on Literature and Culture*. New York: Pantheon Books, 1993. 27-39.

Spivak, Gayatri Chakravorty. "Speculations on Reading Marx." *Post-Structuralism and the Question of History*. Ed. Derek Atridge, Geoff Bennington, and Robert Young. New York: Cambridge UP, 1987.

Spotswood, Jerald W. "Maintaining Hierarchy in *The Tragedie of King Lear*." *SEL* 38 (1998). 266-80.

Spurgeon, Caroline. *Shakespeare's Imagery and What It Tells Us*. Cambridge: Cambridge UP, 1935.

Stainton, Leslie. *Lorca: A Dream of Life*. New York: Farrar Straus and Giroux, 1999.

Steiner, George. *Antigones*. New York: Oxford UP, 1984.

——. *The Death of Tragedy*. New Haven: Yale UP, 1996.

Stockholder, Kay. "*Macbeth*: A Dream of Love." *American Imago* 44 (1987): 85-105.

Stríbrn´y, Zdenek. "Shakespeare as Liberator: *Macbeth* in Czechoslovakia." *Shakespeare and Cultural Traditions*. Ed. Tetsuo Kishi, Roger Pringle and Stanley Wells. Newark: U of Delaware P, 1994.

Strindberg, August. *Seven Plays by August Strindberg*. Trans. Arvid Paulson. New York: Bantam Books, 1960.

Suhamy, Henri. "The Authenticity of the Hecate Scenes in *Macbeth*." *French Essays on Shakespeare and His Contemporaries*. Ed. Jean-Marie Maguin and Michèle Willems. Newark: U of Delaware P. 271-288.

Szondi, Peter. "The Notion of the Tragic in Schelling, Hölderlin, and Hegel." *On Textual Understanding and Other Essays*. Trans. Harvey Mendelssohn. *Theory and History of Literature* 15. Minneapolis: U of Minnesota P, 1986: 43-55.

Tate, Allen. *Essays of Four Decades*. New York: William Morrow, 1970.

——. *The Fathers*. Baton Rouge, LA: Louisiana State UP, 1977.

Tate, Claudia. "Toni Morrison." *Conversations with Toni Morrison*.

Danille Taylor-Guthrie. Jackson: UP of Mississippi, 1994.

Taylor, Carole Anne. *The Tragedy and Comedy of Resistance.* Philadelphia: U of Pennsylvania P, 2000.

Taylor, Charles. *Hegel.* New York: Cambridge UP, 1975.

Taylor, Mark. "Letters and Readers in *Macbeth, King Lear,* and *Twelfth Night.*" *Philological Quarterly* 69 (1990): 31-53.

The Fugitive: April, 1922-December, 1925. Gloucester, MA: Peter Smith, 1967.

Tillich, Paul. *The Protestant Era.* Chicago: U of Chicago P, 1948.

Turner, Victor. *Dramas, Fields, and Metaphors: Symbolic Action in Human Society.* Ithaca, NY: Cornell UP, 1975.

———. *From Ritual to Theater: The Human Seriousness of Play.* Performing Arts Journal Publications, 1982.

———. *The Ritual Process: Structure and Anti-Structure.* New York: Cornell UP, 1991.

Twelve Southerners. *I'll Take My Stand: the South and the Agrarian Tradition.* New York: Harper and Row, 1930.

Unamuno, Miguel de. *Tragic Sense of Life.* Trans. J. E. Crawford Flitch. New York: Dover Publications, 1954

———. *The Tragic Sense of Life in Men and Nations.* Trans. Anthony Kerrigan. Bollingen Series LXXXV, #4. Princeton: Princeton UP, 1990.

Valbuena, Olga. "To 'venture in the rebels' fight': History and Equivocation in *Macbeth.*" *Renaissance Papers,* 1994. Ed. Barbara J. Baines and George Walton Williams. Raleigh, NC: Southeastern Renaissance Conference, 1995. 105-122.

Vernant, Jean-Pierre, and Pierre Vidal-Naquet. *Myth and Tragedy in Ancient Greece.* New York: Zone, 1990

———. *Mortals and Immortals.* Trans. Janet Lloyd. Princeton: Princeton UP, 1991.

Vidal-Naquet, Pierre. "Oedipus Between Two Cities: An Essay on *Oedipus at Colonus.*" Vernant. *Myth and Tragedy in Ancient Greece.* 329-59.

Voegelin, Eric. *Order and History.* Vol. II: *The Greek Polis.* Ed. Athanasios Moulakis. Columbia, MO: U of Missouri P, 2000.

———. *The New Science of Politics.* Chicago: U of Chicago P, 1952.

Whitman, Cedric H. *Sophocles: A Study of Heroic Humanism.* Cambridge: Harvard UP, 1951.

Williams, Raymond. *Modern Tragedy.* Stanford, CA: Stanford UP, 1966.

Wilson, Edmund. "*Philoctetes*: The Wound and the Bow." *The Edmund Wilson Reader*. Ed. Lewis M. Babney. New York: DaCapo P, 1997. 418-36.

Yeats, W. B. *Essays and Introductions*. New York: Collier Books, 1961.

Young, Dudley. *Origins of the Sacred: The Ecstacies of Love and War*. New York: Harper Perennial, 1991.

Zeitlin, Froma I. *Playing the Other*. Chicago: U of Chicago P, 1996.

Index

A

A Doll's House   286

Abelard   279

abgrund   57, 67, 71

abyss   2-4, 11-18, 44-46, 52, 54, 56-57, 65, 67-72, 74-80, 90, 99, 101-103, 106-110, 112, 114, 120, 122, 145-146, 149, 155, 159, 162, 164, 167-168, 174, 177, 182-183, 189, 196-197, 199, 205, 207-209, 213-214, 216, 220, 223, 227, 232-233, 238-243, 245, 251, 255, 257-258, 263, 270, 288-289, 302-305, 315, 335-338, 340, 344-350, 352; darkness and 4, 11-12, 16, 18, 77, 101, 106-107, 111, 114, 159, 167, 199, 205, 255, 258, 303, 335, 346-347; Dionysian state and 65, 67-72, 74-76, 208, 227, 241, 346; hero's confrontation of 4, 11, 70, 90, 101, 145-146, 155, 209, 340, 345, 350; experience of 15, 76, 216, 241, 243; love and 17, 99, 242-243; morality and 233, 238-240, 242, 245, 305; Nietzsche and 67-69, 71-72, 74-75, 77-79, 227, 241; nature and 69-71, 182-183, 189, 196, 238-241, 302; relation to tragedy 2, 10, 13-15, 17, 44, 57, 70, 74, 77, 90, 101, 103, 108-109, 145-146, 167, 177, 182, 189, 196, 207-209, 213, 220, 227, 233, 239, 241-243, 245, 255, 258, 270, 288, 304-305, 336, 340, 345, 347, 349-350, 352;

Achaea   113, 120, 128-129, 134

Acropolis   161-162

action   *see also praxis*   2-3, 5, 7-9, 12, 28, 35, 47-48, 50, 53-54, 65, 71, 99, 109, 112-113, 117, 120, 125, 129, 131, 134-135, 138, 142, 144, 166, 169, 178, 182, 189, 191-192, 201, 210, 213-214, 217-219, 231, 243-245, 250, 266, 268, 270, 282-283, 295, 298-300, 304-307, 310, 323, 326-327, 339-340, 350, 352, 356, 358, 364, 369; Aristotelean 2, 28, 35, 99, 270, 282; comic 183, 307, 327; complete 34, 268; dramatic action 134, 257, 268; heroic 293; human 2, 12, 44, 259, 269, 290, 293-294, 326, 337; imitation of 2, 28-29, 65; tragic 5, 7-9, 48, 144, 165, 183, 213, 243, 268, 282, 307, 310, 327, 337-340, 350, 356

adultery   240, 280, 303

Aegisthus   113-114

Aeneas   1

Aeneid   213

Aeschylus   10, 12, 23, 33, 38, 41, 44, 49-50, 59, 62, 88, 101, 105-109, 111-114, 116-117, 119, 122, 125, 146, 151, 155-156, 172, 174, 213, 278, 334, 359; *Agamemnon* 9-10, 108, 146, 338, 346; *Choephoroe (The Libation Bearers)* 10, 33, 108, 111, 117, 155; *Eumenides, The* 10, 33, 49, 79, 88, 90, 106-108, 116, 121, 149, 151, 156, 159, 172, 174; *Firebringer, The* see also *Prometheus Bound* 2, 10, 15, 49, 69-70, 78, 85, 88, 99, 108-110, 122, 208, 290; *Prometheus Unbound* 10, 78, 109; *Oresteia* 9-12, 14, 41, 49-51, 88, 105-106, 108-110, 116-119, 121-122, 174, 208

aesthetic   40-41, 44, 46, 49, 55

Agamemnon   48, 113, 115-119, 139, 168, 210

E

F

G

H

W

XYZ